Materials
Management

THE IRWIN SERIES IN MANAGEMENT

Consulting Editor   JOHN F. MEE, *Indiana University*

MATERIALS MANAGEMENT

by **DEAN S. AMMER, Ph.D.**
Executive Editor, Purchasing Magazine
Lecturer, Bernard M. Baruch School of
Business and Public Administration
The City University of New York

1962
RICHARD D. IRWIN, INC.
HOMEWOOD, ILLINOIS

First Printing, January, 1962

Library of Congress Catalogue Card No. 62–8739

PRINTED IN THE UNITED STATES OF AMERICA

PREFACE

Materials management problems occur with almost routine frequency in the best-managed companies, but they are rarely called by that name. Instead, managements think in terms of the functional activities concerned with materials management: purchasing, production or material control, traffic, shipping and receiving. Thus, a materials management problem involving scheduling or inventory control becomes a "production control problem," and one concerned with supplier relations becomes a "purchasing problem." This is quite proper, since most companies divide materials management responsibility among several distinct functional departments. In most companies, the production control, purchasing, and traffic departments are not directly linked organizationally, even though each is performing part of the materials management job.

This book treats materials management as an integrated activity. Even though the organization of most companies does not yet reflect this view, I am convinced that integrated materials management is the organizational approach of the future. It has already been adopted by a number of progressive companies, and there are sound economic reasons why it will be commonplace within a generation. As a result, there will be tremendous opportunities for persons trained to think as materials managers rather than as narrow functional specialists in purchasing, traffic, or production control.

Accordingly, this book is written primarily for the future materials manager and only incidentally for the beginner or for the specialist in one phase of materials management. The early chapters are devoted to explanation of the general principles of materials management, organization, and objectives. Discussion of legal phases, planning, and forecasting sets the stage for detailed analysis of the three basic materials functions: inventory control, purchasing, and traffic. Succeeding chapters explore ways in which major objectives in materials management can be achieved and how performance can be measured.

I see materials management as a specialized application of fundamental principles of economics and management. Throughout the text I have tried to relate discussion to these fundamentals. Price negotiation, for example, is related to basic economic principles. Similarly, the principles of materials management organization are treated as specialized applications of general principles of business organization. The student should be able to relate materials management to principles learned in more basic courses. Similarly, the reader who has not been exposed to basic courses in business and economics should realize that materials management didn't appear in a vacuum; it is related intimately to other fields of business.

No book can be all things to all men, and this one is no exception. I believe there is a body of knowledge common to all materials management problems. On the other hand, unique materials management problems are encountered in each company and industry—and in dealing with each major commodity. I have made no attempt whatever to discuss materials management problems unique to certain industries and products—there are just too many industries and products.

In this book you will find no chapters on "capital equipment buying" or "steel purchasing," for example. Instead, you will find discussion of basic principles that can be applied to the purchase of steel, capital equipment, or any other commodity. I believe that the would-be materials manager in any industry not only must be familiar with the general principles of materials management discussed in this book but must also know something about his industry and its products. The materials manager in the chemical industry should know something about chemistry; his counterpart in the auto industry should know something about metalworking, and so on. This specialized knowledge can be acquired partly by taking science and engineering courses and partly through on-the-job experience.

Regardless of the industry, however, the materials manager will encounter many problems that are similar. These are illustrated in the case studies that follow each chapter in this book. The cases are designed to stimulate thinking about real-life materials management problems. Each is a camouflaged version of an actual materials problem encountered by me either when I was an executive engaged in materials work or in the course of my visits to some 200 companies as part of my duties as Executive Editor of *Purchasing* Magazine.

Grateful acknowledgment is made to the hundreds of executives who contributed to this book through personal conversation and correspondence. I have also relied heavily on articles published in *Purchasing* Magazine. While credit is given for all specific references, general acknowledgment must also be made for permission to use material in the many instances where direct reference was not possible. I extend my thanks to Professors John F. Mee and R. S. Stockton of the University of Indiana, who read the complete manuscript and made many helpful suggestions and criticisms. And finally, I extend thanks to my wife, who edited and typed the manuscript. If this book is easy to read and has a minimum of errors, it is largely as a result of her efforts.

Dean S. Ammer

Eastchester, New York
November, 1961

TABLE OF CONTENTS

Chapter 1

INTRODUCTION

Materials management is one of the least-understood activities in business. If one were to ask a hundred top managers in industry to define the term "materials management," one might get a hundred different answers. There is no general agreement about precisely what activities are embraced by materials management. Some managers would associate materials management with their material or production control departments, which schedule materials requirements and may also control inventories of both raw material and in-process material. Others would associate it with the activities of their purchasing departments in dealing with outside suppliers.

Ten years ago, no more than one or two companies had a materials department headed by a materials manager. Today, at least several hundred executives have the title of materials manager. Usually they control their company's purchasing, material control, traffic, shipping, and receiving activities, but their responsibility varies substantially from company to company.

SCOPE OF MATERIALS MANAGEMENT

Every study that has been made indicates that there is no agreement as to precisely what activities should be undertaken by the materials manager. Several years ago, the National Association of Purchasing Agents hired Harbridge House, management consultants in Cambridge, Massachusetts, to make a study on materials management. Harbridge House consultants reviewed all pertinent literature and interviewed top officials in a number of leading companies. Despite these efforts, they were unable to obtain any comprehensive definition of materials management and concluded that many top managers simply didn't know what materials management was.

A survey by *Purchasing* magazine indicated that purchasing executives themselves do not agree as to the scope of materials management even though they are intimately concerned with it. But almost all of them do agree that materials management definitely embraces the purchasing function.[1] About 90 per cent of them feel that materials management should also include material control and inventory control. A majority be-

---

[1] "Will Today's P.A. Become Tomorrow's Materials Manager?" *Purchasing*, August 4, 1958.

lieve it should embrace traffic and receiving, and some feel it should further include production control, shipping, and materials handling. A few would also include receiving inspection.

Since only relatively few companies have a materials department headed by a materials manager, it is not easy to determine precisely who manages materials in most companies. However, the job is most likely to be performed by the top purchasing executive—the purchasing agent, director of purchases, or vice-president in charge of purchases. A study made some years ago by the National Industrial Conference Board of 280 representative manufacturers revealed the following role of purchasing departments in materials management:[2]

	Involved	Primarily Responsible
Scheduling purchases and deliveries	97%	76%
Inventory control	96	43
Incoming traffic control	94	35
Storeskeeping	96	32
Filing transportation claims	96	25
Receiving	94	22
Inspecting incoming material	94	14

When the functions listed above are not part of the purchasing manager's responsibility, they are almost inevitably delegated to departments subordinate to the manufacturing or production manager. The purchasing manager also is often subordinate to the vice-president in charge of manufacturing, but in an increasing number of companies he reports directly to the company's president or general manager. In 1948, a National Industrial Conference Board study of purchasing showed that the purchasing manager reported directly to the president or general manager in 49 per cent of the companies surveyed.[3] Ten years later a similar survey showed that he reported to "top management" in 77 per cent of the companies surveyed.[4]

Thus the purchasing manager's job is growing in importance. One of the major reasons for this is its broadening scope. It is reasonable to conclude that the purchasing manager is most likely to report to the top official in his company if departments other than purchasing are under his jurisdiction.

When most of the functions related to materials management are grouped together organizationally, the purchasing manager becomes a materials manager in fact, if not in title. Eventually managements recognize that the function being performed in this catchall department is no longer purchasing but something else—materials management. They

[2] *Purchasing for Industry*, Studies in Business Policy No. 33 (New York, 1948), p. 7.

[3] *Ibid.*, p. 5.

[4] "Will Today's P.A. Become Tomorrow's Materials Manager?" *op. cit.*, p. 15.

recognize this by changing the purchasing manager's title to "materials manager."[5]

Strategic Role

The materials manager is one of the top officials of the company. His responsibility begins with the receipt of blueprints and specifications for materials, components, or services that are either incorporated directly into the product or used in operation of the business. His responsibility ends when the material is used in production. But after the product is manufactured, the materials manager is once again responsible for it. He sees that it is transported, stored, and finally shipped to a customer. He may also be responsible for packaging the product.

Materials management is a basic function of every business. It is just as essential to survival and profit as the other basic functions: marketing, engineering, finance, manufacturing, and personnel.

The materials management job, however, does vary substantially from industry to industry. In the chemical industry, for example, it is largely concerned with the buying, transporting, and storage of basic raw materials. Once satisfactory materials are available for production, there are few, if any, materials management problems in this industry. In the aircraft industry, on the other hand, materials managers rarely are concerned with basic raw materials. Their major job is providing an adequate supply of components made to precise specifications. Problems often arise in this industry after material has been delivered to the production line. Design changes or manufacturing problems cause previously acceptable material to be rejected, and the materials manager must exercise ingenuity to prevent a shutdown because of lack of material.

Materials management is an important job even when the end product of the organization is a service. For example, governments and educational institutions could not operate without materials management. They spend billions of dollars for thousands of different items—ranging from police cars and complex pieces of experimental equipment to printed forms and paper clips—and each must be purchased and stored until it is needed.

Economic Relationship

Materials management is especially important to manufacturing companies because of its direct relation to their economic success. Each business has a limited amount of capital to invest in plant, equipment, in-

---

[5] It is true, of course, that the purchasing manager is not automatically destined to become materials manager. The new title goes to the executive best qualified for it. He may be, and often is, the former production control manager or a top-flight administrator transferred from engineering, marketing, finance, or manufacturing.

ventories, accounts receivable, and other assets. It is the basic job of management to employ that capital so as to yield the greatest possible profit for the owners. There are two basic ways of doing this: (1) By maximizing the margin of profit on each unit of product that is produced with the capital. (2) By maximizing the number of units of product produced with a given amount of capital.

Successful materials management contributes to both of these objectives. It maximizes profit margins when it reduces the cost of purchased material, and it permits greater output with a fixed amount of capital by efficient scheduling and inventory management.

Bigger Profit Margins. The typical manufacturing company spends about half of its sales dollar on purchased parts, materials, and services.[6] This is roughly twice as much as it spends on total payrolls.

Individual industries and companies may spend substantially more or less than half of their sales dollar on purchases. In the drug industry, for example, few companies spend more than 25 per cent of their sales dollar on outside purchases, while marketing and research expenditures take a disproportionately large share of the sales dollar as compared with the average manufacturing company. In the household appliance manufacturing industries, many companies spend 65 to 70 per cent of their sales dollar on purchased parts and materials. They do relatively little manufacturing, concentrating their efforts on design and merchandising.

In general, companies that either are highly integrated—manufacturing end products from raw materials—or are involved in producing a raw material spend relatively little for purchased material. A crude-oil producer, for example, would need only to purchase tools, equipment, and supplies; he would require no raw materials.

Even highly integrated companies require substantial expenditures for purchased materials. The United States Steel Corporation spends about a third of its sales dollar on purchased materials even though it produces a substantial amount of its own basic raw materials: coal, iron ore, and limestone. The General Motors Corporation operates more than 100 plants and produces almost every major component used in its automo-

---

[6] This estimate may be on the conservative side. The *Sixteenth Census of the United States, 1940—Manufactures*, published by the United States Department of Commerce, indicated that outside purchases comprised 58.1 per cent of aggregate manufacturing cost and 54.7 per cent of national output in terms of finished product cost. Unfortunately, more recent information is not available since over-all data on purchases were not included in either the 1947 or the 1954 census. However, a survey by the First National City Bank of New York (published in the August, 1960, issue of the bank's *Monthly Letter* on business and economic conditions, p. 90) indicated that in 1959 the 100 largest U.S. manufacturing corporations spent an average 52.3 per cent of their sales dollar on purchased materials and services. Since the very largest corporations would tend to be more integrated and make more of their own requirements than smaller firms, presumably all manufacturing corporations spend an even greater percentage of their sales dollar on purchased materials and services.

biles and other products. Yet GM still spends about 50 per cent of its sales dollar (see Figure 1–1) on purchased parts and materials—nearly twice as much as it spends on payrolls even though it employs more than half a million persons.

The average manufacturing company makes a profit of about 9 per cent on sales.[7] Since it spends about half its sales dollar on materials, slight reductions in materials cost exert enormous leverage on profits. If

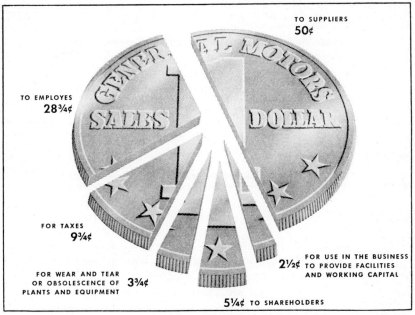

TO SUPPLIERS
50¢

TO EMPLOYES
28¾¢

FOR TAXES
9¾¢

FOR WEAR AND TEAR
OR OBSOLESCENCE OF 3¾¢
PLANTS AND EQUIPMENT

5¼¢ TO SHAREHOLDERS

FOR USE IN THE BUSINESS
2½¢ TO PROVIDE FACILITIES
AND WORKING CAPITAL

Source: General Motors Corp., *Annual Report to Stockholders*

FIG. 1–1. How General Motors Corporation spends its sales dollar.

the company reduces materials costs by just 2 per cent, the profit margin increases from 9 to 10 per cent and total profits go up 10 per cent. Every dollar saved in materials is the equivalent of $11.11 in extra sales with a 9 per cent profit margin. In many manufacturing companies, purchases exert even greater leverage on profits. For example, a one-dollar saving in materials cost is the equivalent of $12.82 in added sales for the Rheem Manufacturing Company (see Figure 1–2).

Greater Working-Capital Efficiency. Every business management tries to increase the return earned on its stockholders' investment. One way to do this is with greater turnover. If a company can produce $1,000 of sales with a 10 per cent profit margin on each $2,000 of its

---

[7] Profit margins vary substantially with business conditions, but 9 per cent is a fairly good average, as indicated in various issues of the *Quarterly Financial Report for Manufacturing Corporations*, published by the Securities and Exchange Commission and Federal Trade Commission.

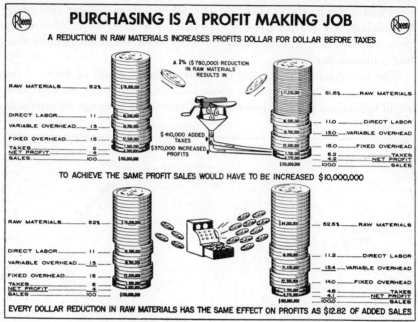

FIG. 1–2.

invested capital, then its profits of $100 provide a 5 per cent return on investment. But if management can figure out how to generate $2,000 in sales at the same profit margin on each $2,000 of assets, then return on investment will double and stockholders will earn 10 per cent.

This is the basic reason why every management tries to make its capital work as hard as possible. For even if there is no demand for the additional output that comes from additional turnover, the capital can still be profitably invested in other products or companies.

Successful materials management can do much to improve the efficiency with which capital is used. The average manufacturing corporation has about 24 per cent of its assets invested in inventories and only 39 per cent in net property, plant, and equipment.[8] (The other assets are cash, accounts receivable, and miscellaneous items.) Inventories are the second most important asset in the average company, and their control is one of the most vital phases of materials management.

If a materials manager can reduce inventories without impairing operating efficiency, he frees working capital that can be employed profitably elsewhere. Good inventory management also boosts profits (or reduces losses) in other ways. With it, the needed items are available in the proper quantities when required. If ten units of item A and five units

---

[8] *Quarterly Financial Report for Manufacturing Corporations.* The exact figures vary from quarter to quarter.

of item B are needed, then one does not stock five units of A and ten of B. With good inventory management there is a smooth flow of material because needs are accurately anticipated. As a result, operations are more efficient, there is minimum loss from spoilage and obsolescence of items not needed, and profits are correspondingly greater.

Successful timing of changes in inventory also can affect profits. If a materials manager adds to inventory and the market price rises, profits are enhanced. On the other hand, if he buys a material at ten cents per pound and the market declines five cents per pound, profits will be less than if he had successfully refrained from buying until the price declined. Most companies find it extremely difficult to anticipate their materials needs and almost impossible to anticipate prices with complete success. As a result, inventory control is one of the most difficult and challenging tasks of management.

If materials management is so important to a company's success, why is so little known about it? Why do so few companies have departments responsible for all phases of materials management? The answers to these questions are at least partly historical.

HISTORY OF MATERIALS MANAGEMENT

The function of industrial materials management is as old as the Industrial Revolution. Early industrialists, of course, were not formally acquainted with the principles of materials management or any other phase of management (although the successful industrialists applied many of the principles intuitively).

The First Factories

The concept of a separate and independent materials activity was a novel one to most managers even as late as 1900, when the United States and the leading western European nations were already heavily industrialized. However, since it is a basic function of the business, the materials management job was being performed. Each shop foreman was pretty much his own materials manager. In most companies, he ran his department like a semi-independent feudal barony with remarkably loose ties (by today's standards) of allegiance to the company as a whole. The foreman scheduled his own production, bought his own supplies, and did his own hiring and firing—all with a minimum of interference from top management if he did the jobs with reasonable competence.

If someone had proposed a separate and independent materials department to the typical manager of about 1900, he probably would have been ridiculed. Why should a company incur extra overhead by hiring a purchasing agent or materials manager to do a job that could be done as well or better by the shop superintendent or foreman? Besides, favors or kickbacks from suppliers were often a substantial part of a shop superintendent's income. If they were eliminated by transferring the buying power to someone else, the company would have to raise the salaries of its supervisors to prevent them from leaving to work for a competitor.

There is no basic need for a separate, independent materials activity if just one premise is accepted: skill in *managing* materials automatically accompanies skill in *specifying* and *using* materials. If one accepts this premise, one accepts the idea that a competent engineer or manufacturing manager is by definition a good materials manager, and materials automatically are managed as their specifications are developed and as they are used in operations. So there is no need for a materials manager.

This premise was widely accepted fifty years ago, and a few companies still accept it today. But modern, progressive managements know it to be false. They believe there is a distinct difference between skill in specifying and using materials and skill in buying them. They know that a professional buyer trained in economics and familiar with the capabilities of hundreds of suppliers can do a much better job than an engineer or foreman whose training and orientation are less suitable for buying.

Although modern managements accept the concept of a separate purchasing activity, only a few have departments responsible for every phase of materials management. One major reason for the lack of integrated materials departments in American industry is historical in origin. It is the almost inevitable result of the evolution of the great corporation from the small family-owned business.

Development of Purchasing Function

Materials management is just as essential to the firm with half a dozen employees as it is to the great corporation with half a million workers. The great corporation has full-time specialists in every phase of materials management (although they are not always grouped organizationally into a single, unified materials department).

In the small business there is little functional specialization. The owner-manager handles all the administrative jobs. He is normally his own materials manager, chief engineer, controller, marketing manager, manufacturing manager, and personnel manager. He can't afford the luxury of full-time staff specialists; about the only "experts" he does have are part-time attorneys and public accountants.

The Two-Manager Stage. When the small business grows, the work load of the owner-manager gets heavier and heavier. Fortunately, profits grow with sales. Eventually, the owner-manager feels prosperous enough (or is sufficiently overworked) to hire someone to help him with his administrative chores. He either hires an "assistant" or someone to supervise fairly well-defined functional areas—i.e., an office manager or "someone to take charge of the shop."

Regardless of the title that is given him, the addition of this second manager is one of the most significant steps in the development of the business. It is at this point that an "organization" begins to develop. With it come problems in communication and division of work. Responsibility no longer centers on just one person. As the organization continues to expand, it becomes far more complex. But the problems and changes are not nearly so far-reaching as when work is divided in some fashion between two full-time administrators in a still minuscule organization.

In the one-manager organization, all materials management responsibility centers on the owner-manager. When a second manager is hired, the owner-manager usually delegates to him part—but not all—of the responsibility for materials management. For example, the second manager may have responsibility for determining materials requirements and buying supplies, while the owner-manager retains responsibility for buying major materials and controlling major inventories. Regardless of how responsibility is divided between the two managers, it is inevitably a permanent division; never again in the typical company are materials managed by a single executive. The job is eventually dispersed among a number of executives working at different organization levels, who report to executives interested in other functions—particularly manufacturing and finance. Most companies enjoy unified materials management only in their infancy; unfortunately, they are then still too small to enjoy the benefits a specialist in the field can give them.

The P.A. Appears. As the company continues to grow and reaches the stage where it has a hundred or so employees, the two-manager type of organization becomes increasingly inadequate. More functional specialization is necessary; full-time managers of finance, production, sales, and engineering eventually appear. Finally, a separate purchasing department is formed. At first it may be run by someone who holds another job, too—that of office manager, controller, company secretary, personnel manager, or the like. But eventually a full-time purchasing agent is hired.

The new P.A. isn't a materials manager by any means. In fact, he rarely even has complete responsibility for purchasing. He buys the less important items, formerly handled by the shop superintendent, various engineers, the controller, and others. He may also take over certain other activities, including operation of the storeroom for supplies, the receiving department, and so on. But the manufacturing manager continues to be responsible for inventory management and top managers usually retain authority over all major contracts with outside suppliers.

At this stage in its growth, the typical company establishes a separate purchasing department mostly as a clerical convenience. The purchasing agent is definitely a second-string manager. He has yet to prove that he can make really significant contributions to the company's success. In fact, more often than not, top managers are still convinced (and in some cases, rightly so) that they can do a better job of buying than the professional buyers in their purchasing department. So they continue to dictate sources of supply for the half-dozen or so major commodities that in most companies comprise as much as 75 per cent of total dollar volume of purchases.[9]

The purchasing agent, at this stage in the development of the company, outranks shop foremen, but he is hardly the equal of the managers of finance, marketing, manufacturing, and engineering. However, if the purchasing agent is a good one, he may eventually convince his management that there is a lot more to purchasing than having lunch with suppliers and supervising a couple of clerks.

Management eventually does accept the idea that there is a distinct difference between skill in buying materials and using them. This takes time, however. By nature, almost everyone from housewife to corporation president not only thinks he knows how to buy things but also rather enjoys it. Even though they accept the theory that professional buyers buy better, many top managers are prone to make themselves exceptions to their own rules and inject their ideas into the company's buying operations.

Recognition of Purchasing

As purchasing grows in importance, the purchasing agent's stature, title, and function gradually change. In many companies the P.A. becomes a vice-president in charge of purchases and thus becomes the organizational equal of the heads of the other major departments. No longer is he a middle-management executive reporting to a manufacturing manager or a controller.

In most cases, the change in title and organization status is a formal recognition of gradual changes that have taken place in the purchasing executive's job over a period of twenty years or more. The process begins as top management gradually grows more confident that the P.A. is the logical man to make the actual buying decisions on major purchased materials and gives him authority to do the job.

If he is a genuine professional buyer, the P.A. can almost always do a better job of buying than those who formerly did it. Since purchases comprise a major part of any manufacturing company's cost, the top purchasing executive must work quite closely with other key managers. As the company's biggest spender, his efforts must be co-ordinated with the controller's department to control cash. Manufacturing depends on him for both the production materials and the supplies it requires. Close co-ordination between manufacturing and purchasing is essential for solving the inevitable problems in quality and delivery of purchased ma-

---

[9] This is still true today in certain industries. In big textile companies, for example, the purchasing department usually buys all needed supplies while someone else, usually the company treasurer, handles the company's most important purchases—the cotton, wool, and synthetic fibers that are woven into cloth.

terials that arise. Since practically every company relies on suppliers of parts and materials for aid in engineering and product development, the purchasing and engineering departments must work closely together on new products in order to enlist supplier assistance.

To do its job effectively, purchasing must be "in the know" regarding almost every activity in the company. It becomes almost essential that the top purchasing executive is a member of the company's key management group—its "operating committee" or "executive committee." Because almost every major decision affects purchasing, he also often winds up being a member of various other committees. These include the scheduling or production planning committee, the make-or-buy committee, the cost-reduction committee, the standardization committee, the product-planning committee, and others.

In companies with top-flight purchasing departments, purchasing personnel make all major buying decisions. They also actively assist engineers by introducing them to suppliers or new products they can use, and sometimes even make specific recommendations on design changes. They assist in inventory control by buying in the most economic quantities, making special arrangements with suppliers to reduce the need for safety stocks, and so on. They assist the sales department with supplier relations programs and, in some cases, with actual sales leads.

EVOLUTION OF MATERIALS MANAGEMENT

To do its job effectively, purchasing must have a particularly close relationship with the traffic and production control departments. In most companies the three departments together control practically all materials management activities.

Production control was originally performed by the foremen, who scheduled their own production and kept necessary records of inventories. Then parts of this job were performed by the superintendent's clerk, who kept necessary records while the superintendent continued to make the decisions. As more and more authority was stripped from line supervision and the scheduling process became more complex, the clerks eventually were superseded by a department of production control specialists.

Before the appearance of the traffic department, the traffic function usually was even more widely dispersed. Carriers were sometimes selected by suppliers, sometimes by the person responsible for the purchase, and occasionally by a top manager on the basis of personal friendship with a carrier representative. The other important functions of the traffic department were often performed casually by whoever selected the carrier or sometimes they weren't performed at all.

Managements in progressive companies now realize that their purchasing, production control, and traffic departments have jobs so closely related that they can work better together to achieve common objectives if they are linked organizationally. With this integrated approach to materials management, all of the jobs encompassed by these activities would be under the over-all direction of a materials manager.

Functions of Materials Management

There is no general agreement on what functions should be unified organizationally for unified materials management. Most would agree, however, that in a typical company they would embrace all activities concerned with materials *except* those directly concerned with designing or manufacturing the product or maintaining the facilities, equipment, and tooling. These would include most, if not all, of the activities performed by the following departments in the typical company: purchasing, production control, shipping, traffic, receiving, and stores.

The specific duties of these departments vary considerably from company to company and industry to industry. In general, however, they would include the following:

1. Production and Material Control. The production control manager helps set the over-all production schedule and is responsible for making certain that manufacturing has the parts and materials it needs to meet it. He directs five basic activities:

a) Computing detailed requirements for parts and materials—both purchased and manufactured—from up-to-date bills-of-material and specifications supplied by the product engineering department.

b) Scheduling production or purchase of parts and materials needed to meet over-all schedules for completed end products. This involves calculation of requirements for each item, taking into account such variables as inventory, lead time, on-order position, and so on.

c) Issuing work orders to manufacturing departments and purchase requisitions to purchasing for parts and materials needed to meet over-all production schedules. This includes following up to make certain schedules are met, and revising schedules when necessary.

d) Keeping detailed records of inventory, on-order status, and potential demand for each production part and material, and making periodic physical counts of stock to verify the accuracy of records.

e) Maintaining physical inventories of all direct (i.e., production) materials[10] in various stages of fabrication and administering controls necessary to maximize turnover and limit losses from spoilage, pilferage, or obsolescence.

---

[10] "Direct" or "production" parts and materials are incorporated directly into the end product. "Indirect" or "nonproduction" material is consumed in making the product but does not physically become a part of it. Screws used to fasten components of a product would be direct material. If the same screws were used for a minor repair in the plant, they would be a nonproduction maintenance supply. Solvent used to wash the product would be an indirect or nonproduction material. A standard package used to ship the product would probably be considered direct material by most cost accountants.

2. Nonproduction Stores. Techniques and procedures used to control nonproduction material (office supplies, perishable tools, and maintenance, repair, and operating supplies) resemble those used for production material, although they are usually less elaborate. Specifically, the stores department:

a) Maintains physical stocks of nonproduction items to be drawn on as needed for operations or maintenance.

b) Manages inventories of nonproduction materials and prepares purchase requisitions for needed material when stocks drop to the reorder point.

c) Keeps records and maintains controls to prevent duplication of inventories, minimize losses from pilferage and spoilage, and prevent stock-outs.[11]

3. Purchasing. The purchasing department buys material in amounts authorized by requisitions it receives from the production control and stores departments. There are four basic purchasing activities:

a) Selecting suppliers, negotiating the most advantageous terms of purchase with them, and issuing necessary purchase orders.

b) Expediting delivery from suppliers when necessary to assure delivery in time to meet schedules and negotiating any changes in purchase schedules dictated by circumstances.

c) Acting as liaison between suppliers and other company departments, including engineering, quality control, manufacturing, production control, and finance, on all problems involving purchased materials.

d) Looking for new products, materials, and suppliers that can contribute to company profit objectives. Acting as the company's "eyes and ears" to the outside world and reporting on changes in market conditions and other factors that can affect company operations.

4. Traffic. While purchasing buys parts and materials, the traffic department buys transportation service. It is always concerned with inbound shipments of purchased materials and is frequently concerned with out-bound shipments of finished products to customers. There are four basic traffic activities:

a) Selecting common or charter carriers and routings for shipments as required.

b) Tracing in-bound shipments of material in short supply as requested by production control or purchasing. Assisting customers in tracing out-bound shipments when asked.

c) Auditing invoices from carriers and filing claims for refunds of excess charges or for damaged shipments when required.

d) Developing techniques to reduce transportation cost. This may involve negotiation with competing shippers, special studies on selecting the most advantageous plant location for new products, analysis of tariffs, and negotiation of any number of special arrangements for handling certain traffic.

---

[11] Pilferage in particular can be a problem in stores management, since many of the items, like small tools, paintbrushes, pencils, and so on, can be used in the home as well as in the plant.

5. Receiving. The receiving department unloads and identifies incoming material, prepares a receiving report, and dispatches the shipment to the area in the plant where it is to be used or stored.

6. Shipping. Responsibility sometimes includes packaging of the finished product. It always includes necessary labeling and loading of end products and other miscellaneous items to the vehicle that will carry them to their destination.

Organization by Function

In most companies the six functions described in the foregoing become separate, but not equal, organization units. Their relative status depends on their importance to the organization as well as on other factors, including custom, habit, and so on.

Purchasing usually has the highest organization status of the six materials functions. The purchasing manager usually reports directly to the president or general manager and is on the second highest level in the organization. In some cases, he may report to the manufacturing manager or finance manager and be on the third level. Very rarely is he on the fourth level.

The production control manager and the traffic manager usually report on the third level. The traffic manager would normally report to the sales manager, purchasing manager, or manufacturing manager; the production control manager almost always reports to the manufacturing manager or works manager. Occasionally, the traffic manager reports directly to the president, and, in a few cases, so does the production control manager. Both are found more often on the fourth level of the organization than they are on the second.

The shipping, receiving, and stores activities rank much lower in the organization. They are almost always fourth level or lower. Their managers usually report—either directly or indirectly—to the production control or the purchasing manager.

Even though the various departments concerned with materials management often are not linked together organizationally nor even are on the same organization levels, the work they do is closely related. Each plays a necessary role at some stage of the materials cycle; this will be examined in detail in the next chapter.

Chapter 2

THE MATERIALS CYCLE

Materials management is concerned with the flow of materials to and from the manufacturing departments. The materials manager regulates this flow in relation to changes in demand for finished products, actual or predicted prices of materials, supplier performance on quality and delivery, availability of material, and other variables. He bases his decisions on information from other departments within his company, suppliers, and other sources, including news in business periodicals.

In its simplest form, most of materials management consists of learning how much to get, when, and from whom. Simple as this sounds, the job can be quite complex, both because of the fantastic amount of detail work involved and, as seen in Chapter 1, because of the tremendous impact of materials management decisions on a company's success or failure.

THE CARPET SWEEPER CASE

Suppose you were a materials manager for a small company making a relatively simple product like carpet sweepers. What would your job encompass? What would be some of the problems you would be likely to encounter?

The job would be more difficult than one might casually suppose. Even though a carpet sweeper is not a very complex product, the products of almost every industry would be needed to operate a carpet-sweeper plant. The carpet sweeper itself would probably have components made of zinc die castings, molded plastics, brushes made of wood, hog bristle, and glue, steel screws made by cold heading, sheet steel stampings, and so on.

In addition, thousands of other nonproduction items would have to be purchased before the first carpet sweeper could be shipped to a customer. Machinery, equipment, and a stock of spare parts to keep them in good repair would be needed, as would all the tools and supplies required to operate and maintain the factory and the office. These would include such diverse items as stationery, fuel for the plant's boilers, packaging supplies for the product, and countless others.

Materials management in even a small business often involves control of 8,000 to 10,000 different items when all supplies are considered. However, the major materials management effort is directed toward the

15

items that are "direct" material, i.e., incorporated directly into the product as parts, particularly the more expensive items. Usually 75 to 90 per cent of the materials expenditures in a manufacturing company are for direct material, and often a few key items account for a large share of direct material expense. Needless to say, materials managers try to spend more time on these major items than on minor ones, and most of them devote 75 to 90 per cent of their time to direct material[1] and concentrate a big part of it on problems involving a few key materials.

Good materials managers try to "manage by exception." They try to organize their departments so that major problems requiring decisions are promptly called to their attention while minor problems are automatically shunted to subordinates for solution. However, some managers delegate a minimum of authority early in the materials cycle, when the product is being designed. At this stage decisions are made that have an important effect upon every succeeding stage. Sometimes they may limit the materials department's flexibility in choosing supply sources for years to come, and bad design decisions can create innumerable problems at every stage of the cycle.

THE DESIGN STAGE

Prime responsibility for design rests with the engineering department, but the materials department plays a vital role. No company is so big that it can afford to have on its payroll scientists and engineers who are experts in the design, application, and processing of every part and material it uses. Suppliers make enormous contributions to every company's design efforts.[2]

The materials department is the company's prime contact with supply sources. It can act as a catalyst in bringing supplier know-how to bear on the company's technical problems. Veteran materials specialists often develop an expertise of their own, both from their educational backgrounds and from their association with suppliers. In some cases, they can assist with design problems that concern their specialities. For example, in a carpet-sweeper company, the materials specialist who handles zinc die castings could be the best-informed man in the company on die-casting technology. Engineers would be primarily interested in more critical parts of the carpet sweeper, such as the brush action, and, especially if the company does no die casting in its own plant, their knowledge of this specialized field could be fairly limited.

---

[1] Naturally this is not the case in educational institutions, in governments, or in companies that sell services.

[2] To a much greater extent than most people realize. For example, in a familiar product like an automobile, spring-steel bumpers, chrome-plated wheel covers, power steering, automatic transmissions, overdrives, and numerous other components were originally developed by suppliers, not by the auto manufacturers themselves.

Usually, the first step in creating a product whose appearance is important—such as a carpet sweeper—is to make sketches of various styles. The final style selected would presumably offer maximum sales appeal for the lowest possible cost. Sales appeal can be determined by previous marketing experience, market research surveys, opinions of top marketing executives, and so on. Cost can be evaluated by comparison of proposed designs.

It is not easy to evaluate relative costs simply by looking at an artist's sketch of a product. At this stage, specifications for materials, dimensions, and processes have yet to be determined. The engineering approach to cost estimating, where material weights are calculated from blueprints and the like, just won't work. The cost estimate becomes, in effect, a well-educated guess. The company's future profits can depend on how accurate the guess is. Once a decision is made and tools are constructed to make a given design, it becomes expensive to make changes.

Experienced materials personnel can estimate relative costs with almost uncanny accuracy because they are (or should be) comparing relative values of materials as a routine part of their day-to-day jobs.

Suppose that stylists propose four different approaches to a design for the outer cover of the carpet sweeper. Competent materials experts would review the designs. From experience, they would probably be familiar with the operations needed to make each cover, and they might also have opinions on relative cost. If they needed help, they could always call on a trusted supplier. With preliminary reviews of this sort, it often is possible to eliminate costly features that contribute relatively little to sales appeal or utility and add features that make a substantial contribution with little additional cost.

Once the style is agreed upon, engineers proceed to translate the stylist's sketches into detailed specifications to guide the manufacture of each component. Materials specialists also should work closely with the engineers at this stage. They can assist by proposing standard components, bringing in suppliers to aid in development work, guiding design decisions, and introducing engineers to new materials and techniques.

Standard Components. If a standard component can be used in a product, it usually costs less. In addition, there may be some saving in engineering and development cost since the standard item is already available. Sometimes the standard item costs less than the special one, even though it may have features that are inherently more costly. For example, if the engineer's calculations in designing the carpet sweeper indicate that a .45 horsepower motor is required, what size motor should be specified? The answer is a ½ H.P. motor. The slightly bigger motor is theoretically more costly but its price is lower because it is a standard size that motor manufacturers are already equipped to produce. Also, the price for the ½ H.P. design may be based on relatively large production volume if other manufacturers buy a motor with the same specifications.

Supplier Development. If the carpet sweeper is a new model, the key components will probably require some engineering development before they can be produced. Because they have the specialized product know-how, it is usually desirable to have suppliers do this for the components in which they specialize. For example, the vacuum cleaner motor might be an adaptation of some supplier's standard design.

In such cases, the company may effectively commit itself to buy from a certain supplier as soon as it asks for assistance on development. The supplier will incorporate his own specifications into the adaptation, and it will not be possible to get competitive bids from other suppliers. For this reason, the materials department should play a strong role in choosing the suppliers needed as engineering works on new product development.

Guiding Design Decisions. Engineers may sometimes have difficulty choosing from a number of acceptable designs and specifications. For example, it might be possible to make satisfactory wheels for a carpet sweeper from wood, molded hard rubber, molded plastics, steel stampings, machined gray iron castings, or die castings.[3]

The engineer can determine which materials and processes will do the job but he can hardly hope to be an authority on the relative cost and availability of each. Nor can he always be guided by previous design decisions. Markets change. While it may have been economic to make a component out of one material a year ago, an alternate material may be more desirable now. Relative prices and availability can change fast.

Introducing New Materials. Good engineers try to keep up to date on all new products and processes that might help them. But even with a simple product like a carpet sweeper, there can be just too many bases for the engineer to cover. Many different industries are involved and no single engineering department can keep up with all of them.

The materials specialist can help engineers by introducing them to suppliers who are promoting new ideas. For example, for the carpet sweeper, the materials specialist might suggest to his engineers that they test such new materials as molded Fiberglas for the exterior of the sweeper. Or he might propose molded nylon or sintered metal for the wheels—or anodized aluminum (instead of stainless steel) for the decorative molding.

Minor Changes. Different suppliers may use slightly different equipment and processes to make identical items. Minor changes in specifications often are necessary to adapt a design to their equipment and processes. The materials specialist (or buyer) must co-ordinate such changes

---

[3] In practice, there are rarely more than two or three acceptable choices among materials or fabrication methods. However, there are remarkably few products that do not have at least one alternative.

with his company's engineering department. Sometimes he also becomes involved in changes to permit quality standards to be met; in this case, he must bring together the supplier with both quality control and product engineers.

THE SOURCING STAGE

When the design is complete, the next basic stage of the materials cycle is sourcing.[4] Since very few manufacturers start with raw materials that they mine or grow themselves, this is largely a matter of determining the stage of fabrication at which a component or material will be purchased. At one extreme, a company may buy basic raw materials and perform all manufacturing and assembly operations in its own factories. At the other extreme, a company may concentrate its efforts on engineering and merchandising its products, and rely on outside suppliers to produce them complete.

Most companies follow a middle course between these extremes. They fabricate some items from raw material and rely upon outside suppliers for others. For example, the typical carpet-sweeper company might buy fasteners, moldings, and die castings as finished components. It might also buy semifinished items, like castings, forgings, copper wire, and sheet steel, which would be fabricated into parts to be assembled into finished carpet sweepers. Since the typical company spends about twice as much on purchased parts and materials as it spends on its payroll, it obviously finds it more advantageous to rely upon outside suppliers for many finished components and assemblies.

Make-or-Buy. The decisions that determine which parts to make in the shop and which to buy from suppliers aren't by any means made exclusively by the materials manager. Since they can shape the company's future for years to come, they are nearly always reviewed by all of the company's top managers. Among the variables that influence make-or-buy decisions are estimated manufacturing costs, purchase costs, technical skills, availability of material, and capital resources.

The materials manager plays a vital role in make-or-buy decisions. Estimates of the variables of the market place (present and future price and availability of materials and components) depend almost entirely upon his judgment. If he's wrong, the company may make a decision that will hurt its profits for years to come.

For example, suppose the carpet-sweeper manufacturer must make a choice between investing in facilities and equipment to make his own

---

[4] This is an oversimplification. In practice, design and sourcing are almost simultaneous operations for a product. Suppliers often are assured of business when the design is in its preliminary stage, although orders usually are not formally placed until the design is complete. Also, individual components may be ordered months before the final design of the assembled product is completed.

sheet steel stampings or molded plastic parts. The materials manager would estimate current purchase prices of both types of part and try to project future price trends. These estimates would be compared with estimates of the company's own manufacturing costs for these items.

The difference between the purchase price and the company's own manufacturing cost would be the company's return on investment should it decide to make the parts. If the purchase price declines in the future because of more competitive market conditions, the company's return on investment would also decline. On the other hand, if outside market prices rise, the return will rise. With a bad make-or-buy decision, the company's funds will be invested in equipment that yields small profits or, at worst, is an actual drain on the company's earning power.

Facilities Procurement. Once decisions have been made as to which products and components will be manufactured and which will be purchased, definite commitments can be made for needed facilities and equipment. Occasionally, buildings will have to be purchased. The materials manager would be partly responsible (along with other top executives) for selecting the site of the new building and letting the contract for its design. He also would handle all dealings with contractors and subcontractors for construction.

Contracts for necessary machinery and equipment would, in most companies, be the joint responsibility of the materials manager and the chief plant or process engineer. The latter would determine the technical specifications for the equipment; the former would handle necessary negotiation with suppliers and administration of purchase contracts.

PLANNING PRODUCTION

Once a company has a product and knows what its manufacturing facilities will be, it is ready to plan production. The planning process starts with a sales forecast, which may be based on market research studies, actual orders from customers, and the judgment of the company's senior marketing executives.

The Master Schedule. The materials manager rarely is directly concerned with the sales forecast but he is part of the group that translates this forecast into a master production schedule. Sometimes the schedule is identical with the market research forecast; usually it is different. The schedule must take account not only of basic market demand but of other factors. A good schedule has a minimum of fluctuations to facilitate economic operation, and it must also take into account availability of labor and materials and basic capacity.

The master production schedule influences the operation of every department in the company. For this reason, its final preparation and approval are usually a committee effort. Represented on the committee are the materials manager, marketing manager, finance manager, manufacturing manager, and other key officials.

Calculating Requirements. Each product has a bill of material that indicates the name, part number, and usage of each component, and, usually, the subassembly in which it is used. Material control clerks "explode" the bill of material by taking the schedule and multiplying the number of units in each product by the scheduled output of that product. They post this information as "demand" on a record card that is kept for each individual component. Records are normally kept on a monthly basis. In posting, the clerk allows a predetermined lead time that is shown on the card.

Suppose, for example, that the company plans on building 10,000 carpet sweepers in the month of August. Five units of a certain fastener are used in a subassembly of the sweeper. When the clerk explodes the bill of material, he knows that 50,000 fasteners will be needed for August production. But since these fasteners aren't used in the final assembly operation, they must be available before August. In this case, the clerk's records might indicate that he should allow 30 days for subassembly operations ahead of final assembly; he then knows he needs 50,000 fasteners during July.

After the clerk posts all future requirements on the master record card for each component, he compares future demand with current inventories and commitments outstanding on purchase orders or work orders. The card should at all times reflect the latest information on demand, supply, and inventory of the part. All changes in production schedules are posted to it, as are all receipts or withdrawals of material from stores and any physical counts taken of material by stock checkers.

Changing Schedules. Although they can be and are changed, schedules introduce inflexibility into the materials cycle. Individual components and the raw materials to make them must be ordered weeks or even months before the end product is assembled. During this period, there is danger that schedules will be disrupted. The demand for end products may change. Production problems with any one component can cause scheduling and assembly problems for countless other components and end products.

Clerks are quite capable of calculating what requirements will be when everything goes according to plan; materials managers must cope with the unforeseen. When one is controlling thousands of individual components, some problems are almost inevitable. There will be strikes at supplier plants, quality control problems, shortages of raw material, tooling difficulties, and so on. Materials management problems also arise when business is unusually good. If demand suddenly spurts, the flow of material must be accelerated. In such cases, materials managers look for the bottleneck items that will be most likely to prevent greater output and give them their personal attention, using techniques that will be discussed in future chapters.

THE ORDERING PROCESS

After a schedule has been determined for each item and requirements calculated, the ordering process begins. Requisitions and work orders are made up for each item. Typically they list unit requirements either for a given customer's order or for total production for several months.

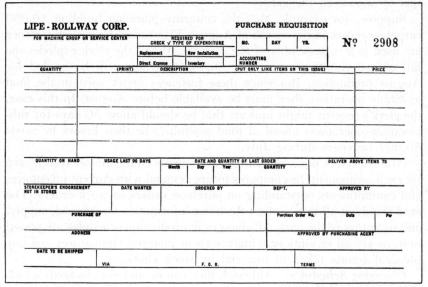

Courtesy Lipe-Rollway Corp.

FIG. 2–1. The purchase requisition is the authority to buy material from an outside supplier.

Purchase requisitions (see Figure 2–1) provide the authority to issue purchase orders (see Figure 2–2) to outside suppliers; work orders authorize the manufacture of components made in the shop. Work orders and requisitions are interrelated. If a work order is to be carried out on schedule, the purchase requisition for the raw material must be executed on schedule.

For example, a work order for a motor assembly for the carpet sweeper may automatically generate a purchase requisition for the bearings used in the motor. It may also generate a second work order, for the motor's commutator assembly, which in turn might create need for a third work order for the individual components of the commutator, which in turn would generate a purchase requisition for the silicon steel needed. Needless to say, a single failure in supply can raise havoc with the entire operation.

To prevent supply failure, materials managers must exercise considerable care in selecting vendors. Before contracts are awarded, suppliers' facilities and reputations are carefully investigated. Materials managers also review their companies' own records of how suppliers have handled previous orders; they naturally favor vendors who have

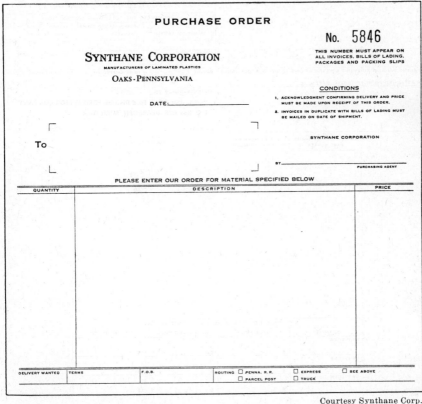

Courtesy Synthane Corp.

FIG. 2–2. The purchase order authorizes the supplier to ship and invoice for material in accordance with its terms and provisions.

done a good job for them in the past. But they also like to reduce prices they pay for materials, so they are prone to experiment with new suppliers who are willing to cut prices.

Placing the Order. Buyers send quotation request forms (see Figure 2–3) to three or more competing suppliers when they believe they can reduce prices by competitive bidding. Often there are substantial differences between the quotes of the high and low bidders. If the high bidder has an excellent record on quality, delivery, and service, while the low bidder's record is more dubious, the materials manager has a problem. To whom should he award the business?

To find the answer, he must compare the saving made by buying

FORD DIVISION
Ford Motor Company,

REQUEST FOR QUOTATION
BIDDER MUST FILL IN COMPLETE NAME AND ADDRESS

Gentlemen.

Please submit your price (less trade discounts) and terms of payment on materials listed below.

Omit Sales and Use Tax from your price, but include all other applicable taxes. Sales and Use Tax status will be indicated on the Purchase Order or Release. If you are legally required to pay this tax, we shall reimburse you for it in addition to the quoted price.

If unable to supply amount specified, please show hereon the quantity you can supply and your guaranteed deliveries.

Please insert unit price opposite each item and mail copy, properly signed, to this Company, retaining bidders' copy for your reference.

Quotation must remain open for acceptance for thirty days after receipt.

COMPLETE THE FOLLOWING INFORMATION

F.O.B.	TRANSPORTATION TERMS	PAYMENT TERMS
☐ CARRIER, SELLER'S PLANT	☐ COLLECT	☐ NET 20TH PROX.
☐	☐	☐

MINIMUM RUN (IN PIECES)	MIN. SHP. GUAN. (IN PIECES)	BEST DELIVERY DATE

PACKAGING AND/OR SHIPPING SPECIFICATIONS TO BE IN ACCORDANCE WITH ATTACHED FORM FD-1882-A. DATED

WEIGHT	TO BE SHIPPED VIA	SHIPPING POINT

ADDRESS REPLY TO:

Purchasing Office, Ford Division FORD MOTOR COMPANY
P.O. Box 628, DEARBORN, MICHIGAN

ATTENTION _____ ROOM _____ DATED _____

PARTS AND ACCESSORIES PART NUMBER	ENGINEERING PART NUMBER	PART NAME

FURNISH QUOTATIONS AS SHOWN BELOW

QUANTITY	PIECE PRICE	PACKAGING PRICE	TOTAL PRICE
IN PIECES	$	$	$
IN PIECES	$	$	$
IN PIECES	$	$	$

PPR. NO.

☐ BLANKET ORDER	$	$	$	BLUEPRINT DATE
INITIAL REQM'TS (PIECES)	AVG. MO. REQM'TS (PIECES)	DELIVERY REQ'D BY	DELIVERY REQUIRED AT	BID REQUIRED BY

IN ADDITION TO OUR STANDARD TERMS AND CONDITIONS, THE FOLLOWING WILL APPLY

ANY SUGGESTIONS RELATING TO PROPOSED CHANGES IN THE SUPPLIER COVERED BY THE REQUEST FOR QUOTATION WHICH YOU BELIEVE WILL RESULT IN IMPROVEMENTS IN THE SUPPLIER OR THEIR USE WILL BE WELCOMED. FORD MOTOR COMPANY ACQUIRES NO RIGHTS UNDER YOUR PATENTS BUT YOU ACKNOWLEDGE THAT SUCH SUGGESTIONS ARE NOT SUBMITTED ON A CONFIDENTIAL BASIS AND THAT ALL RIGHTS, CLAIMS AND REMEDIES IN RESPECT OF THEM (OTHER THAN THOSE ARISING FROM SUCH PATENTS) ARE WAIVED. PLEASE ADVISE US OF YOUR LOWEST QUOTATION FOR SUPPLIES CONFORMING TO BOTH THE BLUEPRINT DESIGN AND ANY SUGGESTED CHANGED DESIGN.

FIRM SUBMITTING QUOTATION

SIGNED BY AUTHORIZED REPRESENTATIVE   DATE

Courtesy Ford Motor Co.

FIG. 2–3. Quotation request forms are filled out by potential suppliers for any purchases in which there is price competition among producers.

from the low bidder with his estimate of the cost and greater probability of supply failure that might result from awarding the business to the low bidder. Since risks of this sort cannot be estimated precisely, such decisions are not easy to make. They depend to a great degree on the judgment and experience of the materials manager.[5]

The purchase order formally confirms the choice of supplier. It becomes, when accepted by the supplier, a contract between buyer and seller. Before the contract is finally accepted by both parties, there sometimes are legal problems to iron out. Special contract conditions may be negotiated, clauses may be added to the order, and so on. The materials manager must know enough about contract law to negotiate and write simple clauses. He must also recognize his own limitations and know when to call on an expert attorney for help with the more complex ones that occasionally arise.

Follow-up. The buying job does not end with the placement of the order. Not infrequently the supplier has difficulties with specifications, tooling, and so on. Even if there are no problems, a buyer cannot risk issuing a purchase order for an important item and then forget about it. He often follows the supplier's progress on the order in great detail to make sure that nothing happens to prevent delivery on schedule. If the item is in particularly short supply, the buyer may even go so far as to stay in the supplier's plant and watch work on the order progress so as to be assured that delivery will be made when promised. If the supplier has trouble getting raw material, the buyer may exert his pressure along with that of the supplier's buyer on the raw material producer.[6]

Packaging and Transportation. Before the supplier can deliver, he must be given instructions as to how to package and ship. In some cases, there is no problem since the delivery may be in the supplier's truck and the product may require no packaging. In other cases, the packaging specifications and/or the transportation routing may be quite complex. Because transportation and packaging are so costly, many companies

---

[5] They also depend on the materials manager's personality and the attitude of his superiors. Some materials managers are more willing to gamble on unknown suppliers than others. Most will back their bet on a new supplier either by protecting themselves with a larger-than-normal inventory or with a second source of supply. When neither of these alternatives is practical, some managers won't gamble on a new source regardless of the benefit. In big business and big government, the penalties for supply failure are quite real while there may be little or no reward for brilliant success when the gamble pays off. A smart management encourages intelligent risk taking.

[6] Buyers occasionally use spectacular and rather flamboyant methods to assure delivery. Use of chartered planes is not unheard of when material is in short supply. One of the most imaginative buying feats was performed by a General Motors buyer during the Korean War, when nickel was in short supply. He managed to buy substantial quantities of Chinese coins, which were then melted down, and the nickel in them presumably wound up being plated onto Chevrolet or Buick bumpers and other parts.

make elaborate studies and sometimes discover ingenious ways to reduce expenses.

Despite the most intensive cost-reduction efforts, transportation and packaging are still expensive,[7] and if their costs are reduced too much other problems result. Service is slower and damage in shipment is greater. As with the selection of suppliers, the materials manager must compare the savings from lower-cost packaging and shipping with the greater risk of loss that he assumes. Even if transportation and packaging are specified without regard to cost, there are problems. Shipments go astray or are damaged in transit. Claims must be made against the carrier for damages and bills must be audited for errors.

THE RECEIVING PROCESS

When material is shipped, the supplier encloses a packing slip. The common carrier (if one is used) encloses a bill of lading and an invoice for freight. All of these documents identify the material when it arrives at the buyer's plant. The receiving clerk checks them against his file of open purchase orders. He then physically checks the shipment to make certain that it actually contains the material indicated on the supplier's packing slip and the buyer's purchase order. This check involves weighing or counting the shipment, along with a general identification; it does not involve investigation of the material's quality to assure that specifications have been met.

The Receiving Report. The receiving clerk customarily fills out a separate receiving report (see Figure 2–4) for each shipment. In it, he describes the material being received, the number of the purchase order that authorized the shipment, and the name of the supplier. If there is a discrepancy between the quantity on the purchase order or supplier's packing slip and the quantity actually received, it is noted on the receiving report. Copies of the report accompany the material and also are sent separately to the purchasing department, the user of the material, and the accounting department.

Inspecting the Material. The next step in the receiving process is inspection. In many companies, the quality control inspector works in the same area as the receiving clerk. He compares the quality of incoming material with its specifications and blueprints, using gauges, laboratory tests, visual inspection, and other techniques. He reports his findings on an inspection report, which may be a separate form (see Figure 2–5) or part of the receiving report.

Copies of the inspection report usually go to both the buyer and

---

[7] Probably 10 to 15 per cent of the cost of the average product is transportation and packaging. In some cases, of course, transportation or packaging is the major cost. Sand and gravel cost more to ship than they do to quarry, and a toothpaste tube is worth more than the toothpaste it holds.

FIG. 2–4. The receiving report is used by the receiving department to notify interested departments of delivery of purchased material.

FIG. 2–5. The inspection report indicates whether or not purchased materials conform with specifications.

the supplier (although sometimes the supplier does not get a copy if the material meets specifications), as well as to other departments in the buyer's company. If the material is rejected, the buyer will contact the supplier and ask him how it should be disposed of.[8] The supplier may wish to have the material returned to him for either reworking or scrapping. If shipping costs are high, he will probably prefer to have the buyer either scrap the material or rework it himself at the supplier's expense.

If purchased material is returned to a supplier, the buyer must prepare a shipping notice that is, in effect, a purchase order in reverse, since it calls for the supplier to buy back the material he has sold. If the buyer reworks or scraps the material, he must negotiate an agreement with the supplier on the charges or credit for scrap.

Quality Problems. If an item fails to meet the buyer's specifications, the major problem usually is not an administrative one. Rather, the materials manager may, as a result of the rejection, have a shortage that can disrupt production. Suppose, for example, that a supplier of carpet-sweeper motors needs five weeks' lead time to complete each order he gets for motors. A shipment of motors arrives for the current month's production and is found defective. How does the materials manager prevent a shutdown of the carpet-sweeper assembly due to lack of motors?

Sometimes he can't prevent a shutdown, of course. But he can usually get good motors from an alternate supply source, from inventory, by reworking the defective motors, by having suppliers work overtime at their plants (which raises the question of who pays for the premium paid to workers for overtime—the buyer or the supplier), and other measures.

Needless to say, vendors aren't happy when their shipments are rejected. If the defects are their responsibility, the loss to them can be substantial, particularly if the parts cannot be reworked and are a total loss. Occasionally, vendors will challenge the buyer's quality control procedures and maintain that specifications actually were met on the shipment. Or they will maintain that the defects were not their responsibility—either that they weren't told certain specifications had to be met or that the parts were damaged after they left the supplier's plant.

The buyer must investigate all such complaints to make certain that the supplier has been treated fairly. He always should try to preserve amicable relations with suppliers even if this sometimes means going more than half way in reaching a compromise. He should also make certain that the supplier is familiar with his company's specifications and quality control procedures and will make an honest effort to correct quality discrepancies on future shipments.

---

[8] Buyer and supplier often have standing agreements on how material with certain types of defect should be handled, in order to reduce the volume of letters and phone calls.

INVENTORY CONTROL

If a shipment passes inspection, the receiving clerk usually prepares a "move" ticket that indicates to what area of the plant the material should go next. This ticket is physically attached to the shipment along with the receiving report and the inspection report. The material is then transported either directly to the user or to a storage area.

If the material goes into stores, which is true of almost all routine purchases, it becomes part of the company's inventory. It is carried on the company's balance sheet as an asset until it is incorporated into an end product that is sold to a customer.

Safety Margin. Without inventories, the typical materials manager's job would be hopeless. Every minor delay in every minor component would cause a serious shortage. Production rates of components and subassemblies would have to be perfectly synchronized.

Inventories provide a safety margin for defects in scheduling and errors in forecasting the demand for and supply of materials. If its stocks are big enough, a company can operate for months without buying any raw materials at all.[9] In-process inventories provide a cushion between manufacturing operations. Without them, the entire plant might be shut down if a single machine tool failed to operate. In-process stocks also facilitate synchronization of production. If one machine produces 200 units per hour while another machine produces 400 units, production can be balanced only by building up stock from the faster machine and then shutting it down to permit the slower operation to catch up.

Cost of Inventories. Although inventories solve many materials management problems, there are strong incentives for maintaining minimum stocks. Companies have a limited amount of cash to invest in inventories. Also, it costs as much as 20 to 30 per cent per year to store materials.

The materials manager must have material available when needed. But he can't afford to carry extra-large stocks just to make his job easier. He must balance the cost of carrying stock against the cost of possible shortages. His objective is the lowest over-all average production cost.

To achieve it, materials must flow smoothly through the plant. The proper quantities—no more, no less—of each of thousands of different items must be available at all times. Raw material stocks will be larger than the minimum only if there is some special advantage to be gained. In-process stocks should be the minimum necessary to prevent serious

---

[9] Steel companies normally have at least six months' stock of iron ore each fall in order to avoid costly rail shipments during the winter months, when the Great Lakes freeze over and water shipments from Lake Superior ports are cut off. Similarly, steel users always stock millions of tons of steel shortly before the contract between the steel industry and its union expires. Thus they usually are prepared to operate for two to three months on inventories if there is a strike.

production problems; the tighter the scheduling and material, the smaller the protective stocks needed.

Companies with poor materials management have both big inventories and frequent shortages. Their inventory doesn't prevent shortages because it's not balanced. There's enough stock of some items to last for months or even years, and no stock of one or two critical items.

THE FINAL STAGES

When material is delivered on schedule to the manufacturing organization, the materials manager has done his most important job. When manufacturing completes processing and assembles the final product, the materials cycle is almost complete. All that remain are the packaging, storage, and shipment of the end product.

These final stages rarely create as many problems for the materials manager as the earlier stages. Packaging must usually be synchronized with the production process.[10] The major effort on the part of the materials manager is directed toward improving packaging materials and equipment.

The storage of finished products is similar administratively to storage of raw materials. The materials manager would normally supervise the foreman in charge of the finished goods warehouse. But he would not control finished goods inventories. Such stocks exist to protect customers and give them better service, to permit more efficient operation of manufacturing plants,[11] or because demand for end products was lower than anticipated when schedules were made up. Decisions concerning finished goods inventories are normally made by a top-management committee of which the materials manager is a member.

The materials cycle for direct material ends with shipment of finished products to a customer. The materials department would always be responsible for loading the finished goods into the carrier and preparing necessary shipping documents. If the customer does not have a traffic department, it may also be responsible for routing the goods to their destination.

MANAGING INDIRECT MATERIAL

The problems of managing indirect material are similar to, but rarely as complicated as, the problems of managing direct material. The cycle

---

[10] In such cases, the workers who do the actual packaging may be under the supervision of a foreman or superintendent reporting to the manufacturing manager. The materials manager, however, retains responsibility for package procurement and may also be responsible for package design.

[11] Sometimes, for example, demand for finished products is seasonal, so the only way to operate the plant economically on a year-round basis is to build up stocks of finished goods during the slack season.

for indirect material starts with the initiation of the need for the material in any department of the company—manufacturing, personnel, marketing, engineering, finance, or the materials department itself.

Nonrepetitive Items. Each department needs certain materials and supplies in order to operate. It gets them by filling out a purchase requisition form if the item is not carried in stock. A buyer reviews this requisition against his purchase records, gets quotations, and issues an order to a supplier.

Thus, the materials cycle to this point is quite similar to that for direct materials. There is one basic difference, however. Direct materials are almost always purchased in accordance with definite engineering specifications. This is not always the case with indirect materials; many of them are bought the way the housewife buys—by brand name. For example, if a buyer gets a requisition for a desk calculator, he doesn't send a set of blueprints to each calculator manufacturer. Instead, he and the user of the material must evaluate various brands of calculator and compare their performance, features, and prices.

The purchase order will be for a specific brand of calculator. The materials cycle ends when the machine is delivered to the requisitioner who ordered it and operates satisfactorily.

STORES REQUISITION

NO. 89994 DATE__________

SHIP TO— ACCOUNT NO. EQUIP NO.

INTERNATIONAL MINERALS AND CHEMICALS CORP.

STOCK NO.	QUAN.	UNIT	DESCRIPTION

ORIGINATOR AUTHORIZATION

Courtesy International Minerals & Chemicals Corp.

FIG. 2–6. This form authorizes material to be drawn from stores and is later posted to the stores record.

Repetitive Items. The conventional procedure for buying nonrepetitive items like desk calculators is wasteful if there is a continuing demand for the item. For example, it would be ridiculous to issue a separate purchase requisition and purchase order each time a light bulb burned out. Commonly used nonproduction items are bought in fairly large quantities and stocked in a storeroom. Users withdraw them from stores by presenting a stores requisition (see Figure 2–6) to the stores clerk.

The clerk posts withdrawals from stock to his stores record (see Figure 2–7). When his stock drops to a certain reorder point, he issues a purchase requisition to authorize another buy. The purchasing procedure is similar to that for other items. Some nonproduction items are used in sufficiently high volume to justify a lot of time and effort in their buying.

Some companies even go to the trouble of making elaborate specifications for key nonproduction items. No longer do they buy by brand

INVENTORY RECORD										
Min. Point	Min. Quantity		Order Point	Order Quantity						
DATE	RECEIVED	DISBURSED	DISBURSED TO DATE	INVENTORY BALANCE		DATE	RECEIVED	DISBURSED	DISBURSED TO DATE	BALANCE INVENTORY
CODE NUMBER		ITEM								

FIG. 2–7. Receipts and withdrawals from stores for each item are posted to perpetual inventory record cards.

name. Instead, they invite a number of qualified suppliers to quote in accordance with their own specifications. This usually cuts costs. It also eliminates the problem of brand preference by users. If the materials department is forced to buy a specific brand, its efforts to get competitive bids are inhibited. In addition, inventories may be higher. If Supervisor X insists on Brand A and Supervisor Y insists on Brand B of the same item, then the item is duplicated in inventory.

Duplication is always a problem in nonproduction stores. It is almost impossible to draw up exact specifications for every item, and suppliers' descriptions and code numbers can be misleading. Stores personnel try to cope with these problems by using classification systems, periodic reviews of stock, standardization programs, and so on. But no system or program is foolproof. The only lasting solution is constant vigilance by alert and intelligent materials personnel.

CASES

CASE 2–1.   ZERO CORPORATION

ESTABLISHING AN INDEPENDENT MATERIALS DEPARTMENT

The Zero Corporation was founded in 1946 by George Frost, a former superintendent of a company that manufactured auto parts. The company commenced operations in a rented garage with a total of five employees. Because of its low overhead and Frost's manufacturing know-how, it was able to underbid larger competitors for contracts let by the "Big Three" auto manufacturers for small components used in their lower-volume truck lines.

Zero grew steadily. By 1959 its annual sales were $600,000 and there were about 70 persons on the payroll. Because the company got its business by being low bidder in a very price-conscious industry with excess capacity, profits didn't increase nearly as fast as sales. They were only $25,000 in 1955, the company's best year.

For all his work during this period, Frost had succeeded in paying himself only a moderate salary ($15,000 per year) and meeting obligations to his creditors. By 1959, he concluded that he was in the wrong business and began to look for a product where there was less price competition. He became acquainted with Robert Blank, a salesman for a firm making household refrigerators. Blank proposed to Frost that he manufacture refrigerated frozen-food display cabinets for grocery supermarkets. Although several other companies were already in the field, Blank was convinced that it was growing fast enough to support a newcomer.

Blank proposed that Frost hire him as sales manager with a special salary and bonus arrangement. He also suggested that Frost hire Harold Brown, a young engineer who worked for the same large company as Blank, to head the design department. Frost talked to Brown, liked him, and suggested that he prepare a preliminary design proposal on a consulting basis in his spare time.

Frost then studied Brown's preliminary designs. He decided that he was equipped to produce some of the sheet-metal components of the cabinets and that he could assemble them with a minimum of additional investment—no more than $600,000 for plant, equipment, and inventory.

Meanwhile, Blank had not been idle. He discovered that a major grocery chain was contemplating a complete renovation of a number of its stores and would be in the market for as many as 10,000 cabinets. The chain planned to buy them piecemeal from a number of manufacturers. Frost suggested that Blank approach the chain's fixtures buyer and propose a contract arrangement for the entire 10,000 cabinets. The stores would not only get a lower price but would also get a design that was uniquely tailored to their needs.

The buyer was impressed with Blank's presentation and suggested that Zero Corporation present a formal proposal. Frost, Blank, and Brown went to work immediately. Working from Brown's preliminary specifications, Frost got quotations from major suppliers for such key components as compressors, electrical accessories, steel, and so on. He then estimated his fabrication and assembly costs and added a moderate profit.

The store's buyer and director of purchases reviewed Frost's proposal and asked for additional price concessions. Frost complained that his estimated profit was already very modest and showed the buyers his cost estimate. A summary of the cost estimate indicated the following:

Purchased parts and materials	$405.30
Direct labor	72.60
Manufacturing overhead	90.75
Manufacturing cost	$568.65
Sales, engineering, and administrative expense	33.45
Profit	66.90
Unit selling price	$669.00

Frost pointed out that practically all of the $66.90 profit would be needed to amortize the special tooling that Zero would have to invest in for the new contract. He observed that the company would have to make an investment of $600,000 in facilities, tools, and equipment, so it would do little more than pay off this investment on the first order for 10,000 cabinets.

The prospective buyers considered this to be Frost's risk in doing business. They pointed out that about two thirds of Zero's sales dollar would go to outside suppliers. They felt that it wasn't enough just to solicit bids from a few leading companies when making a cost estimate. In their opinion, Zero should be able to get its material at least 10 per cent cheaper by shopping around, and unit material cost should actually be no more than $360. They also suggested that since Zero had no previous experience in the field, the chain store was entitled to an extra-close price for risking its business with a new supplier. The buyers finally succeeded in persuading Frost to accept the contract at a unit price of $600, which would provide Zero with no profit at all unless actual costs were less than the estimate.

Frost accepted the order because without it he would find it almost impossible to raise the money to go into the refrigeration business. With the chain-store order in hand, Frost went to an investment banker and asked for help in raising the $600,000 he needed. The banker arranged a $300,000 loan and, late in 1959, another $300,000 was raised with a stock issue. Zero was in the refrigeration business.

Blank and Brown immediately became full-time employees of the company; the sales and engineering functions were well taken care of. Frost himself intended to devote his time to general management with special interest in the finance and manufacturing areas. He already had a capable accountant and shop superintendent to assist him.

While the company was in the auto parts business, the job of materials management had been pretty much divided between Frost and the shop superintendent, Richard Howard. The job was not too complex, since the company's only product was steel stampings made to auto company specifications.

When the company quoted on a job, Frost studied the blueprint. From experience, he could readily estimate the blank size and cost of material. He then determined the manufacturing operations that would be required and noted the equipment he would use if he got the order. He then sent his estimated operation sheet and the blueprint to a friend of his who ran a tool shop for an estimate of the cost of special dies that would be needed.

If he got the order, Frost ordered sufficient steel to handle the contract from a nearby mill. The superintendent scheduled production in accordance with requirements on customer orders. His system was simple. He kept a separate record for each piece of equipment and then "reserved" time on it for each job. For example, if a customer wanted 2,000 parts delivered during the month of August, the superintendent might schedule a press for the first operation on the 4th and 5th of the month, the second operation on the 6th, the third on the 7th, and so on.

Both the superintendent and the accountant purchased materials and supplies that they needed to do their work. They got Frost's approval for any unusual purchases, but bought everyday items as the need arose. The accountant had a cabinet in which he stored office supplies; employees got supplies by coming to him. The superintendent had a storeskeeper who doled out material to the workers and the two job foremen as required. Materials that were bulky and not subject to pilferage were stored in open plant areas.

Frost realizes that materials management will become more important now that the company is entering the refrigeration business. It will be necessary to buy equipment and tooling to fabricate the stampings and assemble the completed units. The volume of purchases will increase and will also become more diverse. For the first time, the company will be buying components, ranging from compressor assemblies consisting of several hundred components and costing about $60 to fasteners with a unit cost of a few mils.

The company will have to deal with at least a hundred suppliers for production parts and materials, with plants located in many different areas. Formerly, it purchased its basic production material—steel—from two mills. Because of the wider diversity of operations, Frost believes that a greater variety of nonproduction materials will have to be purchased. Inventories of both production and nonproduction materials will increase, both because of the expected increase in volume of business and because of the greater complexity of the product.

Frost wonders if the materials management system that has worked quite well in the past will continue to work under these new conditions. He explains his doubts to his informal operating committee, consisting of the sales manager, the chief engineer, and the shop superintendent.

Both the superintendent and the chief engineer believe that the old system will continue to work best because, under it, administrative overhead will be minimized. The superintendent believes that he can schedule production and buy necessary tools and supplies just as he has done in the past. He thinks he may need a clerk to help him. The chief engineer points out that he will have to work with suppliers in developing final engineering details of the refrigeration equipment, and that it will take but little effort on his part to follow through and actually place the orders for components.

The sales manager disagrees with this view. He believes that materials management is a separate function of the business and should be handled by a materials manager.

Questions

1. Bearing in mind that the company wishes to keep administrative overhead at a minimum, what are some of the arguments that Blank, the sales manager, should advance for the establishment of a separate materials organization at Zero?
2. What functions should the materials department at Zero embrace? What should be the materials department's relationship with the production and engineering departments?

Chapter 3

THE OBJECTIVES OF MATERIALS MANAGEMENT

Managers always should direct their efforts toward achievement of the general objectives of the business. The two most general economic objectives are survival and profits. A business has other noneconomic objectives, of course. These may include favorable community relations, maximum service to customers, pleasant working conditions and opportunities for advancement for employees, technological lead, and others.

Each function of the business should work to achieve these objectives. The materials function is no exception. It contributes to survival and profits by providing materials at the lowest over-all cost. There are many ways it can achieve this over-all objective. The most obvious is to pay minimum prices for materials. But doesn't the materials function also help achieve this objective when it boosts inventory turnover or gets material of superior quality? In both cases, the true cost of material is reduced, in one because of less investment and in the other because of fewer rejections due to failure to meet specifications.

Let us now examine in detail some typical objectives of materials management. Each, in some way, will contribute to the achievement of some over-all company objective. If the contribution is one made directly by the materials function, we shall call it a "primary" objective. If it is indirect and results from the materials department's assisting some other department in achieving its objectives, we shall call it a "secondary" objective.

Primary Materials Objectives

Almost every materials department has at least nine primary objectives. These are low prices, high inventory turnover, low cost of acquisition and possession, continuity of supply, consistency of quality, low payroll costs, favorable relations with suppliers, development of personnel, and good records.

Low Prices. This is the most obvious materials objective and certainly one of the most important. If the materials department reduces the prices of the items it buys, operating costs are reduced and profits are enhanced. This objective is important for all purchases of materials and services, including transportation.

High Inventory Turnover. When inventories are low in relation to sales (inventory turnover = sales ÷ average inventories), less capital is tied up in inventories. This, in turn, increases the efficiency with which the company's capital is utilized, so that return on investment is higher. Also, storage and carrying costs of inventories are lower when turnover is high.

Low-Cost Acquisition and Possession. If materials are handled and stored efficiently, their real cost is lower. Acquisition and possession costs are low when the receiving and stores departments operate efficiently. They also are reduced when shipments are received in relatively large quantities (thereby reducing the unit cost of handling) but naturally are increased if average inventories are boosted with the large shipments.

Continuity of Supply. When there are disruptions in the continuity of supply, excess costs are inevitable. Production costs go up, excess expediting and transportation costs are likely, and so on. Continuity of supply is particularly important for highly automated processes, where costs are rigid and must be incurred even when production stops because of lack of material.

Consistency of Quality. The materials department is responsible for the quality only of the materials and services furnished by outside suppliers. The manufacturing department is responsible for quality control of manufacturing processes. When materials purchased are homogeneous and in a primitive state (e.g., sand and gravel), quality is rarely a big problem for materials personnel. But when the product is in a highly advanced stage of manufacture and specifications are a tremendous challenge for suppliers to meet consistently (e.g., components of interplanetary missiles and rockets), then quality may become the single most important objective of materials management.

Low Payroll Costs. This objective is common to every department in the company. The lower the payroll, the higher the profits—all other factors being equal. But because no department can do its job without a payroll, the objective of low payroll must be viewed in proper perspective. It pays to spend $1.00 on additional payroll if earnings can thereby be boosted $1.01 through achieving other objectives.

Favorable Supplier Relations. As was pointed out in Chapter 1, manufacturing companies rely on outside suppliers to a far greater degree than is generally recognized. This makes favorable relations with suppliers extremely important. A company's standing in the business community is to a considerable degree determined by the manner in which it deals with its suppliers. A company with a good reputation in supplier relations is more likely to attract customers than one with a bad name.

Suppliers also can make a direct contribution to a company's success. Their product development and research efforts can be of tremendous assistance to their customers. Although such efforts naturally help the supplier too, it is important to remember that suppliers are human beings and respond to fair treatment. If a company has good relations with its suppliers, it will be far more successful in its efforts to stimulate superior performance from supplier personnel—extra service, co-operation on cost-reduction projects, a willingness to share new processes and ideas, and so on.

One of the major problems of materials management is sudden shifts in the demand for materials, requiring either rapid cancellation of existing commitments or extra output to prevent shortages. Co-operative suppliers can do much to help the materials manager with such problems.

Development of Personnel. Every department in the company should be interested in developing the skills of its personnel. And each department head should devote special effort to locating men in junior posts who have the leadership potential the company needs for continued success and growth. They should try to develop these high-potential men as the company's future executives; the company's future profits will depend on the talents of its future managers.

Good Records. Paper work is a means to an end, not an end in itself. So it may be surprising that good records are considered a primary objective of materials management. How can they contribute to the company's survival and profits?

The fact is that records and paper work contribute only indirectly to the materials department's contribution to profits. They are necessary and useful; they help materials personnel do a better job. This can also be said of office equipment, yet the maintenance of the materials department's stock of typewriters, adding machines, and the like would hardly be considered a primary objective. Good records, however, must be considered a primary objective in the purchasing and traffic phases of materials management for the same reason that they are a primary objective in the accounting department.

Buyers spend company money and can be subject to tremendous temptation. Suppliers may wine and dine them and give them gifts for Christmas and other holidays. Although perhaps 99 per cent of all buyers are above corruption, the opportunity does exist. Good records, along with well-planned administrative controls and periodic audits, can discourage corruption. They also partly remove the onus of suspicion from a completely honest individual working at a job that is popularly associated with graft and corruption.[1]

Secondary Objectives

The secondary objectives of materials management are not nearly so limited in scope and variety as the primary objectives. Since they repre-

---

[1] This is particularly true in government procurement. But all buyers probably suffer some loss of social prestige because their jobs are unjustly associated with graft in the public mind. Groups like the National Association of Purchasing Agents have done much to boost the prestige of the buyer by establishing ethical standards.

sent the materials department's contribution to the achievement of the primary objective of some other department, they can vary widely from industry to industry.

There are literally hundreds of possible secondary objectives in materials management. Among the more common ones are reciprocity, new materials and products, economic make-or-buy decisions, promotion of standardization, product improvement, good interdepartmental relations, and accurate economic forecasts.

Favorable Reciprocal Relations.   When a company deliberately buys from its own customers as much as possible, it is practicing reciprocity. Sound reciprocity involves a balancing of the advantages and disadvantages of using one's buying power as an instrument for getting sales. Similarly, suppliers will use their buying power as customers as a sales tool.

In the consumer-goods industries, reciprocity is rarely a problem; sales are spread among many users. In producer-goods industries, however, reciprocity is a way of business life, particularly among industries where there is little product differentiation and prices are uniform. The materials department in such industries often co-ordinates its purchases with the sales department to make certain that company customers get favored treatment.

New Materials and Products.   Engineering and manufacturing managers are always interested in new products and materials that will help them operate more efficiently and thereby achieve one of their primary objectives. The materials department can help. Its personnel deal regularly with the suppliers responsible for the new developments. Whenever they learn of anything of interest, they can call it to the attention of the interested parties in manufacturing, engineering, or other departments.

Economic Make-or-Buy.   Make-or-buy decisions are often sparked by materials personnel since they are the group most intimately concerned with the selection of supply sources. But by no means are they solely responsible. As pointed out in the previous chapter, make-or-buy decisions should be a committee effort, representing the points of view of all departments in the company. The materials department, in its regular reviews of cost and availability of materials, often will spot the need for new make-or-buy decisions and should refer them to the committee for action.

Standardization.   The fewer the items that need be controlled, the simpler and more efficient the materials management process. Thus it is to the selfish interest of materials personnel to promote standardization and simplification of specifications. The engineering groups are primarily responsible for standards and specifications. But materials personnel can make a substantial contribution. They can periodically review stock to weed out nonstandard items; they can promote the incorporation of standard components into product designs to reduce cost; and they can promote standardization with suppliers.

Product Improvement. This is perhaps the single most important objective of the engineering department. Materials personnel can assist, however. Their economic knowledge can supplement the technical skills of the engineers on programs to boost profits through product change. The engineering of practically any product is basically a compromise between design and economic objectives. Materials personnel can help engineers achieve their design objectives more economically by suggesting materials or components that will do a better or equivalent job at lower cost.

Interdepartmental Harmony. The materials department deals daily with every other activity in the business. It not only can contribute to the success of every other department, but its own success depends on how successful it is in gaining the co-operation of personnel in other departments. In practice, most materials managers are fully aware of the importance of good interdepartmental relations. To prevent disputes, they are careful to define departmental responsibilities clearly (this will be discussed later in this chapter) and also try to familiarize others with materials objectives, policies, and organization.

Forecasts. To manage materials well, one must have some conception of the future outlook for prices, costs, and general business activity. Some sort of forecast is required. In large companies, professional economists make forecasts that are used for both sales and purchase planning. Materials personnel translate these general forecasts into specific forecasts for purchased materials. They may also provide the economists with "raw material" for forecasts because, more than any other group in the company, they are intimately familiar with the market and general business conditions through their daily contacts with suppliers.

In the smaller company that can't afford a staff of professionals, the materials manager may double as company economist. In such a case, good forecasts become a primary, not a secondary, objective of materials management.

ACHIEVING OBJECTIVES

The primary and secondary objectives that we have discussed would be applicable to most manufacturing companies. However, objectives would vary in relative importance from industry to industry and even among companies within an industry. One company may devote considerable effort to one objective while another may concentrate most of its efforts on a different one. Here are three examples to illustrate this point:

Price Objective Paramount. In the tanning and woolen textile industries, the raw material is always available at a price. But price fluctuations can be violent. Wool and hides (and other commodities, like crude rubber, zinc, and copper) have been known to double or triple in price within six months or decline by a proportionate amount.

For users of the material, the key objective is to pay minimum prices for material. It overshadows all others in importance. A shrewd materials manager can save ten—or even a hundred—times as much by intelligent timing of purchases as he can hope to save through achievement of other materials objectives.

Reliability Required. In the aircraft and missile industry, consistency of quality (i.e., reliability) is all important. Almost any minor component can cause a $1,000,000 missile to malfunction. The odds favor failure because of the very complexity of the product. Even a 99.9 per cent quality standard may be inadequate. With this standard one part in 1,000 will be unsatisfactory. Since each missile contains more than 1,000 parts, it is likely that each will contain a component that will fail.

Too Much Inventory. In companies making a wide range of complicated products (instruments, machine tools, and similar items), the key problem usually is inventory turnover. Not only must the company have thousands of items available for production, but often it stocks tens of thousands of repair parts for customer service. If demand is erratic, there is always the danger that inventories will become unbalanced. So the materials manager strives to prevent stockouts without tying up too much of the company's capital in inventory.

Effect of Business Changes

Objectives also can vary within the same company. When sales are expanding, the materials manager may concentrate on continuity of supply and consistency of quality. He may be less interested in inventory turnover or low prices since the economic expansion should bring both higher sales and higher prices, and so these objectives will be achieved automatically.

But when business slumps, the story is different. Sales are dropping faster than output, so the materials manager is hard pressed just to keep turnover from dropping and he must be nimble to avoid being greatly overstocked when the business cycle nears the bottom. During this period, he is also under considerable pressure to reduce prices because his company is often under pressure to cut the prices of its end products despite slipping profit margins and lower sales volume.

Similarly, during a war or some other period of extreme scarcity, the simple act of locating sources of supply may become the single most important materials objective. This is also true when a key supplier is shut down because of labor trouble. Even under reasonably normal conditions, there can be an unpredicted upsurge in the demand for a finished product that can put considerable pressure on the materials manager to locate additional sources of supply fast enough to satisfy the demand.

In a young company that is growing rapidly, cash is perpetually short. All earnings and all borrowings are plowed back into plant and equipment. Some must be invested in inventory, of course. But the materials manager is under considerable pressure to get along with as little stock as possible in order to make cash available for other purposes. To boost inventory turnover, he may buy in small quantities, even if this means he must forego quantity discounts and raise his cost of acquisition because of the greater number of receivals necessary to operate on a hand-to-mouth basis. He also may buy from suppliers with slightly higher prices, provided they will deliver with little advance notice.

Balancing of Objectives

The examples above provide clues to one of the most basic parts of the materials manager's job: balancing of objectives. Objectives vary in im-

TABLE 3–1

INTERDEPENDENCE AND POTENTIAL AREAS OF CONFLICT
IN PRIMARY OBJECTIVES OF MATERIALS MANAGEMENT

Primary Objective	*Other Objectives Adversely Affected*
1. Low prices for purchased items	High inventory turnover, low cost of acquisition and possession, continuity of supply, consistency of quality, favorable relations with suppliers.
2. High inventory turnover	Low cost of acquisition and possession, low prices for materials purchased, low payroll costs, continuity of supply.
3. Low cost of acquisition and possession	Low prices for purchased materials, high inventory turnover, good records.
4. Continuity of supply	Low prices for purchased materials, consistency of quality, favorable relations with suppliers, high inventory turnover.
5. Consistency of quality	Low prices for purchased materials, continuity of supply, favorable relations with suppliers, low cost of acquisition and possession, high inventory turnover.
6. Low payroll costs	Concentration on this objective can readily restrict achievement of all other objectives.
7. Favorable relations with suppliers	Low prices for purchased materials, high inventory turnover, continuity of supply, consistency of quality.
8. Development of personnel	Low payroll costs.
9. Good records	Low cost of acquisition and possession, low payroll costs.

portance. During certain periods, the materials manager may concentrate on one objective, and at other times he may concentrate on another objective.

Achievements Bring Sacrifices. Efforts to achieve one primary objective almost necessarily involve relaxation of efforts to achieve some other objective. The materials manager who concentrates on inventory turnover pays higher prices and has higher costs of acquisition because he must buy more frequently in smaller quantities.

On the other hand, if a materials manager goes all out to get lower prices, he will buy in larger quantities to get quantity discounts. This will reduce inventory turnover. The higher average inventories will inevitably raise costs of possession, although unit costs of acquisition will probably decline because of the greater average size of each shipment. Continuity of supply and consistency of quality also may be affected. The materials manager will be tempted to go to "cheap" suppliers who cut prices and also cut corners on quality and don't live up to their delivery promises. The objective of favorable supplier relations will suffer because of the shifting of business to the "cheap" suppliers and because of the steady pressure for price reductions.

Basic Principle.   All materials objectives are interrelated. As illustrated in Table 3–1 (see preceding page), a gain in one objective brings sacrifice on other objectives. In materials management you never "get something for nothing."

The materials manager must always be ready to re-evaluate his objectives when business conditions change or when they are affected by top-management decisions.

POLICIES AND PROCEDURES

After the materials manager determines the relative importance of his objectives, he devises a program to achieve them. In directing the program, the materials manager wants to manage by exception if possible. That is, he wants to delegate the achievement of the program completely to his subordinates. If everything goes according to plan, the materials manager does not interfere. But if something goes wrong because of a basic defect in the plan, the materials manager wants to learn of it. He may have to re-evaluate the objectives and devise a new plan or take other remedial steps.

Definition.   Written policies and procedures permit management by exception. They guide routine performance. With them, management decisions are needed only when an exceptional problem arises. Policies are broad, over-all guides to performance. Procedures are the specific administrative actions needed to carry out policies. Policies define in general terms the basic jobs of each department and its relation to other departments; they are derived from the general goals and objectives of the department itself and the company as a whole. Procedures are derived from policies. They describe routine operations in great detail.

An Example.   One big aircraft and auto parts manufacturing company includes low prices and favorable vendor relations among its materials objectives. To achieve these objectives, it has a written policy that "negotiations with vendors regarding price, terms, quality, etc. should be initiated, conducted, and concluded by the purchasing department."

This policy might be carried out with the following procedures: (1) A buying procedure whereby no purchase commitment is valid unless it is approved by a member of the purchasing department. (2) A procedure that prohibits anyone in departments other than purchasing from interviewing supplier salesmen without written approval of the purchasing agent.

Similarly, if a company were to have a policy of stimulating maximum competition among suppliers (in order to achieve an objective of low prices), it might have a procedure calling for a minimum of three bids on each purchase.

Advantages of a Manual

Progressive materials departments have these and literally hundreds of other policies and procedures codified in manuals that sometimes are hundreds of pages long. They invest in hundreds of hours of a high-priced specialist's time in preparing the manual. Moreover, such manuals are no good unless they are kept up to date, so frequent revisions are necessary as well.

After all this work, what usually happens? Nine policy and procedure manuals out of ten may not be referred to for months or even years. They just gather dust on supervisors' bookcases.

Very few persons in a well-managed company ever have much need to refer to a manual. Each knows his job, and if he has any questions he simply asks his supervisor for the answers. New employees don't have much use for manuals, either. They normally learn their jobs by observing their fellow workers and through verbal instructions from their supervisors.

Yet the best-managed companies have manuals for materials policies and procedures. They have them because manuals promote good interdepartmental relations (a secondary materials objective), make supervision easier, encourage standard practices, improve procedures, and aid in training.

Interdepartmental Relations. Even the best organization structure represents, to some extent, a rather artificial division of work. Departmental responsibilities overlap. Each department must work with the others if the over-all job is to be done. Written policies and procedures define interdepartmental relationships. Thus they prevent many unnecessary jurisdictional disputes and also can prevent duplication of effort.

Written materials policies are particularly important because the materials department must work with other departments on problems where it is sometimes hard to determine jurisdiction. For example, although the materials department is responsible for selecting suppliers, using departments certainly have a right to receive the materials they need and to solicit suppliers for advice. Without written policies, jurisdictional disputes are almost inevitable when two departments are independently working with the same vendor on the same problem.

Make Supervision Easier. With written policies and procedures, a supervisor need not develop original solutions to routine problems. Nor need he even explain routine procedures to his subordinates (although he may wish to do so to make certain they understand them). The answers are in the manual. In most cases, the manual need not be referred to because employees already know what is in it. But were there no manual as a basic record, employees would gradually forget certain details of little-used procedures and the load on supervisors would be correspondingly greater.

Develop Standard Practices. Without written policies and procedures, each supervisor would devise procedures to fit his superior's not-always-consistent instructions. As a result, eventually the same job would be performed in many different ways. Operations would be less efficient, communication slower, and supervision poorer. With written policies and procedures (called "standard practices," because that is exactly what they're designed to promote), supervisors will still deviate from routine when necessary, but they will have basic guides to make them aware that they are deviating, and these in themselves will tend to prevent them from making unnecessary changes in routine.

Improve Procedures. When a manual is prepared, procedures are subjected to close scrutiny, which they may never have received before. Improvements are almost inevitable. Unnecessary paper work can be eliminated. Tighter controls can be instituted if necessary. Periodic review and revision of the manual can prevent sloppy practices from creeping back into the system.

Training Aid. Although new employees are often lazy readers and prefer to get their training by watching and talking with fellow employees, the manual is still helpful for reference. It is also useful to employees in other departments.

The job of preparing or revising a manual can be a training vehicle in itself. There is no better way to give a new, high-potential man a good grasp of the over-all workings of the department, and also permit him to apply his imagination and resourcefulness to improvements in procedures.

Preparing the Manual

The materials department probably has more need for a policy and procedures manual than any other department in the company. The main reason for this is its contact with outside suppliers. Difficulties arise because almost everyone in every department likes to buy and feels particularly competent to buy the items he uses. Controllers like to buy their own accounting machines, maintenance superintendents prefer to select brands of cleaning compounds, and product engineers feel they should select suppliers of parts and materials.

Because of these difficulties, preparation of a materials manual is an especially long and tedious job. Since most of the important policies and procedures affect other departments, the person writing the manual must submit a draft of the proposed policy to each affected department head for approval. In many cases, hours may be spent discussing precisely how a given policy should be worded so that each department's prerogatives are protected.

The usual procedure in preparing a manual is first to determine what is being done and then to describe each operation in writing. Existing procedures are analyzed critically. Then the materials manager and his staff try to put down in writing what they would like to have done. This includes both policies and procedures. Existing procedures are then modified to fit these goals and drafts are submitted to all interested department heads for approval. The whole process always takes a few months and occasionally more than a year.

The effort is worthwhile, however. Written objectives, policies, and procedures provide the framework within which the materials organization does its job. But they're useless, of course, if the materials department does not also have the organization it needs to achieve the objectives. The principles of building a materials organization will be discussed in the next chapter.

CASES

CASE 3–1. GENERAL ELECTRIC COMPANY
Determination of Materials Objectives

The General Electric Company is one of the largest manufacturing corporations in the world. It employs about 250,000 persons, and its sales are more than $4 billion. Volume of purchases is more than $2 billion, and more than $600 million is invested in inventories. The company makes thousands of different products in hundreds of plants, including numerous consumer products, heavy capital goods, components and materials for industrial customers, and various defense products.

Organizationally, the company is broken up into more than a hundred different operating departments. Each department specializes in a certain product line; for example, the company's Home Laundry Department in Louisville, Kentucky, makes washers and driers for the home. Each department is operated, to the greatest extent possible, as an independent business. Department managers have considerable latitude in choosing their staff, negotiating for materials with suppliers, developing their own product and marketing strategy, and so on. The company's headquarters group, centered in New York City, exercises a minimum of authority over the departments. However, it does lay down over-all policies that the department managers are supposed to follow. For example, the company has a mandatory policy requiring each of its department managers to comply fully with all government regulations and laws, including the antitrust laws.

In general, however, the headquarters staff tries to give the department managers maximum freedom to operate within the framework of company policy. The performance of managers is measured as much as possible in terms of the over-all objectives of the company. These objectives are:[2]

1. To carry on a diversified, growing, and profitable world-wide manufacturing business in electrical apparatus, appliances, and supplies, and in related materials, products, systems, and services for industry, commerce, agriculture, government, the community, and the home.

2. To lead in research in all fields of science and in all areas of work relating to the business, including managing as a distinct and a professional kind of work, so as to assure a constant flow of new knowledge and of resultant useful and valuable new products, processes, services, methods, and organizational patterns and relationships; and to make real the Company theme that "Progress Is Our Most Important Product."

3. To operate each business venture to achieve its own favorable customer acceptance and profitable results; especially by planning the product line or services through decentralized operating management, on the basis of continuing research as to markets, customers, distribution channels, and competition, and as to product or service features, styling, price range, and performance for the end user, taking appropriate business risks to meet changing customer needs and to offer customers timely choice in product and service availability and desirability.

4. To design, make, and market all Company products and services with good quality and with inherent customer value, at fair prices for such quality and value.

5. To build public confidence and continuing friendly feeling for products and services bearing the Company's name and brands through sound, competitive advertising, promotion, selling, service, and personal contacts.

6. To provide good jobs, wages, working conditions, work satisfactions, and opportunities for advancement conducive of most productive performance and also the stablest possible employment, all in exchange for loyalty, initiative, skill, care, effort, attendance, and teamwork on the part of employees—the contributions of individual employees that result in "Value to the Company" and for which the employee is being paid.

7. To manage the enterprise for continuity and flow of progress, growth, profit, and public service through systematic selection and development of competent managerial personnel for effective leadership through persuasive managerial planning, organizing, integrating, and measuring for best utilization of both the human and material resources of the business; using a clear and soundly designed organization structure, and clearly expressed objectives and policies, as a vehicle for freeing the abilities, capacities, resourcefulness, and initiative of all managers, other professional workers and all employees for dynamic individual efforts and teamwork, encouraged by incentives proportionate to responsibilities, risks, and results.

---

[2] As cited by General Electric's president, Ralph J. Cordiner, *New Frontiers for Professional Managers* (New York: McGraw-Hill Book Co., Inc., 1956), pp. 119–21.

8. To attract and retain investor capital in amounts adequate to finance the enterprise successfully through attractive returns as a continuing incentive for wide investor participation and support; securing such returns through sound business and economic research, forecasting, planning, cost management, and effectively scheduled turnover of all assets of the enterprise.
9. To cooperate both with suppliers and also with distributors, contractors, and other facilitating distribution, installation, and servicing of Company products, so that Company efforts are constructively integrated with theirs for mutually effective public service and competitive, profitable progress.
10. To adapt Company policies, products, services, facilities, plans, and schedules to meet continuously, progressively, foresightedly, imaginatively, and voluntarily the social, civic, and economic responsibilities commensurate with the opportunities afforded by the size, success, and nature of the business and of public confidence in it as a corporate enterprise.

Department managers at General Electric have considerable latitude in developing their organizations. There is no "standard" way to organize a General Electric department. However, most GE departments have materials managers who supervise the purchasing, production control, traffic, shipping, and receiving activities. These materials managers are expected to help their department achieve their over-all objectives.

Question

What specific objectives might General Electric materials managers develop to help their department achieve their general objectives?

CASE 3–2.   LAWTON PRODUCTS COMPANY

DETERMINING MATERIALS MANAGEMENT OBJECTIVES

The Lawton Products Company was formerly known as the Lawton Camera Corporation. The new name was adopted in 1946 to reflect the company's broadened product line. Lawton was founded in 1915 by Howard F. Lawton, Sr., to manufacture and market a relatively expensive line of cameras designed especially for the amateur photographer. The company grew at first by widening its line of photographic equipment. Home movie cameras, movie and slide projectors, and a best-selling line of 35-millimeter "candid" cameras were introduced between 1920 and 1935.

The company prospered in the camera business not only because its products were of high quality and well merchandised but also because the company successfully avoided the problem of foreign competition with its products. Until World War II, the market for high-quality cameras was dominated by German manufacturers who had gained world-wide acceptance for quality and dependability. Although they were protected by an extremely high tariff, American manufacturers were hard put to compete even in their own market. Their products usually were not so widely accepted as the leading German brands. In addition, their costs were much higher; American camera workers were no more productive than German workers but their wages were more than twice as high.

Lawton's solution to the problem of German competition was to buy major components from Japanese manufacturers, who could undersell both American and German firms. Lawton confined its efforts to design, assembly, and marketing.

The company was extremely successful, and by 1938 it had sales of $10 million with profits of nearly $600,000 after taxes. In 1938, however, Howard Lawton became increasingly fearful of the threat to the company's survival if war should cut off his supplies of Japanese components, and so he decided to diversify. At that time, the company was doing almost no manufacturing. While Lawton desperately wanted to acquire manufacturing know-how on camera equipment, he had no desire to cut off his Japanese suppliers if he didn't have to. His solution was to buy the Abramson Company, a small manufacturer of optical instruments. In Abramson, Lawton got a profitable company with experience in optical equipment, which could easily be converted to manufacture of camera components if necessary. The Abramson plant was located just a few miles from the Lawton plant, so there was no difficulty in integrating Abramson into the Lawton organization.

Pearl Harbor not only cut off Lawton's source of components, but it also cut off all manufacture of cameras for amateur photographers. The Lawton Corporation expanded its instrument line to serve the war effort. It also became one of the U.S. Navy's major contractors for optical fire-control equipment and gained considerable experience with the elaborate electric and electronic controls used in this equipment.

After the war, Lawton was able to use much of its expanded manufacturing capacity to broaden its line of photographic equipment. It also was able to apply its wartime skills in optics and electronics to a greatly expanded instrument line. In 1950 the company developed a closed-circuit television unit for industrial process control and added another line of process-control instruments to use with its TV systems. In 1951, the company reactivated its fire-control business when it got several major Navy contracts, and by 1960 the company had become a major supplier of fire-control and missile-guidance equipment for both the Navy and the Air Force.

The company's 1960 sales were $165 million or more than sixteen times as great as in 1938. Profits did not keep pace, however; they grew less than 500 per cent in this period. The company's after-tax margin has deteriorated steadily since 1955, and in 1960 the company earned only 2 per cent on sales and just over 5 per cent on net worth. This was substantially below the 1960 average after-tax returns of all durable goods manufacturers (about 4 per cent on sales and 8 per cent on net worth).

In an effort to get to the bottom of the problem of declining profit margins, Howard Lawton, the company's president, has hired the management consulting firm of Smith, Martin, and Conrad to make a broad survey of the company's organization, policies, and procedures.

The company's organization has grown a great deal since the 1930's but its structure has changed very little. Reporting directly to Howard Lawton are vice-presidents in charge of sales, engineering, manufacturing, and finance.

Reporting to the sales vice-president are an administrative assistant, advertising manager, public relations manager, sales personnel manager, general sales manager, and four product managers. The general sales manager supervises regional sales managers responsible for sales of all of the company's products except cameras.

The product managers for instruments, defense products, and electronics each supervise a small staff. They are responsible for:

1. Co-ordinating complaints from customers with manufacturing and engineering.
2. Liaison with engineering on new products and design changes.
3. Production and materials planning, including the breaking down of orders from customers, preparation of purchase requisitions and factory work orders for parts, and preparation of over-all schedules.
4. Preparation of quotations on new business from data secured from the cost department and interested activities.

Sales of camera equipment are handled somewhat differently. Since cameras are marketed through consumer channels, an entirely separate sales force is needed. It is under the direct supervision of the camera product manager. The manager is also responsible for market research on cameras, styling, co-ordination with engineering on new product development, and purchase of all imported purchased components and complete products.

The company's purchasing manager, who reports to the vice-president in charge of manufacturing, is responsible for buying all raw materials used in the company's products, as well as all nonproduction materials. Reporting to him are two buyers (one for direct material and the other for indirect), supervisors of the storerooms for both production and nonproduction materials, and the company's general foreman in charge of receiving inspection. In addition, the purchasing manager supervises a small data-processing group that keeps records of all the company's inventories, including finished goods and in-process stocks. He also is functionally responsible for the purchasing specialists in the engineering department and provides them with forms, clerical services, and so on.

Also reporting to the manufacturing vice-president are the superintendents of the company's two plants, the production planning and control manager, the traffic manager, the factory personnel manager, the master mechanic, the cost estimating manager, the work standards manager, and the quality control manager.

The planning department prepares schedules, requisitions, and work orders for cameras from sales forecasts it receives from the camera product manager. It also participates in, but is not directly responsible for, production planning for other products.

The foremen of the shipping and receiving departments report to the traffic manager. Their activities require only a small amount of the traffic manager's time, most of which is spent on traffic problems on outgoing shipments of camera products and occasionally on assisting customers for other products when they do not specify any routing. The company has always relied on its suppliers to handle all in-bound shipments. Even foreign suppliers take all responsibility for getting their shipments to Lawton and handle all details of shipping, customs, and so on.

The engineering department is organized almost entirely by product. There are chief product engineers for each of the company's lines. Reporting to each chief product engineer are various engineers who specialize in certain details of the product. Each chief engineer also has one or more buyers working for him, who handle most routine contacts with suppliers. Individual engineers also work closely with the company's suppliers. On new products, they often rely on the supplier for substantial assistance in development. Suppliers do not charge for this service. They are rewarded indirectly, however, since the final specifications for the item usually are tailormade to their processes, and, in some cases, they even indicate that the component should be purchased from the supplier who assisted in its development.

The engineering department is responsible for about 40 per cent of the company's $110 million purchase volume. About 25 per cent is spent by the camera department product manager on imported products and components, 30 per cent is spent directly by the purchasing manager, and the balance is spent by the office manager for office supplies and by the master mechanic for machine tools and equipment.

The office manager reports to the general accounting manager, who in turn reports to the vice-president in charge of finance. Also reporting to the general accounting manager are the supervisors in charge of office personnel, accounts payable, and accounts receivable. Invoices from suppliers go directly to accounts payable, where they are logged into a register and then sent for approval to the department responsible for the purchase. The department that made the purchase compares the invoice with the receiving report and the receiving inspection report and approves it if everything is in order. The approved invoice is then returned to accounts payable for payment. During an average month, accounts payable processes invoices for more than $9 million and manages to take discounts for prompt payment on all but about $500,000. Terms vary, but most suppliers offer a 1 to 2 per cent discount if bills are paid within ten days.

Questions

1. Should Smith, Martin, and Conrad recommend any changes in Lawton's approach to materials management?
2. What are Lawton Company's probable materials management objectives?
3. How can it better achieve these objectives?

Chapter 4

ORGANIZING FOR MATERIALS MANAGEMENT

Someone in every organization must make materials management decisions. Since, as we saw in Chapter 3, materials objectives are inter-related, it is desirable to give one person authority over all activities concerned with materials management. Otherwise, no one—other than the president of the company—can be held responsible for materials decisions.

Suppose, for example, that materials authority is dispersed among a number of departments in a company (see Figure 4–1). A purchasing

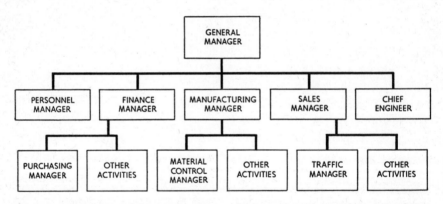

FIG. 4–1. Divided responsibility for materials management. In this organization, the general manager is the only person responsible for all phases of materials management, including purchasing, material control, and traffic. Since he is involved with many other problems, materials don't get managed as well as they should.

agent reporting to a finance manager is in charge of buying parts and materials. A traffic manager reporting to the sales manager buys trans-portation services. A material control manager reporting to the manu-facturing manager schedules materials and controls inventories.

Now suppose that one of the company's immediate objectives is to reduce materials cost by 5 per cent. If the objective is actually achieved, the material control manager, purchasing agent, and traffic manager—and their respective bosses—all can share the credit. But who is respon-sible if the objective isn't achieved? Each has a legitimate alibi. The material control manager is not responsible for negotiating prices of materials and services. The purchasing agent buys in amounts determined by the material control department, and his prices and bargaining power are determined by the quantities he buys. The traffic manager can't cut freight costs if purchasing insists on buying from suppliers in distant cities.

The only person who can be held responsible for results in achieving materials objectives is one who has authority over all phases of materials management (see Figure 4–2). In companies that don't have integrated materials departments, this is the president of the company. Unfortunately, he usually is too involved in other company problems to be able to do a good job of materials management. So a materials manager is essential for successful materials management.

The materials manager should be a top official of the company. The materials point of view is critical in many over-all policy decisions. Also, the materials manager should be fully informed of all company plans.

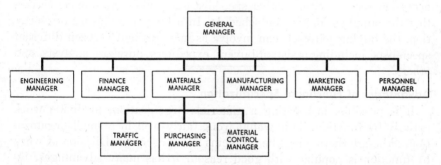

FIG. 4–2. Division of work by function. The over-all job of management is delegated by its major functions. Division of work at the third level is also usually functional. For example, the materials management job is divided functionally into its traffic, purchasing, and material control elements.

He must be in a position to change his program to cope with changes in over-all company policies and objectives.

Almost every materials manager requires a staff to help him achieve his objectives. Materials management is a big job. In a fairly small concern it may require 20 or 30 persons; in a big corporation, hundreds or even thousands will be needed. The over-all materials job must be divided up into many different jobs under some sort of organization structure. In the ideal organization, objectives are consistently achieved at low cost and with a minimum of confusion. This ideal is hard to achieve, for organization is hardly an exact science. Two different managers will build entirely different organization structures, even though there are relatively few ways in which work can be divided in creating an organization. Among those that are feasible for a materials organization are division of work by: (1) function; (2) location; (3) product; and (4) stage of manufacture or process.

ORGANIZATION BY FUNCTION

The most widely used organization technique is division of work by function (see Figure 4–2). The principle behind it is a sound one: jobs should be organized so as to promote maximum specialization of skills. With functional specialization, jobs are broken up so that they are as narrow as possible in scope. Each man is an expert in some highly specialized area.

There is considerable functional specialization in every materials organization. Breaking up the over-all materials job into its components (purchasing, traffic, material control, and so on) is a form of functional specialization. Within these groups, there is even more specialization. For example, purchasing may be broken up so that one person receives purchase requisitions and prepares the records for a buyer. Another person, the buyer, contacts suppliers and actually places orders. Another specialist may do nothing but type purchase orders, and another files the necessary records. Still another specialist may follow up to make certain that the suppliers deliver on schedule. In a large purchasing organization, the buying job itself can involve as many as half a dozen different specialists, including assistant buyers, expediters, purchase analysts, and others.

Advantages of Functional Specialization

It is possible, in creating a materials organization, to divide work entirely by function. This would work fairly well in a small organization, although there might be problems in a larger one. Division of work by function is popular with good reason. It has many advantages, including:

1. Economic Use of High-Salaried Help. With functional specialization, jobs can more readily be broken up into highly skilled and less skilled elements. A well-paid buyer doesn't type his own purchase orders (he probably wouldn't have this skill anyway); he relies on a typist whose salary is substantially lower. This permits the buyer to use his special skills more effectively. Functional specialization also makes it economic to hire specialists whom the organization could not otherwise afford.

For example, in the typical company, buyers in the purchasing department and various marketing executives all can make profitable use of periodic forecasts by a professional economist. By setting up a separate economics department to serve the entire company, each executive can get the benefit of an expert's advice. An additional function, economic forecasting, is created to serve a number of departments. Each executive served by the economist in effect delegates part of the forecasting element of his job to the economist, so that there actually has been a division of work by function.

2. More Efficient Operation. With functional specialization, it is possible to become extremely adept at one particular job. A girl who runs a calculator all day in production control is bound to be more accurate and efficient in her work than one who uses the same machine only occasionally.

3. More Flexible Organization. An organization with a maximum of functional specialization can adjust more readily to changes in business volume. The reason is that it makes the most effective use of a few highly skilled persons who are always needed. When volume is low, they handle both skilled and unskilled jobs. When it expands, less skilled persons can be hired to take over elements of their jobs. There is no need to hire additional highly skilled people, who might not even be available in a period of business expansion.

Disadvantages of Functional Specialization

Unfortunately, excessive application of the principle of functional specialization can cause serious weaknesses in the organization. Among them are:

1. Employee Dissatisfaction. People get bored when their jobs become too specialized. They like variety. Also, with specialization, the general objectives of the business can become too remote from the jobs of those who are supposed to achieve them. People may become so engrossed in their specialties that they begin to regard them as ends in themselves and not as means of reaching some broader company objective.

2. Bureaucratization. If jobs become too specialized, everyone is liable to "pass the buck" and disclaim responsibility for solving a problem that isn't routine or for an error that is made. Also, an organization with a great deal of functional specialization is often "deep"—with many layers of supervision. This makes for a long chain of command and causes the decision-making process to be slow and complex.

ORGANIZATION BY LOCATION

In a large organization with many plants, the need for some application of the principle of organization by location is self-evident (see Figure 4–3). Each plant requires a materials organization, and at least part of that organization must be physically located at the plant. Therefore division of responsibility by location is essential.

Organization by location is also practical in companies that operate only one plant. Many plants have more than one receiving, shipping, or stores department. In such cases, division of responsibility usually is by location, with each unit serving a given part of the plant.

When the materials organization is by plant, materials personnel can work more closely with the other departments in that plant. They become more intimately familiar with the plant's problems. The major disadvantage of organization by plant is that it tends to disperse the materials organization. Some of the advantages of specialization are lost, and buying power is often diluted.

Organization by plant is naturally essential for some elements of the materials job, notably shipping and receiving. Organization by area served is similar. In the materials department, it is particularly applicable to field expediters and traffic clerks. Field expediters can deal with suppliers in given areas. For example, one California aircraft company has field expediters in Cleveland, Ohio, and Hartford, Connecticut, to expedite needed shipments from Eastern and Midwestern suppliers. If a traffic clerk specializes in shipments from a given area, he will rapidly all but memorize tariffs of carriers serving that area and so will be able to do his job more efficiently.

For other parts of the materials department, organization by location is rarer. The disadvantages of this form of organization in purchasing, for example, usually outweigh the advantages.

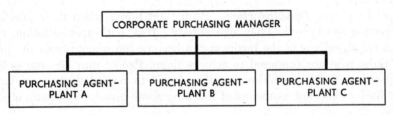

FIG. 4–3. Division of work by location. When similar functions are being performed in areas remote from each other, division of work by location is desirable at some level in the organization.

ORGANIZATION BY PRODUCT

Since the materials organization exists to help make some product or service more profitably, breaking up materials activities by product is logical (see Figure 4–4). Each materials group is assigned to some product or group of products. For example, the purchasing departments of the General Motors Corporation are set up on a product basis. There is a separate purchasing department for each product division: Chevrolet, Pontiac, Frigidaire, and so on.

Within the materials departments, division of work by product or commodity is quite common. Purchasing departments often are organized so that each buyer specializes in a few commodities. (This is a combination of functional specialization and product specialization.) One buyer may specialize in castings and forgings, another in sheet steel, and so on. The production control organization frequently follows the same pattern. In a cruder fashion, so does stores. Raw materials often go to one stores department, finished parts to another, and so on.

The big advantage of organization by product is that it permits personnel to become really familiar with the problems of a single group of products. As a result, they should be able to do their work more effectively. When the over-all materials organization is broken up into a number of product groups, as it is at General Motors, each member's job is more closely related to the profit objectives in a particular product line.

The main disadvantage of organization by product is that it tends to disperse the over-all materials effort. In a company as large as General

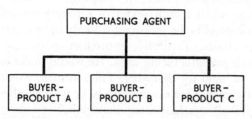

FIG. 4–4. Organization by product. There is no better way to make a man conscious of profit margins than to give him responsibility for performing a vital function in the manufacture and marketing of that product.

Motors, this dispersal probably is no handicap. But it would be highly uneconomic, by contrast, to have the traffic organization broken up into product groups in a company employing 1,000 persons and making 100 fairly similar products.

ORGANIZATION BY STAGE OF MANUFACTURE

Organization by stage of manufacture (see Figure 4–5) is consistent with our basic concept of materials management as the administration of the flow of materials to and from production equipment. And some might regard the functional division of materials responsibility into purchasing, traffic, production control, and other components as also being a division by stage of manufacture. Responsibility passes from department to de-

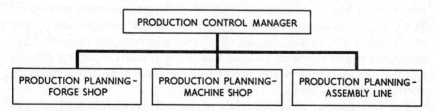

FIG. 4–5. Organization by stage of manufacture. The manufacturing organization is almost always by stage of manufacture. Materials personnel are able to work more closely with manufacturing when they are organized in a similar manner.

partment as the material or component moves from the idea stage to fabrication in the vendor's plant through the buyer's receiving and stores to the point where it is utilized in his manufacturing process.

Carried to its extreme, application of the principle of division of work by stage of manufacture to the materials organization would require an individual materials manager for each stage of the manufacturing process. For example, one materials manager would be responsible for raw materials, another for the early stages of the process, and so on. This form of organization is impractical, of course, since most materials functions are best set up so that they serve an entire plant. (It would be especially impractical to break up shipping, receiving, and traffic into separate groups so that each served a separate manufacturing area.)

Production control is the group most likely to be organized on a stage-of-manufacture basis. Typically, a production control man might be assigned to each manufacturing area. He would make certain that there was material on hand for that area. This, in turn, would involve liaison either with purchasing, for raw materials, or with another manufacturing area that supplied semifabricated materials.

The principal advantage of a stage-of-manufacture organization is that it brings materials personnel into intimate contact with manufacturing problems, where they are in the best position to suggest new products and materials to boost efficiency. The major disadvantage of stage-of-manufacture organization is that the benefits of functional or commodity specialization are often lost and bargaining power with outside suppliers becomes too widely dispersed.

SPAN OF CONTROL

We have seen that there are four major ways in which to divide work in the materials organization. But before we can build a materials organization, there is one other principle with which we must become familiar. It is called "span of control." We already know how we can divide work. But without understanding the principle of span of control, we do not know how many divisions we should make.

If we have a materials organization with 100 persons, should we have one general materials manager and 99 assistant materials managers? If so, we are assuming that the general materials manager has a span of control of 99, that is, he can effectively supervise 99 persons. Most managers would not want to have that many persons reporting directly to them. In fact, they would prefer to have fewer than ten persons reporting directly to them.[1]

For this reason, most materials organizations with a staff of 100 would more likely have some half-dozen "assistants" reporting directly

---

[1] Management authorities sharply disagree over the limits of effective span of control. One authority, Col. Lyndall Urwick, maintains that no supervisor can manage directly the work of more than six subordinates. See Urwick's *The Elements of Administration* (New York: Harper & Bros., 1943). Peter Drucker, on the other hand, believes span of control is limited only by "the number of people a supervisor can help reach the objectives of their own jobs." He believes that one manager can directly supervise 100 or more subordinates. See Drucker's *Practice of Management* (New York: Harper & Bros., 1954).

to the general materials manager. Each of the assistants, in turn, might have half a dozen persons reporting to him. And these "third-level" people would in turn have subordinates. So we might wind up with 100 persons at four distinct organization levels.

This does not mean it is desirable to have an organization with many levels. On the contrary, such an organization has many disadvantages, and there are many reasons why an organization should be kept as "flat" (i.e., with a broad span of control and relatively few levels) as possible.

The "Flat" Organization. Morale tends to be higher in the "flat" organization (see Figure 4–6) than in the deep one. Most people are much closer to the top echelon than they would otherwise be. They are more likely to have a better grasp of the problems of the business as a whole. And they are less likely to become so immersed in their own specialties that they lose sight of over-all objectives. The flat organiza-

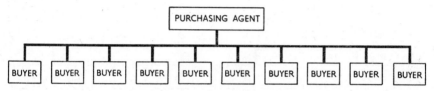

FIG. 4–6. A purchasing agent with a broad span of control.

tion is more democratic. To a greater degree, everyone is his own boss and is forced to make his own decisions.

Since people are on their own to a much greater degree, individual skills must be greater in the flat organization. And, of course, the flat organization is a much better training ground for future top executives, since they get a chance to make decisions at a much earlier stage in their careers.

The "Deep" Organization. Don't, however, discount the "deep" organization (see Figure 4–7 on next page). In practice, most companies have fairly deep organizations, and they have them because they work. Proponents point out that there is a place for everyone in the deep organization. Highly routine, unskilled jobs can easily be found for the inexperienced and relatively inept at the bottom of the pyramid. And the skills of the highly specialized and extra talented can be utilized to a much greater degree in some position near the top of the pyramid. Fewer experts are needed in the deep organization. And, since there is a greater breakdown of work by skill, the services of everyone in the organization are used in the most economic manner.

The deep organization has faults, too. It tends to be bureaucratic; decisions are passed upward from echelon to echelon. It can be inefficient; it requires more supervision than the flat organization does and, if carried to an extreme, this can reach the point where there are literally more "chiefs" than "Indians." The deep organization also tends to discourage individual initiative; it is inherently more autocratic than the flatter organization. Promotions may be slow in the deep organization. In extreme cases, it can take exceptionally able persons years to reach jobs with sufficient responsibility for their skills to be recognized.

On the other hand, in a deep organization, supervisors are more likely to have time to train and counsel each of their subordinates on an individual basis. And it is possible to have tighter control over everyone's actions.

Wide or Narrow Span? In practice, every organization structure represents a series of compromises. This is the case with span of control.

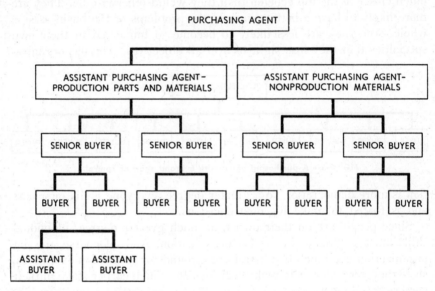

FIG. 4–7. A "deep" purchasing organization with a narrow span of control.

Some factors tend to widen span of control; others tend to narrow it.

It is possible to have a flat organization with broad span of control when:

1. Job objectives are clearly spelled out. A man who knows exactly what is expected of him obviously requires less supervision than one who knows what he is supposed to do only by frequent contact with his boss.
2. Job performance can be measured. When there are objective measures of performance, the supervisor's job is easier. It is no problem to determine the contribution of each subordinate to the business.
3. Jobs supervised are similar and repetitious. The less complex the job, the fewer the supervisor's problems. And, of course, the supervisor's job is much simpler if he supervises persons doing almost identical jobs, all relatively unskilled, than if he supervises persons who are highly skilled, each of whom is doing a different job.
4. Supervisors and supervised both are above average in job skill and administrative skill. In other words, exceptional supervisors can effec-

tively handle more subordinates, and exceptional subordinates can get along with less supervision.

5. Errors aren't serious. If a man's mistakes don't have too much effect on the company's profit and survival, there is naturally a greater inclination to put him in a spot where he can learn by making his own mistakes. If errors are too costly, supervision must be more intense.[2]

Span of control in the ideal organization is neither too broad nor too narrow. In such an organization, the manager tries to get some of the initiative that the flat organization encourages while retaining the ease of supervision of the deep structure.

In the typical materials organization, the span of control varies from 4 or 5 to 15 or 20. The top materials manager usually has fewer persons reporting to him than any other supervisor in the department. Receiving and shipping foremen may supervise as many as 15 or 20 men.

LEVEL OF ORGANIZATION

It is possible to build an effective organization simply by applying the principles of division of work to each major job within the limits of span of control. Managers whose activities embrace a big part of the organization would then report to major officials while their subordinates would include managers with narrower responsibilities.

Of course, everyone would prefer to report to the president of the company. Because of the limits of span of control, this isn't possible. As we have already mentioned, usually only those in charge of the primary functions of the business—marketing, materials management, engineering, finance, manufacturing, and personnel—customarily report to the chief executive. Similarly, only the managers of the key functions of purchasing, material control, and traffic would report directly to the materials manager.

But there are exceptions. The materials manager may have lower-ranking employees reporting to him as matter of convenience. These might include a secretary or administrative assistant, for example. They might include the manager of some activity that provides a service to the entire materials department—perhaps a clerical group that handles filing or provides stenographic services.

The materials manager may want to have a certain executive reporting directly to him because he wishes to give particular attention to a certain area. For example, suppose a company spends a large percentage

---

[2] This is the basic reason why supervisors in a purchasing department may have an extremely limited span of control. Each individual buyer may be spending hundreds of thousands or millions of dollars. Obviously, the company can't afford too many mistakes, so his work is checked and rechecked by various supervisors. On the other hand, work in a receiving department is less vital to the profits of the business. An error made on a receiving report will undoubtedly cause confusion and could be expensive. But it's unlikely to be as critical as an error in buying. Therefore it is possible to have a broader span of control in receiving.

of its purchase volume on a key raw material—crude rubber in a tire company, cloth in a clothing company, crude petroleum in an oil refining company. The materials manager may want to have the buyer of the key material report directly to him, along with the purchasing agent, traffic manager, and others. Theoretically, the buyer of the critical material should report to the purchasing agent along with the rest of the company's buyers. But the material is so important that it's worth extra attention and also may be worth the skills of an extra-talented buyer who, in salary and responsibility if not in title or nominal authority, is every bit the equal of the purchasing agent.

APPLYING ORGANIZATION PRINCIPLES

Now that we have discussed the basic principles of organization, let us apply them. The materials organizations of the Lycoming Division of the Avco Manufacturing Company and the Jet Engine Division of the General Electric Company are excellent examples for this purpose. They are similar in many ways. Both make aircraft engines. Each has a materials manager responsible for every phase of materials management.[3] Each is too big to be typical (although the organization structure of either could be satisfactorily adapted to a company with only a few hundred employees), having several hundred persons in its materials department.

Despite these similarities, their materials organization structures are quite different. In the Avco organization, division of work by function is emphasized. In the General Electric organization, division of work is mostly by product.

The Avco-Lycoming Organization

The director of materials reports to the general manager of the Lycoming Division of Avco Manufacturing Co. (see Figure 4–8). Division of responsibility at this level is by function; the materials director is responsible for all materials management functions in the plant.

Managers of the four major materials activities at Lycoming—purchasing, expediting, traffic and transportation, and material control—report to the director of materials. Thus, division of responsibility is on a functional basis also at this level. Let us now examine the organization of the departments headed by these four managers:

Purchasing. Reporting to the purchasing manager is a purchasing agent for production materials and another for nonproduction materials. One purchasing agent is responsible for all the parts and materials that

---

[3] In this respect, both organizations are atypical. At least 90 per cent of all big companies have yet to adopt a completely unified approach to materials organization. Some still have organizations resembling that shown in Figure 4–1 on page 54.

are directly incorporated into the plant's products, the other for all the materials and services used in manufacturing and administration. Thus division of responsibility is essentially by product.

This is also true at the buyer level in the organization. The principle of commodity specialization is followed as much as possible. Each buyer handles a group of commodities. (This is not shown on the chart in Figure 4–8.) For example, one buyer may handle castings, another machined parts, and so on. With this type of organization, which is almost universally used in purchasing departments, buyers can become more familiar with suppliers, costs, manufacturing processes, and so on of the commodities in which they specialize. They can keep informed on all

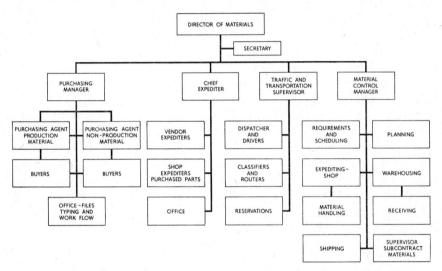

FIG. 4–8. Division of work in the materials department of the Lycoming Division, Avco Manufacturing Co., is almost entirely by function. Managers of the four subdepartments divide work by function; division of work at lower levels is also predominantly by function.

new technological and economic developments in their specialties.

A third person reporting directly to the purchasing manager (in addition to the two purchasing agents) is the office manager. His department handles all filing, typing, and miscellaneous clerical chores for the purchasing department. It frees the buying groups as much as possible from clerical duties, so they can concentrate their efforts on the buying process itself. Thus there is a functional division of the buying job, since much of the clerical phase is handled by a separate group. Lycoming feels this boosts efficiency. Routine clerical jobs can be more closely controlled if they are supervised by someone who is not distracted by other duties. In addition, certain records, such as copies of the purchase orders issued, must be kept centrally for the entire department, so the work must be organized on a department-wide basis.

Expediting. Many materials organizations do not have expediting departments. They consider expediting a basic part of the buyer's job. They believe that his responsibility does not end until acceptable material is actually delivered from the supplier. Buyers retain basic responsibility for on-time delivery of purchased material at Lycoming, too. But a separate expediting department helps them with the clerical chores of expediting—another case of division of work by function. The expediting group is divided into three sections (see Figure 4–8): vendor expediting, shop expediting on purchased parts, and office.

The division of work between vendor expediting and shop expediting is essentially by stage of manufacture. The vendor-expediting group deals with the supplier before the purchased part is manufactured or delivered. Shop expediting takes over when the part is delivered to the Avco receiving desk. If a part is on the critical shortage list, the shop expediter speeds its movement through inspection to the area in the plant where it is needed.

The office group in the expediting department is like its counterpart in purchasing. It handles typing, filing, and so on, and thus is a functional subdivision of the over-all expediting job.

Traffic and Transportation. This department is divided by function into its three basic sections (see Figure 4–8): dispatching and drivers of company-owned cars and trucks, classifying and routing of inbound shipments from suppliers, and reservations. The first group operates the company's trucks. The second handles the conventional traffic department jobs: selecting common carriers and routes for in-bound shipments and tracing shipments when necessary. The third group makes plane and hotel reservations for company executives when they travel.

Material Control. The eight groups within the material control department at Avco-Lycoming reflect a combination of the stage-of-manufacture and the functional approaches to organization.

The requirements-and-schedules group translates customer orders into requirements for parts and materials. The planning group translates these requirements into purchase requisitions, taking account of quantities currently in inventory and on order. The receiving department unloads purchased material when it is delivered and issues a receiving report. The warehousing group stores material until it is needed. The shop-expediting group co-ordinates shortages that develop within manufacturing (i.e., when one manufacturing operation gets behind schedule and holds up the succeeding operation). The materials handling group is responsible for moving materials in manufacturing from operation to operation. The subcontract-materials group is responsible for seeing that major subcontracted assemblies are available on schedule for final assembly. And the shipping group is responsible for packaging and shipping the finished product.

Thus, there is a separate group for each stage in the materials process.

However, the organization is also functional, since each group performs a basic function in the over-all materials job.

Although it is not shown on the chart, there is further functional division of responsibility within the material control department. For example, as with purchasing and expediting, separate little groups in planning and other sections within the material control department handle various specialized activities, such as typing and filing.

The General Electric Approach

The General Electric Company has experimented with a new approach to materials management in its Evandale, Ohio, jet-engine plant. Reporting to the plant's materials manager are materials supervisors who are in charge of materials management for each of the plant's major products. Also reporting to him are a purchasing agent, a supervisor of shipping, receiving, and stores, and two staff supervisors (see Figure 4–9). The purchasing agent is in charge of buying all items used

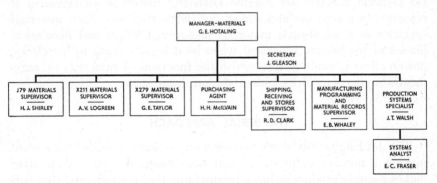

FIG. 4–9. The materials department of the Jet Engine Division of General Electric is organized by product as much as possible. Materials supervisors handle all phases of materials management for each product. Division of work at the lower levels is also by product or type of material.

throughout the plant (maintenance supplies, stationery, etc.). The staff assistants handle systems and procedures, manufacturing programing, records, and so on.

Product Groups. The unique feature of this organization is the product groups. Each group is responsible for all phases of materials management for a particular product. It must:

1. Get basic requirements and design data from engineering.
2. Locate supply sources.
3. Determine required delivery dates and purchase quantities necessary to meet the requirements of the over-all program.
4. Place orders.
5. Expedite and follow up with suppliers to make sure that delivery promises are kept.

    6. Maintain necessary property and inventory control records.
    7. Schedule assembly build-ups in the plant and handle necessary liaison on engine-test programs.

In other words, each group is responsible for virtually all phases of materials management except shipping, receiving, and stores, and non-production buying. These remain centralized and continue to serve the entire plant.

Within the product groups, the same organization approach is used. "Materials specialists," who report to the supervisor of the product group, are responsible for various groups of commodities. Each has over-all materials management responsibility and is assisted by clerical help.

The major difference between this organization and the more conventional materials organization, represented here by Avco, is in the emphasis on functional specialization. At Avco, materials management is regarded as a series of related, but functionally distinct, activities. In the General Electric Jet Engine Division,[4] materials management is regarded as a separate and almost indivisible function. Each materials specialist is a small-scale materials manager. Clerical and nonclerical phases of his job are separated when he delegates work to his clerks, but no effort is made to distinguish the functions of materials management—buying, expediting, material control, and so on.

THE SERIAL APPROACH

The Jet Engine Division's materials organization is suited for a plant making a number of products. But what about the plant that either makes a single product or has a product mix that is so diverse[5] that it is not practical to have a materials specialist for each product? In such cases, division of responsibility within the department might be serial, that is, by stage of manufacture (see Figure 4–10).

Divisional materials managers, reporting to the plant materials manager, would be responsible for all phases of materials management in certain areas of the plant. For example, one materials manager might serve the company's foundry, another the press shop, a third the assembly line, and so on. A divisional materials manager for nonproduction items would serve the entire plant and would also supervise the operation of the nonproduction storeroom.

Each materials manager would be responsible for determining his

---

    [4] Most other General Electric divisions have materials organizations similar to that of Avco-Lycoming.

    [5] For example, oil refineries and chemical plants make many products from common raw materials. Similarly, a job shop might make so many products and change them so frequently that it would be impractical to have a materials specialist for each.

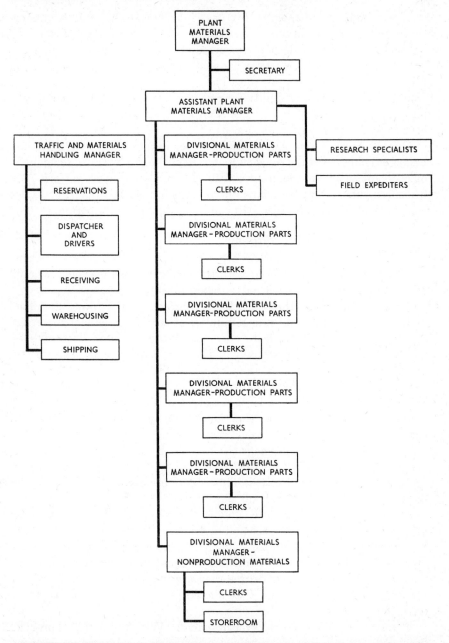

FIG. 4–10. In the smaller materials organization that is either dedicated to a single product line or to many products made on a job-lot basis, organization by product is not practical. Organization by stage of manufacture is a good substitute in many cases, however.

own requirements, managing his own inventories (but not managing the actual storeroom in most cases), placing his own orders, and doing his own expediting. The supervisor of traffic and materials handling could assist each division materials manager with traffic, materials handling, and packaging problems, but the division materials manager would have basic responsibility for results. The traffic supervisor would also supervise plant-wide services such as receiving, warehousing, reservations, dispatching, and so on.

One or more research specialists reporting to the plant materials manager could assist the division materials managers with value analysis or economic analysis. Such specialists might also develop performance measurements so that the contribution of each materials manager to the achievement of over-all objectives can be evaluated and reported.

Advantages of Serial Organization

The serial type of materials organization has both advantages and disadvantages when compared with the conventional functional type of materials organization. The advantages include:

1. Management by Objectives More Feasible. By breaking the plant materials organization up into a number of semi-independent materials groups, it becomes possible to correlate the interrelated objectives of materials management discussed in Chapter 3 at a lower level in the organization. With the functional type of organization, on the other hand, each buyer or production control planner or traffic clerk is dedicated to his own specialty. He loses sight of the over-all objectives of materials management. The functional type of organization develops specialists, the serial type "generalists."

2. Performance Measurement Easier. With the serial type of organization, it becomes more practical to devise techniques to measure performance in meeting objectives. This is true because individual jobs are more closely related to over-all objectives.

3. Greater Job Satisfaction. People don't like to feel like cogs in a giant machine. They like to see and understand the results of their work. To a much greater degree (particularly in a big organization), the serial approach permits materials personnel to think in terms of the over-all materials job. To a greater degree they are like managers of their own little businesses. As a result, they should get greater satisfaction from their jobs.

4. Improved Management Development. With the serial approach, the "materials specialists" or "division materials managers" are getting useful training for future middle- and top-management responsibilities, and they are getting it at a fairly low level in the organization. They learn to think like managers even when their own responsibilities are not too great. In the conventional organization, buyers and other materials personnel tend to think like specialists. They're very interested (usually) in their own particular job, but only rarely are they encouraged to think in terms of its impact on over-all production and profits.

5. *Closer Interdepartmental Relations.* Materials personnel must work closely with practically every other department in the company— particularly with quality control, manufacturing, engineering, and accounting. A serial approach can facilitate this. A materials manager serving one area in manufacturing can develop a very close relationship with the production and quality control supervisors concerned with that area. Since he need not concern himself with problems in any other part of the plant, he can afford to give these supervisors all of his attention. Similarly, relations with the engineering department can be more effectively cemented if the materials organization is set up on the same pattern as that used in engineering. One of the reasons for the success of the GE Jet Engine materials organization is that it parallels the organization structure of the engineering department, thereby improving communication on engineering problems.

6. *Less Communication Required.* With the serial approach, each materials specialist is making, by himself, materials decisions that used to involve a buyer, material control planner, and others. This not only eliminates the need for many telephone conversations but also makes it possible to get along with fewer memos, records, and so on.

Advantages of Functional Organization

The conventional, functional type of materials organization, which is almost universally used in industry today, also has special advantages. They include:

1. *Concentration of Buying Power.* In the conventional materials organization, buying assignments are normally made on the basis of commodity specialization. One buyer handles stampings, another handles office supplies, and so on. With this approach, the buyer not only becomes an expert in his field but the plant's entire buying power is concentrated for each commodity instead of being dispersed among a number of "materials specialists" or "divisional materials managers." This can make for better procurement and lower costs.

2. *Better Use of Manpower.* Compare the organization charts for the two types of materials organization (see Figures 4–8 and 4–9). Note how many more different jobs there are in the functional organization; the skills of almost everyone can be successfully applied. A few highly skilled men at the top make the key decisions.

In the serial type of organization, on the other hand, responsibility is dispersed. Each divisional materials manager makes decisions. Lack of trained personnel with initiative, willing and able to make decisions, will prevent many companies from adopting the serial type of materials organization without a great deal of costly preparation—training programs, recruitment, and so on.

THE DECENTRALIZED MATERIALS ORGANIZATION

The three materials organizations discussed in this chapter could theoretically be expanded to serve a company with sales of hundreds of millions (or even billions) of dollars. The expansion process is quite simple. Each supervisor adds subordinates until the limits of his span of control are reached. Then another layer of supervision is added. When these new supervisors reach the limits of their span of control, still another layer of supervision is added.

For example, the purchasing department at Avco's Lycoming Division (see Figure 4–8) can be doubled by increasing the purchasing manager's span of supervision from two purchasing agents to four. It could be redoubled by adding a new level of supervision. Each purchasing agent would hire two assistant purchasing agents, each of whom would supervise a department identical to that formerly supervised directly by the purchasing agent.

Decentralization. Many small firms have grown to giant corporations by following this process. Eventually they may wind up with an organization twelve or thirteen levels deep. The organization becomes cumbersome and bureaucratic. It responds slowly to change, and there is a lot of red tape in even the simplest transactions.

Managements of giant corporations lick the problem of size with decentralization. They break up the corporation into a number of smaller divisional units, each of which operates as a semi-independent business. Decentralization has many advantages. It brings managers closer to the objectives of the business. It permits tighter control of costs. It provides a better environment for training future managers. It helps stimulate improvements in products and methods.

Diluted Buying Power. Decentralization also creates a major materials management problem: diluted buying power. One of the major advantages of a big corporation over a smaller one is its greater buying power. Big buyers can purchase in carload lots. In some cases they can buy a major proportion of or even the total output of supplier factories. With this buying power, they can get big price concessions. In addition, vendors often provide superior quality, delivery, and service to their very biggest customers.

With decentralization, management faces a dilemma. Should it go only part-way and continue to have a headquarters buying staff responsible for all major purchases? Or should it completely decentralize the materials activities along with the rest of the organization? With the former approach, it preserves its buying power. With the latter, it gives the managers of the decentralized "little businesses" authority over all phases of their operations, including materials management. This is consistent with the management principle that you can't hold a manager responsible for profits unless he has authority over all phases of his operation.

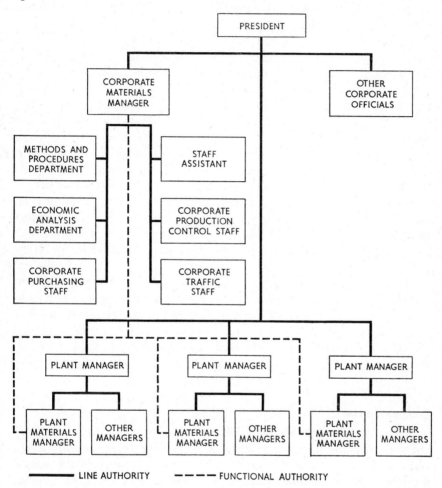

FIG. 4–11. The line-and-staff approach to organization is widely used in very large corporations. A corporate materials manager co-ordinates policy and functionally supervises plant materials managers who report directly to their respective plant managers.

STAFF AND LINE

Only a few giant corporations operate with a single, highly centralized buying department. A few others are highly decentralized, with a number of buying departments completely independent of each other. Usually corporations that use similar or identical parts or materials at a number of plants tend to have a centralized buying organization to exploit their buying power.[6] On the other hand, those that make a number of products with little resemblance to each other tend to have a decentralized buying organization.[7]

Most major companies try to compromise. They try to get the advantages of both centralization and decentralization. They do it with the so-called "staff-and-line" approach[8] (see Figure 4–11 on previous page). At the top is a corporate staff, often headed by a corporate director of purchases or materials manager. At this level, division of responsibility is by function. The materials manager, who often is a vice-president, reports to the president or executive vice-president. Usually strictly a staff executive, he is responsible for over-all materials policies and plans but has no responsibility for the basic "line" activities of materials management.

Directly responsible for "line" activities are materials managers in each plant or division. These managers usually do not report to the corporate materials executive, although they do rely on him for advice on corporate-wide buying policies and procedures and for assistance on special problems. Instead, they report directly to the general managers of their respective plants or divisions. This is consistent, of course, with the principle of making the general managers responsible for every phase of their job.

With the staff-and-line organization, most of the advantages of centralized buying are preserved. The corporate purchasing staff is able to consolidate purchases of all items used by a number of plants in order to get the lowest possible prices. Usually it makes over-all contracts directly; occasionally it restricts itself only to making available information on savings that might be made if the plants chose to pool their buying power.

Staff Activities

Although the corporate materials manager in a big corporation does not supervise the plant materials managers directly, he usually has a small staff under his direct supervision. The staff provides specialized services to both the plant materials managers and top management.

---

[6] For example, most chemical, steel, and petroleum companies have a centralized buying organization, both to permit corporation-wide buying of key raw materials and to facilitate handling of reciprocity problems.

[7] Good examples are the Borg Warner Corporation and American Machine & Foundry. Both companies have buying departments in each of their divisions that operate independently. It is significant that both corporations make a wide variety of products that are frequently unrelated to each other in terms of technology and markets.

[8] The reader should note that the staff-and-line approach isn't unique to the very large, multiplant materials organization. It can readily be adapted to a small materials organization. For example, Figure 4–10 illustrates a plant materials organization with two staff activities, research and expediting.

Among its major services are value analysis, administrative planning, and economic analysis.

Value Analysis. Value analysis refers to a series of techniques that are designed to reduce costs. The value analyst is a specialist with substantial training in engineering, cost estimating, and manufacturing methods. He assists buyers and others in the materials organization with cost-reduction projects.

Administrative Planning. The over-all materials cycle is complex. Procedures, policies, and organization structures must be planned carefully. Records must be kept of the performance of every materials executive in every plant. Training programs must be administered. Budgetary controls are necessary. All these jobs and many others can be handled by a competent administrative assistant to the materials manager.

Economic Analysis. When and how much should a company buy? How much inventory should it carry? The answers to these questions depend on more than just the company's internal costs. They depend also on the external economic environment and on the trend of both over-all and individual prices and costs. Economic analysis is essential in modern materials management, and a staff economist or statistician can provide invaluable assistance to the materials manager. (Specific applications of economic analysis to materials management are discussed in more detail in Chapter 6.)

Other Specialists. The three types of staff specialist mentioned so far are the most common in industrial materials organizations. However, there are many others. A staff specialist on "trade relations" (i.e., reciprocity) is quite common in industrial purchasing departments. He works closely with the company's sales department and helps determine policies governing how far the company will extend itself in making purchases from suppliers who are also customers.

A number of big companies with thousands of suppliers have staff specialists handling vendor-relations problems. These specialists investigate complaints from suppliers who feel they haven't been treated fairly by company buyers and also do everything they can to bolster supplier good will.

Many large companies find it convenient to have field expediters in key cities where there are a number of suppliers. These men expedite items in short supply for any buyer requesting their services. They investigate new suppliers, and they also help to get information about quality problems. Because they serve the entire materials department, they must report directly to the director of materials or to one of his immediate assistants.

Problems of Staff

Breaking a department into line and staff activities provides additional functional specialization. Skilled specialists can be hired to serve the entire materials department. In addition, staff work provides excellent training for high-potential junior executives. They can be exposed to top-level decision making without the company's having to suffer the consequences of their mistakes.

The staff executive almost always has problems. To get anything done, he must work through line personnel and persuade them to co-operate. With strong staff men, dual subordination frequently results, that is, the line supervisor winds up reporting both to a staff executive and a line executive. Some writers on management charge that since staff has no real responsibility to contribute directly to the objectives of the business, it is inherently wasteful.

THE ORGANIZATION OF THE FUTURE

Staff specialists are useful and there will always be a need for them, especially in large materials organizations. But the writer believes there will be a smaller staff in future materials organizations. These organizations, he believes, will have a decentralized, serial type of structure similar to that illustrated in Figures 4–9 and 4–10. Since they treat materials management as an integrated concept, there should be less need for staff experts in a variety of functions.

At present, there is by no means universal agreement that the serial structure is even theoretically superior. And general agreement about its theoretical merits need not necessarily bring wide adoption. Successful companies are extremely reluctant to make a drastic change in their organization structures. Not only do they hesitate to break up a team that gets results in exchange for an untried concept, but in every basic organization change some executives invariably get jobs with less authority and prestige than those they had previously. Why make these men unhappy and create internal dissension when the company is operating smoothly and profitably? Unsuccessful companies usually don't like to change their basic organization either. They often feel that they can't afford the risk of trying something new and relatively untested. They usually prefer to imitate their more successful competitors.

Despite the resistance, there are strong forces favoring the eventual adoption of the decentralized, serial type of organization by many companies. They are:

1. The pressure on supply created by highly automated factories.
2. Increasing adoption of electronic data processing with programing that makes an integrated approach to materials management essential.
3. Increasing availability of highly trained personnel able to assume responsibility in a decentralized organization.

These forces are discussed in greater detail in the final chapter of this book.

CASES

CASE 4–1.   ALABAMA AIRCRAFT CORPORATION

Organizing for a New Product Line

Alabama Aircraft Corporation was founded in 1928. It has always specialized in fighter planes for the U.S. Air Force, and its products served the country well in both World War II and the Korean War. By 1959, the company employed 8,000 workers and its sales were almost $200 million. The company now faces one of the major turning points in its history. New orders for military aircraft are off sharply because of the growing use of missiles instead of fighter planes. Although the company may continue to produce airplanes indefinitely, management doubts that its airplane business will ever be as good as it once was. Missile orders will take up part of the slack, but the company will still be left with a tremendous unused investment in facilities and equipment to fabricate aluminum and steel.

Fortunately, the company's engineers had some advance warning of this problem and have been working for several years on a host of new products designed to fill the gap left by a slowdown of the aircraft business. Among these products are prefabricated aluminum highway bridges, house trailers, and a line of aluminum boats.

Alabama's marketing department expects that these new products will account for 25 per cent of the company's sales volume almost immediately and will ultimately account for as much as 50 per cent. The company already has substantial contracts with distributors and mail-order houses for some of these products, and it is convinced that the others will gain rapid acceptance. It anticipates few problems in selling products as long as its prices are competitive. But costs are a major problem. The company is used to producing aircraft-quality components where it would willingly pay as much as $1.00 for a simple bolt manufactured to aircraft standards. Now it must manufacture to entirely different standards and can't afford to spend more than five cents for a bolt that would superficially look not much different from an aircraft bolt even though it was made from lower-cost material to looser tolerances.

Harry Spooner, the company's materials manager, anticipates that an entirely different approach to materials management may be necessary if the company is to keep its costs in line. He believes that an entirely different group of suppliers may be needed for the company's new civilian products. Aircraft suppliers are used to such high-quality standards that they may not be able to cut prices enough to compete for civilian business.

Spooner is also apprehensive about quality problems on the new line. He fears that Alabama's quality-control department is so indoctrinated with aircraft quality standards that it will reject components from his new suppliers. He knows that although instruments can be used to measure quality objectively on certain dimensions, quality is at least partly a matter of the inspector's judgment. If inspectors apply their aircraft background to civilian parts, they may set such high standards that Spooner will be forced to pay higher prices. Since purchases will comprise about 60 cents out of every sales dollar on the civilian line (about the same ratio as the military line), obviously the company can't afford to pay higher prices for components than its competitors do. On the other hand, if the company's inspectors set realistic quality standards for the new products, they may get too lax for the company's military line.

Spooner is responsible to management for meeting cost objectives on the new product line. But he is virtually at the mercy of the quality-control department in achieving them, since with a high reject rate he will have to insist that vendors institute more rigid controls over their manufacturing processes and inspect outgoing shipments more carefully. Inevitably, he will have to pay for this extra work.

Spooner believes that the best solution to the problem is to set up a separate receiving inspection department under his control that is staffed with inspectors who will work exclusively on the new product line. Currently, Spooner has a conventional materials organization. Reporting to him are managers of traffic, production control, and purchasing. The traffic department, the smallest of the three, has six transportation specialists working on routing, tracing shipments, and so on. In addition, the traffic manager supervises a foreman, who in turn supervises the company's trucks and drivers. The production control manager has seven supervisors reporting directly to him. One supervises shipping, receiving, and nonproduction storerooms; others supervise production raw materials, purchased parts, and a "bond room" in which parts are stored after they have passed inspection; and there is a supervisor in charge of in-process materials in each of the plant's main manufacturing areas. The purchasing agent supervises five senior buyers, each of whom specializes in a given group of commodities. Working for each senior buyer are three to six buyers, each of whom supervises an expediter and a secretary.

While Spooner is convinced that receiving inspection for the new line should be under his jurisdiction rather than that of the company's quality control manager, he is less certain about how he should reorganize his department to handle the new product line. Moreover, he believes that changes will be necessary, particularly in the purchasing department, where he wants buyers to be more price conscious on the new line.

Questions

1. Should management accept Spooner's recommendation that a new receiving inspection department be established for the new line and be put under the materials manager's jurisdiction? What are the pros and cons? What are the alternatives?

2. How should the materials department be reorganized to cope with the new product? Support your recommendation with a new organization chart.

CASE 4–2.   ALBERT ELECTRONICS CORPORATION

Centralized versus Decentralized Materials Management

Albert Electronics is a New England firm that has gradually grown until it presently operates more than 20 plants from coast to coast. Last year's sales were more than $200 million, up 10 per cent from the previous year. The company has hit a new sales record in nine of the last ten years. But profits have not kept pace. The company earned nearly $8 million after taxes six years ago, when its sales were only $100 million. Last year it earned only $10 million. A 100 per cent increase in sales has brought a mere 20 per cent increase in profits during a period when the company has also almost doubled its investment in plant and equipment.

This year the outlook is even bleaker. Mr. Watson, vice-president in charge of finance, predicts that profits will actually drop off a little even though sales are scheduled to rise to about $220 million. In addition, the company is going to need more money to finance the extra inventories required by expanded sales. Current inventories total about $24 million. Mr. Watson estimates that they will rise to $27 million, and the company's cash position will tighten so much that it will have to draw on its line of credit at several large banks.

The company has grown so rapidly that it has been forced to rely on outside suppliers for an abnormally large part—68 per cent—of its sales dollar. The company has a small top-management staff consisting of a president, two executive vice-presidents, and vice-presidents in charge of sales, engineering, manufacturing, personnel, and finance, and a small group to assist these top officials. The two executive vice-presidents each supervise ten of the company's twenty plant managers. The other vice-presidents have no direct responsibility for operations but serve primarily in an advisory and policy-making capacity in their specialties.

Each of the company's plants is responsible for making its own purchases. Organizations within the plants vary, since Mr. Albert, the founder of the company, believes in giving his plant managers maximum autonomy so long as they achieve their profit objectives. In most cases the plant materials management job is divided among a purchasing department, a traffic department, and a production control department. Typically the purchasing agent reports directly to the plant manager, while the production control manager and the traffic manager report to the plant's manufacturing manager. However, in the largest plant (the Cleveland Works), which has a purchase volume of nearly $50 million, there is a materials manager who reports to the plant manager. This materials manager supervises separate production control, purchasing, and traffic departments.

No formal efforts are made to co-ordinate company-wide purchases. However, the Cleveland Works materials manager has made some informal efforts. Because his volume is so much greater than that of any other plant, he can sometimes get special concessions from suppliers on various mill supplies and other nonproduction materials. When he gets an especially good deal, he sends a memo to the purchasing agents of the other plants so they can call the supplier and demand the same terms on the basis of being part of the same corporation as the Cleveland Works. No one knows how many plant purchasing agents have taken advantage of these occasional opportunities.

Mr. Albert is becoming concerned because, while the company is successful in expanding its sales, its profit margin has gotten progressively narrower and now even total profits are threatening to drop off. He has engaged Merrill, Johnson & Connors, management engineers, to study the problem. In its preliminary report, Merrill, Johnson & Connors has suggested that a detailed study be made of the company's purchasing operations. Since the company spends nearly $140 million on purchases, it pointed out that relatively small improvements in this area can have a considerable effect on the company's over-all profits. It believes that substantial savings could be made by consolidating purchases of certain materials.

Questions

1. Suppose you were a consultant working for Merrill, Johnson & Connors. What changes would you recommend in Albert Electronics' approach to purchasing?
2. Draw a new organization chart in which you show your suggested changes in the purchasing organization.
3. Compare the relative merits of the present completely decentralized purchasing organization at Albert Electronics with those of a completely centralized organization.

Chapter 5

LEGAL ASPECTS OF MATERIALS MANAGEMENT

Each purchase order that the materials manager approves is a contract. The materials manager need not be a lawyer. He can readily get advice from the company's legal staff on any special problems that arise. But since he does approve more than 99 per cent of the contracts into which his company enters, he should be familiar with the general principles of contract law.

The basic steps in making a purchase contract are quite simple:

1. Each verbal or written quotation by a supplier is an offer to sell, which is usually subject to acceptance at the time the buyer issues the purchase order.
2. Each purchase order either is an acceptance of the seller's offer or, if its terms and conditions differ somewhat from the supplier's quotation, is in effect a counteroffer.
3. Each acknowledgment of a purchase order by the seller confirms the contract and makes it binding, provided that the seller accepts all of the terms and conditions of the order. If the seller takes exception to any of them, he is in effect making a counteroffer, which must be accepted by the buyer before the contract is binding. If the seller does not acknowledge the order formally, he does so informally when he complies with its terms and ships the goods or services the order calls for.
4. Every purchase order change subsequently agreed to by buyer and seller becomes a part of the purchase contract.

Many firms follow the procedure outlined above almost unwittingly year after year. About 40 per cent of all manufacturing companies don't even bother to include any terms and conditions in their purchase orders. They don't worry about legal "fine points." And they never have any problems. Any misunderstandings that arise are worked out in friendly negotiation with suppliers; lawsuits are almost unheard of.[1]

In contrast, federal government procurement is carried out in a highly legalistic atmosphere. Procurement officials are governed by thousands of regulations (the Armed Services Procurement Regulations alone consist of hundreds of pages), and their every action must be within the precise letter of the law.[2]

---

[1] "How Legal Should Purchase Orders Be?" *Purchasing*, May 11, 1959, p. 11.

[2] Some government agencies don't feel they should relax even the seemingly insignificant regulations. For example, at least one agency will flatly refuse to accept any bids that arrive even one minute after the deadline. It feels that to do so would be to discriminate against the bidders who do obey all the rules.

Most private corporations take a middle ground. Their materials managers almost never get involved in legal hassles with suppliers, and they are inclined to be lenient if suppliers sometimes fail to comply with all purchase order terms and conditions. They recognize that with good supplier relations, a highly legalistic approach is both unnecessary and unprofitable. But they also recognize that it is extremely important to define the terms and conditions of each contract as precisely as possible, not only to prevent misunderstanding but also to protect the company from a number of potential liabilities. That is why good materials managers carefully review each contract as it is placed and make absolutely certain that it has the proper terms and conditions.

There are four basic areas where legal problems can arise between the buyer and either the seller or a third party. They are price, quality, delivery, and compliance with various laws.

PRICING TERMS

Most purchase orders are for goods that are available for almost immediate delivery. The price and quantity desired are indicated on the order,[3] the vendor ships and bills in accordance with the order, and the contract is fulfilled.

Problems arise when delivery is not "off the shelf" but must be made some time after the order has been placed. Prices of labor and raw material can change during this period, as can general economic conditions. In addition, if the item is made to order, the supplier's actual costs of production may be either substantially higher or lower than his estimate. So either buyer or seller may wish to change the price on the order. But neither can do so in the absence of mutual agreement or some advance provision that permits change. *A purchase order that has been unqualifiedly accepted by the seller legally binds both parties to the prices and quantities shown on the order unless the order's terms and conditions specifically provide for changes.*

Many companies issue or accept purchase orders for delivery of material over a long period of time with no provision whatever for change in prices. Occasionally they will negotiate price changes on these orders. In such cases, the provision for change is in effect made informally, as a result of a long-established friendly relationship.

---

[3] Many purchasing departments follow the practice of issuing unpriced purchase orders for inexpensive minor items. The supplier's invoice goes directly to the buyer who placed the order. If the price is consistent with previous prices paid for the material, the buyer approves the invoice. If it is not, he either negotiates with the vendor, or, on rare occasions, returns the material for credit. Although many departments have followed this practice for years without difficulty, this is not good purchasing. For reasons brought out in this chapter, it is always good practice to define every purchase-order term and condition as clearly as possible for every purchase.

Some private companies and all government bodies are more cautious. All orders they issue or accept have provisions for price changes incorporated in them if they anticipate the need for change. Most governments and government prime contractors employ standard provisions determined by regulation. Most private firms are more flexible. The terms and conditions they use are limited only by their imagination and their acceptability to suppliers. However, these terms and conditions, like those used by government bodies, fall into four general categories: open-end pricing, cost-plus, escalation, and price redetermination.

Open-End Pricing. When there is an established free market for a material, it is possible that neither buyer nor seller will want to commit himself to a specific price for a long period of time. The purpose of the contract is to assure a supply of material for some time in the future at the prevailing market price. In such cases, the purchase order need not be priced (although it may be convenient to list the current price for reference purposes). Its terms indicate that the supplier is to charge the "price in effect at time of delivery."

Open-end pricing is used for basic raw materials whose prices are determined on commodity markets by impersonal supply-demand forces. It also is frequently used for other purchases simply because the producers refuse to sell unless there is open-end pricing. Producers of steel, aluminum, and other materials whose prices are not determined on commodity markets insist on open-end pricing. So do most suppliers of patented items.

Buyers avoid open-end pricing whenever possible because it limits their flexibility. With open-end pricing, the supplier gets, so to speak, a blank check.

Cost-Plus Contracts. Sometimes a purchase contract is made for something that is so novel that neither buyer nor seller knows what the cost should be. In such cases, some sort of cost-plus contract may be the only solution. The seller agrees to do the job either at some fixed price per hour of work performed or at his cost plus some extra fee as profit. Such contracts should be avoided whenever possible. Under them, suppliers have little incentive to keep down costs. In fact, waste can even become profitable for the supplier, especially if he can successfully pad his "costs" to include some profit.

When cost-plus contracts are necessary, they should be controlled and circumscribed as closely as possible. Provision should be made for a detailed audit of the supplier's cost. It also is preferable to fix the supplier's profit on such contracts, so that there is no incentive for him to waste time. With a cost-plus-fixed-fee contract, for example, the supplier would recoup his exact cost plus some predetermined fee. With a straight cost-plus contract, he would recoup his costs plus some percentage profit on cost; the more the supplier spends, the more he makes.

Military procurement officers frequently use cost-plus-fixed-fee contracts for research and development of new weapons. They avoid them whenever possible, however, and always try to change a supplier's contract from cost-plus-fixed-fee as soon as the weapon is sufficiently developed to permit a price to be negotiated.

Escalation Contracts. Almost every long-term contract must have some provision for price change. But a wise buyer or seller tries carefully to define the areas of price escalation; otherwise, he is likely to lose all the benefits he hoped to gain from entering into the long-range contract. For example, buyer or seller may invest millions of dollars in plant and equipment on the strength of some long-range contract.[4] Unrestricted escalation can make such investments unprofitable.

Escalation clauses permit a change in price if a key element of cost changes. Usually this is labor or material cost, or both. Construction contracts often permit escalation if wages paid to the various building-trade workers change. Contracts issued by automobile manufacturers for electric storage batteries, on the other hand, may permit escalation if the prices of the key raw materials (lead and antimony) change. Sometimes escalation is linked to changes in some well-known price index issued by the Bureau of Labor Statistics or some other agency.

To prevent disputes, the formula for escalation should be completely clear. It should be based, whenever possible, on widely available economic information and not upon the seller's internal costs. For example, if there is an escalation clause to cover supplier wage increases, it is best to agree on a price adjustment for each cent-per-hour change in the Bureau of Labor Statistics average wage for the supplier's industry. This not only prevents arguments about the effect of a wage change on a supplier's cost but also gives the supplier an incentive to resist wage increases in collective bargaining that will make his prices higher on future bids.

When it is not feasible to base the escalation on some widely available cost data information and the supplier's individual cost data must be used, then the method whereby costs are determined should be agreed upon in advance. Also, it is usually desirable to have some top limit to escalation incorporated in the contract; 10 to 15 per cent of the original price is typical.

---

[4] A classic case is a contract between the Tennessee Valley Authority and the Peabody Coal Co. TVA has invested $100,000,000 in a steam-electric generating plant on the strength of a contract with Peabody to supply 65,000,000 tons of coal worth $191,750,000 over a period of seventeen years from a nearby mine. TVA's basic reason for locating its plant next to the Peabody mine is the favorable price it has negotiated for the coal. The cost is only $2.95 a ton, one-fourth less than TVA pays on the average for coal for its other steam plants. Obviously, the contract must have some provision for price escalation because of its long duration. But escalation clauses must also be restrictive; uncontrolled price increases could conceivably raise TVA's costs to the point where its $100,000,000 investment could become uneconomic.

Price Redetermination. Normally only government agencies and their contractors use formal price-redetermination clauses. On many contracts for complex items, such as jet planes and aircraft carriers, it is impossible to have truly competitive bidding. One supplier has all the tools and know-how and could readily underbid all competitors and still make excessive profits. Also, sometimes the supplier has not had sufficient experience to know his costs thoroughly. The best solution is a negotiated selling price based on the best available cost data. As work progresses on the contract, prices are "redetermined" by review of incurred costs and negotiation between buyer and seller.

Private companies sometimes also use price-redetermination clauses. They are particularly useful when a company subcontracts an entire product. For example, a department store chain may issue a contract for its own brand of lawn mower to a manufacturer. If the supplier has never made lawn mowers before, he may not know precisely what his costs will be. He may also expect to reduce costs after he has more experience with lawn mowers, and costs will be especially low if the lawn mowers sell well. In this case, a price-redetermination contract might be ideal. Sometimes it will include an agreement permitting the buyer to audit the supplier's cost and to recoup any profits in excess of some predetermined percentage of sales. For example, Sears, Roebuck & Co. has allowed certain suppliers an 8 per cent profit on sales.

Price-redetermination contracts are superior to cost-plus contracts because they provide for better control over prices. But, like cost-plus, they can encourage waste; higher costs almost automatically bring higher prices. Armed forces procurement officers try to get around this weakness by close control and periodic audits. They sometimes also use incentive-type contracts that permit cost-cutting suppliers to make bigger profits. For example, the Navy's Bureau of Ships permits contractors to keep 55 per cent of any savings they make from value analysis; only 45 per cent need be passed on to the Navy as a price reduction.

Despite the incentives in price-redetermination contracts to prevent waste, military procurement officers still feel there is no substitute for competitive bidding when it is feasible. And they prefer to issue fixed-price contracts whenever possible.

OTHER ECONOMIC TERMS

Payment Terms

The cost of materials contracted for is not determined solely by the unit price of the material and the quantity. Someone, usually the buyer, must pay for transporting the material to the buyer's plant. In addition, suppliers usually offer customers a trade discount of 1 to 2 per cent if they pay for the material within ten days of its receipt instead of within the customary thirty days. The buyer should always be certain that the trade discount is included in his contract. Sometimes this discount is negotiated between buyer and seller; usually it is a standard discount that the supplier offers to all of his customers.

Payment terms can become quite complicated on construction contracts and equipment purchases. Usually suppliers insist on progress payments to be made at specified stages. For example, on a contract to design and build a machine tool, the order might call for payments to the supplier when the design is complete, when the machine is ready to be tried out, and final payment when the machine is operating in accordance with performance specifications.

Who Pays Freight

F.O.B. Our Plant. Responsibility for transport of the material should always be clearly assigned in the contract. Contracts for low-value materials purchased from local suppliers are customarily made "F.O.B. our plant."[5] In such cases, the buyer takes title to the goods only when they are delivered to the loading dock at his plant; the supplier must pay any transportation charges. In addition, if the goods are damaged in transit, the supplier—not the buyer—is responsible for making a claim and negotiating a settlement with the carrier.

F.O.B. Shipping Point. When the contract is big and transportation charges are substantial, the terms are usually "F.O.B. shipping point." The buyer takes title when the seller loads the goods onto a common carrier. The buyer pays transportation charges directly to the carrier and also negotiates all freight damage claims and the like with the carrier. Most companies prefer to buy major materials "F.O.B. shipping point" because then their traffic departments can completely control inbound shipments. As a result, they often can cut freight charges substantially.

Cost-Insurance-Freight. C.I.F. and c.a.f. (cost and freight) contracts are also quite common. With them the seller includes in his price an allowance for freight and insurance. The buyer takes title to the goods when the documents are conveyed to him, not when the goods are delivered. So he must handle all damage claims (or loss claims) with the carrier even though the seller is paying freight charges. Such arrangements are not uncommon in export-import transactions. Some buyers prefer to buy "ex-dock" on imports, however, because they don't take title to the goods until they are actually unloaded from the shipment. The shipper, not the buyer, is then responsible for claims against the carrier if there is damage in transit. Shippers often charge slightly higher prices when they sell "ex-dock" because of the slightly greater risk of loss that they assume.

---

[5] If the buyer serves more than one plant or there is some reason why such brief terms would create confusion, then more explicit terms should be incorporated.

Freight Equalization. Producers of uniformly priced commodities,[6] such as aluminum, steel, and cement, will often equalize freight charges with competitors whose plants are located closer to customers. For example, if the freight rate is 50¢/cwt from the plant of Supplier A of a given commodity and only 25¢/cwt from the nearest supplier, Supplier A will offer a 25¢/cwt "freight equalization" adjustment to the buyer. The buyer's purchase order to Supplier A would then read "F.O.B. shipping point; 25¢/cwt freight equalization adjustment allowed." The buyer would pay the common carrier the full 50¢/cwt freight charge but would deduct the 25¢/cwt adjustment when he paid his invoice to Supplier A.

REJECTION OF DEFECTIVE GOODS

If goods are not satisfactory or do not meet specifications, buyers normally return them for credit. Sellers almost never object if returns are made promptly. In many states, the Uniform Sales Act[7] governs warranties; in these states, almost all goods may be returned provided the seller is promptly notified of rejection.

The buyer has the right to conduct reasonable tests upon merchandise. If the merchandise is unsatisfactory, he should promptly notify seller of breach of warranty. His statement should identify the transaction (by purchase order number and shipment), describe the defect to the seller, and indicate that the buyer is asserting his legal right to reject the shipment.[8] If the buyer delays inspection and rejection of material for an "unreasonable" period of time, or if he notifies the wrong person in the supplier organization, his warranty may not be valid. Frequently goods are rejected but can be put in good order by the buyer. In such cases, the seller should agree in advance to any repair charges made by the buyer; naturally, he can normally request return of goods if he feels the charges are unreasonable.

---

[6] Usually because of oligopolistic pricing, such commodities carry identical prices F.O.B. shipping point. With such a pricing structure, the lowest delivered price is naturally always obtained from the nearby producer. For example, a metal-working firm in South Bend, Indiana, would always get lowest delivered prices on steel from mills in the Chicago-Gary area. A Pittsburgh mill can get business in South Bend only by offering the South Bend firm the same delivered prices as Chicago mills. But it doesn't want to reduce its F.O.B. shipping-point price, since it doesn't wish to cut prices to nearby customers. Therefore, the only solution is to reduce the freight charge to South Bend artificially by allowing the South Bend customer an allowance equal to the difference between the Pittsburgh–South Bend freight rate and the Chicago–South Bend rate.

[7] This law regulates almost every phase of purchases and sales. It was first written more than fifty years ago in an effort to set a uniform commercial code that would be applicable in every state. To date, most states have adopted it in its entirety and all states have adopted most of its provisions.

[8] The supplier is normally notified of a rejected shipment with an inspection report form, which may be sent to him separately or may accompany the rejected goods if they are returned for credit.

Specifications. There is rarely a legal problem because of poor quality on purchases of standard, off-the-shelf items. In such cases the company's right to reject the merchandise is recognized. A company's relations with its suppliers for such materials are like a housewife's relations with a department store. If the merchandise is not satisfactory, it is returned for credit. The supplier then either sells the merchandise to another customer or returns it to his supplier.

Quality problems are not so simple when a company makes a product to the buyer's specifications. In such cases, the buyer may be the only user of the product. If he rejects a shipment, the supplier may suffer a substantial loss. Because of this, the buyer should incorporate specifications for the item in the purchase order. If the item is made to a blueprint, the purchase order should indicate that material is to be made in accordance with a particular blueprint number or specification accompanying the order. In such cases, the buyer need only accept the material if it meets the requested specifications.

With some purchases it is not possible to describe the product with detailed specifications. In buying machinery, for example, the buyer is interested not in the supplier's design of the equipment but in the performance of the equipment. So he uses a performance specification. Typical is this performance clause incorporated into a contract issued for a machine developed for Chesebrough-Pond, Inc. by one of its suppliers:[9]

The machine is to be guaranteed to produce at a minimum linear speed of 240 inches per minute, using a specific material, sample rolls of which were tested by the supplier. The seals produced by the machine are to withstand a minimum of 20 inches of vacuum at 70° F. Furthermore, the machine is to be test-run, prior to shipment, with representatives of our company present. In addition, agreement is to be reached for a specific delivery date, stemming from the date of final confirmation of all details.

FAILURE TO DELIVER

The date that delivery is required should be clearly indicated on the buyer's order. If the seller accepts the order, he binds himself to deliver by that date. What happens if he fails to deliver? The Uniform Sales Act says that if "seller wrongfully neglects or refuses to deliver the goods, the buyer may maintain an action against the seller for damages for non-delivery."

If the goods that a seller fails to deliver are readily available, the buyer may collect general damages. Such damages are limited to the difference between the contract price and the price the buyer must pay on the open market.[10] If the goods are not readily available, the buyer may

[9] As described in *Essentials of Machinery Procurement and Development*, Special Report No. 14 (New York: American Management Association, 1956), p. 7.

[10] Suppose a supplier accepts an order for material at 30¢/lb. and then fails to deliver. If the buyer must pay 40¢/lb. for the material, he may collect 10¢/lb. damages from the supplier who failed to deliver.

USEFUL PURCHASE ORDER TERMS

BASIC CLAUSES

(1) Time is of the essence on this order. Purchaser reserves the right to cancel this order, or any part thereof, without obligation, if delivery is not made at the time(s) specified.

(2) Seller warrants that there has been no violation of copyrights or patent rights in manufacturing, producing, or selling the goods shipped or ordered, and seller agrees to hold the purchaser harmless from any and all liability, loss, or expense occasioned by any such violation.

(3) All goods shipped against this order must have been produced in compliance with the requirements of the Fair Labor Standards Act of 1938, as amended, including Sections 6, 7, and 12, and regulations and orders issued under Section 14 thereof. Seller must certify this compliance on each invoice submitted in connection with this order.

OPTIONAL CLAUSES

In addition to the three basic clauses above, there is an almost infinite number of special clauses that purchasing agents may want to add to their orders. Among the more common are the following:

(1) The terms and conditions of sale as stated in this order govern in event of conflict with any terms of seller's proposal, and are not subject to change by reason of any written or verbal statements by seller, or by any terms stated in seller's acknowledgment, unless accepted in writing by us.

(2) We reserve the right to inspect all shipments after delivery to us and to reject any material that may be defective or not in accordance with specifications as to quality or performance.

(3) If price is omitted on order, except where order is given in acceptance of quoted prices, it is agreed that seller's price will be the lowest prevailing market price and in no event is this order to be filled at higher prices than last previously quoted or charged without purchaser's written consent.

(4) In the event any article sold and delivered hereunder shall be defective in any respect whatsoever, seller will indemnify and save harmless purchaser from all loss or expense by reason of all accidents, injuries, or damages to persons or property resulting from the use or sale of such article or which are contributed to by said defective condition.

(5) If seller performs services, or constructs, erects, inspects or delivers on buyer's premises, seller will indemnify and save harmless buyer from all loss or expense by reason of any accident, injury or damage to persons or property occurring in connection therewith.

(6) Purchaser may at any time insist upon strict compliance with these terms and conditions, notwithstanding any previous custom, practice, or course of dealing to the contrary.

These terms were suggested in an article in Purchasing ("*P.O. Terms: How to Comply with the Labor Laws,*" *March 30, 1959*) *by Lyle Treadway, purchasing agent, Federal Glass Co. Mr. Treadway is a graduate lawyer and also a former vice-president of the National Association of Purchasing Agents.*

FIG. 5–1.

recover special damages. To do so he must prove that the damages he suffers from nondelivery could reasonably be anticipated by both buyer and seller. He must also be able to justify the amount of the damages.

Late delivery can often cause as much damage to buyer as no delivery. But if the buyer does not indicate a specific delivery date on his purchase order, the seller is bound by the Uniform Sales Act to deliver only within a "reasonable" time. Courts differ in the interpretation of the word "reasonable." Many buyers protect themselves against late deliveries by inserting a clause in their purchase orders saying that "if shipment is not made at the time specified, seller reserves the right to cancel the order, or any part of it, without obligation."

OTHER LEGAL PROBLEMS

When a buyer issues a purchase contract, he may be innocently violating some law, infringing upon someone else's rights, or otherwise subjecting his company to possible lawsuits. Among the possible legal pitfalls for the buyer are patent infringement, the Fair Labor Standards Act, the Robinson-Patman Act, and others.

Patent Infringement. A patent gives the inventor a legal monopoly for 17 years. If anyone manufactures, sells, or uses a patented device during this period without permission, the patent owner may sue and collect damages for infringement. Purchasers may innocently buy an item made by a supplier who is infringing upon the inventor's patent and still be liable for damages because they used the patented device.

Many buyers try to protect themselves against unwitting patent infringement by inserting in their orders clauses such as those in Figure 5–1 (on preceding page). Such clauses do not enable them to transfer liability for infringement from themselves to the seller. But they can give the purchaser a basis for a claim against the seller in the event he is forced to pay damages to the inventor.

Fair Labor Standards Act. The "hot-goods" clause (Section 15) of the F.L.S.A. says that it is unlawful to buy and resell goods made in violation of the act. (The Fair Labor Standards Act regulates child labor and wages and hours.) Another section of the act permits a buyer to protect himself against innocent violation of the act by getting certification from seller that the act has been complied with.

Such certification should consist of a clause in the purchase order (similar to that in Figure 5–1) indicating that the seller must comply with the act in producing the goods specified in the order. In addition, the buyer should insist that the supplier certify on each of his invoices that he has complied with the act.

Robinson-Patman Act. This law is designed to prevent a seller from unfairly discriminating among customers. It makes it unlawful, under most circumstances, for a seller to offer identical merchandise in similar quantities to different customers at different prices. One section of the Act also makes it unlawful for buyers to accept such discrimination. The act is not designed to prevent buyers from seeking lower prices under most circumstances. In general, a buyer does not violate the act if he accepts a lower price, in good faith, in order to: (1) Permit a seller to meet a competitor's bid that was also made in good faith. (2) Secure the benefit of purchases in bigger quantities or of some other arrangement that reduces seller's costs.

In practice, the Robinson-Patman Act has not been troublesome for buyers. Most cases brought against them have been dismissed by the courts. On the other hand, the act has helped curb monopolistic practices of certain sellers.

EXEMPTION CERTIFICATE

PURCHASES FOR FURTHER MANUFACTURE
UNDER SECTION 4220 OF I.R.C.

*Date:*_____196___

The undersigned hereby certifies that he is a manufacturer or producer of articles taxable under Chapter 32, sub-chapter A, of the Internal Revenue Code, as amended, and holds certificate of registry number 20 issued by the Director of Internal Revenue at Cleveland, Ohio, and that the article or articles specified in the accompanying order will be used by him as material in the manufacture or production of, or as a component part of, an article or articles enumerated in sub-chapter A to be manufactured or produced by him.

It is understood that, for all the purposes of such sub-chapter A, the undersigned will be considered the manufacturer or producer of the articles purchased hereunder and (except as specifically provided by law) must pay tax on resale or use, otherwise than as specified above of the articles purchased hereunder. It is further understood that the fraudulent use of this certificate to secure exemption will subject the undersigned and all guilty parties to revocation of the privilege of purchasing tax-free and to a fine of not more than $10,000 or to imprisonment for not more than five (5) years or both, together with costs of prosecution.

This certificate covers Purchase Order No._____dated_____.

This certificate covers purchases from_____to_____.

THE B. F. GOODRICH COMPANY

*By:*_____

*Title:*_____

FIG. 5–2. Many states have sales or use taxes and the federal government has excise taxes on various products. Production parts and materials purchased for resale are exempt from these taxes provided the buyer either includes the appropriate exemption certificate with his order or files it with the appropriate taxing authority. Above is an exemption certificate used by the B. F. Goodrich Company for purchases subject to federal excise tax.

Damages in Supplier Plants. Suppose a company sends equipment or material to a supplier and it is damaged or destroyed while in the possession of the supplier. Naturally the company feels the supplier is responsible. Some companies like to clarify this situation in advance with a clause in the purchase order. For example, the B. F. Goodrich Company has a clause in its purchase orders that states: "Whenever Seller shall, by virtue hereof, have in its possession any property belonging to Buyer and/or Buyer's customer, Seller shall be deemed an insurer thereof and shall be responsible for its safe return to Buyer."

Workmen's Compensation and Liability Insurance. When a company has a contractor working on its premises, it may be liable for any injuries inflicted on others by the contractor's workers or vehicles in accidents. Therefore, it should insist in its purchase terms that contractors be covered by liability insurance. Some companies go further; they demand to see copies of the insurance policies before they will let the contractor start work. A company can also be responsible for injuries suffered by a contractor's employees. It protects itself by making certain that the contractor has workmen's compensation insurance.

Tax Exemption. Certain goods are subject to federal excise tax if they are used by the purchaser. But if they are purchased for further manufacture—as is the case with all production parts and materials that are incorporated into some end product—they are exempt from tax. To avoid the tax, the buyer must add an exemption certificate to his purchase order. Figure 5–2 (on the preceding page) illustrates the certificate used by the B. F. Goodrich Company.

A company also may purchase materials for direct resale without using them in manufacture. In this case, it is also exempt from the federal excise tax and should add an exemption clause to its purchase order. A special exemption clause would also be added if the material is to be exported.

Many states also have sales or use taxes. But if a material is purchased for resale, incorporation into another product, or export, it will normally be exempt from the tax. However, special clauses must be added in each case in accordance with the laws of the state in which the buyer does business.

CONTRACT CANCELLATION

Every materials manager issues purchase orders that he later must cancel because the goods are no longer needed.[11] When a buyer cancels

---

[11] In technologically dynamic industries, purchase contract cancellations are frequent because materials and components rapidly become obsolete on account of product changes. In the materials departments of the big aircraft companies, as many as 50 persons may be employed full-time on cancellations.

an order before its completion, it is called "anticipatory breach." If the merchandise for which he has contracted is salable but only at a lower price, the Uniform Sales Act says that buyer is liable to seller for the difference between this lower price and the contract price.

If buyer cancels an order for materials made to his specification, he is liable for all of the costs incurred by the seller—including the seller's liability to his suppliers of materials and services used in carrying out the contract. In addition, the buyer is liable for the normal profit the seller would have made on the contract.

Buyers should terminate contracts without delay once they determine that the material on order is no longer needed. They are liable only for costs incurred (less salvage value) by the supplier prior to termination. Once supplier has acknowledged termination, the buyer cannot change his mind and demand reinstatement of the contract unless the supplier concurs.

All major contracts should include a termination clause. Terms of payment for all potential liabilities should be defined as clearly as possible. Procedures used to determine costs of inventories, depreciated value of special tools, and so on, should be agreed upon in advance. It is usually wise to make provision for an audit of termination costs. Both buyer and seller are protected on termination of big contracts if there is agreement when the original contract is made. And there is no danger of unpleasant misunderstandings arising between them that will mar relations on future contracts.

AGENT, NOT LAWYER

The Law of Agency permits a materials manager, purchasing agent, or buyer to act as his company's agent in making contracts; his word or signature can be a binding contract for the company.[12] Although he may make thousands of contracts, he is not a lawyer. *Specific legal problems on purchase contracts should always be reviewed by company attorneys.* Every nonroutine agreement should have the approval of the buyer's legal staff. In addition, lawyers, not materials managers, should draft all of the clauses used for routine purchases.

Good materials managers study the principles of contract law so they can recognize possible legal problems as they occur and so they can work with attorneys on their solution. Even those materials managers who are graduate lawyers rarely attempt to solve their own legal problems. They know they are better taken care of by full-time lawyers who are alert to the latest changes in the law.

---

[12] Salesmen may be, but frequently are not, legal agents for their companies. Buyers are safe in assuming that a salesman's price adjustment or delivery promise is not binding until it is accepted and confirmed in writing by the home office.

CASES

CASE 5–1. SOUTHERN ELECTRONICS CORPORATION

PURCHASE-ORDER ACKNOWLEDGMENTS

The Southern Electronics Corporation is an important prime contractor for the U.S. Air Force for missile guidance systems. All major purchases must be approved by the Air Force contracting officer, and periodic audits are made by the government's General Accounting Office to check conformance with procedures.

Most of the orders issued by Southern Electronics have contained no provision for price escalation. In almost every case, bidders have quoted fixed prices and the business has been awarded to the low bidder. Because government regulations are quite strict, the company is careful about maintaining good records. Clerks even keep track of each purchase-order acknowledgment. If the acknowledgment copy of the order is not returned within two weeks after the order is placed, the supplier gets a form letter requesting that he return it.

Once this procedure was set up, Errol Walters, the materials manager, and Clark Bedell, the purchasing agent, ceased to worry about acknowledgments. However, two incidents involving acknowledgments have recently been called to their attention:

(1) An audit of the acknowledgment copy file shows that several suppliers have taken exception to the terms and conditions of the company's purchase orders when they have acknowledged them. Most notably, the Apex Metals Corporation, one of the biggest companies in the world, insists on acknowledging Southern's orders with its own sales acknowledgment forms, which have terms and conditions quite different from those on Southern's purchase orders. The contracting officer flatly refuses to accept Apex's terms. He particularly objects to Apex's clause: "Price subject to change without notice." He correctly points out that this condition, if accepted, would give Apex the right to charge almost any price it pleased when it actually delivered the order. Apex points out that it is against its policy to accept any restrictions on its pricing, or any terms but its own. It also points out that it has always been extremely conservative in pricing, and under no circumstances has it ever consciously sold its products at prices higher than those of its competitors. It says flatly that it must ask Southern Electronics to cancel its orders if it will not accept Apex's terms.

Unfortunately, Apex is the only supplier that can meet Southern's quality and delivery requirements. In addition, Apex's price is competitive and no other producers in Apex's rather oligopolistic industry will offer better terms. Nevertheless, the contracting officer insists that Southern should not give Apex a blank check.

(2) Another Southern supplier, the Moon Screw Products Company,

accepted Southern's fixed-price order without qualifications. Now Moon finds that its costs on the order are much higher than anticipated. The order calls for it to receive only $10,000, and Moon claims that its total costs are $60,000 and the small company is now having trouble meeting its payroll. The specifications on the order have been much more difficult to meet than Moon anticipated. Bedell checks Moon's story by getting bids from other suppliers with experience on items similar to those made by Moon and finds that he would be lucky to get the parts for $60,000 from an experienced supplier. Now Moon is threatened with bankruptcy if Southern tries to force delivery at the contract price. In addition, Southern won't get delivery of the parts when it needs them if Moon doesn't have money to meet its payroll.

Questions

1. What contract changes, if any, should Walters and Bedell recommend to the Air Force contracting officer on the Apex and Moon orders?
2. What, if anything, should Walters and Bedell have done before they placed their first orders with Apex and Moon?

CASE 5–2. ZERO CORPORATION

THE USE OF ESCALATION CLAUSES

The Zero Corporation (see Case 2–1 on page 33 for additional history and information about the company) has redesigned the fan it uses to cool its compressors. The fan was formerly an assembly consisting of several steel stampings that were screwed to a gray iron casting. The new design is a one-piece aluminum die casting that costs substantially less.

The supplier, Broderick Zinc and Aluminum Corporation, suggested the new design and is willing to sell at a guaranteed unit price of 70 cents. However, Mr. Allen, the Broderick sales representative, suggests that this may not be the best possible deal for Zero. When it guarantees a price, Broderick must include some allowance to protect itself against fluctuations in raw materials prices. Currently, secondary aluminum alloy (No. 108) sells for 26 cents a pound. However, price changes of as much as five cents a pound during the course of a year are not at all uncommon. Since the casting weighs 0.9 pounds and Broderick must allow an additional 5 per cent in calculating the weight of material used because of dross losses, the firm must obviously include some "fat" in any fixed-price quotation to protect itself.

Allen says that his firm is willing to cut its price to 67 cents provided that Zero is willing to accept risks from price fluctuations in secondary aluminum. The 67-cent price is based on 26-cent 108-alloy, and Allen proposes that provision be made to adjust the price either upward or downward when the price of 108-alloy, as reported in the *American Metal Market*, changes. He suggests that the price be adjusted in exact multiples of one cent and that no adjustment be made unless the cost of aluminum used in the casting changes by at least that amount.

In addition, Broderick is willing to amortize the costs of molds used in making the die casting in the piece price. In other words, the $2,000 cost of the molds can be spread over the first order of 20,000 units with a 10-cent price increase. This arrangement permits Zero to pay for the tools as it makes savings from the use of the new lower-cost design, and it need not make a big cash investment in tools. Both Zero and Broderick agree that since tools are being amortized, there should be a special cancellation clause in the contract that permits Zero to cancel only if it: (1) Accepts responsibility for any parts that it authorized to be fabricated against the order. (2) Compensates the supplier for the balance of tool cost not yet amortized in the piece price at the time of cancellation.

Questions

1. Should Zero buy the die casting on the basis of a 70-cent fixed price or a 67-cent price subject to escalation due to changes in secondary aluminum prices? Justify your answer in terms of the price trend that has prevailed for 108 secondary aluminum alloy during the last year.
2. Suppose you are the Zero buyer negotiating this contract and you conclude that it is advantageous to accept the 67-cent price with escalation and also wish to amortize tooling in the piece price. Draft the escalation and cancellation clauses that you would submit to your company's legal department for approval.

Chapter 6

THE ECONOMICS OF MATERIALS MANAGEMENT

No materials manager is expected to be a professional economist. But every materials manager should be familiar with business statistics and know how they apply to his job.

Many big corporations have full-time, professional economists on their staffs. In such cases, the materials manager should know how to apply the forecasts of the company's economists to materials management. Also, he often can supply the economists with much useful information gleaned from his contacts with thousands of suppliers in many industries.

In the overwhelming majority of companies, however, the materials manager is strictly on his own as far as business forecasting is concerned. There are no staff economists to help him. He must read and interpret his own data and make his own decisions. In these smaller firms, particularly those with a limited number or type of customers, the materials manager is in the best possible position of anyone to act as company economist. He often is the only member of management with contacts outside the particular company's industry. Also, he is the manager most directly concerned with economic forecasts in the course of his day-to-day work.

Why must management be familiar with the business outlook? Because in most industries, general business conditions play a vital role in determining the prices, availability, and demand of purchased materials.

Prices. When business booms, prices tend to rise; when it slumps, they tend to decline. If a materials manager is sure of the business outlook, he can make substantial profits for his company. If he believes prices are going to rise, he will increase inventories with forward buying. If he believes they are going to decline, he will hold off buying and operate with minimum inventories.

Availability. When business is booming, many industries are operating near capacity and materials take longer to get. In some cases, supplies become inadequate to satisfy the demand of all users. If the materials manager can successfully anticipate shortages, he can either stock up in advance or locate alternate sources of supply to protect his company against shortages.

Demand. Demand for a company's end products is at least partly determined by general business conditions. If the materials manager knows that general business will decline, he can cut back on purchase commitments since less material will be needed. If he anticipates better business, he can increase commitments. Without good forecasting, it is easy to make serious errors in commitments for materials. Many items must be ordered months before they are needed, and if demand changes, the company either is stuck with excess stocks or loses sales because of lack of inventory.

It is no exaggeration to say that if the materials manager could forecast business conditions with absolute certainty, his job would become largely routine. So far no one has figured out a sure-fire forecasting technique. All the materials manager can do is to study certain key business barometers and make the best possible decisions.

GROSS NATIONAL PRODUCT

To see how the materials manager can use business data for forecasting, let us start with the biggest, broadest business indicator of all, gross national product.[1] GNP is the estimated total spending for all goods and services; it is prepared quarterly by the Bureau of Labor Statistics of the U.S. Department of Commerce. Its components and their approximate relative importance (as a percentage of total GNP) are:

    Personal consumption expenditures..........................66%
    Net balance of foreign trade (difference between exports and im-
      ports)... 1% or less
    Government spending for goods and services (federal, state, and
      local)...20%
    Gross private domestic investment..........................14%

As the term implies, the personal consumption expenditures component of GNP is estimated total consumer spending for goods and services. Although it is the biggest component of GNP, it is one of the easiest to predict. Individuals spend a consistent percentage of their incomes. Big fluctuations in consumer spending come only on durable goods (automobiles, refrigerators, and so on) where consumers can postpone spending without great hardship.

Foreign trade, the second GNP component listed above, rarely has much effect on the American economy. Exports normally exceed imports by a few billion dollars. The difference between them is the net contribution to GNP and it is rarely more than 1 per cent of the total.

Government spending, on the other hand, is a very important component. It now comprises about 20 per cent of our economy and shows no sign of declining in importance. Government spending poses few prob-

---

[1] The reader is reminded that this is a book on materials management, not one on economic theory. If explanations of economic phenomena seem either confusing or too superficial, it is suggested that he refer to one or more of the books listed in the bibliography that deal entirely with economic theory and business cycles.

lems for the forecaster, however. It is voted in advance by Congress and by state and local legislative bodies.

INVESTMENT SPENDING

So it is no great task to predict what three out of four segments of GNP will be. Would-be forecasters fall flat on their faces only when they try to predict the fourth major component, gross private domestic investment. In a private-enterprise economy, business investment spending is a not-too-small tail that wags the over-all GNP dog. Cutbacks in investment spending touch off recessions; increases spark booms.

During the 1957–58 recession, for example, investment spending dropped $11 billion while over-all GNP declined only $3 billion. When the economy recovered from the recession in 1959, GNP rose, personal consumption expenditures were up just 5 per cent, and gross private domestic investment zoomed up 38 per cent in the same period.

The Multiplier Principle. The reason why the level of investment spending determines GNP and total economic activity is a common-sense one. To understand why this is so, let us compare the economic activities of a farmer raising pigs to those of a bricklayer.

When the farmer sells his pigs on the market, he increases the supply of nondurable consumer goods. When he spends his income from the pigs, he is increasing the demand for consumer goods by a like amount (assuming that he spends all of his income). The net result is that GNP rises by the exact amount of the revenue that the farmer gets from the pigs.

When the bricklayer cashes his paycheck, he also increases the demand for consumer goods. But the product of his labors, a new office building or factory (i.e., investment spending), has no immediate effect on the supply of consumer goods. So the bricklayer's economic activity produces an imbalance in the supply of and demand for consumer goods. His net increase in demand is a call for additional production and investment; the whole economy expands.

Thus, spending for pork increases GNP by the exact value of the pork. Spending for a bricklayer's services increases it by more than the value of his services because there is a net increase in the demand for consumer goods (since the bricklayer's production cannot be used for immediate consumption). This is what economists call the "multiplier principle." It is one of two basic reasons why investment spending is so important to the over-all economy. The second reason isn't hard to deduce: it is easy to postpone investment spending, but it is hard to postpone consumption spending. As a result, investment spending virtually determines over-all output of the entire economy.

Every long-range, over-all economic forecast is really an attempt to determine the level of the three basic types of gross private domestic in-

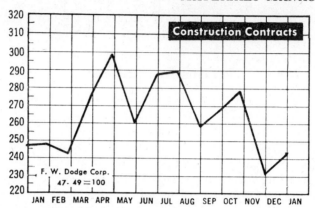

FIG. 6–1. F. W. Dodge Corp. statistics on construction contract awards are useful to the business forecaster because they indicate future capital expenditures.

vestment: new construction, producers' durable equipment, and changes in business inventories.

The best barometer of new construction activity is the monthly report of contract awards by the F. W. Dodge Corporation. It is particularly useful since contract awards are indicators of future investment spending. It must be interpreted carefully, however. Construction activity is highly seasonal (see Figure 6–1). It reaches a peak late in spring and is at a seasonal low in January and February. In analyzing contract awards, it is best always to compare current with year-ago figures; otherwise the analysis may well be distorted by normal seasonal fluctuations.

The U.S. Department of Commerce and the department of economics of the McGraw-Hill Publishing Company both run quarterly surveys on future plant and equipment spending. These surveys are widely reported and are extremely useful to the business forecaster. Materials managers in metalworking industries are keenly interested in the monthly report of the National Machine Tool Builders' Association on new orders and shipments of machine tools (see Figure 6–2). New order statistics are

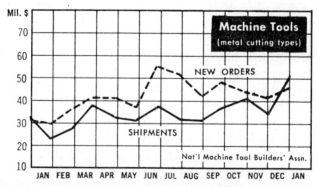

FIG. 6–2. A drop in machine-tool orders can signal a general business downturn. When machine-tool orders rise, the economy is usually already booming.

especially interesting for forecasting purposes since they are an excellent barometer of future investment in producers' durable equipment. The association's report is quoted widely in many publications. It should be read not only by materials managers interested in making a business forecast but by machine-tool buyers, who will find it a good indicator of the industry's ability to deliver promptly on new orders.

INVENTORY CHANGES

Inventories are by far the most unstable component of investment spending. The reason is obvious. Businesses can change direction in in-

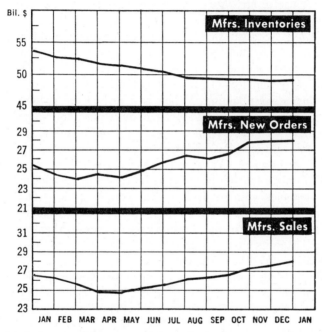

FIG. 6–3. U.S. Department of Commerce estimates of sales, inventories, and new orders help confirm forecasts made from other statistics that are available sooner.

ventory investment much more rapidly than they can in spending for construction or equipment. When business gets better, they can boost inventories in a period of weeks. But it can take months (or even years) to get new plant and equipment.

Relatively rapid changes in inventories by business are the single most important factor in the business cycle. We have already seen how the 1957–58 recession was caused by an $11 billion drop in investment spending. Roughly half of this drop was due to inventory liquidation. Of the $20 billion increase in investment that sparked the recovery from the recession, about $14 billion resulted from change in business inventories.

No one is closer to inventory policy than the materials manager. But even the materials manager can profitably supplement his unique know-how on inventory trends with data on changes in inventory in the entire economy.

The U.S. Department of Commerce issues monthly statistics on business inventories that are excellent leading indicators of future business conditions. Their only fault is that they come out six weeks late; that is, inventory figures for September, for example, are not available until about November 15.

So forecasters try to guess approximately what inventories will be during the current month. A number of business barometers provide clues. Particularly useful are figures on new orders, freight carloadings, retail sales, and certain commodity prices.

New Orders. Statistics on new orders are issued simultaneously with inventory figures by the Department of Commerce (see Figure 6–3 on preceding page). So they, too, are at least six weeks late. But they are still useful as barometers of future spending. Changes in order backlogs influence inventory planning. When new orders are rising, inventories eventually will rise as business stocks go up to meet anticipated new business. On the other hand, when new orders drop, business is likely to cut inventories in anticipation of lower business volume.

Freight Carloadings. When business activity is high, carloadings are high. This is not a leading barometer, however; it does not indicate what future inventories will be. It is useful mainly because it is available weekly for the previous week. Properly interpreted, carloading statistics can provide clues to inventory trends weeks before the Department of Commerce issues its monthly report on sales, inventories, and new orders.

Retail Sales. Weekly Department of Commerce estimates of department-store sales also provide clues to inventory trends at the retail level. When retail sales are rising, department-store orders to suppliers will also rise, and this in turn will affect industrial sales, orders, and inventories.

Both retail sales and carloadings are subject to wide seasonal fluctuations (see Figure 6–4), so the forecaster must be careful in making week-to-week comparisons. For example, retail sales always plunge during the last week of the year. This doesn't mean the beginning of a recession; it's just the end of the Christmas shopping season.

Commodity Prices. Industrial materials traded on commodity exchanges generally fluctuate widely in price. Slight changes in supply or demand are almost immediately reflected. By watching these prices, the economist can deduce what changes in inventory policies are going on. If commodity prices rise, inventories are probably rising. When they're dropping, users of the commodity may be buying less than they are consuming.

Unfortunately, inventory changes are not the only factors that influence commodity prices. So it's easy to be misled by price changes in individual commodities. For this reason, forecasters rarely take commodity price changes too seriously in making over-all forecasts unless other barometers confirm the trend of prices. It is especially hazardous to rely on any one commodity as a barometer of the general business trend. Speculation can cause the price of a commodity to move counter to the general trend. For this reason, indexes such as the Dow-Jones commodity index

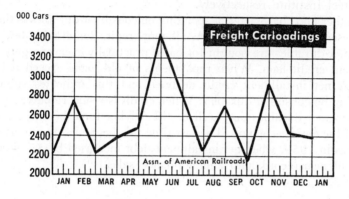

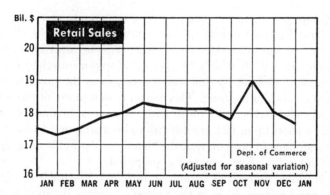

FIG. 6–4. Retail sales and freight carloading statistics are especially useful because they are available weekly. Allowance must be made for seasonal variation, however.

are useful barometers, for they reflect the prices of a group of various commodities.

Consumer Durables. If personal consumption expenditures are determined primarily by investment spending, why should we analyze spending for durable consumer goods in making a business forecast? The answer is that consumer durables are an exception to the general rule for an important reason. Consumers have a hard time postponing expenditures for the nondurables and services (food, clothing, electricity, telephone, etc.) that comprise about 85 per cent of total personal consumption expenditures. But they can and do postpone spending for consumer durables. For example, if Detroit's car models are real hits with the public, the entire economy can boom as a result. On the other hand, if the public decides to make the "old buggy" last another year, over-all production and national income will be adversely affected.

Weekly figures for automobile production and for steel output provide good clues as to spending on consumer durables. These are issued by *Ward's Reports*, an auto industry publication, and by the American Iron and Steel Institute respectively.

Another good barometer of spending on consumer durables is the Federal Reserve Board's report on installment credit. Remarkably few major consumer durables are bought for cash; practically everyone gets an installment credit loan. When repayments of old loans exceed new borrowing, net installment credit declines and this indicates subnormal spending on consumer durables. When credit is rising rapidly, spending for consumer durables may well be the driving force behind an expansion of the entire economy. The last time this happened to any great extent was in 1959, when net installment debt increased by $5 billion because of near-record auto and appliance sales.

LEADING INDICATORS

The materials manager should watch the trends of all the economic barometers discussed so far in this chapter. In addition, he should watch all production and price statistics dealing with his own industry or with those industries with which he deals for major purchased materials. Unfortunately, despite all this study, changes in the business cycle will still often catch him napping. The reason is that many of the barometers discussed so far either: (1) move with the general business cycle or lead it by only a short time; (2) are difficult to interpret; or (3) have statistics that take so long to prepare that the "lead" they provide on general business is lost while they are being prepared.

The National Bureau of Economic Research has made detailed analyses of every business cycle in the nation's history. Its studies show that certain indicators usually—though not always—lead changes in general business conditions by several months to a year or two.[2] Watch these indicators and you'll know where general business will be six months to a year from now. The leading indicators are:

1. Average hours worked per week in manufacturing.
2. Gross accession rate, manufacturing.
3. Layoff rate, manufacturing (inverted).
4. New orders, durable-goods industries (value).
5. Housing starts (number of new dwelling units).
6. Commercial and industrial building contract awards.

[2] See Geoffrey H. Moore (ed.), *Business Cycle Indicators*, 2 vol. (Princeton: Princeton University Press, 1960).

7. Net change in number of operating businesses.
8. Business failures, liabilities, industrial and commercial (inverted).
9. Corporate profits after taxes.
10. Common stock price index—industrials, rails, and utilities.
11. Change in business inventories.
12. Industrial materials spot price index.

MARKET SENTIMENT

All intelligent businessmen follow the trend of business. They carefully read comments on the business outlook by professional economists. Many of them analyze the business statistics that we have just discussed. Yet in general, businessmen are wrong on business forecasting more often than they are right. One reason they are wrong is that forecasting is far from an exact science and it is extremely easy to make serious mistakes. A second reason is even more basic. Forecasts can be self-defeating if they gain wide acceptance.

Suppose every economist and businessman agreed that we will be in for the biggest boom in history next year. What would happen? Each would prepare for it by expanding plant, equipment, and inventories. The surge in demand would push up prices and employment. The boom would no longer be a year away; it would already have arrived. In fact, in a year the expected boom might prove to be a mirage, for there would be a slump as soon as business was completely prepared for the coming boom and tapered off its capital investment.

Investment decisions are not based on current activity but on businessmen's estimates of future activity. Business forecasting is the art of anticipating future business decisions. Analyzing current statistics isn't enough; the forecaster must predict how businessmen will react to these statistics and the forecasts on which they are based. If he has a knack for it, the materials manager is in a much better position to do this than the professional economist is. Economists can be expected to catch swings in business sentiment only when they show up in news releases and business statistics. The materials manager, on the other hand, is in daily contact with leaders of the business community—his suppliers. If he is an intelligent listener, he can sense changes that won't be reflected in gross national product statistics for months to come.

PRICE FORECASTS

From statistics, his evaluation of the market sentiment, and the forecasts of professional economists, the materials manager reaches his own conclusions as to the future course of the economy. He then tries to translate this general forecast into specific forecasts for various key commodities.

Most materials are always available at a price. Materials that are bought and sold in commodity markets are always available; the price automatically equilibrates supply and demand. Even scarce materials whose prices are "administered"[3] are available if the materials manager is willing to pay enough. For example, although steel was scarce when ordered through regular supply channels at published prices right after World War II, it was almost always available from "gray market" dealers at prices 50 to 100 per cent higher than those charged by the major producers.

But what materials manager wants to pay premium prices for materials? His job is to get the required materials at minimum prices. And, to the greatest extent possible, he wants to be able to predict what prices will be in the future so he can plan his purchases accordingly.

The materials manager can influence the prices of most of the items he buys. All parts and a few raw materials have "administered" prices; in most cases, they are established by negotiation between buyer and supplier. While the materials manager will make use of economic forecasts when buying such items, he is not at the mercy of an impersonal market, and in practice he can predict such prices with considerable accuracy.[4]

Free Market Commodities.   When he buys many raw materials, however, the materials manager can almost never influence price. He is one of many buyers and sellers. Prices are determined by the interaction of demand and supply. The general business outlook and cost of production ultimately affect demand and supply, but over a short term prices are determined entirely by sellers and buyers whose bids and asks determine prices on commodity exchanges.

Among the free market commodities are cotton, wool, copper, lead, sugar, zinc, crude rubber, tin, wheat, and soy beans. In addition, the prices of other commodities, like steel scrap, secondary aluminum, glycerine, hides, and various oils and chemicals, are determined almost entirely by supply and demand even though these commodities are not formally traded on any exchange.

Demand for these commodities fluctuates considerably. When the business outlook is basically bullish, businessmen not only buy for current production but also add to inventories. When businessmen are pessimistic about the future, they will "live off" their inventories and buy practically nothing even for current production. Demand depends more on business sentiment and expectations than on actual business conditions.

While demand is subject to extremely wide swings, supply changes quite slowly. It takes time to bring additional facilities into production in response to high prices. And businessmen are reluctant to shut down

---

[3] That is, set by a few big producers whose pricing decisions are based on demand, competition, cost of production, and other factors.

[4] Techniques used in forecasting administered prices are discussed in Chapter 7 and the administered pricing process is discussed in Chapter 16.

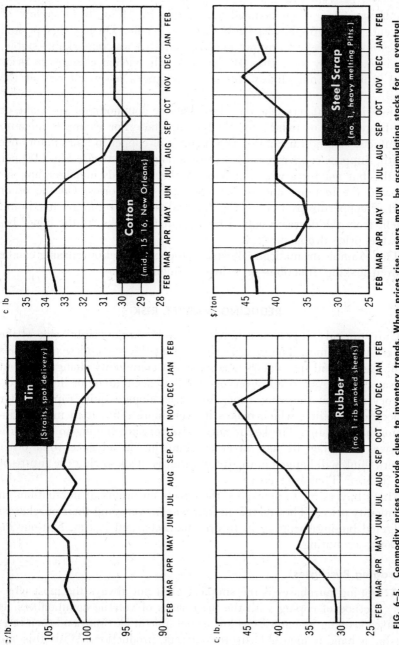

FIG. 6–5. Commodity prices provide clues to inventory trends. When prices rise, users may be accumulating stocks for an eventual increase in output. When prices fall, they are most likely cutting their inventories.

marginal facilities until prices fall to ruinously low levels. The result of this supply-demand situation is highly unstable prices (see Figure 6–5).

Copper Prices.   For example, copper sold for as much as 46 cents per pound in 1956, when demand was high. In 1958, it hit a low of 24 cents. By 1960 it was back up to 33 cents. During this period, domestic copper refinery output (i.e., the supply) was remarkably stable; it did not vary by more than 10 per cent. The violent changes in price were brought about almost entirely by changes in inventories of the metal.

Materials managers who buy these volatile commodities can make or lose large sums of money for their companies. For example, an auto manufacturer might use 2,000,000 pounds of copper in its radiators per month. Suppose copper goes up 4 cents a pound. Costs rise $80,000 per month—but not for a while, at least, if the materials manager has anticipated the increase and so has increased inventories. On the other hand, if copper drops 4 cents, the materials manager can get maximum benefit from the decrease only if he has cut his stocks "to the bone" before the price dropped.

This example dramatically illustrates the axiom that purchasing can be a profit-making function—or a loss-producing one.

REDUCING MARKET RISK

Unfortunately, it is almost impossible to be on the "right" side of the market at all times. The general rule is that the economic expectations of all users of and speculators in a particular commodity change at about the same time. As a result, everyone tends to accumulate or liquidate inventory at about the same time. So prices change quite rapidly after periods of stability, which makes it even more difficult to manage inventories profitably. The key to successful forward buying in commodities was described by one buyer as "knowing in advance what other buyers think will happen in the future; that is, it's knowing the future of the future." That isn't easy.

Many buyers try to neutralize the effects on profits of fluctuations in commodity prices. They do this in four ways: averaging their purchases; budgeted buying; hedging in futures markets; and last-in, first-out inventory accounting.

Averaging Purchases

Averaging purchases is the simplest (but not always the most effective) method of coping with the price risks of volatile commodities. It involves keeping inventories as low as possible at all times and then buying on a hand-to-mouth basis for current production. With this approach, the average cost of the commodity used in production will be about the same as the average price for that commodity during the year.

The average-purchase technique permits a company to concentrate its efforts on making and selling a finished product without giving a thought to commodity market fluctuations. It works well only when: (1) the commodity is not too important in relation to over-all product cost; or (2) increases in the cost of the commodity can be passed on immediately to customers buying the end product; or (3) the commodity is not subject to particularly violent fluctuations; *and* (4) the commodity is not produced abroad or under other circumstances where supply lines are long and complex and likely to be disrupted by political upheavals,[5] labor trouble, and the like.

Budgeted Buying

If prices regularly fluctuate around some mean, it is possible to beat the market with budgeted buying. The materials manager budgets regu-

TABLE 6–1

AVERAGING PURCHASES VERSUS BUDGETED BUYING

| | | | Averaging Purchases | | Budgeted Buying | |
Month	Market Price	Quantity Required (in lbs.)	Quantity Purchased (in lbs.)	Cost	Quantity Purchased (in lbs.)	Cost
January	10¢	120,000	120,000	$12,000	120,000	$12,000
February	9	120,000	120,000	10,800	133,333	12,000
March	8	120,000	120,000	9,600	150,000	12,000
April	10	120,000	120,000	12,000	120,000	12,000
May	11	120,000	120,000	13,200	109,090	12,000
June	12	120,000	120,000	14,400	100,000	12,000
Total			720,000	$72,000	732,423	$72,000

lar amounts to be spent for the material regardless of its selling price. As a result, the company automatically buys more when prices are low and less when they are high.

Table 6–1 illustrates a budgeted policy for a commodity whose usage is 120,000 pounds per month. The materials manager assumes that the price will fluctuate around a mean of 10 cents per pound, so he calculates that, on the average, he can get required quantities by spending $12,000 a month on the material. When the price is higher than 10 cents, he buys less than 120,000 pounds and draws on inventories for production requirements. When the price is lower than 10 cents, he spends $12,000 anyway and buys more than 120,000 pounds.

Table 6–1 covers a commodity over a six-month period in which its price averaged 10 cents per pound and varied from a high of 12 cents

---

[5] It is for this reason that users of crude rubber, tin, and other materials produced in politically unstable countries thousands of miles away traditionally carry extremely heavy inventories, often amounting to enough for production needs of a year or more.

to a low of 8 cents. When purchases are averaged, requirements of $120,-000 pounds were purchased each month at the market price. During the six-month period, they totaled 720,000 pounds and the cost was $72,-000. With budgeted purchases, $12,000 was spent each month for material at the market price and total purchases were 732,423 pounds, or 12,423 pounds in excess of use. This addition to inventory, worth $1,490.76 at the June market price, is the "profit" earned through budgeted purchasing in this period as compared with averaging purchases. In both cases total expenditures were $72,000, but with budgeted purchasing it was possible to buy 12,423 pounds of additional material.

Unfortunately, a budgeted-buying program is successful only when the materials manager can predict the average price that will prevail with reasonable accuracy. For example, suppose prices declined steadily for a long period of time. The materials manager simply could not afford to continue to buy in excess of current requirements indefinitely, and he would be stuck with a large inventory worth, at market prices, less than he had paid for it. Similarly, if prices went up steadily for a long period, a budgeted-buying program would not work. Month after month the materials manager would be buying less than the amount being consumed and eventually he would run out of inventory, which he would then have to replenish at peak prices.

Despite its shortcomings, budgeted buying is a useful technique for certain commodities—especially when the materials manager is reasonably certain what the over-all price trend will be.

Hedging in Futures Markets

If a company must carry large inventories of a commodity for various reasons, it is always in danger of suffering substantial losses when the commodity drops in price. This is strictly a "paper loss" as long as the company is not forced to reduce the selling prices of its products when the commodity drops in price. In such cases, the "loss" is the additional profit that would have been made if the company had postponed its purchase and got the commodity at lower prices, thereby making its profit margin bigger.

The loss becomes more painful if the company must cut its prices when the commodity drops in price.[6] For if the company has a big stock of material, its costs will be much too high at the new market selling price for its finished products.

With some commodities, the buyer can avoid this risk by hedging in the futures market. He can sell a contract for future delivery of an amount equal to the quantity in his inventory. Then, for the period of

---

[6] This would be the case with a brass mill, for example. Brass prices move up and down in unison with copper prices. Contrarily, if a steel mill takes an inventory loss when steel scrap drops in price, this is merely profit that is lost since steel prices don't fluctuate with scrap prices.

the contract, he will neither lose nor make money on his inventory.

A Typical Transaction. Suppose, for example, a company has a contract to make auto tires for a mail-order house. The price agreed upon is fixed in every respect except that it will be adjusted to reflect changes in the market price of crude rubber.

Now suppose the company has approximately 1,000,000 pounds of crude rubber in stock for this contract at the time it is signed. The cost was 30 cents per pound. Suppose the average price for crude rubber during the life of the contract is only 20 cents. Then the company must adjust its prices to the mail-order house accordingly. But its costs are now lower, since its crude rubber was bought at a price that was 10 cents a pound higher. Consequently, the company's profits are reduced by 10 cents per pound multiplied by 1,000,000 pounds, or $100,000.

The company need not have taken this loss. Instead, it could have sold a futures contract for delivery three, six, nine, or twelve months hence for 1,000,000 pounds of rubber. When it sells such a contract, it accepts payment for the commodity at the prevailing price and agrees to deliver it at some time in the future.

Preventing Losses. Suppose the company sells 1,000,000 pounds at 30 cents per pound[7] for delivery twelve months hence. If rubber then drops to 20 cents a pound during the term of the contract, it will be possible to buy rubber in the spot market (or simply to sell the futures contract at a profit) at a price 10 cents per pound lower. So the company will collect $300,000 for the rubber it sold for future delivery but will have to pay only $200,000 for it when the contract is completed. This exactly offsets the $100,000 the company loses on its inventory, so that profits on the contract with the mail-order house are exactly as anticipated.

Similarly, if rubber had advanced from 30 cents to 40 cents during the life of the contract, the company would have lost $200,000 on its futures contract. It would have sold the rubber for future delivery[8] and received 30 cents for it. And it would have had to purchase in the spot market at 40 cents to cover, thereby incurring a loss of 10 cents a pound on the transaction. However, this loss in the futures market would be offset by increased profits. The company, by the terms of its contract for the tires, would be able to increase its prices because of the price rise in

---

[7] To simplify the example, the futures price of 30 cents was made identical with the spot price. In practice, this isn't usually the case. Spot and futures prices are not determined by completely identical supply and demand forces. Therefore they are rarely identical. However, they are almost always within 3 or 4 per cent of one another. Otherwise, it becomes profitable for traders to buy in one market and sell in another.

[8] Traders call this a "short" sale, i.e., the commodity is sold when the seller is "short" of it (doesn't own it) and the seller promises to deliver the commodity he has sold at some future date. It is the opposite of a "long" purchase, where the buyer gets immediate delivery on the commodity he has bought and paid for.

rubber, even though its costs did not go up since it already had the rubber in stock.

The mail-order house, if it desired, could hedge on its purchases of tires to avoid paying a price higher than that based on the 30-cent cost of rubber.[9] Its action would be precisely the opposite of that of the manufacturer. It would buy a futures contract instead of selling one short. That way, if rubber went up in price, the house's profits on the futures contract would offset the higher price it would have to pay for tires. And vice versa if crude rubber prices declined.

Disadvantages of Futures Hedging.   Many materials managers make little or no use of futures contracts. Although brokerage commissions are nominal on individual transactions (less than 1 per cent of the value of the contract), they become significant if a company does a lot of trading. Most managers simply prefer to swing their inventories up and down with the business cycle. With last-in, first-out accounting (LIFO), companies that can vary their selling prices with raw material costs needn't worry too much about the effect of inventory losses on the profit-and-loss statement anyway.

Last-in, First-out Accounting

Conventional accounting procedures are based on a first-in, first-out (FIFO) treatment of inventory. In other words, the items that are received earliest are regarded as being used first. In some businesses, this handling of inventory literally fits practice. In a grocery store, for example, every effort is made to turn over stock physically on a first-in, first-out basis. That way there's no spoilage, provided that not every housewife tries to beat the system by reaching for the fresher merchandise at the back of the shelf.

In a manufacturing business, the first-in, first-out concept isn't as logical. A stock of raw material is just as vital as plant and equipment in a company making, for example, zinc die castings. And zinc slabs received a couple of years ago are just as useful as those received yesterday. This basic stock is regarded almost as a permanent investment in the business and is carried on the books as original cost. Purchases are regarded as almost immediate operating expenses; cost of production is charged the most recent purchase cost.

Effect on Profits.   When material costs vary a great deal, reported profits can be affected substantially by the inventory accounting method used. For example, suppose a company making zinc die castings has

---

[9] This is purely a hypothetical example. In practice, it would be extremely foolish for both buyer and seller to hedge in a commodity market. It would be far wiser for them to make a contract wherein all market risks would be taken by one party, which could then do the hedging for both of them. Hedging isn't free. Brokerage commissions and other costs are incurred. With intelligent management, these are minimized.

1,000,000 pounds of zinc in its inventory. Let us assume that 500,000 pounds were bought when the price of zinc was 15 cents a pound, and at a later date an additional 500,000 pounds were purchased at a price of only 10 cents a pound.

Now suppose that the company gets an order for finished die castings in which 100,000 pounds of metal will be used. The order price is based on the current market price for zinc, 11 cents a pound. So, the total cost of metal will be as follows:

> At market price: 100,000 lbs. at 11¢/lb. = $11,000.
> Cost on FIFO basis: 100,000 lbs. at 15¢/lb. = $15,000.
> Cost on LIFO basis: 100,000 lbs. at 10¢/lb. = $10,000.

Naturally, the company's prices must be based on the current market for materials; otherwise, it is liable to lose out to competitors who can offer finished castings made of metal bought at the prevailing low price. But what happens if it keeps its books on a FIFO basis? Then its cost of production will be based on the prices paid for the "oldest" metal in the inventory, that bought at 15 cents a pound. Thus costs will be $5,000 higher than anticipated.

If accounts are kept on a LIFO basis, this won't happen. If the materials manager decides not to increase inventories because of this order, production cost will be based on the "last" zinc received, which will be "used" in that order. As a result, costs will be 1 cent a pound lower than anticipated and the company will show an added "profit" of $1,000 ($.01 × 100,000 lbs.) on the order. Finally, if the company decides to increase inventories because of the order and buys more zinc at 11 cents, it will make the anticipated profit if its records are kept on a LIFO basis.

With last-in, first-out accounting, changing prices for raw materials have considerably less effect on stated profits. This takes some of the pressure off the materials manager to time purchases properly. However, even with LIFO, profits over a long term will be affected just as much by timing of purchases as with any other accepted accounting system. LIFO can only keep the full impact of an unfavorable swing in inventory prices from being reflected immediately in the profit-and-loss statement. It also, of course, prevents a big rise in raw materials prices and consequent "paper" gains in inventory values from being immediately translated into higher profits.

CASES

CASE 6–1. OHIO BATTERY COMPANY

Forecasting Lead Prices

The Ohio Battery Company makes automobile batteries for the replacement market. As with all battery manufacturers, its single most important cost is the lead that is cast into plates in the battery. For example, the company has the following costs for one of its cheaper, more popular batteries:

Lead (22 lbs. @ 14¢/lb.)	$3.08
Other materials	1.97
Direct labor	.36
Overhead	.72
Manufacturing cost	$6.13
Sales and distribution cost	1.35
Total cost	$7.48
Profit	.32
Selling price to dealers	$7.80

Prices to dealers are revised periodically to reflect changes in cost. Ohio Battery never tries to be the price leader. Instead, it waits for its larger competitors to adjust prices and follows with an identical price change a few days later. Major swings in the lead market always bring price adjustments on batteries. Producers can't afford to absorb a substantial increase in lead prices, and competition forces them to pass on major reductions in lead costs to their customers.

Changes in the lead market provide Ohio Battery with unusual opportunities for both profit and loss, since the company does not have to adjust its prices until its competitors adjust theirs. For example, if the company has a large inventory of lead acquired at low prices and competitors raise prices to reflect higher costs, Ohio Battery can also raise prices and enjoy high profits while it uses up its low-cost inventory. On the other hand, if the company has a high-cost lead inventory and competitors cut prices because of a declining lead market, the effect on the company's profits can be almost disastrous. For example, the price breakdown above is based on lead at 14 cents a pound. If the lead market declined to 12½ cents and competitors cut prices by 33 cents (22 lbs. × 1½¢/lb.), the company's profits would be wiped out completely until it managed to use up its inventory of 14-cent lead.

The company tries to protect itself against such violent fluctuations in stated profits with a last-in, first-out inventory control system. As a result, gains and losses in the lead market are not immediately reflected in the company's income statement. Lead inventories, with the oldest inventory first, are currently valued as follows:

10,000 lbs. @ 10¢	$ 1,000
90,000 lbs. @ 9¢	9,000
11,000 lbs. @ 12¢	13,200
6,000 lbs. @ 14¢	840
Total	$24,040

Demand for the company's products is seasonal. The peak is in fall, when dealers stock up for the wave of battery failures that come with the first cold weather, after four months of summer doldrums. The company anticipates the following pattern of lead usage:

January....................................	100,000 lbs.
February.................................	100,000
March....................................	100,000
April.....................................	70,000
May......................................	60,000
June......................................	60,000
July......................................	60,000
August...................................	60,000
September................................	100,000
October..................................	120,000
November.................................	120,000
December................................	100,000
Total...........................	1,050,000 lbs.

Questions

1. Prepare a one-year price forecast for lead based on *current* spot and futures prices, refiners' stocks, production, consumption, general economic outlook, and analysis of price trends in lead and other commodities.
2. Prepare a plan of purchase based on your price forecast. Assume that the company president is willing to carry as much as three months' inventory provided that you can convince him that it will be worthwhile.
3. On the basis of your forecast and plan of purchase, calculate the difference between the company's stated profits with its last-in first-out system and a first-in, first-out system of inventory control.

Chapter 7

MAKING THE MATERIALS PLAN

Planning is a major part of the materials manager's job. Plans are made from day to day. In addition, more formal plans are made at less frequent intervals. Usually a materials manager submits a broad plan to management at the beginning of each fiscal year. This plan is not developed on the spur of the moment, by any means. Typically, a materials manager might start to work on his plan three to six months before he submits it to top management for approval. In the course of the next three months, he may have to make several revisions in his plans to bring them in line with the plans of other activities of the business and also to reflect changes in basic assumptions. After the plan is approved, there may be further changes. If the assumptions on which the plan is based change during the year, the materials manager would again revise his plans. Also, during the course of the year he would report progress in achieving objectives of the plan.

ACHIEVEMENT OF OBJECTIVES

The materials planning process always should be in terms of objectives. In his plan, the materials manager should indicate how he proposes to achieve each of his basic objectives. For example, suppose that his objectives are identical with those listed in Chapter 3. (Remember, however, that objectives vary from company to company and industry to industry; each materials manager must determine his own.) Here are some typical ways in which a materials manager might plan to achieve them.

Low Prices. Individual plans of purchase incorporate price objectives. But the materials manager also should have an over-all objective. Based on his economic forecast, knowledge of competitive conditions, and so on, he may wish to set an over-all target for cost reduction—e.g., 2 per cent of total purchase volume, or $300,000 total savings.

High Inventory Turnover. To achieve this objective, the materials manager might institute programs to reduce the number of items carried in stock, to persuade vendors to carry special stocks available for immediate delivery, to work on tighter lead times, and similar techniques that will be discussed in later chapters of this book. By consolidating his plans of purchase for various commodities, the materials manager can readily estimate what planned inventories will be. He then can compare the probable turnover rate and inventory level with those for previous years. As a result, he may wish to set a target for tighter control.

Low Cost of Acquisition and Possession. This objective can be achieved with various programs to reduce the cost of in-bound freight, using techniques that will be discussed in the chapter on traffic management. It also can be achieved through methods improvements in the handling and storage of materials—materials handling equipment, better controls, and so on.

Continuity of Supply. To a considerable extent, this objective should be achieved when plans of purchase are made for various commodities, since it is largely dependent on selection of suppliers and inventory policies. But it also can be achieved in part by improved liaison with other departments in the company that use materials, so that changes in their needs can rapidly be communicated to suppliers.

Consistency of Quality. If quality is a problem, this becomes one of the most important objectives. The materials manager may propose joint programs with the quality control department to educate suppliers concerning the company's quality standards. He may propose a program of statistical quality and vendor certification. If the quality problem becomes serious enough, he may plan on introducing new suppliers who can meet specifications, or propose a joint program with engineering to develop alternate designs whose specifications suppliers can better meet.

If quality is not a problem and vendors are likely to continue meeting specifications, the quality objective may require almost no planning by the materials manager. In fact, it is possible that he may go even further and propose that suppliers with lower quality standards be introduced if he feels the company is paying for quality it doesn't need.

Low Payroll Costs. The materials manager should plan on introducing laborsaving equipment, such as electronic data-processing equipment, in order to keep his clerical costs as low as possible. He also should review his organization at least once a year to make certain that changes in its structure will not permit jobs to be done by fewer personnel. He certainly should also try to prevent overtime expense by planning work ahead to even out work loads, hiring additional personnel if necessary, and improving organization and methods.

Good Supplier Relations. A program to improve supplier relations may include "supplier days" on which vendors are invited to tour company facilities, hear speeches, and so on. It also may include efforts to prevent favoritism in buying, stimulate supplier interest in developing new products for the company, and even institute improvements in parking, lobby facilities, and the like to make the salesman's calls pleasanter.

Development of Personnel. On-the-job training programs and night courses for high-potential personnel can help achieve this objective. So can plans for a more informal development of personnel. Ideally, the materials manager should include in his report evaluations of all key personnel and steps planned to improve their job skills. He also should include plans to prepare for job openings that may come with expansion, retirements, and so on.

Good Records. Each record and procedure should be subjected to "regular trials for life," and those that are unnecessary should be eliminated. Periodic studies also may indicate a need for new records or better record keeping.

Other Objectives. The objectives that have been discussed so far are very basic ones. Most materials managers will have other objectives as well. These might include favorable reciprocal relations, better relations with other departments, improved liaison with engineering on new products and design changes, promotion of standardization, and better make-or-buy decisions. In each case, the materials manager should present the objective and indicate how he plans to achieve it. If other departments in the company are involved, this should be made clear in the plan. Naturally, these departments must concur with such a plan before it is put into action.

THE MATERIALS PLAN

The materials manager must supplement his broad plan to achieve objectives with highly detailed plans directly related to his basic jobs of buying, storing, and moving materials. The materials planning process starts with an economic forecast. Using the forecasts of professional economists and applying the principles discussed in the previous chapter, the materials manager tries to predict the general trend of prices, wages, and costs for at least a year ahead. He must also make certain assumptions about his company's sales and production prospects for the coming year (and even further in the future if possible). He must be informed about his company's expansion plans, product development efforts, and all major changes contemplated by other company departments.

From these broad forecasts and plans, the materials manager tries to develop specific predictions and plans. He is careful not to misuse his forecasts. For example, if his forecasts indicate that over-all wholesale prices will rise 2 per cent, can he then conclude that the average prices he will pay for materials and components will rise 2 per cent? Of course not. Some of the prices he pays will rise; others will decline. The change in his average prices may be greater or less than an over-all average. To make an intelligent forecast, the materials manager should divide his commodities into groups. Such a division for an office-equipment manufacturer is shown in Table 7–1.

The materials manager should develop forecasts for each major commodity. Allowances should be made for changes in both price and availability. For example, if steel is a major commodity—as it is for the office-equipment manufacturer whose commodities are listed in Table

7–1—then the materials manager should be concerned about expiration of union contracts in the steel industry and possible strikes. He might also try to estimate whether or not demand for steel will be strong enough to permit a price increase after new contracts are negotiated.

No materials manager can hope to forecast price or availability perfectly. With a material whose price is administered, such as steel, availability is likely to be more difficult to forecast than price. Prices of such materials respond quite slowly to changes in supply and demand

TABLE 7–1

MAJOR PURCHASED COMMODITIES FOR A MANUFACTURER OF BUSINESS MACHINES
AND EQUIPMENT

I. Production parts and materials
    A. Semifinished and raw materials
        1. Plastic molding compounds
        2. Zinc
        3. Sheet steel
        4. Gray iron sand castings
        5. Steel forgings
        6. Miscellaneous materials
    B. Component parts and assemblies
        1. Sheet steel stampings
        2. Ball and roller bearings
        3. Fractional horsepower electric motors
        4. Plated zinc die castings
        5. Miscellaneous components and assemblies
II. Nonproduction materials
    A. Machine tools and equipment
    B. Maintenance, repair. and operating supplies
        1. Perishable tools
        2. Lubricants and cutting oils
        3. Other supplies
    C. Construction
III. Transportation costs

since producers exercise considerable discretion in price administration. On the other hand, availability can be a problem either when over-all demand exceeds supply or when producers are shut down because of labor trouble or other reasons.

The situation is just the opposite with materials whose prices are determined almost entirely by impersonal supply-demand forces. As we saw in Chapter 6, these materials are almost always available at a price. When supply is reduced or demand is heavy, prices can rise precipitously. Demand will then drop not because buyers are unable to get the material but because they are unwilling to pay the going price. Unfortunately, for reasons discussed in Chapter 6, it is no easy job to forecast prices of such materials. Nevertheless, the materials manager who uses them is forced to make some sort of forecast whether he wants to or not. This is true even of materials managers who deny that they attempt to predict what the market will be. A materials manager's buying and stocking pattern is intrinsically based on market assumptions, whether he wants to admit it or not.

Of course, as we saw in Chapter 6, a materials manager can say, "I don't know what the market is going to do," by using various buying and accounting techniques designed to reduce risk. These include averaging of purchases, budgeted buying techniques, last-in, first-out accounting, and hedging. All these techniques prevent bad timing of purchases and poor forecasting from being immediately reflected in the profit and loss statement. But few materials managers would deny that they can boost profits substantially through shrewd timing of purchases, particularly when dealing with commodities that fluctuate a great deal in price.

TIMING PURCHASES

How does one go about timing purchases? To successful materials managers, timing is both an art and a science. They try to make the timing process as scientific as possible, using forecasts, statistics, and so on. But, as one materials manager pointed out, "There is no formula that will tell me when and how much to buy. The best I can do is to review all available information, try to interpret it as best I can, make my decision, and then hope I'm right." He adds, "Regardless of how long you've been in the business, you're often wrong."

It is almost impossible for any materials manager to be consistently "smarter" than the market. All buyers are constantly analyzing general business conditions and supply-demand relationships in particular commodities. So are thousands of speculators. As a result, changes in sentiment are almost immediately reflected in prices. Buyers tend to reach the same opinion regarding future prices at almost the same time. Consequently, their total buying—or lack of buying—tends to cause prices to readjust to the new conditions. Therefore buying tends to be heavy when prices are high and light when prices are low. Obviously only a minority of buyers are in the market when they should be, i.e., when prices are low.

There is good reason for this situation. The materials manager's prime mission is to provide needed raw materials for operations. Unfortunately, he usually needs materials least when prices are low. Prices generally slump with over-all business, and most materials managers must cut back purchases because of a drop in their company's sales. When prices are high, on the other hand, the materials manager often must buy regardless of whether or not he thinks the material can be bought more cheaply at a later date. His factory is running full blast and it needs raw materials to keep it operating.

There is no single right formula that can be applied to timing of purchases in all situations. However, most successful materials managers do follow these general procedures:

1. Estimate Materials Needs. The usual approach is to try to make a rather firm estimate of materials consumption for at least several quarters and possibly a year ahead. In addition, the materials manager tries to get a more tentative estimate of materials needs for a five-year or even a ten-year period. Both the long- and short-term estimates are revised at periodic intervals to bring them in line with the latest sales projections supplied by the company's market research department.

At all times, the materials manager's estimates should be based on the best available forecasts. During the period of the estimate, the materials manager knows he will have to buy at least enough material to satisfy estimated use (less any reduction in inventories that might be desired). So purchases must always be timed to meet use requirements. In other words, the materials manager can buy "ahead" of materials requirements. But he cannot afford to buy "behind" actual requirements; he must always have material available when it is scheduled to be used.

2. Develop Tentative Plan of Purchases. At this stage in his planning, the materials manager ignores the effect of future price changes and the like on his purchase timing. He breaks up his requirements into economic lots and programs their delivery, allowing sufficient lead time to prevent shortages from delivery failures.

Suppose, for example, that usage of a given material is estimated as follows: January, 10,000 pounds; February, 60,000 pounds; March, 100,000 pounds; April, 60,000 pounds; May and every month thereafter, 50,000 pounds.

Let us further suppose that this material is shipped most economically in carload quantities with 50,000 pounds in each box car. Also, there is a lapse of 30 days between the time the material is ordered and when it is received, and the materials manager is interested in maintaining inventories at present levels.

Under these conditions, the materials manager would have to order his first carload of material early in December for early January delivery (in practice, he'd probably give himself a small safety margin and order a few weeks earlier than this). He would have to order the second carload in the second or third week of January for delivery later in February, and so on.

In practice, the materials manager would allow also for a minimum safety stock to prevent a stockout should unforeseen circumstances cause deliveries to be delayed or usage to be increased.

3. Watch for Buying Opportunities. Whenever prices look unusually favorable, the materials manager should consider buying in excess of requirements. He should work closely with his company's financial officials on forward buying. Most companies have limited funds available for forward buying, and the amount available can vary from month to month.

When a buying opportunity does appear, the materials manager is still faced with a timing problem. Should he buy ahead now, should he spend all the money available for forward buying, or should he hold off? No materials manager can hope to be right on timing all of the time. Many try to average their success through various timing formulas. Here's how one such plan might work:

The materials manager expects the price of a material to average 30 cents a pound during the year. He makes up a buying plan[1] based on this assumption. If the price is 30 cents or more, he will buy only the absolute minimum of material needed for production. But for every 1-cent drop in price below 30 cents, he will use 10 per cent of his forward-buying fund to accumulate inventory. He does this cumulatively. For example, if the price drops 1 cent he spends 10 per cent of the fund; if it drops an additional cent (to 2 cents below the estimated average of 30 cents), he uses another 20 per cent of the fund; and so on.

The advantage of this formula is that it encourages stock accumulation when prices are low and discourages it when they are high. However, the buyer is not protected against severe price drops, since he will use up his fund before the bottom is reached. Nor will he be buying most advantageously should prices inch up progressively throughout the year. Formulas, when they are used, must be developed on a "tailor-made" basis to suit the needs of the materials manager applying them. They can never be used as substitutes for the judgment of a skilled and experienced materials manager.

FORECASTING PARTS PRICES

Timing of purchases isn't nearly as difficult for parts and price-administered materials as it is for those materials whose prices are determined almost entirely by the workings of impersonal supply-demand forces. The timing problem on price-administered items is simplified because prices of such items can often be predicted with considerable precision. To forecast prices of such items, the materials manager uses techniques not too different from those used for free-market items. He takes account of the broad economic changes that affect all prices and then reviews the probable cost and supply-demand situation that exists in particular industries.

Suppose, for example, the materials manager is trying to estimate the future price of gray iron castings. He should consider:

---

[1] Note that this plan is based on the principle of budgeted buying described in Chapter 6.

1. Effect of General Business Conditions. He should consider the effect of the predicted gross national product on the industries that use gray iron castings. If GNP rises 3 per cent, demand for gray iron castings may not rise at all or it may rise substantially more than 3 per cent. The materials manager often can guess quite accurately what the over-all effect of a change in GNP on demand for castings will be by studying what happened in previous years.

2. Estimated Changes in Supply. By using general business statistics and also drawing on his knowledge of the expansion plans of key suppliers in the industry, the materials manager can deduce how much additional capacity is planned.

3. Cost Trends in the Industry. If contracts between foundries and the unions representing their workers are being renewed, the materials manager should estimate the cost of the settlement and its probable effect on the foundries' cost of production. He also should be familiar with the probable trend of the prices of key raw materials in gray iron castings: pig iron, scrap iron, coke, and so on. And further, he should try to estimate what effect new equipment and various laborsaving devices will have on suppliers' costs when they are introduced.

4. "Temper" of the Market. The materials manager and his buyers should be in regular contact with all important suppliers. In this way they are always apprised of the state of the market. If producers are extremely confident, the near-term outlook is probably for firm prices. Sophisticated buyers know how to evaluate their suppliers' comments on the market. They are sharp enough to spot market weakness when the optimists sound a little less optimistic and the pessimists moan a little louder than usual.

5. Prices on New Contracts. If the materials manager has been successful in making new purchases at lower-than-expected prices, the market is obviously weakening. Similarly, if prices are rising slightly, the market is firmer. When current prices are changing, the materials manager can safely predict a change in total prices in the same direction, and rarely will he be wrong. Price trends take time to reverse themselves. In addition, not all prices paid reflect the effects of new prices at the same time; prices usually are adjusted only when a new purchase is made and deliveries are made. For these reasons, purchase price indexes (which will be discussed later in this chapter) can be extremely useful tools for predicting short-term trends in prices.

Subjective Evaluation. The materials manager's evaluation of the five factors that influence the price of gray iron castings is primarily subjective—although it should be based on objective data as much as possible. The materials manager may wish to assign a percentage weighting of the importance of each factor in making his final estimate of the probable price change in castings. This may give the estimate an appearance of objectivity, but the final decision remains highly subjective and depends almost entirely on the materials manager's skill and experience.

THE PLAN OF PURCHASE

When he has made his forecasts of both raw material and parts prices and reached tentative conclusions on timing of purchases, the materials manager is ready to make his final plan of purchase. He analyzes his current inventory position and studies the production forecast. He then plans exactly how much material he intends to buy in coming months. He must always have enough material on hand to meet minimum production requirements, and he may wish to have substantially higher inventories.

Let us see how a plan of purchase might be made for one of the major components of a product. The first step in developing the plan would be to calculate the minimum quantities that are needed to sustain production. As long as production schedules do not fluctuate, this can be done simply by multiplying the usage of each item in the end product by the end-product production schedule.[2] Whether or not the materials manager decides to buy more than this minimum depends on predicted price and availability.

A Typical Plan. Suppose, for example, that gray iron castings are an important commodity for a company. Assume that the sales forecasts show that 1,200,000 pounds of castings will be needed for production of various components and that the current price is 10 cents per pound. The forecast indicates that there is a strong possibility of labor trouble at key supplier plants in July and that higher costs and strong demand may push prices up 10 per cent by the end of the year.

What should the plan of purchase be? First, the materials manager calculates minimum requirements. Then he modifies this plan to take into account predicted changes in price and availability.

Table 7–2 shows a purchase plan that might satisfy the assumptions we have made. During the first six months of the year, inventories will increase at the rate of 50,000 pounds per month. The build-up is spaced over this period because of limitations of supplier capacity and because patterns for the castings cannot be utilized more intensively than this. By July 1, inventories will be 300,000 pounds greater than normal. All available storage space is used and the company has invested an additional $30,000 in raw materials inventory.

With this build-up, the company is protected against a 90-day strike. Without it, it would either have to locate new suppliers in a tight, strike-bound market or cease operations. The inventory accumulation also

---

[2] If the production schedule varies from month to month, the calculations become more complicated. Scheduling and inventory management problems are discussed in detail in Chapters 8, 9, and 10.

postpones the effect of any price increase. If prices go up 10 per cent in August as anticipated, the company will have saved $2,250 by stocking up at lower prices.[3] Its only direct cost (assuming that storage space is available without any additional cost) will be a $30,000 investment for an average of six months. Thus, the company theoretically will earn a return of 15 per cent per annum on its investment during this period. The return is offset by all the risks (not the least of which is an inaccurate forecast) of carrying excess inventories.

TABLE 7–2

THEORETICAL PLAN OF PURCHASE OF GRAY IRON CASTINGS

Month	Actual Production Requirements		Suggested Purchases	
	Quantity	Cost	Quantity	Cost
January	100,000	$ 10,000	150,000	$ 15,000
February	100,000	10,000	150,000	15,000
March	100,000	10,000	150,000	15,000
April	100,000	10,000	150,000	15,000
May	100,000	10,000	150,000	15,000
June	100,000	10,000	150,000	15,000
July	100,000	10,000	50,000	5,000
August	100,000	11,000*	50,000	5,500*
September	100,000	11,000	50,000	5,500
October	100,000	11,000	50,000	5,500
November	100,000	11,000	50,000	5,500
December	100,000	10,500†	50,000	5,250†
Total		$124,500		$122,250

* Ten per cent price increase assumed to be effective August 1.
† Giving effect to planned negotiated price reduction or savings from introducing new supplier.

Cost Reduction. Each commodity purchase plan should allow for buyers' cost-reduction efforts. For example, in the plan of purchase outlined in Table 7–2, the materials manager assumes that his buyers will succeed in reducing the 10 per cent price increase (predicted for August 1) by 50 per cent through negotiation, introduction of new suppliers, and so on.

Cost reduction is a basic part of every purchase plan. It should be considered not only when making plans for individual commodity groups but also on a consolidated basis with recommendations as to how to achieve definite goals by application of certain cost-reduction techniques (which are discussed in later chapters).

But lower costs are not the only objective of materials management. As we saw in Chapter 3, there are a number of primary and secondary objectives. These objectives are interrelated; success in achieving one

---

[3] The chapters on inventory management describe in some detail various formulas that provide quantitative guides to buying decisions in fluctuating markets.

may impair performance in achieving one or more of the others. The art of materials management is successful balancing of objectives into a coordinated plan and then achieving the goals of the plan.

Conflict of objectives is illustrated in the plan of purchase for gray iron castings in Table 7–2. In this case, the objective of high inventory turnover is deliberately made secondary to achievement of objectives of low prices and good delivery performance. Stocks are built up in anticipation of higher prices and possible shortages. In making his purchase plan for each major commodity group, the materials manager is really balancing achievement of various objectives. When making the plan, he should consciously consider its effect on prices, inventory turnover, continuity of supply, relations with suppliers, quality, and low cost of acquisition and possession.

KEY PARTS CONTROL

The plan of purchase indicates exactly how much the materials manager plans to spend on a certain commodity. If the materials manager made a plan of purchase for every individual item, he could readily anticipate exactly what his inventory position would be during the period of the plan. All he would have to do is to add up each plan of purchase to get a total.

In practice, this is never done. It isn't practical to make detailed plans of purchase for each item. Usually materials managers make plans only for major items; other less important materials are ordered and stocked in accordance with the principles discussed in Chapters 8, 9, and 10. Also the plan of purchase may be too general to be really useful in forecasting product costs. For example, a plan of purchase might be made (as it was in Table 7–2) for gray iron castings used in all of a company's products. This plan would be extremely useful for inventory planning and allocating purchases of castings among suppliers. But it would not necessarily be useful for forecasting product cost since the castings might be used in dozens of different products.

The solution to this problem is obvious. All the materials manager need do is to make over-all plans of purchase for his major commodity groups and then break these plans down in detail into plans and forecasts for each product. In a typical materials department, this is almost an impossible job. It would be necessary to keep extremely accurate records and make rather elaborate calculations for literally thousands of different items. The cost would be high and errors frequent.

80 Per Cent Buys 15 Per Cent.   A more workable approach is to keep special price records of a sample of key items in each commodity group. Usually, 80 to 90 per cent of the money is spent on only 10 to 15 per cent of the items. If careful records are kept of these "big-money" items, over-all changes can be accurately estimated with a minimum of paper work. This is the "key parts" approach to cost control and forecasting.

Suppose a company finds that its key parts sample (which may be 15 per cent of all items) represents exactly 90 per cent of total expenditures. If prices of the items in the sample increased exactly 1 per cent, the value of *all* items has increased 0.9 per cent even though there were no changes at all in the prices of the nonsample items. In practice, of course, the nonsample items change in proportion to the sample items. A carefully selected sample not only includes the expensive items but is also reasonably representative of the over-all sample as to type of material, industry, method of fabrication, and so on.

TABLE 7–3

BUDGETED MATERIALS COST CHANGES
Product XYZ for the Year 196?

Month	Beginning Cost	Negotiation	Product Change	Materials Cost	Supplier Change	Other	Total Change
January	$100.00	(.42)	(.22)	.14	(.05)		(.55)
February	99.45	(.28)	.60	.75	(.35)		.72
March	100.17	(.40)			(.10)		(.50)
April	99.67	(.40)			(.10)		(.50)
May	99.17	(.40)			(.10)		(.50)
June	98.67	(.40)			(.10)		(.50)
July	98.17	(.40)		1.05	(.10)		.55
August	98.72				(.10)		(.10)
September	98.62				(.10)	3.10*	3.00
October	101.62				(.10)		(.10)
November	101.52				(.10)		(.10)
December	101.42				(.10)		(.10)
Total at end of year	$101.32	($2.70)	$.38	$1.94	($1.40)	$3.10	$1.32

* Addition of new parts to sample formerly made in the shop, and purchased from outside suppliers effective September 1, 196?.

The mechanics of preparing a key parts index are not hard to understand although the job itself is long and tedious. It is necessary to compile a complete list of every item purchased and compute the value of the usage of each by multiplying unit price by usage. The high dollar-volume items are then culled from each commodity or product group so that the sample represents approximately 80 to 90 per cent of the dollar volume.

Controlling Product XYZ. Key parts control is normally by product for production parts and materials because management needs product information for pricing and cost-control purposes. Table 7–3 shows key parts control for hypothetical product XYZ. It is a summary of groups of key parts for each commodity group. The sample's value on January 1 is $100. The materials manager classifies the changes affecting price and projects them for the coming year.

The total price reduction of $2.70 for "negotiation" for the year is his estimate of savings that can be made. The total is based on individual forecasts of economic and competitive conditions for major commodity groups and on estimates of probable success that buyers will have in applying the cost-reduction techniques discussed in later chapters of this book.

The predicted $.38 cost increase due to "product change" is based on the materials manager's estimate of the cost of design changes that are planned. The $3.10 change classified as "other" arises from a make-or-buy decision. Both of these changes affect product mix. Since they are not economic, they will not be used to measure the success of the materials department in achieving its cost-reduction objectives.

An increase of $1.94 per unit is anticipated because of higher materials costs. This could include both increases in the cost of purchased raw materials and increases in prices of components as suppliers pass along higher raw material costs. In calculating the effect of increases in materials costs, the materials manager would estimate the amount of the increase per unit of raw material (using techniques that have already been discussed) and multiply by the amount of raw material in the product. For example, suppose that a 2 cents per pound increase in the price of copper were anticipated in January. If there were 7 pounds of copper used in the product—either in shop-made or purchased components—the unit product costs would rise by 14 cents,[4] as indicated in Table 7–3.

The final price change column in the materials plan is one that allows for "supplier change." It is an estimate of savings that will be made by bringing in new suppliers who charge lower prices than existing suppliers. It is based on both an evaluation of competitive conditions and an estimate of how successful buyers will be in performing one of the basic parts of their job.

COMMODITY PRICE INDEXES

Key parts systems work well in companies that produce a limited number of products in large volume. They are used, for example, by several leading automobile manufacturers.

They won't work well in companies that produce many products on a job-order basis. In such cases, individual products are manufactured intermittently and it simply isn't worthwhile to maintain key parts control

---

[4] In practice, this would rarely be literally correct. In many cases there is a lag of at least a month between the time a raw material increases in price and the time suppliers of parts fabricated from the material request a price adjustment. To allow for this, the materials manager would allow for two adjustments because of a change in materials costs: one for the material purchased directly and a second, later adjustment for parts made of the material.

over every product. Management is interested primarily in the over-all trend of costs; it needs information that will help it do a better job of estimating costs on new jobs that come in.

A commodity price index is best suited for this purpose. It is similar to key parts control except for two basic differences: index numbers are used instead of actual dollar costs, and cost data are classified entirely by commodity instead of by product.

To see how such an index might be set up, let us take the example of a hypothetical manufacturer of highly specialized, custom-made business machines that require the commodities listed in Table 7–1. Such a company might buy as many as 20,000 different items and make 100 different products even though it employs no more than 1,000 persons. Almost every customer would require a product that was engineered specifically for his needs.

Selecting the Sample. The mechanics of compiling the index would be much like those used in developing key parts control. Average monthly expenditures for each commodity would be calculated from purchase records and the more expensive items would be selected for the sample. However, in developing the index, it will be necessary to take particular pains to select a sample that is a truly representative cross section of the commodities purchased. Because the company makes so many different products in relatively small quantities, it is no longer true that 10 to 15 per cent of the most expensive items account for 80 to 90 per cent of the dollar volume of purchases. It might be necessary to work with a sample that comprises only 30 to 40 per cent of total dollar volume.

The procedure used in calculating the base cost of the index sample is different from that used in key parts. Usage is not taken into account. Base cost is calculated simply by adding the unit prices of each item in the sample. This makes it vital to allow for relative usages when choosing the items represented in the sample.

For example, suppose the business-machine manufacturer compiles an index of castings costs. If he used an average of two small castings as miscellaneous components for every larger casting used for the machine base, then the sample should be divided 67 to 33 between the large and small castings.

Making the Index. After the sample is selected, price changes are tabulated. The technique is similar to that used in Table 7–3. Let us imagine, in fact, that Product XYZ in Table 7–3 is an index of castings costs for our hypothetical business-machine manufacturer. The beginning cost in January is $100. The unit price changes during January on the castings in the sample reduce total cost of the sample by $.55— as in Table 7–3—to $99.45. But since this is an index, we do not use dollar amounts but the index number of 99.45. We use index numbers because the total value of our sample has no significance; unlike a product index, it is merely the sum of current prices for a selected group of materials. It is easier to judge the effect of price changes with index numbers that automatically indicate the number of percentage points in change from the base period. Actual dollar figures rarely come to the convenient $100 figure of our example.

With a commodity index, it is simple to estimate the effect of price changes on over-all costs. For example, if a company were spending an average of $10,000 a month for castings, a drop in the castings price index from 100.00 to 99.45 would indicate a saving of $55.00 per month.

Commodity indexes can be used for both production and nonproduction items. However, when they are used to measure changes in cost of a

TABLE 7–4

COMPOSITE INDEX OF MATERIALS COSTS—MACHINE TOOLS

Component Group	Per Cent Weight	January		February		March	
		Index	*Extension*	*Index*	*Extension*	*Index*	*Extension*
Electrical............	35%	100.00	35.00	102.00	35.70	101.00	35.35
Castings.............	20	100.00	20.00	90.00	18.00	90.00	18.00
Bearings.............	5	100.00	5.00	100.00	5.00	99.00	4.95
Hydraulic...........	15	100.00	15.00	96.00	14.40	97.00	14.55
Miscellaneous........	25	100.00	25.00	100.00	25.00	94.00	23.50
Composite index..			100.00		98.10		96.35

nonproduction group such as maintenance, repair, and operating supplies, the sample must be constructed with extra care because such a wide variety of items with erratic usage patterns falls into this category.

Composite Indexes. Commodity indexes also can be used to build product indexes of composite products. If a company makes a wide variety of products on a job-order basis, it cannot afford to keep cost indexes for each product. But it can construct an index of a composite product; the company's various products are sufficiently similar so that cost changes of each would follow similar patterns.

A composite index is made up of indexes for major commodities; it is weighted by the relative importance of each commodity in the typical end product. Table 7–4 shows the construction of such an index for a hypothetical machine tool manufacturer. Studies might show that the average purchased material cost for each machine tool is divided as indicated in the second column of the table: 35 per cent for electrical, 20 per cent for castings, etc. The monthly price index for each commodity group is then multiplied by its per cent weight (e.g., multiplying the electrical component index of 100.00 by its 35 per cent weight gives an extension of 35.00), and the products are added to get the composite index.

Table 7–4 shows that material for a composite machine tool in January cost its precise base price of 100.00. In February and March, prices of components declined until the index reached 96.35, indicating an average 3.65 per cent reduction in materials cost of machine tools.

USES OF INDEXES

Indexes and key parts cost controls are expensive. They can take hundreds or even thousands of man-hours of work to set up, and even a relatively simple system can take 500 man-hours of work a year to maintain. Cost is undoubtedly one of the main reasons that indexes are not used more widely in materials management. But companies that do use them rarely abandon them; they are convinced that they are worth their cost. Indexes and key parts controls permit more accurate forecasting of costs, stimulate superior materials performance, and help make the materials management job easier.

Accurate Forecasts. An index or summary of key parts cost is based on prices currently being paid for materials. But because of supplier and manufacturing lead times and inventories, there is always a considerable lag between the average order date for material and the date when the material is actually incorporated into an end product. In some industries, today's purchases appear in products six months hence; in few industries is this lead time less than two months. Indexes or key parts systems permit material costs to be forecast with 99.99 per cent accuracy during the lead time. When they are combined with the materials manager's price projections, it is possible to predict materials costs with considerable accuracy a year or more in advance.

The company controller can use projections of key parts prices to plan his cash flow, to develop a projected profit and loss statement based on the sales estimate, and to develop data for pricing. Composite price indexes cannot be used so directly. But they are useful in forecasting cost trends. For example, if a composite index drops 3.65 per cent (as in Table 7–4) and materials cost constitutes 50 per cent of the sales dollar, management knows it can reduce average prices by 1.82 per cent (i.e., 50 per cent of 3.65 per cent) in bidding for new business without narrowing its profit margin. It also can plan on spending 3.65 per cent less for materials for the same physical output and can budget its cash accordingly.

Stimulate Performance. Index and key parts information provides a convenient yardstick for performance measurement. Comparison of actual key parts prices with projected prices or with general price indexes indicates how well materials personnel have done their work and also stimulates improvement.

Simplify Management. Materials management involves thousands or even millions of individual transactions each year. Materials managers can do their job effectively only if they avoid the distraction of numerous unimportant details and concentrate on significant problems. Price indexes help them function more effectively because they summarize the exact effect of thousands of materials transactions on cost and profits. They also make it easy to evaluate accurately the effect of future changes in materials prices on operating costs.

For example, suppose management becomes concerned about a possible price rise for a key raw material. With key parts or index data, it is an easy matter to calculate what product costs will be at various price levels for the raw material. It also is possible to calculate precisely when it pays to change to a substitute material or initiate a program to redesign the product so that it no longer requires the material.

Indexes can also simplify inventory management. It is often practical to make plans of purchase for each index item. When the materials manager adds up the projections in these plans, he knows exactly what 80 to 90 per cent of his inventory investment will be months in advance. If he must change his plans because of faulty sales or price forecasts, he knows almost exactly how rapidly he can change with a minimum of detail work. For example, suppose a materials manager's current inventory of index items is equal to two months' production and he is already committed to a build-up to three months' stock. Because of a shortage of cash, management decides to cut back to one month's stock. The materials manager can do the job quickly and efficiently by concentrating his attention on the index items that comprise the biggest part of his costs. Indexes and key parts control systems can be linked with some of the selective inventory control techniques that will be discussed in the next three chapters.

CASES

CASE 7–1. DONALDSON CHEMICALS, INC.

Poor Forecasting Eliminates Profits

Donaldson Chemicals, Inc. is a "middleman" in chemical manufacturing. It buys basic chemical raw materials and converts them into more complex chemicals, which it sells to manufacturers of chemical end products. For example, it buys a basic material like napthalene and converts it into a product such as pthalic anhydride, which it sells to other companies for making paints and for other uses.

Donaldson has grown rapidly in its specialized business. In 1960, its sales were $99 million—up 67.4 per cent since 1956. The story on profits has not been quite so impressive. In 1960, Donaldson's management forecast a $5 million profit, but actual profits were only $3 million —less than they were in 1956. The drop in profits could be traced to a single cause: the high cost of napthalene.

Napthalene is one of Donaldson's single most important raw materials. Steel companies are the biggest source of supply. They generate napthalene as a by-product when they convert coal into coke in their coke ovens. Naturally, the steel companies try to get the best possible price for their napthalene. But they have little or no direct control over the amount of napthalene they produce. If napthalene prices are high, the steel mills will not make more coke just to get napthalene. Their sales and profits come primarily from steel. When demand for steel is strong, the mills produce more coke and, consequently, more napthalene. When demand for steel is weak, the steel mills can't afford to stockpile coke so their napthalene production falls off, even though napthalene prices may be relatively high.

In 1960, demand for steel was weak. In January, the steel industry was operating at about 90 per cent of capacity. By June it was operating at less than 60 per cent of capacity, and operations continued below 60 per cent capacity until April, 1961. Although the demand for steel had fallen, the demand for chemicals made from napthalene was stronger than ever. As a result, the price of napthalene soared from about 6 cents per pound late in 1959 to 17 cents by December, 1960.

Donaldson uses about 100 million pounds of napthalene per year. An increase of 10 cents per pound in napthalene prices can thus raise costs by $10 million per year. To some extent, Donaldson can pass on higher materials costs to its customers. But it must always meet competitors' prices. If competitors do a better job of buying napthalene, the effect on Donaldson's profits can be almost disastrous.

Donaldson experienced just such a disaster in the first quarter of 1961. In late 1960, Donaldson's management was desperate for napthalene to keep its plant operating. It had held off buying napthalene in more than hand-to-mouth quantities for months. It had hoped that steel production would rise (and napthalene prices fall), so it had gradually used up its inventories. Steel operations were at less than 50 per cent of capacity in December, 1960, and napthalene cost 17 cents per pound. Unfortunately, Donaldson had to have napthalene or go out of business. So it purchased 25 million pounds—enough for its first quarter's needs—at 17 cents.

Because it was using high-priced napthalene, Donaldson's operating costs were abnormally high throughout the first quarter. Unfortunately, selling prices could not be raised without losing business to competitors. As a result, Donaldson had one of the worst quarters in its history. It lost $200,000 on sales of $24 million.

Ironically, while Donaldson was eating up its profits with its 17-cent napthalene, the market price of napthalene was declining. By May, when Donaldson used the last of the 17-cent material, the price had dropped to 7 cents. And by July, it reached 6 cents as the steel industry's operating rate reached more normal levels.

The 1960–61 gyrations in the price of napthalene are reasonably normal. The steel industry is highly cyclical, and this automatically makes for wide fluctuations in napthalene production and prices. To some extent, of course, napthalene output does respond to demand. Usually demand for napthalene is greater when the business cycle is at its peak and steel mills are running full tilt. And it is weakest when the cycle is nearing bottom and steel production is in a slump. However, napthalene demand does not fluctuate as much as steel demand. As a result, it is relatively cheap and plentiful at the peak of the business cycle and scarce and expensive at the bottom of the cycle.

Napthalene need not be a by-product of the steel industry, of course. It can be made from almost any hydrocarbon. If the price of napthalene is sufficiently attractive, oil companies, for example, are perfectly willing to make it from crude oil. In August, 1961, partly as a result of its unhappy experience in the previous year, Donaldson signed a contract for napthalene with the Wabash Oil and Refining Company. The contract calls for delivery of 20 million pounds of napthalene per year at a price of 11 cents per pound. The price is subject to escalation should crude oil prices rise or decline. But escalation is limited to 15 per cent in either direction for the five-year term of the contract. One of Donaldson's competitors has signed a similar contract with another oil company. Another competitor continues to buy all of its napthalene in the open market.

Question

Based on today's market conditions, what plan of purchase would you propose for Donaldson Chemical, Inc.?

CASE 7–2. OWEN ELECTRIC COMPANY

Developing a Plan of Purchase

The Owen Electric Company is a small manufacturer of fractional horsepower electric motors. In the fall of 1958, despite depressed business conditions, it is about to complete a record business year with sales of $5 million. The company's marketing department predicts that business in 1959 will be even better, with sales reaching $6 million.

The general business outlook is equally bullish. The economy is showing strong signs of recovery from the recession that prevailed early in the year. The Federal Reserve Board's index of industrial production has advanced to 138 (1948–49 = 100) from its April low of 126. Copper prices have advanced 5 cents per pound in the same period, and other sensitive commodities have moved up by similar amounts. Inventory liquidation has virtually ceased; the most recent figures show inventories of durable-goods manufacturers to have been almost unchanged for three months at about $28 billion.

Richard Owen, Jr., Owen Electric's purchasing manager, is particularly concerned about the outlook for copper and steel, the company's two major commodities. The company's sales increased faster during the year than Owen had anticipated, and it was necessary to draw on inventories. Currently, the company is operating on almost a hand-to-mouth basis.

The production forecast indicates that 10,000 pounds per month of copper magnet wire will be required through June 30. During the summer months, requirements will drop to 7,000 pounds per month, and, if sales are as high as current plans indicate, they will rise again to 13,000 pounds per month during October, November, and December. Over-all steel requirements will be proportionate: 50 tons per month through June 30; 35 tons per month until September 30; and 65 tons per month for the balance of the year.

Since inventories currently are barely adequate to maintain production and shortages have been a problem, Owen already has allowed for some build-up early in the year. He has ordered 170 tons of steel for first quarter rolling and also has ordered 22,000 pounds of copper for delivery during January and February. Owen Electric uses several different types of copper magnet wire. At present, their weighted average cost is 45 cents per pound. Richard Owen estimates that this will probably increase by 1.2 cents for every 1-cent increase in the price of ingot copper, as copper fabricators attempt to pass on the cost of wage increases. On the other hand, he believes that fabricators will be forced to pass on to their customers the full benefit of any drop in ingot prices.

Copper producers freely predict higher prices. Deliveries of refined copper in the United States totaled 120,793 tons in October, 1958—a sharp increase over the 86,982 tons in August and the 101,064 tons in September. This is the best October that copper refiners have had since 1955, when the demand for ingot was so heavy that prices were pushed to more than 40 cents per pound. Copper consumption frequently reaches a seasonal peak in spring because of heavy usage in the auto industry and other areas. Owen anticipates no difficulty in buying copper wire in any reasonable quantity with two months' lead time at the price in effect at time of delivery.

The delivery situation on steel may be more difficult. The contract between the major steel producers and the steelworkers' union expires on July 1. Most commentators believe that the odds favor a strike. The last steel industry strike, in 1956, lasted about three weeks. This year the steel industry's attitude toward what it regards as inflationary wage increases seems to have stiffened. If there is a strike, many believe it will be a long one. If the workers win a substantial wage increase, a price increase is almost inevitable. Steel prices have advanced every year since 1946. This year the steel companies not only will be faced with higher wage costs but also will feel the effects of much higher scrap prices. The Pittsburgh price of No. 1 heavy melting steel scrap has advanced about $10 a ton from its low of $35 earlier in the year. Steel companies use varying amounts of scrap in their open-hearth furnaces, but a charge of 50 per cent scrap is not unusual.

Owen's current weighted average price for the various types and grades of steel it uses is $148 per ton. Richard Owen anticipates an increase of about 5 per cent regardless of whether or not there is a strike.

The anticipated price increase and the possible strike both provide an incentive for Owen to stockpile steel. Unfortunately, storage space is limited. In fact, Owen's current open orders for 170 tons—20 tons in excess of expected usage—will use up all available storage space in the plant. Any further additions to inventory must be stored in an outside warehouse. The storage cost is $1.50 per ton per month, plus $2 per ton to move the steel from the warehouse to the Owen Electric plant.

There is no storage problem for copper, but the company's cash position is not ideal. The controller advises Owen that no funds are available for inventory accumulation beyond the extra 20 tons of steel for which the company is already committed. However, the controller anticipates no difficulty in getting an additional $150,000 short-term loan at 6½ per cent interest should the company's board of directors approve an inventory build-up.

Questions

Develop a plan of purchases for Owen Electric's requirements of copper wire and steel for the year 1959. Use the data provided; state any additional assumptions that must be made. Prepare a defense of your plan for the company's board of directors. Indicate the cost of your plan to the company, based on:

1. Your own assumptions of price and availability of copper wire and steel.
2. No change in the price or availability of copper and steel.
3. Higher copper prices: a 6-cent advance during the year, spaced as a 1-cent increase every two months starting in January.
4. Lower copper prices: a 2-cent increase in price in January followed by three 2-cent decreases in April, July, and October.
5. A 5 per cent increase in steel price in July with: (*a*) no strike, (*b*) a three-week strike, (*c*) a three-month strike. (In evaluating the cost of stockouts, assume that the company loses $2,000 per day that cannot be recouped when it is shut down).

Chapter **8**

PRINCIPLES OF INVENTORY MANAGEMENT

The average business has about 30 per cent of its working capital tied up in inventories. This is about 70 per cent of its investment in plant and equipment.[1] In the typical company, inventory management is even more important than these statistics indicate. In fact, it is no exaggeration to say that inventory control can make or break a company. Yet even the most successful companies, for reasons we shall discuss, are rarely able to manage their inventories as well as they would like to. Either they have too much inventory, too little, or, most frequently of all, a combination of both—too many of some items and too few of others.

When companies have too little inventory and run out of stock, manufacturing efficiency or customer relations is bound to be hurt. Stockouts of essential materials can't help but cause some interruption of production, which raises costs. They may also delay delivery of finished products to a customer. After a few such delays, even the most patient customer will start looking for a supplier who will give him better service.

The situation is almost as bad for the company that carries too much inventory. It may have material available when it is needed, but its costs will be so high that it won't make any profit on the business it gets by having material available. Inventories tie up a company's capital; they generate storage costs; and they deteriorate or become obsolete in storage. In all, as will be discussed in greater detail in Chapter 10, inventories may cost as much as 25 per cent per annum to carry. In other words, it can cost a company as much as $250,000 per year (and sometimes even more) to carry a $1,000,000 inventory. Obviously, therefore, if through intelligent materials management the same company can get along with just $500,000 invested in inventory, the savings will be substantial.

Since a company with a $1,000,000 inventory may have sales of no more than $8,000,000 and profits of only $800,000, it doesn't take too much imagination to grasp how clever inventory management can make a tremendous contribution to company profit objectives. Similarly, one can easily guess what will happen to company profits if costs are raised

---

[1] *Inventory Management in Industry*, Studies in Business Policy, No. 88 (New York: National Industrial Conference Board, 1958), p. 7.

137

5 or 10 per cent because of frequent delays in manufacturing due to lack of inventory, or what happens to both sales and profits if customers find they can get prompter service from a competitor who is able to have material on hand when it is needed.

Thus, as in all the other phases of materials management, there is a conflict of objectives in inventory management. The objective of high inventory turnover (discussed in Chapter 3) conflicts with the objective of continuity of supply and other objectives. Of all business assets, inventories are the least stable and most difficult to control. Unfortunately both for their profits and for the economy as a whole, American corporations do a rather bad job of inventory management. Their inventories tend to be high when they should be low, and vice versa. Bad inventory planning has been one of the major causes of almost every business recession.

In the typical business cycle, inventory accumulation helps push business activities to a new high. Business then tapers off, but inventories continue to rise. Stocks become excessive. Businesses not only stop buying in excess of needs but buy substantially less than current consumption. This underbuying causes production to drop even more and so helps accelerate the downturn. Finally, equilibrium is reached at the bottom of the business cycle and recovery begins. The recovery catches business unprepared. Sales temporarily exceed production and inventories drop further. At last production catches up with and eventually exceeds sales. Inventories start increasing and the cycle begins all over again.[2]

NATURE OF THE PROBLEM

Why do businesses have so much difficulty managing their inventories? The major reason is inability to forecast accurately. When a materials manager adds to inventory, he is anticipating a need for the material. In many cases, the need comes later than anticipated and sometimes it never materializes at all. The result is excessive inventory. Or, if demand comes sooner or is stronger than anticipated, the inventory is inadequate.

The materials cycle is remarkably sluggish. Typically, more than a year may pass before a quantity of raw materials is transformed into a finished product. Theoretically, it would take less than a week to perform every operation necessary to transform various raw materials into a product like a television set. But chances are that the iron ore, copper ore, bauxite, and other minerals used in making the TV set completed

---

[2] This obviously is a greatly oversimplified explanation of the effect of inventory changes on the business cycle. More thorough explanations can be found in almost any text on business forecasting and business cycles. The reader is particularly directed to Moses Abramovitz's study, *Inventories and Business Cycles* (New York: National Bureau of Economic Research, 1950).

today were mined nearly a year before. The materials spent months either in various stockpiles or in transit between operations or plants. It may take only a few seconds to drill a hole in a small component on the TV set, but the material can sit on a factory floor for two days waiting to be scheduled on a machine that will perform this operation. Even completely automated processes have "pipelines" full of material awaiting processing.[3]

THE NEED FOR INVENTORY

No business can operate without inventories. It needs them as a protection against uncertainty, for efficient processing of material, and to permit transit and handling.

Protection against Uncertainty. Because the materials cycle is long and complex, the materials manager must anticipate his needs at each stage. Inventories protect him against unforeseen failures in supply or increases in demand. Without inventories, a large plant would cease operations each time a motor on a machine tool failed. Even a flat tire on a supplier's delivery truck could interrupt production if it delayed a shipment of needed material. Inventories protect production against unanticipated delays.

Similarly, inventories also protect against sudden upsurges in demand. Even with the most advanced market research techniques, few manufacturers can estimate demand accurately—particularly for various individual models of their products. The room air-conditioner industry is an extreme example of this. Sales are greatly affected by both season and weather. During a hot, humid summer, sales may be 50 per cent higher than during a cool summer. Air-conditioner manufacturers must not only guess how many air conditioners the public will want but which models it will prefer. And these decisions must be made in fall and winter, months before the public is in a buying mood. If a company wants to sell as many air conditioners as the market will absorb, its only protection against a really hot summer—and soaring demand—is an extra-heavy inventory.

Efficient Processing of Material. Unit costs normally are lowest when material is purchased, handled, and processed in large quantities, which in turn generate larger inventories. In addition, inventories act as a "cushion" between operations or processes. Production at various stages of a manufacturing cycle can never be synchronized perfectly; inventories take up the slack when one stage operates at a rate different from that of the preceding or succeeding stage.

The components of any product are manufactured at widely varying

---

[3] In an automated process, material must be moved between operations by some sort of conveying mechanism that is loaded with in-process inventory.

rates of production. For example, it may be possible to make the fasteners used in a television set at the rate of 20,000 pieces per hour. TV assembly lines might operate at the rate of about 200 sets per hour. It would be completely impractical to synchronize fastener production with TV set assembly. In practice, fasteners are assembled onto the TV sets from an inventory strategically located near their point of use on the assembly line.

Transit and Handling. Materials sometimes are transported thousands of miles before they are incorporated into an end product. Jamaican bauxite may travel by ship to British Columbia to be made into aluminum ingot. From there it may be shipped to New Jersey to be rolled into aluminum sheet. From there it may move by rail to Detroit to be fabricated into a component for an automobile. From there it may move by truck to rail to an auto assembly plant, whence it is finally trucked to a dealer as part of a finished auto that eventually is sold to its ultimate user. All the time it is in transit, which may be a period of several months, this material is part of someone's inventory.

For the reasons given above, every manufacturer must carry a certain minimum inventory. In practice, almost every manufacturer carries an inventory that is substantially greater than this minimum. He does so because:

1. His sales and manufacturing departments find it convenient to have stocks that are more than ample.
2. He expects prices of materials to rise and therefore stocks up at lower prices.
3. Scheduling, production control, and inventory management are more difficult and costlier when stocks are kept at optimum level. The manufacturer may lack the skills necessary for such control or be unwilling to incur the control costs, so he carries extra inventory in order to prevent stockouts.

DETERMINING INVENTORY LEVELS

The amount of inventory a company carries is determined by three basic variables: order quantity, lead time, and reliability of forecasts of materials usage.

Order Quantity

The greater the order quantity, the greater the average inventory. Suppose a company uses 100 units of an item per week and orders in lots of 200 units whenever it runs out of stock. In this case, its maximum inventory would be 200 units right after a new shipment is received and its minimum inventory would be 0 units when the stock is used up. Since usage is steady, its average inventory would be 100 pieces—exactly halfway between the maximum and the minimum. If inventory were plotted against the time, the result would look like the sawtooth pattern illustrated by the upper part of the drawing in Figure 8–1 (on next page).

What happens if the company doubles its order quantity while usage remains unchanged? Its maximum inventory doubles; there now are 400 pieces in stock immediately after a shipment is received. It takes twice as long—four weeks instead of two weeks—to use up the inventory. As a result, the average inventory also is twice as great. It consists of two weeks' stock, or 200 units, instead of just one week's stock.

Lead Time

There is always some interval between the time that the need for material is determined and the time the material is actually manufactured and delivered. This period is the lead time. For example, if an office manager requisitions an electric calculator on February 1, a buyer issues a purchase order on February 3, and the calculator is delivered on February 11, then the total lead time for the purchase is ten days. The total lead time has two components, administrative lead time and supplier lead time. In the case of the calculator, these are two days and eight days respectively.

Lead Time Varies. The shortest lead-time items are those that a local supplier has in stock for immediate delivery. Even in such a case, a company will usually allow a week's lead time between the day the purchase requisition is prepared and the actual delivery of the purchase. The lead time permits both buyer and supplier to process the order efficiently and economically. When there is an immediate need for an off-the-shelf item, however, the lead time usually can be shortened to less than one day.

Much longer lead times are necessary for items made to order by out-of-town suppliers, and the more complex the item, the longer the lead time. Steel mills normally will accept orders with a lead time of 60 to 90 days. Auto companies often allow their parts suppliers—who fabricate steel and other raw materials into finished components—as much as five months' lead time. And the lead time for a complex piece of custom-made equipment may be two or three years.

Lead times also vary for identical items. One supplier may require a greater lead time for a given item than another supplier. The same supplier may have different lead times for a given item at various stages of the business cycle. When business is depressed and the supplier is operating well below capacity with almost no new orders coming in, lead time will be short. When the supplier is working at capacity and has a huge order backlog, the lead time will be long. Variations in lead time can be quite substantial. For example, machine tool manufacturers may require only two months' lead time when business is depressed, but at the peak of a boom the lead time may stretch to a year or more.

Changing lead time is one of the most difficult problems of materials management. Suppose, for example, the normal lead time for an item is four weeks. If a buyer orders material on February 1, he can expect delivery on February 28. What happens if the lead time changes and the buyer isn't aware of the change? If the lead time increases, the order that the buyer places on February 1 won't be delivered when it is needed on February 28. At best this will be an inconvenience; at worst it can cause an entire factory to shut down temporarily.

Effect on Inventory Levels.   If lead time suddenly decreases, the effect is not quite so bad. Suppose the lead time shortens by 50 per cent and the item that is due February 28 is actually delivered on February 14. In that case, the buyer's plant won't shut down because of lack of inventory. On the contrary, it will be carrying substantially more inventory than is needed, for when lead time shortens the need for inventory also is reduced.

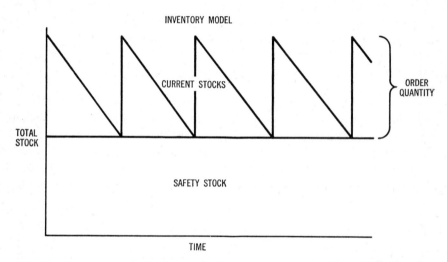

FIG. 8–1.   Inventories normally do not drop below the safety stock level. They reach their peak when a new shipment is received, when they usually equal the order quantity plus the safety stock. When usage during the lead time is greater than planned or when deliveries are late, the safety stock protects against a stockout.

In order to prevent a stockout, a company must have an inventory that is at least adequate for usage during the lead time. If lead time is four weeks for an item with a usage of 100 units per week, there must be at least 400 units in inventory when the order is placed in order to prevent a stockout. This means that the lowest possible average inventory is 200 units (with an order quantity of 400 units). On the other hand, if lead time drops to two weeks, there need be only 200 units in inventory before it is necessary to place an order to replenish stocks. In this case, the lowest possible average inventory is 100 units, which happens when 200 units are ordered every two weeks.

Safety Stocks

If usages and lead times could be predicted exactly, it would be possible to limit maximum inventory of an item to the order quantity and we would have the usage pattern described above. A new shipment would arrive just as the last unit of the existing stock was used. Maximum inventory would equal the order quantity; average inventory would equal one-half the order quantity; and minimum inventory would be zero. In practice this can't be done. Suppliers fail to keep delivery promises, and usage forecasts are inaccurate. Extra inventory is needed to protect against unreliable forecasts. This extra inventory is called "safety stock."

When forecasts of lead time and usage are accurate, the maximum inventory is equal to the order quantity plus the safety stock, and the minimum inventory is equal to the safety stock (see Figure 8–1). If usage is steady, the average inventory equals half the order quantity plus the safety stock. For example, if order quantity is 400 units and safety stock is 50 units, then average inventory is 250 units.

JOB-LOT ORDERING

Companies that manufacture on a job-lot basis have the easiest job of inventory control. Each customer order is, in effect, treated as a brand-new product. The materials department reviews the bill of material for the customer's order and buys what is needed to do the job. If its timing is perfect on lead times, the company's raw material inventories are negligible. Materials are incorporated into semifinished products almost as soon as they are received.

The purest examples of job-lot ordering are found in the construction industry. When a construction firm wins a contract, its materials personnel must go to work immediately to get the material needed for the contract. There usually are no inventories to draw on since construction firms almost always have suppliers deliver raw materials directly to the site. It would not be economic for a construction firm to carry an inventory of bricks, for example, since there would be too much handling expense in storing the inventory between jobs. It is much cheaper to buy the bricks needed for each contract and have the supplier deliver them to the site as needed.

Manufacturers of products that are largely made to customer specifications—machine tools, various types of equipment, special instruments, and so on—have problems similar to those of construction firms. Although they do their work at the same location, each order is substantially different from its predecessors. It becomes almost impossible to anticipate materials needs. Many firms don't even try; they simply calculate what material is needed for each order and then buy it.

Problems. With a system of job-lot control, each order must be scheduled separately. Different materials and components for the job are needed at different stages of construction or manufacture. The long lead-time items needed at earlier stages naturally get top priority. Materials personnel usually deliberately hold off buying short-term lead-time items until they have to. For example, they may know in January that an item with a lead time of three weeks will be needed in June, but they will make no commitment for the item until, perhaps, the last week in April, and even then they may request that the vendor hold up delivery

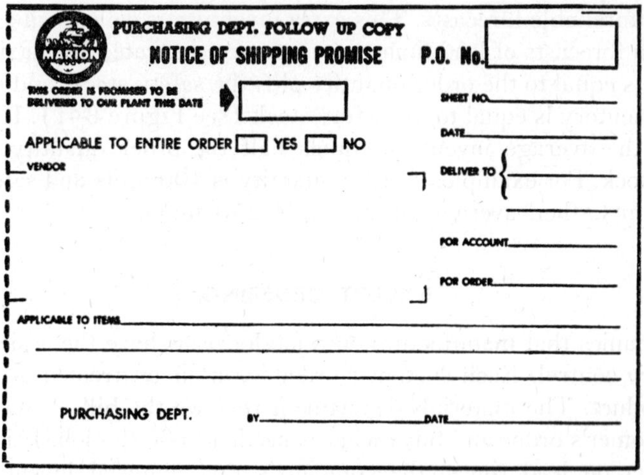
MARION
PURCHASING DEPT. FOLLOW UP COPY
NOTICE OF SHIPPING PROMISE
P.O. No.
THIS ORDER IS PROMISED TO BE DELIVERED TO OUR PLANT THIS DATE
SHEET NO.
DATE
APPLICABLE TO ENTIRE ORDER ☐ YES ☐ NO
VENDOR
DELIVER TO
FOR ACCOUNT
FOR ORDER
APPLICABLE TO ITEMS
PURCHASING DEPT. BY DATE

Courtesy Marion Power Shovel Co.

FIG. 8–2. Lead times and delivery dates of purchased material are extremely important in a job-lot ordering system. The purchasing department of the Marion Power Shovel Co. uses this form to advise the production department of supplier shipping promises.

until early June even if he actually can deliver a few weeks ahead of schedule.

With good material control, in a job-order system materials are committed for and delivered only when they are needed. This keeps liabilities to a minimum should an order be canceled, reduces the cost of last-minute changes in specifications, and ties up a minimum of storage space for materials not needed immediately.

Problems arise when the lead time turns out to be different from the plan. Frequently an entire order can be held up because a supplier fails to deliver on schedule. Materials personnel try to spot lead-time problems as far in advance as possible. They also try to use all possible expediting methods (discussed in Chapter 14) to bring the lead time back to normal. Should a shortage develop, they immediately inform the manufacturing and sales departments so that the job can be rescheduled. A typical form used for this purpose is shown in Figure 8–2.

Order quantity also can be a problem in job-order systems. Theoretically, the materials department simply can order the material specified in the bill of material for each job and there are no problems. But what happens if usage is greater than anticipated because of miscalculations, spoilage in manufacturing, or shrinkage? Unless this is allowed for by ordering a little extra material, production may be plagued with work stoppages due to lack of material. It is no easy job to determine in advance how much extra material will be needed. And any material that is not used for the job may be wasted.

Another problem in ordering is that suppliers sometimes insist on certain minimum quantities. If a company needs 100 cotter pins for a job, it usually must buy 1,000 or more. With some items, the company simply can't afford to pass up the lower prices gained by buying in

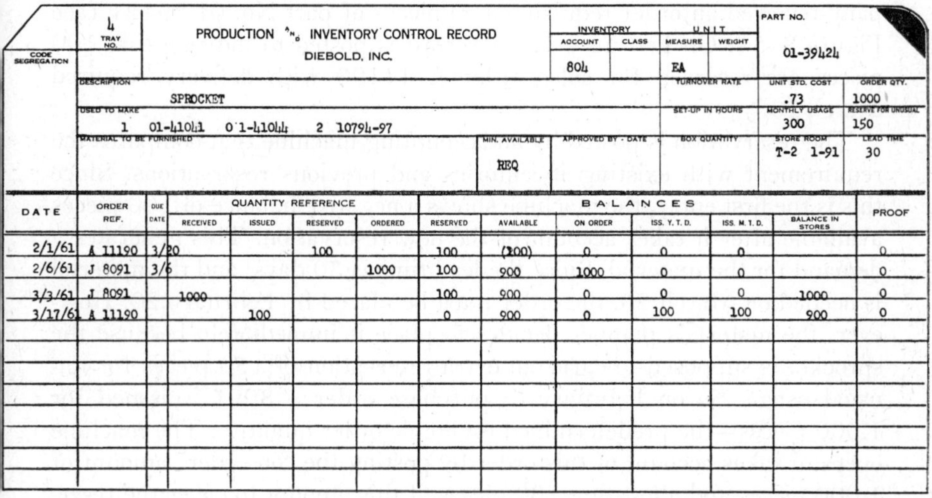

PRODUCTION AND INVENTORY CONTROL RECORD
DIEBOLD, INC.

TRAY NO. 4 — CODE SEGREGATION — INVENTORY ACCOUNT 804 — CLASS — UNIT MEASURE EA — WEIGHT — PART NO. 01-39424

DESCRIPTION: SPROCKET — TURNOVER RATE — UNIT STD. COST .73 — ORDER QTY. 1000

USED TO MAKE: 1 01-41041 01-41044 2 10794-97 — SET-UP IN HOURS — MONTHLY USAGE 300 — RESERVE FOR UNUSUAL 150

MATERIAL TO BE FURNISHED — MIN. AVAILABLE REQ — APPROVED BY - DATE — BOX QUANTITY — STORE ROOM T-2 1-91 — LEAD TIME 30

DATE	ORDER REF.	DUE DATE	QUANTITY REFERENCE: RECEIVED	ISSUED	RESERVED	ORDERED	BALANCES: RESERVED	AVAILABLE	ON ORDER	ISS. Y. T. D.	ISS. M. T. D.	BALANCE IN STORES	PROOF
2/1/61	A 11190	3/20			100		100	(100)	0	0	0		0
2/6/61	J 8091	3/6				1000	100	900	1000	0	0		0
3/3/61	J 8091		1000				100	900	0	0	0	1000	0
3/17/61	A 11190			100			0	900	0	100	100	900	0

Courtesy Diebold, Inc.

FIG. 8–3. Inventory control card for the modified job-lot ordering system used by Diebold, Inc. Sales orders are posted as demand for material; purchase orders or manufacturing work orders supply this demand.

quantity. In such cases it makes every effort to consolidate requirements for a number of different orders so that common items are ordered simultaneously.

Modified Job-Lot Control. Many companies have developed material control systems designed to reduce the costs of job-lot ordering and to eliminate some of its basic defects. Each customer order is regarded as a demand on a portion of a common pool of materials and components. While no materials and components are stocked until an order comes in to generate a demand, customer orders are not handled so independently that it is impossible to pool requirements and so reduce cost.

Figure 8–3 illustrates the production and inventory control record used by a manufacturer of a widely diversified line of office equipment. The company's sales volume of $15 million a year comes from more than 500 different products, and material control involves more than 15,000 different items.

The company cannot afford to manufacture so many different products to stock nor is it economic to stock all the materials and components it uses. Thus job-lot material control is essential. Some of its disadvantages are eliminated by using as many common parts as possible in each product. Requirements for each individual item are combined by listing each item on a separate card so that purchases reflect the demand of each product in which the item is used.

When the company receives an order for its machines, this generates a "demand" that is posted to the record. For example, suppose the company received an order requiring 100 pieces of part No. 01-39424 (see Figure 8–3). On February 1, the record is posted to indicate that 100 pieces are reserved for sales order A 11190 with delivery required March 20.

The reservation is posted by an accounting machine that compares the requirement with existing inventories and previous reservations. Since this is the first entry, the machine shows a negative balance of 100 pieces available after it takes account of the new reservation. This generates a demand for the material. Since the lead time is 30 days[4] and the material is needed on March 20, the order must be placed by February 20. However, the materials planner decides to place it immediately because the sprocket is supposed to carry an extra reservation of 150 pieces for unusual usage. So on February 6, purchase order J 8091 is issued for 1,000 pieces—the predetermined economic order quantity. The machine operator takes account of this order by posting the "on order" amount of 1,000 pieces and allocating 100 pieces of this amount to cover the reservation and 900 "available" for future reservations.

When the order is delivered on March 3, the records are posted to eliminate the 1,000 pieces on order and add 1,000 to the "balance in stores" column. On March 17, 100 pieces are drawn out of stores to be used for sales order A 11190 and the reservation that was made for this order on February 1 is canceled.

ORDERING FOR INVENTORY

Even a modified job-order system has weaknesses. Material is not purchased until there is a definite need for it, so it often is not on hand for emergencies. There is no way to plan ahead and anticipate requirements so that large quantities of materials may be purchased at

---

[4] Shown in the upper right-hand corner of Figure 8–3.

lower prices. Also, manufacturing costs are high and customer service is slow. Because of these disadvantages, companies use job-order systems only when they are forced to do so because it is impossible to predict materials requirements for each order. Even companies that make thousands of semicustom-made products avoid job-order material control whenever possible. All material that is common to a number of products is carried in stocks that are drawn on as needed.

Two-Bin System. The oldest and simplest system of inventory control is the "two-bin system." One bin holds a reserve supply of material equal to the amount that will normally be consumed during the lead time plus an extra amount for safety stock. The other bin holds the balance of the inventory. When stock in the second bin is used up, the order point is reached. A clerk requisitions a new supply of material and then draws on the reserve supply for his needs. When the order is delivered, the reserve supply is brought up to its former level and the balance of the order is put into the other bin to be drawn on for immediate needs.

The two-bin system is simple to operate because there is no need for records. And, in most cases, there is no need even for two bins. The only requisite for successful operation of the system is that the order point of reserve stock be physically separated from the balance of the stock. This often can be done quite simply.

For example, suppose the item being controlled is pencils. Suppose usage averages four boxes a week and maximum lead time is one week. The reserve supply in a two-bin system might then be five boxes, including one box as safety stock for unexpected changes in usage or lead time. This supply need not be kept in a separate bin. It can be identified simply by putting a rubber band around it and then using up the other boxes in the inventory first. When the stock drops down to the point where it is necessary to use the boxes held by the rubber band, the order point has been reached.

The two-bin system is best suited for items of low value, fairly consistent usage, and short lead time. It is most commonly used for office supplies, and in smaller plants it also is used for maintenance, repair, and operating supplies. It rarely is suitable for production materials because it doesn't provide any record of stock on hand and is not sensitive to changes in demand or lead time.

Perpetual Inventory. The two-bin system actually is a primitive version of a conventional perpetual inventory control system.[5] The main difference is that in the regular perpetual system, there is no need to segregate stock. Control is maintained with record cards (see Figure

---

[5] Also called a "max-min" system, because inventories fluctuate between a maximum equal to the order quantity plus the safety stock and a minimum equal to the safety stock.

8–4)[6] for each item. All materials transactions are posted on these cards.

The stores clerk disburses material only when he gets a storage requisition. Data from requisitions is later posted to the record cards. Similarly, when an order point is reached, the clerk prepares a purchase requisition and posts the "on order" section of his record card. When material is received, the clerk posts the record card from his copy of the receiving report.

Each transaction can be substantiated by some document such as a receiving report, requisition, or the like. As a result, the clerk can be

MATERIAL DESCRIPTION									LOCATION	COMMODITY NUMBER	
FORM-M 135 BEPCO			NON-PRODUCTION MATERIAL RECORD								
USED FOR OR BY									ORDER QUAN.	UNIT OF MEAS.	
			MONTHLY USAGE								
JAN.	FEB.	MARCH	APRIL	MAY	JUNE	JULY	AUG.	SEPT.	OCT.	NOV.	DEC.	MIN. BAL.	ORDER TIME
DATE	REFERENCE	QUAN. ON ORDER	QUAN. RECVD.	QUAN. DISB.	BAL. IN STOCK	DATE	REFERENCE	QUAN. ON ORDER	QUAN. RECVD.	QUAN. DISB.	BAL. IN STOCK

FIG. 8–4. Typical nonproduction inventory control record. This card provides a perpetual inventory of the item. All receipts and additions to stock are posted; the balance is periodically verified with a physical count of stock on hand.

held responsible for any discrepancies between his records and actual inventories. Losses from pilferage or unauthorized use are minimized. In addition, the records always show the balance on hand and on order, so it is possible to calculate the value of the stock at any time. While the perpetual inventory system is much more expensive to operate than the two-bin system without records, its cost usually is more than justified for relatively valuable items subject to losses from pilferage. Companies use perpetual inventory systems both for general maintenance, repair, and operating supplies, and for production parts and materials.

---

[6] The form shown in Figure 8–3 also can be used in a perpetual inventory control system. The order point is indicated in the "Min. Available" box on the form. A new order is issued whenever the balance on hand and on order drops below this minimum.

INVENTORY RECORDS

Classification. Even small companies may carry thousands of different items in inventory. Obviously some system of classification is essential to prevent duplication of stock and to permit each item to be located readily. Almost every company assigns individual part numbers to its production parts and materials, and most companies also have some classification for nonproduction items.

The principles of classification are the same for all items. In every case, the best approach is first to classify inventory items into broad general categories and then progressively reclassify within each category. For example, one very broad category might be "tools"; a subcategory would be "machine-powered cutting tools," of which one type might be "milling machine cutters." The final classifications identify the specific classifications by size and type. For example, the specification number for a particular tool might be 18–26 444. The first digit might indicate that the item was a tool, the second digit that it was a machine-powered cutting tool, the next two digits that it was a milling machine cutter, and the last digits would identify the particular cutter.[7]

Classification systems permit similar items to be stored in close proximity to one another, both for convenience and to facilitate joint ordering of similar items. Assignment of classification numbers also helps prevent duplication of inventories. Master lists indicate specifications of each item and the brands that meet specifications.

Chrysler's System. For example, the Chrysler Corporation assigns its specification No. NPUV 204 to an iron valve gate with outside screw and yoke, capable of withstanding pressures of 125 W.S.P. and 200 W.O.G.[8] Chrysler does not have valves made to order; it uses standard types supplied by a number of manufacturers. Each supplier also has its own specification number. For example, the Chrysler NPUV 204 valve is the equivalent of the 465½ valve supplied to Chrysler by Crane, the 1430 valve furnished by Lunkenheimer, the 651-A of Jenkins, and so on.

In the Chrysler storeroom, certain Jenkins, Lunkenheimer, or other valves may be sitting side by side under the same Chrysler specification number. If Chrysler did not use its own numbers, it could readily carry duplicate stores. For example, if a Lunkenheimer 1430 valve failed in service, the stores clerk might think it necessary to buy another 1430 valve; he wouldn't necessarily know that the Crane 465½ valve would

---

[7] Some classification systems are so highly refined that the last digits also have very special meaning. For example, they may indicate the particular size of the tool, the parts or products on which it is used, and so on.

[8] Chrysler Corporation Standards, Valve & Cook Specification Index, January, 1958, p. UV 3.

do the same job, unless there were some classification system to group together like products of competing manufacturers.

Even the best inventory systems aren't perfect. Constant vigilance by materials personnel is necessary to prevent duplication and obsolescence of inventories. From time to time, engineers will specify new parts and materials when the job can be done with items already stocked. Or requisitioners will insist on slightly different brands and automatically increase the number of items in stock. These problems are discussed in detail in Chapter 18.

Inventory Accounting. All purchases and withdrawals from stock must be accounted for. In addition, company accounting departments issue periodic reports on inventories. The materials department uses these reports but usually is only indirectly concerned with their preparation. In most cases, the accounting department keeps separate records and gets copies of all documents concerned with materials transactions.

Accounting systems vary widely, and since this is not a text on accounting they will not be discussed here. However, essential to every system is some periodic review to make certain "theoretical" inventories indicated by stock records and the like correspond with actual inventories. This review usually is made by materials personnel (with assistance from other departments). Since it normally involves a physical count of all inventory items, it often is done during a vacation shutdown to prevent disruption of operations. Discrepancies between actual inventories and theoretical balances shown on records are a reflection on the company's inventory controls and the efficiency of its materials personnel. For this reason, many companies do not like to have physical inventories counted by the same person responsible for keeping the records of the stock. They prefer an independent check by an accountant.

CASES

CASE 8–1. QUEENSTOWN CHEMICAL COMPANY

DEVELOPING AN INVENTORY-REDUCTION PROGRAM

The Queenstown Chemical Company is a leading producer of specialty chemicals. It makes thousands of different compounds for almost all of the major drug and fine chemical producers. George Mead, Queenstown's director of purchases, is responsible for both raw-material and finished-goods inventories in addition to directing the company's purchasing activities. At present, his biggest single problem is managing finished-goods inventories, which in the last year have increased from $2 million to more than $10 million. Not only is the company running short of storage space, but its cash position is getting tight.

There is no easy solution to the problem. Queenstown's customers are aware that chemical shortages are a thing of the past, and they insist that the company stock their needs for immediate delivery. Where customers formerly carried 30 to 60 days' inventory to allow Queenstown plenty of lead time on new orders, they now insist on getting delivery in 10 days or less. If they don't get this rapid service, they can buy from Queenstown's competitors, who are willing to carry stock for their customers. Unfortunately, competition and overcapacity are facts of life in Queenstown's industry, and everyone believes it will be many years before producers can once again require customers to allow adequate lead time so they can schedule their production for each order and carry minimum finished-goods inventories.

It occurs to Mead that he might try the same approach on his suppliers and get them to carry inventories for Queenstown. At present the company has $1 million invested in nonproduction inventories and $6 million in raw materials. Usage of nonproduction items is about $100,000 per month, and usage of raw material is about $2 million per month. Queenstown uses a perpetual inventory system. All materials transactions are posted to inventory records for each item. Clerks set order points based on past usage, lead-time estimates they get from purchasing, and their own experience. Whenever there is a shortage, they increase the safety stock. In general they are criticized for shortages, but, except for occasional campaigns to reduce inventories, management has rarely expressed concern over excess stocks.

Mead believes that inventories can be reduced substantially by requiring suppliers to carry inventories. "If we carry inventories for our customers, there is no reason why our suppliers shouldn't be willing to carry them for us," he declares at a meeting of the corporation's executive committee. He proposes that Queenstown make contracts with each of its major suppliers that call for them to maintain certain minimum stocks of materials available for immediate delivery. Queenstown won't pay for the material until it is delivered, but it will guarantee the supplier a market for it eventually.

For example, in its processes Queenstown uses a "9280" type of valve that must be replaced periodically. Usage of this valve varies widely from month to month but averages about 400 valves per year. Currently, Queenstown reorders when its inventory drops to 20 valves and delivery takes about two weeks. Mead believes that the division could get along with just two valves if it had a deal with the valve distributor guaranteeing that 30 valves would always be on hand for overnight delivery. Since these valves cost $150 each, Mead's plan would reduce inventory investment by $2,700 on this item alone.

Mead's assistant, Robert Stark, disagrees with his boss's plan. He points out that it costs the supplier just as much to carry inventory as it does Queenstown. In addition, Mead's plan would require more frequent ordering, which raises costs for both buyer and seller. The result would be that costs would be higher over all than they are at present.

He grants that Queenstown would probably be able to persuade its suppliers to stock without having to pay a premium. However, he feels that in the long run the division has to pay for every service it gets from its suppliers. As an alternate solution, he suggests that Queenstown discuss the problem with its suppliers and try to persuade them to offer lower prices because Queenstown is not requiring them to carry inventories. He admits, however, that this approach may not work too well on items that are price-fixed.

Stark also suggests that Queenstown might be able to reduce inventories by trying to schedule its needs for maintenance items in advance. For example, the life of the "9280" valves can be accurately predicted. If the maintenance department were to schedule replacement far enough in advance, there would be no need to carry inventory. Orders could be placed for each job, and it wouldn't be necessary to carry more than two or three valves in stock.

Question

How do you evaluate Mead's and Stark's proposals? Develop an inventory-reduction program for Queenstown.

Chapter 9

ORDER-POINT AND PERIODIC CONTROL SYSTEMS

The inventory control systems discussed so far are all fixed reorder-point systems. That is, when stocks drop to a certain level (the safety stock), a new order for a fixed quantity is prepared. With these systems, stocks fluctuate in a pattern like that illustrated in Figure 8–1 (page 142).

As has already been pointed out, the average inventory balance is determined by order quantity, safety stock, and lead time. These three factors also influence the probability of a stockout. The greater the order quantity, the less frequent the exposure to risk of stockout. For example, when order quantities are so great that it is necessary to order only once a year, then the only stockout per year is risked when inventories drop to the reorder point. The safety stock reduces the stockout risk as inventories drop to the reorder point. It also takes up the slack if there are unanticipated changes in demand during the lead-time period, when additional stock is on order but has not yet been delivered. This period, which is the only time during the inventory cycle when there is risk of a stockout, is equal, of course, to the total lead time. Stockout risk also is reduced by selecting suppliers with short and consistent lead times who never fail to keep delivery promises. (This is discussed further in Chapters 12, 13, and 14.)

A PROBLEM IN ORDER-POINT CONTROL

Let us now apply the principles of order-point control. When demand can be predicted with reasonable accuracy and the value of the item is not too great, it is fairly easy to determine safety stock and order quantity. Common-sense rules can be applied.

Suppose, for example, that a company uses 20 typewriter ribbons per week in its offices and can get a 10 per cent extra discount if it buys them in lots of one gross. Total lead time is only a week (or less, since the ribbons are available from a local office-supply distributor). What should the order quantity, safety stock, and order point be?

Determining Order Quantity. The order quantity is easy to determine. It should be 144 ribbons in order to get the discount. By buying just a little more than seven weeks' supply with each order, costs are

154 MATERIALS MANAGEMENT

reduced 10 per cent. This means that at the maximum the company is carrying three and a half weeks' more inventory than it would if it operated on a hand-to-mouth basis on typewriter ribbons. The 10 per cent saving earned in three and a half weeks is equal to an annual return of more than 100 per cent. In addition, it is more convenient and administrative costs are lower when the company buys in larger quantities.

What if there were no quantity discount, if the price for the typewriter ribbons were the same regardless of the quantity purchased? Chances are that most companies would still choose to buy in lots of roughly 144 ribbons if their usage were about 20 ribbons per week. With this order quantity and usage, average inventories of ribbons would be roughly four weeks' supply including safety stock. Most managers would feel that it wouldn't be worth the trouble and clerical expense to order such a minor item much more often than six or seven times a year even if this policy did result in carrying somewhat larger stocks of ribbons than absolutely necessary.

However, this attitude would be quite different if the ribbons were an extremely expensive material that accounted for a large percentage of their inventory investment. In such cases, materials managers are quite willing to order weekly or even daily in order to minimize their inventory investment. Most materials managers, as we shall discuss in detail later in this chapter, classify inventory items by dollar value of usage and then establish rules for determining order quantity. For example, a materials manager might not permit an order quantity greater than two weeks' usage for an item whose dollar value of usage is $10,000 per month, while he would require a minimum order quantity equal to twelve weeks' usage for an item whose dollar value of usage is only $10 per month.

Determining Safety Stock. The safety stock is determined by analyzing the past pattern of usage. Suppose that weekly usage during the past year has been as follows:

Number of Ribbons Used	Number of Weeks with This Usage
15 or fewer	6
16	3
17	4
18	6
19	7
20	12
21	5
22 to 30	8
30 to 40	0
More than 40	1

Suppose, with the pattern of usage above, that the reorder point were set at 20 ribbons. At this point, there would be no safety stock at all, since 20 ribbons are used on the average during the one-week lead time.

How many stockouts would there have been because of variations in demand?

The first answer that might come to the student is 14, since there were 14 weeks in which actual usage was greater than the average lead-time usage of 20 ribbons. On second thought, he might come up with a different answer when he considered that the order quantity were 144 ribbons. This is equal to more than seven weeks' usage, so it is only necessary to order between seven and eight times per year. Thus, at the very most, a stockout is risked no more than eight times per year with the usage pattern above; at any other times stocks are more than ample.

In actual practice, there would be considerably fewer than eight stockouts for an item with this usage pattern, an order quantity of 144 units, and no safety stock. The week when the previous order was almost used up would have to coincide with the week when usage was greater than 20 units. Chances are (the probability can be calculated with precision, of course) that this would not happen more than two or three times per year.

With this pattern of usage and an order quantity of 144, a typical inventory planner would probably set the safety stock at 10 ribbons. The order point thus would be reached when stock dropped to 30 ribbons. With a safety stock of 10, there would be an occasional stockout (perhaps once every seven years) during the rare week when usage was greater than 30 ribbons and when the order point would have been reached even if usage had been normal.

A good case could be made for setting a safety stock even lower than 10 units, were the cost of the ribbons not so low that the saving from the reduced investment in safety stock probably would not offset the inconvenience of an occasional stockout. For example, a safety stock of 5 ribbons might bring one or two stockouts per year. This might cause slight inconvenience but certainly no serious problems. Typewriter ribbons simply aren't that critical. They can be bought in a few orders on a rush basis. Chances are that the typists wouldn't actually need fast service anyway; they often keep a spare ribbon in their desks.

THE ABC SYSTEM

Materials managers rarely, if ever, worry much about stockouts of typewriter ribbons. This is not the case with many other items, particularly production parts and materials. In many cases a stockout of even a minor production part can be just as costly as one of a major one. For example, the bolts that hold the engines to the wings are just as important to an air-frame manufacturer as the engines themselves. Production is held up if either item is out of stock. But the engines may cost $100,-000 each, while the bolts may be no more than a few dollars each. A safety stock of eight bolts would cost only a few dollars a year to maintain, while a safety stock of eight engines would cost thousands of dollars a year. Obviously the investment in safety stock for the bolts is a much better value than investment for the engines, since it provides the same protection at a fraction of the cost.

Safety stocks almost always are a better value for low-cost items than they are for expensive ones. Modern inventory control systems take this into account by classifying items by value of usage. The high-value items have lower safety stocks because the cost of protection is so high. The low-value items carry much higher safety stocks.

10 Per Cent of Items, 70 Per Cent of Value. This is the basis of the "ABC" approach to inventory control, which provides maximum over-all protection against stockouts for a given investment in safety stocks. In every company, a big percentage of the investment in inventory is concentrated on relatively few high-value items. The first step in the ABC approach[1] is to estimate average weekly usage for each item in inventory and multiply this figure by unit cost to determine value of usage. Then expenditures are listed in order of importance, with the greatest dollar-volume item topping the list. The items are separated into three groups. The 10 per cent that are most costly are "A" items; the next 20 per cent are "B" items; and the balance are "C" items. In every case the "A" items will account for a heavy percentage of total expenditures and the "C" group will account for a surprisingly small percentage. The following relationship is not untypical:

Category	% of Items	% of Value
A	10%	70%
B	20	20
C	70	10

Although there are one-seventh as many "A" items as there are "C" items, seven times as much is spent on "A" items as on "C" items. Thus, the average expenditure for an "A" item is 49 times greater than the average expenditure for a "C" item. Investment in safety stock for the "A" item must be 49 times greater than for a "C" item in order to afford the same protection against stockouts (provided that all other factors are equal).

Selective Control. The ABC system permits selective inventory control. Safety stocks are kept low for the high-value items, which should be subject to extremely close control by materials personnel anyway.[2]

---

[1] The "ABC" approach or some variation of it is covered in almost every book on inventory management and in various articles, including Julius Kneitel's "It's Easy to Take the Guesswork Out of Buying," *Purchasing*, February 2, 1959, pp. 60–65.

[2] The high-value items often are controlled with a periodic reorder system, and if stock checks are frequent enough there need be less concern about safety stocks.

The low-value items get less attention from materials personnel; stockouts are prevented by maintaining much higher safety stocks.

With ABC control, it is possible to risk fewer stockouts and reduce investment in inventories. This is proved by comparing ABC control with over-all control. Inventories are divided into three classes: the expensive "A" items account for 10 per cent of the total and roughly 70 per cent of the value; the "B" items for 20 per cent of the total and about 20 per cent of the value; and the "C" items for 70 per cent of the total and about 10 per cent of the value.

Suppose, for example, that a company stocks 1,000 items in inventory and that its average investment is six weeks' usage, or $1 million, of which $200,000 is safety stock. Average order quantity is eight weeks' usage, and there is two weeks' safety stock. With this order quantity and safety stock, let us assume that the company experiences ten serious stockouts every five years. These are distributed at random among the 1,000 items carried in inventory, and they are equally effective in disrupting production.

Let us now suppose that the company classifies its inventory by the ABC system. It breaks down as follows:

	Number of Items	Average Inventory Investment	Investment in Safety Stock
"A" items	100	$ 700,000	$140,000
"B" items	200	200,000	40,000
"C" items	700	100,000	20,000
Total	1,000	$1,000,000	$200,000

Since the ten stockouts we expect every five years are distributed at random among all the items, we can safely expect the following: one stockout on the 100 "A" items; two on the 200 "B" items; and seven on the 700 "C" items. But note the enormous difference in the "price" we pay for protection against stockouts. We have $700,000 tied up in inventory, including $140,000 in safety stock, to hold the stockout rate to 0.2 per cent per annum (i.e., once every five years) on "A" items. With "C" items, on the other hand, we get the same rate of protection at one seventh the cost.

We can get the same or better protection against stockouts at much lower cost by concentrating our investment on the cheaper items, where we can buy protection more cheaply. For example, we might decide to get along with no more than two weeks' average inventory of "A" items, of which only one-half week is safety stock. The "B" items we might not change at all, while we would double safety stocks of "C" items, leaving order quantities unchanged. If we do, we get the following:

	Number of Items	Average Inventory Investment	Investment in Safety Stock
"A" items..............	100	$233,333	$ 56,667
"B" items..............	200	200,000	40,000
"C" items..............	700	110,000	40,000
Total..............	1,000	$543,333	$136,667

Note that we have succeeded in reducing our inventory investment by $456,667—almost 50 per cent. For reasons explored in detail in the next chapter, this could reduce our operating costs by as much as $100,000 per year. Despite this spectacular cost reduction, we may actually have increased protection against stockouts. We probably reduced our stockout rate on "C" items by more than 50 per cent when we doubled the safety stock. So we can expect no more than three stockouts of these items in the next five years, instead of seven. Our rate on "B" items remains unchanged. So we wind up ahead even if we tripled our stockout rate on "A" items (three stockouts every five years, instead of just one) with our sharp reductions in both order quantity and safety stock, which cut average inventory by two thirds.

In practice, we probably need not suffer any increase in stockouts of "A" items. With the ABC approach we not only have different inventory policies for the more expensive items but also different control procedures. Because there are so few "A" items, it may be economic to review their inventory status almost daily to spot deviations in demand and to maintain extremely close follow-up on suppliers to make certain they adhere to lead times. In other words, we substitute tight control for the protection of inventory of costly items. This is economic, since it permits substantial reductions in inventory investment.

With the low-cost items, it is cheaper to carry inventory than to pay the salaries of the personnel needed for close control. It would take seven times as much effort to maintain tight control over the 700 "C" items as it would for the 100 "A" items. And, for our pains, we would be able to reduce our investment in "C" items by only one seventh as much as we could reduce the investment of "A" items. With the "B" items we would probably follow a middle-of-the-road policy. We would have some control, but we would also rely to a greater extent on inventories to protect against stockouts than we would with the "A" items.

DETERMINING LEVEL OF CONTROL

The student should not conclude from the above that inventories are always essential to prevent disruption of production. In some cases a company using an order-point control system can operate successfully without any inventory investment in many key parts and materials.

Suppose, for example, that a company makes a product *A* whose sales lead time is six weeks. Product *A* is assembled from subassemblies *B* and *F* and purchased component *T*. Subassembly *B* consists of manufactured components *C*, *D*, and *E*, which in turn are made from purchased parts and materials *Y* and *Z*. Similarly, subassembly *F* consists

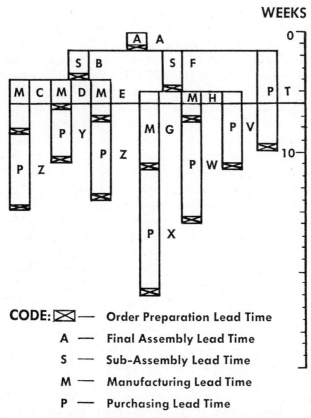

WEEKS

FIG. 9–1. The time-cycle chart makes it easy to determine which inventories require safety stock protection. For example, if sales lead time is six weeks, the parts C, D, E, G, and H require protection at manufacturing in-process level while purchased parts stocks are required of V and T. No other safety stocks are needed. (This chart was used in a talk given by R. L. Van D. Mark to the 1960 Annual Convention of the American Production and Inventory Control Society in Detroit on November 3, 1960.)

of manufactured components *G* and *H* and purchased component *V*. Then *G* and *H* in turn are made from purchased materials *X* and *W*.

Each material, component, and assembly requires some lead time. If we start with the lead time for final assembly of the product and then add the lead times of the components, we can construct a time cycle chart like that shown in Figure 9–1. The chart shows that, starting from scratch with no inventories at all, we would need about 22 weeks' lead time before we could produce a finished product. The bottleneck item is material X, which must be fabricated into G, which in turn is assembled into F, which becomes part of A.

Obviously, we must have inventories if we are going to offer delivery to customers in six weeks. We could carry protective stocks at every stage of manufacture. But there is an easier way, which involves less control and usually will also reduce inventories. Stocks are maintained for only a few critical items; the others are purchased or manufactured only when there is a definite demand for them.

This concept is best explained graphically. Note that there is a horizontal line in Figure 9–1 at the six-week mark that represents our sales lead time. We need stock only those items whose lead time intersects this six-week line. These include components C, D, E, G, H, V, and T.

For example, suppose we decide from experience that a safety stock of 100 units each of C, D, E, G, H, V, and T will permit us to take care of all foreseeable demand from our customers. To simplify our arithmetic, let us assume that we are operating entirely on a job-lot basis; except for our safety stock, we buy or fabricate exactly enough material to complete each order we receive from a customer.

Suppose a customer orders 20 units of product A. We draw components C, D, E, G, H, V, and T from stock. In order to deliver within six weeks, our chart shows that we must start work on subassembly F within one week. If it suits our convenience (and it may, since every factory manager likes to even out work loads in order to get more efficient operation), we can hold off starting work on subassembly B for two weeks. Or, of course, we can start work immediately and give the customer extra-prompt service.

We must also take steps to replenish our safety stock. Therefore we order materials and parts T, V, W, X, Y, and Z in sufficient quantities so that they ultimately can be manufactured into the key components for which we carry safety stocks.

The example above is greatly oversimplified. The assumption that we could carry identical safety stocks of the various key items is not correct. In actual practice, we would certainly carry a much greater safety stock of parts G, whose raw material X must be ordered 22 weeks ahead of final assembly, than we would of T, which requires a total lead time of only 10 weeks. If we had a 100-unit safety stock of T, we would probably require a 220-unit safety stock of G to get the same protection against stockout, because of the difference in lead time.

Also, we probably would not find it convenient to operate strictly on a job-lot basis. We would buy or fabricate certain items in excess of actual requirements, both for convenience and to reduce costs.

It is not difficult to see how this selective control system can be applied to any of the inventory control systems described in this chapter and the previous chapter. It can also be used in conjunction with an ABC system. The components and materials that we control selectively could be classified according to their value. Inventory levels would then be adjusted to afford varying degrees of protection in accordance with the ABC rules already described.

LIMITATIONS OF MAX-MIN SYSTEMS

Problem of Demand Change. All of the inventory control systems discussed so far have been order-point or "max-min" systems. Control can be improved and inventory investment reduced through application of ABC systems, selective control, and other techniques. But these systems still have one fundamental weakness: they work well only when the lead time and the demand for material during the lead time can be predicted with reasonable accuracy. Unfortunately, usage and lead times of many items do vary enormously. Many companies increase their production by 50 per cent in an exceptionally prosperous year, and demand for individual products can change even more. Let us see what happens when demand suddenly surges upward on an item under a max-min system of inventory control.

Let us assume that an item normally has a usage of 1,000 units during its one-month lead-time period and that the previous year's usage pattern indicates a safety stock of 250 units to be more than adequate. If demand rises by 50 per cent during the year and, as is often the case when business is increasing, lead times lengthen slightly, a whole series of stockouts is possible. The first stockout will come when usage during the lead time is 25 per cent greater than normal. The inventory planner may consider usage abnormal and not increase safety stocks after this first stockout.

A second stockout will almost certainly touch off an analysis of the item's usage. Usually both order point and safety stock will be increased. Suppose that the item that used to have an average usage of 1,000 units a month has these usages for six months: 1,050, 1,100, 1,400, 1,250, 1,300, and 1,400. The planner notes that average usage during this six-month period was 1,250 units, or 25 per cent above normal. He also notes that maximum usage was 1,400 units. He may decide to increase the safety stock to 300 units and increase the order point to 1,500 units.

If demand continues to rise, the inevitable result is another stockout. If the company is controlling thousands of different items with a simple max-min system, it will be plagued with stockouts. Eventually, however, order points and safety stocks are increased to the point where inventories are more than adequate to cope with peak demand.[3] For example,

---

[3] It is probable, in fact, that they will be increased well beyond this point. In a period of rising demand, inventory planners are subject to almost daily harassment from production and sales executives because of shortages and stockouts. On the other hand, there will be few immediate complaints if they raise order points and safety stocks to the point where stockouts are highly unlikely regardless of how much usage increases.

an item that once had an order point of 1,250 units and a safety stock of 250 might wind up with an order point of 2,000 and a safety stock of 500, even though record consumption might not exceed 1,800 units. Eventually, planners would attempt to anticipate increased demand and build up stocks ahead of usage.

If this increase in demand were temporary, the results would be expensive. Suppose, for example, that on account of a business depression or some other cause the company's usage dropped well below its old norm of 1,000 units to 700 units a month. In such a case, its investment in inventories would initially be at least three times greater than necessary, and would continue to be substantially excessive until max-min quantities were gradually adjusted back to the old levels.

Basic Weaknesses of Max-Min. Few companies experience such a stable demand for materials that they can rely entirely on a max-min perpetual inventory control system such as that described above. Companies surveyed by the National Industrial Conference Board in a study of inventory control[4] indicated that they believed maximum-minimum stock levels were no substitute for effective inventory management. According to the NICB study, max-min control has the following weaknesses:

1. Stock levels are actually set by clerks, since managers do not have the time to study inventory levels of individual items.
2. Reorder points and safety stocks often are not changed for years on end.
3. Delay in posting records makes them useless for control. Reorder of a critical item can be held up until the clerk gets around to posting the last withdrawal, indicating that the reorder point has been reached.

PERIODIC REORDERING

For the reasons given above, many companies do not use max-min or order-point systems to control inventories of their most important materials. Instead, they use periodic reordering systems.

All the inventory systems discussed so far have been order-point systems. With them, a certain quantity of material is ordered whenever stocks drop to the reorder point. Inventories are regulated by the period between orders; the order quantity is fixed. Periodic reordering is just the opposite: inventories are regulated by the quantity ordered and the period between orders is fixed. In other words, orders are placed at regular intervals for amounts needed to bring stocks up to the desired level.

Applications. Periodic reordering is commonly used when one or more of the following conditions prevails:

1. The item is ordered frequently and expenditures for it are sufficient to warrant tight control.

---

[4] *Inventory Management in Industry*, Studies in Business Policy, No. 88 (1958), p. 23.

2. Inventory balances are determined only periodically, making an order-point system impractical.
3. Many items are ordered from the same supplier and ordering jointly reduces prices, transportation, or paper work.
4. Usage is discreet or irregular. For example, an item may be withdrawn from stock just one day in a month.
5. The item is purchased in large quantities and requires a substantial percentage of a supplier's capacity.
6. Either price does not vary with quantity purchased or quantity discounts are available even though an order is scheduled for partial shipments.

Periodic reordering is used almost always by companies that make a limited product line in large quantities. For example, it is widely used to control production parts inventories in the automobile and appliance industries. In these industries, where identical products are finished on assembly lines day after day, inventory management is regarded as the regulation of a flow of parts and materials. It is not thought of as a series of additions to and withdrawals from stock, as it is in job-lot systems or perpetual-inventory systems used for nonproduction material.

An Example. This flow concept is best illustrated by an example. Suppose an appliance manufacturer has scheduled 10,000 units of a particular model each month and requires a component that is unique to that model. The supplier quotes on the basis of 10,000 units per month but, usually, the purchase order itself does not authorize him to fabricate any parts or buy any raw material. This is authorized by releases that amend the order. A system of releases with periodic ordering limits the buyer's liability for raw materials and finished stock should production be cut back. It also makes it easier to increase orders should requirements temporarily be greater than planned.

Table 9–1 (next page) shows the pattern of weekly usage, inventory, and releasing for our manufacturer. In week No. 1, which is several months after the purchase order was placed, the supplier is authorized to ship 2,500 pieces. He had previously been authorized to fabricate two months' usage (20,000 pieces) and buy raw material for five months' usage. In week No. 2, the buyer authorizes the supplier to make another shipment of 2,500 pieces, and the supplier has already given him the routing and car number for the first shipment, which is in transit.[5]

In week No. 3, the first shipment is received and a third shipment of 2,500 pieces is authorized. In week No. 4, production starts. A stock checker makes a count of stock on hand and a usage of 3,000 pieces is indicated. The buyer notes that usage has been greater than planned because of rescheduling. He warns the supplier but does not increase

---

[5] Companies that buy identical parts and materials for a number of plants sometimes reroute shipments in transit if shortages develop at a particular plant. Even companies with a single plant like to keep tabs on shipments in transit so they can request the carrier to trace them if there are any delays.

TABLE 9–1

MATERIAL CONTROL WITH A PERIODIC ORDERING SYSTEM

Week No.	Weekly Data					Cumulative Data				
	On Hand	In Transit	Received	Apparent Usage	Released	Fabrication Authorized	Material Authorized	Released	Received	Used
1	0	0	0	0	2500	20,000	50,000	2500	0	0
2	0	2500	0	0	2500	20,000	50,000	5000	0	0
3	2500	2500	2500	0	2500	20,000	50,000	7500	2500	0
4	2000	2500	2500	3000	2500	20,000	50,000	10,000	5000	3000
5	1800	2500	2500	3200	3500	30,000	60,000	13,500	7500	6200
6	1800	3500	2500	2500	3500	30,000	60,000	16,000	10,000	8700
7	4800	2500	3500	500	1500	30,000	60,000	16,500	13,000	9200

Note: With a periodic ordering system, stock levels are checked and orders placed at regular, predetermined intervals. In this example, suppliers fabricate approximately two months' usage of material and purchase raw material for an additional three months' usage. They then make weekly shipments of the exact amount of material that is needed.

his weekly shipping authorization. In the following week usage jumps again to 3,200 pieces, and the shipping release to the supplier is increased to 3,500 pieces in order to build up stocks that are now below normal.

Since it is the end of the month, the supplier's fabrication and material authorizations are reviewed. No changes in usage are predicted, so the supplier is authorized to buy material and fabricate an additional month's usage of 10,000 pieces. This increases cumulative fabrication authorizations to 30,000 pieces and material authorizations to 60,000, and the supplier continues to have a lead time of two months for fabrication and five months for materials.

During the sixth week, stocks remain unchanged and 2,500 units are received; thus usage is 2,500 units. The following week there is a wildcat strike at the plant, and the stock checker's report indicates that line stocks are up to 4,800 units and usage therefore is down to 500 units. The buyer now cuts the supplier back to a shipment of 1,500 units.

Despite the extremely close control it offers, periodic ordering does not eliminate the need for safety stocks. As with order-point systems, some protective stock is needed between the time material is ordered and when it is delivered in order to allow for unanticipated delays in delivery or for extra usage. The process of determining safety stock is not unlike that for order-point systems. As with order-point systems, investment in safety stocks can be reduced through application of ABC systems. The high-priced "A" items have the smallest safety stock. Protection against stockouts is achieved by reducing the period between orders. For example, stocks of "A" items might be checked for reorder twice weekly, "B" items every other week, and "C" items once a month.

Using the ABC approach with periodic ordering, automobile assembly plants make daily checks of stocks of high-priced materials such as engines, transmissions, and major body components, but check stock weekly or even monthly for minor items such as upholstery tacks. The principles of selective control can also be applied to periodic ordering. Suppose, for example, that Figure 9–1 illustrated the lead-time cycle of an assembly controlled with periodic ordering. If the entire manufacturing process were so interrelated (through conveyor lines, automated equipment, and so on) that in-process inventories were automatically regulated, then it would be pointless to control anything but purchased parts and materials. In this case, there would be periodic control of all items marked *P* only. Inventories of other items would always be exactly equal to the space they occupy on conveyor lines and in-process equipment less any scrap that was generated.

Close Control, High Cost. Applications of periodic ordering are limited almost entirely to mass-production industries, where enormous quantities of a relatively limited number of items must be controlled.

Periodic ordering permits such companies to operate with minimum inventories that are often only a fraction of what would be required with order-point control. Periodic ordering also has major disadvantages (which is why its applications are limited). It is expensive to operate, since it requires more clerical manpower than order-point systems do. Also, it usually is not practical unless usage is high or the item is extremely expensive. Otherwise it costs too much, because more frequent ordering can raise both unit shipping costs and prices of materials.

TOP-MANAGEMENT CONTROL

Regardless of the system used, periodic ordering or order point, top managers cannot hope to control the thousands of items in inventory on an individual basis. This is a job for clerks or computers. Management can only hope to control inventories on an over-all basis. One of the best ways to do this is through standards used in conjunction with an over-all materials plan.[6]

For example, suppose the plan assumes that production and sales will be $1 million per month for the first three months of the year and then will increase steadily to a peak of $1.5 million in June. Obviously some inventory build-up is necessary to accommodate the sales increase. However, it is not necessary to increase inventories in proportion to the increase in output.[7] Plants can operate with higher stock-turnover ratios as production increases to near-capacity levels.

With a 50 per cent increase in sales, it might even be possible to get along with as little as a 20 per cent increase in inventories of purchased parts and raw materials. Inventories might increase, for example, from $500,000 in January to $600,000 by May 1. Then a drop in inventories to $400,000 might be projected through July. In other words, during the peak production period, management might anticipate cutting inventories if sales are expected to drop sharply when the peak is passed.

Once the plan is agreed upon, managers can maintain control by comparing the standards set in the plan with reports of actual performance. Since it normally takes a rather elaborate study to calculate precisely what inventories are, managers usually maintain control with weekly or daily reports of purchases, receivals, and output, which can provide approximate inventory balances. When these reports indicate deviation from standard, the materials manager investigates and takes necessary corrective action.

Should actual output vary substantially from the plan or should the sales forecast change, the materials manager must be ready to set new standards quickly. If he doesn't move fast, there either may be shortages

---

[6] Over-all materials planning was discussed in some detail in Chapter 8.

[7] F. Beaman Todd and Irving Scharf, "Profitable Inventory Levels," *Harvard Business Review*, September–October, 1953, pp. 101–8. This article discusses techniques to determine required stock-sales ratios at various levels of sales and production.

or inventories will build up rapidly because of accumulated commitments. Suppose, for example, that sales and production in June are actually $1 million instead of $1.5 million. This automatically means an inventory build-up if there has been no advance warning, since it is impossible to cut back commitments too much within the procurement lead time. The materials manager must then devise a plan to get stocks back in balance. If sales are greater than expected in succeeding months, his problem is solved almost automatically. But if they are less than expected, new purchases may have to be cut back sharply for a number of months before a new equilibrium is reached.

When there are no unexpected changes in either demand or supplier lead times, the inventory management process can be made largely automatic. In many cases, optimum inventory levels can be calculated with tremendous precision through the use of various analytical techniques. These techniques are discussed in detail in the next chapter.

CASES

CASE 9–1

A PROBLEM IN ORDER-POINT CONTROL

Suppose you work for a company that controls its inventories on a max-min basis, using perpetual inventory cards. Your company is introducing a new line of products that will result in greatly increased usage of a particular component. You analyze the sales forecast for this new product line and calculate that it will cause demand for the component to rise by about 800 units per month. Naturally, you decide to analyze the history of the component to determine what lead time and order quantities should be. You note the following data on the perpetual inventory card:

Date	Purchase Requisition Issued	Receipts	Disbursements	Balance on Hand
1/2............				922 (balance carried forward)
1/7............			400	522
1/12...........	500			
1/29..........			400	122
2/10..........		500		622
2/15..........	500			
3/13..........		500		1,122
3/16..........			400	722
5/1...........1,000			722	0
5/18..........		1,000		1,000
5/19..........			278	722
7/12..........	500		400	322
8/10..........		500		822
10/26.........			600	222
10/27.........	500			
11/18.........		500		722
12/12.........			200	522

It is expected that demand for the component from the new product will be more regular than demand from other products, which will continue to vary erratically as it has in the past. The unit price of F.O.B. buyer's plant is $1.00 in lots of 100 to 499 pieces, $.95 in lots of 500 to 999 pieces, $.92 in lots of 1,000 to 4,999 pieces, and $.90 in lots of more than 5,000 pieces. Normal lead time is four weeks, but in emergencies you can get delivery in two to three weeks by doing a great deal of expediting.

Question

Calculate purchase quantities, safety stock, and order-point quantity, based on the data above.

CASE 9–2. HOMEWOOD MACHINE TOOL CORPORATION

ANALYSIS OF SAFETY STOCKS

The Homewood Machine Tool Corporation is a medium-sized producer of lathes used both in tool rooms and in production. Although the company offers a standard product line in its catalogue, most of its products are adaptations of standard models to meet special customer requirements. Because of high product costs (the lathes cost from $6,000 to $18,000 each), the company schedules its factory on a job-order basis. In slack times, it can deliver a finished lathe about three months after it gets an order from a customer. In boom periods, it may have as much as a two-year backlog of orders.

The company prefers to purchase major components—motors, electric and hydraulic controls, and the larger castings—only after it gets an order from a customer that requires them. Even so, it stocks some of these more widely used items, both to reduce reordering and to enable prompter service to customers requiring repair parts. Commonly used minor components are stocked on a max-min basis. This permits the company to offer overnight service to its customers on many rush orders for repair parts and also provides a stock on which the production department can draw for building machines. In all, about 16,000 different items are stocked, and the company's investment in inventories is about $4 million. The company's sales are about $21 million. Its major competitor manages to turn over its inventories about eight times per year, and Homewood's president, Mark Roberts, can't understand why his company can't at least equal this competitor's performance on inventory management.

Roberts has called on Donald Albers, his materials manager, to make a detailed study of the company's inventory policies to see if some improvement can't be made. Roberts' timing is appropriate, since the company has just reorganized its entire materials department coincident with the retirement of George Blough, Albers' predecessor.

Blough is proud of his record with the company. The company's production has not been held up because of lack of material since 1951, when the industry was plagued by shortages caused by the Korean War. On reviewing the company's inventory, Albers discovers that about half of it, or $2 million, is safety stock to protect against unanticipated surges in demand during the lead-time period. This safety stock is spread fairly evenly over all items in inventory; protection against stockout is quite uniform. According to Albers' calculations, the typical inventory item has a safety stock adequate to prevent a stockout more than once every ten years. The carrying cost of this safety stock is about 20 per cent per year. Further analysis shows that safety-stock investment is divided as follows:

```
Low-value items (comprising 70% of total)............$  250,000
Medium-value items (20% of total)...................    750,000
High-value items (10% of total)......................  1,000,000
    Total estimated safety-stock investment.........$2,000,000
```

Estimates on the cost of a stockout vary. The accounting manager estimates that a "typical" stockout costs perhaps $100. Most stockouts cost almost nothing, he points out. The purchase lead time for the item is so short that the stockout causes very little delay. In many cases, he feels, a stockout would neither inconvenience a customer were the order for a repair part nor cause any serious delay in the production department. However, he does admit that a few stockouts—particularly on long lead-time items—can be quite costly. If a customer's machine must shut down because Homewood fails to supply a repair part promptly, the cost in good will can be quite high. If the stockout holds up production on a new machine, the cost can also be high if the stockout causes the plant to get badly behind schedule. A serious stockout may cost $1,000 or more.

The sales manager and the production manager believe that the accounting manager's estimate of $100 for the cost of a typical stockout is too conservative. They suggest that the company must assume a loss of $500 for each stockout.

Question

What changes should Albers make in Homewood's inventory management practices? Support your recommendations with an analysis.

CASE 9–3. BLUE MOTORS CORPORATION
A PROBLEM IN PERIODIC ORDERING

Production and inventory control is not an easy job at Blue Motors, a large auto manufacturer. The company's investment in raw material and in-process inventories exceeds its investment in plant and equipment and thus is the company's biggest single asset. Control of production parts and materials inventories is particularly difficult at the company's automobile assembly plants, where the proper components to assemble hundreds of different trim and color combinations of the company's models must be on hand when needed. The company cannot afford to stop its assembly line because of a supply failure. On the other hand, storage space is limited. The company could not carry more than a few days' inventory of such bulky components as engines, radiators, and seat springs even if it were not the least bit concerned about tying up too much of its working capital in inventories.

The company tries to limit inventory investment with an "ABC" system. It carries less than a week's inventory of the bulky and expensive "A" items—engines, bodies, transmissions, and similar components. "B" items normally are limited to about two weeks' stock, and plants may carry as much as three months' stock of "C" items, although they try to hold it to thirty days' stock.

Blue Motors uses periodic ordering for all production parts and materials. Suppliers are authorized to purchase materials five months in advance and to fabricate two months in advance. Blue Motors stock checkers make periodic counts of material on hand. This information is compared with data on the number of parts that are on order and in transit. The total available supply is then compared with the demand indicated by the production schedule. Suppliers then get each month new production releases that authorize them to fabricate and buy material for an additional month's requirements. The ordering and inventory control procedure used by Blue Motors is much like that shown in Table 9–1 on page 164.

The stock checkers use different review periods for different types of item. Any item that is in critical supply is reviewed daily, regardless of its value. Most "A" items are reviewed daily. "B" items are usually reviewed twice a week, and "C" items always are reviewed at least once a month.

Until recently, all of Blue Motors' basic products have been assembled in reasonably large quantities. The company's lowest-volume item has been its convertible coupe, whose output has dropped as low as two units per day at certain of the company's assembly plants. The company's newest product is what its advertising department calls a "customized" sports car. The new product is designed to compete with the sports cars turned out by various European manufacturers. Its price will be about $12,000. The company's marketing strategy is tailored to relatively few buyers who wish to own a high-quality automobile with unique design features. The company already has widely advertised that production of the new car will be limited to 200 units per year in order to "protect the investment of its discriminating owners."

Current plans call for assembly of the car at the company's main plant in Detroit. Its production volume is so low that practically all of the components, few of which are interchangeable with the company's other cars, will be purchased. The company's own manufacturing plants prefer to concentrate on the more profitable, higher-volume components of the company's other products.

Suppliers of major components have been reluctant to accept orders unless they are authorized to fabricate an entire year's requirements in one production run. Since production is limited to only 15 units per day during the period of peak demand, in spring, and will probably drop to 5 units during the slack season, the company's normal ordering procedures for "ABC" items may not be applicable. For example, a supplier might object to shipping small screws in lots of 50 or 100. Similarly, it would be costly to use a supplier truck to deliver only 10 units of an "A" item like a radiator. On the other hand, the company wants to tie up as little of its valuable factory floor space as possible on the new program. Also, if an item cannot be delivered directly to the assembly line, where there is a limited amount of space, it must be stored in some other area of the plant and a second handling will be necessary. This would raise costs, particularly for high-volume components.

Question

Recommend an ordering system for Blue Motors' new sports car. In making your recommendations, assume that a radiator is a typical "A" item, a door handle a typical "B" item, and a fastener a typical "C" item.

Chapter 10

ANALYTICAL INVENTORY CONTROL TECHNIQUES

Average inventory levels are determined by both order quantities and safety stocks. Order quantities are influenced by price and ordering cost. Safety stocks are influenced by certainty of demand and lead time. Businessmen have known these principles for years and have developed the inventory control systems described in Chapters 8 and 9. These systems work reasonably well, but one would hardly describe them as analytical.

It is only in recent years that the average company has made any effort to determine quantitatively the safety stocks and order quantity that yield maximum profits. Modern analytical techniques have taken much, but by no means all, of the guesswork out of inventory management. No longer need stock levels be determined by habit, hunch, or accident. Formulas are available to determine order quantities, and statistical probability theory can be applied to determine safety stocks.

Many students may be surprised to learn that relatively few companies —probably no more than 10 per cent of all manufacturers, large and small—have adopted these quantitative techniques. In most cases, the reasons for not using them have not been valid ones: ignorance, resistance to change, and the like. Relatively few men have been trained in modern materials management techniques. Undoubtedly there will be wider adoption of these techniques when the supply of trained personnel comes anywhere near meeting the demand. However, there is no denying that some companies (mostly very large ones) are thoroughly familiar with the techniques discussed in this chapter but refrain from using some of them because they feel that their advantages are more than offset by their cost, as well as by other disadvantages.

This chapter is organized much as the previous chapter was. The difference is that it is devoted to discussion of analytical approaches to various problems, while the previous chapter was confined to general principles and basic techniques. We shall discuss order quantities and safety stocks as applied to order-point systems. Then we shall discuss more precise methods of determining safety stocks with ABC control and forecasting of demand. Finally, we shall discuss the application of these quantitative techniques to a periodic ordering system.

DETERMINING ORDER QUANTITY

As we have seen, the bigger the order quantity, the bigger the average inventory. A policy of buying in large quantities also has its virtues. Unit prices usually are lower. In addition, the larger the order quantity, the fewer the number of orders that must be processed and the fewer the shipments that need be handled. This reduces costs.

Consequently the materials manager is torn between a desire to keep inventories low by ordering in small quantities and a desire to reduce costs by buying large quantities. The cost of carrying inventories is called "cost of possession," and the cost of purchasing and processing the order is called "cost of acquisition." One of the most important goals in materials management is to strike the most economic balance between cost of possession and cost of acquisition in determining order quantities.

Cost of Possession

Many companies estimate that it costs as much as 20 to 25 per cent per year to carry inventories, that is, each $1 million in inventory costs $200,000 to $250,000 per year to maintain. There are three major costs of possession: storage, obsolescence, and capital cost.

Storage Cost. This is the most obvious inventory carrying cost. It includes rent for storage facilities, salaries of personnel and related storage expenses, taxes, and so on. Storage costs vary widely with the type of material stored, type of storage facilities used, and so on. Usually they are equal to at least 5 per cent of the value of material stored per year.

Obsolescence. When there are no inventories, there can be no obsolescence. But when many items are stored, it is inevitable that some of them won't be used, will shrink or disappear, or will spoil. Needs can't be estimated with perfect accuracy even with the most rigid inventory control systems. Well-managed companies ruthlessly weed out surplus inventory and dispose of it. The general rule is never to hold inventories for which there is no immediate need. In fact, companies sometimes dispose of materials even when there is a definite future need for them. If stocks are held long enough, the accumulated carrying charges will exceed their value.[1]

Although some obsolescence is inevitable, it can't be predicted (or it would be prevented simply by not investing in inventory). Therefore a

---

[1] Suppose a company has $100 invested in a certain material for which there will be no use for at least two years. Carrying costs are 20 per cent a year, or $40 for two years. It pays the company to sell the material immediately if it can find a buyer willing to pay $60 for it. In practice, many companies would be willing to sell the material for less than $60 because they prefer to have capital in cash rather than in inventory, and also because there is always some uncertainty in predicting a need for material a year or more in advance.

part of the cost of possession is an allowance or "insurance premium" to cover losses from obsolescence. The charge naturally varies widely, but few companies can hold it to less than 1 per cent of the value of the inventory per year.

Cost of Capital.   Inventories tie up a company's most versatile asset, cash. Every business has a limited amount of capital available to it from its owners and creditors. Each tries to use it as efficiently as possible to earn bigger profits. One barometer that shows how efficiently capital is being used is inventory turnover: the ratio of sales to inventory. A company can raise this ratio either by reducing inventories or by increasing sales without a corresponding increase in inventories. In either case, its earnings on investment are boosted.

Suppose, for example, that a company's sales are $1 million with total assets of $200,000—including $100,000 in inventories. If its profit margin on sales is 5 per cent, profits of $50,000 provide a 25 per cent return on assets. Inventory is turned over ten times a year ($1,000,000 ÷ $100,000). If the turnover rate can be doubled, the company's sales will be $2 million with the same assets. Profits increase to $100,000 and return on investment is 50 per cent.

Capital never is so readily available that it can be invested in inventory at no cost. Were it not in inventory, it could always earn a return at least equal to the interest on government bonds. In many cases, it could get a much higher return.

The "opportunity cost" approach[2] is one of the best ways to estimate the cost of the money tied up in inventory. With it, one assumes that the capital costs whatever it would earn were it invested in the most advantageous alternatives. The minimum opportunity cost is the 4 to 6 per cent return the capital would earn if it were invested in short-term securities or used to reduce the company's debt. The maximum can be much higher—even 50 per cent or more—if the company is very pressed for cash and has many opportunities to employ capital profitably.

Opportunity cost varies widely not only from company to company but also from year to year (or even month to month) within a company. Because of this, a company's cost of possession can vary widely.[3] Inventory management, never an easy job, becomes an almost impossible job to perform perfectly when changes in the cost of possession are taken into account.

---

[2] The reader interested in a detailed explanation of opportunity cost and other approaches to capital budgeting should study Joel Dean's *Managerial Economics* (New York: Prentice-Hall, Inc., 1951).

[3] In a company subject to wide swings in business, carrying costs can be extremely high at the peak of the business cycle, when there are many very profitable alternative investments available for the capital tied up in inventory. And it can be quite low in a business slump when few investment opportunities are available. When a company's business is seasonal, its carrying costs (with the opportunity cost approach) also will vary seasonally, being very high at the peak of the season and low off season.

Cost of Acquisition

Despite their desire to use capital efficiently and minimize storage cost and obsolescence, most companies deliberately carry inventories substantially bigger than they need be for protection against stockouts. They do this to reduce their cost of acquisition, since by ordering and buying large quantities they reduce both purchase cost and ordering cost.

Purchase Cost. When a company buys in larger quantities, it usually pays lower unit prices. Suppliers will cut prices because their costs are lower when they get a single large order instead of several small ones. Not only are their administrative expenses reduced, but they also can often manufacture in larger lots and reduce unit costs. In addition, the buyer's bargaining power is increased by placing a large order and it is easier to wangle concessions from suppliers.

Ordering Costs. Not only do bigger buys often reduce purchase costs but they also reduce most other costs of acquisition—the cost of making the purchase, expediting, receiving, and paying for the material, interplant and intraplant transportation, packaging, and so on.

Suppose, for example, a company decides to buy material in two separate lots rather than in one big lot. It costs just as much to issue the purchase order for the smaller lot as for the bigger one. Therefore purchase order costs double, since two orders are required to buy two lots. There also is twice as much paper work in the accounting, receiving, and inspection operations. Physically it will usually take more time to handle two smaller shipments than a single large one.[4] And, in most cases, a single big shipment can be packaged more economically and shipped for a lower tariff than two smaller shipments. Thus, the bigger the amount purchased, the lower the unit ordering cost.

Ordering cost is insignificant only with purchases of very high value. For example, one large corporation made a study that revealed it costs its purchasing department $14.60 for each order it issued and it costs $3.86 to receive and inspect each shipment.[5] Higher ordering costs make it desirable to carry rather large stocks of low-value items.

E.O.Q. Formulas

Many formulas have been devised to weigh the variables of cost of acquisition, cost of possession, and usage in order to determine the most economic order quantity (E.O.Q.). If usage doesn't vary much

---

[4] The difference varies with the bulk and weight of the shipments. It usually takes nearly twice as much time to handle two 5-pound shipments as it does for one 10-pound shipment. But it takes about twice as much time to unload a two-carload shipment as it does a one-carload shipment.

[5] Ordering costs in some companies are even higher. The cost per order of the purchasing department of the Ford Division of the Ford Motor Company is $58. See Dean Ammer, "The Purchasing Department: Ford's Cost Control Center," *Purchasing*, May 23, 1960, p. 54.

from week to week, the formulas are not too complex mathematically. When the usage pattern is complex, so are the formulas. The formulas used in this book all assume reasonably steady usage.

E.O.Q.—No Quantity Discount. The following formula can be used to determine economic order quantity when unit price is the same regardless of order quantity:

$$\text{E.O.Q.} = \sqrt{\frac{2 \times (\text{Annual Usage in Units}) \times (\text{Order Cost in \$/Order})}{(\text{Unit Cost of Material in \$/Unit}) \times (\text{Carrying Cost in \%/Yr.})}}$$

Suppose, for example,[6] annual usage of a material is 1,200 units and it costs $10 to handle an order for this material. The price is $1 per unit regardless of quantity purchased, and carrying cost of inventory is 24 per cent per year. Then

$$\text{E.O.Q.} = \sqrt{\frac{2 \times 1,200 \times 10}{1.00 \times 0.24}} = 333 \text{ units.}$$

Quantity Discount. If, as is so frequently the case, the price does vary with the quantity purchased, it is more difficult to calculate economic order quantity. A separate table for each carrying cost and order cost used is required. It consists of tabulations of total procurement cost (purchase cost plus ordering cost plus carrying cost) for a series of order quantities and annual usages.

Calculations to compile such a table are not difficult to make. For example, let us assume that a certain material has an annual usage of $1,200 and each purchase covers a three-month supply. With a $10 order cost and a 24 per cent carrying cost, total annual procurement cost is $1,276 and consists of the following components:

Purchase cost	$1,200
Order cost (4 orders @ $10/order)	40
Carrying cost (24% of $150)[7]	36
Total annual procurement cost	$1,276

When these calculations are made for various values of annual usage and order quantities, a table similar to that in Figure 10–1 can be constructed and used to determine minimum annual procurement cost when purchase price varies with quantity purchased.

---

[6] This and subsequent examples of inventory management formulas appeared in slightly different form in a series of articles by Dr. Spencer B. Smith in *Purchasing* (Nov. 10, 1958, Nov. 24, 1958, and Dec. 8, 1958).

[7] The student should note that, even though $300 worth of material is ordered every three months, average inventory is $150, not $300. When the order is received at the beginning of the period, inventories rise by $300. Halfway through the period (after one and a half months), half of the order, or $150 worth, has presumably been consumed. At the end of the period, the entire order has been used. Average stock carried during the period therefore is $150 if usage has been reasonably regular.

	TOTAL ANNUAL COSTS (IN DOLLARS)						
VALUE OF ANNUAL USE	1	2	3	ORDER QUANTITY IN MONTHS' SUPPLY 4	5	6	7
$ 100	221	162	143	134	129	126	124
102	223	164	145	136	131	128	126
104	225	166	147	138	133	130	128
106	227	168	149	140	135	132	131
108	229	170	151	142	137	134	133
1,050	1,181	1,131	1,122	1,122	1,127	1,133	1,141
1,060	1,191	1,141	1,132	1,132	1,137	1,144	1,151
1,070	1,201	1,151	1,142	1,143	1,148	1,154	1,162
1,080	1,211	1,162	1,152	1,153	1,158	1,165	1,173
1,090	1,221	1,172	1,163	1,164	1,169	1,175	1,183
1,100	1,231	1,182	1,173	1,174	1,179	1,186	1,194
1,110	1,241	1,192	1,183	1,184	1,190	1,197	1,205
1,120	1,251	1,202	1,194	1,195	1,200	1,207	1,216
1,130	1,261	1,213	1,204	1,205	1,211	1,218	1,226
1,140	1,271	1,223	1,214	1,216	1,221	1,228	1,237
1,150	1,282	1,233	1,225	1,226	1,232	1,239	1,248
1,160	1,292	1,243	1,235	1,236	1,242	1,250	1,258
1,170	1,302	1,253	1,245	1,247	1,253	1,260	1,269
1,180	1,312	1,264	1,255	1,257	1,263	1,271	1,280
1,190	1,322	1,274	1,266	1,268	1,274	1,281	1,290
1,200	1,332	1,284	1,276	1,278	1,284	1,292	1,301
1,210	1,342	1,294	1,286	1,288	1,295	1,303	1,312
1,220	1,352	1,304	1,297	1,299	1,305	1,313	1,323
1,230	1,362	1,315	1,307	1,309	1,316	1,324	1,333
1,240	1,372	1,325	1,317	1,320	1,326	1,334	1,344
19,750	20,068	20,205	20,383	20,570	20,762	20,955	21,150
19,800	20,118	20,256	20,434	20,622	20,814	21,008	21,203
19,850	20,169	20,307	20,486	20,674	20,867	21,061	21,257
19,900	20,219	20,358	20,537	20,726	20,919	21,114	21,310
19,950	20,270	20,409	20,589	20,778	20,972	21,167	21,364
20,000	20,320	20,460	20,640	20,830	21,024	21,220	21,417

FIG. 10–1. This table shows total annual cost for various values of annual use and various order quantities when carrying cost is 24 per cent and ordering cost is $10. Total annual cost equals the sum of the value of annual use, the order cost, and the carrying cost.

Using the Table.   An example illustrates how the table is used. Suppose a supplier has the following price schedule:

Order Quantity	Unit Price
1–499	$1.00
500–999	.95
1,000 or more	.925

If usage is 1,200 units per year, the value of the usage is $1,200 at the price of $1.00, $1,140 at the $.95 price (i.e., 1,200 × $.95), and $1,110 at the $.925 price.

Using the table, we note that minimum total procurement cost for a

usage value of $1,200 per year is $1,276. This minimum is achieved
with a three-month order quantity (i.e., 300 units per order).

With a usage value of $1.140, we must order at least five months'
supply (500 units) to get the $.95 price. Looking at the table, we see
that total procurement cost is $1,221 with five months' supply and higher
still if we have bigger orders. Similarly, to get the $.925 price and
$1,110 annual usage, we must order ten months' supply at the minimum.
In this case, the student can readily calculate a total annual procurement
cost of $1,233. Obviously it pays to buy in lots of 500 at a unit price of
$.95.

Making E.O.Q. Fit the Budget

So far, we have dealt only with the applications of E.O.Q. formulas to
individual items. They also can be useful tools for top-management control of over-all inventory levels.

Suppose that you are a materials manager, and at a meeting of your
company's executive committee it is agreed that inventories should be reduced by 10 per cent. Your company is short of cash or the committee
feels that sales and earnings will drop off sharply in coming months. If
you were an "old-style" materials manager, you might have your staff
review every item in stock to see where stocks could be reduced by ordering more frequently, or you might even make rather arbitrary cuts in
safety stocks and order quantities.

E.O.Q. formulas permit a more analytical approach. What, in effect,
has management decided when it makes a decision to cut inventories? In
the economist's jargon, its liquidity preference has increased. It has
raised the interest rate on which it bases its investment decisions. This
means that the inventory carrying cost in the E.O.Q. formulas should be
increased to reflect this higher "cost" for the use of the company's capital.

Suppose inventory is $1,200,000, including a $200,000 safety stock.
Management wants a 10 per cent (or $120,000) reduction without any
change in safety stock. This means that the average inventory due to
order quantity must be reduced from $1,000,000 to $880,000. It's easy
to determine our new carrying cost. From our formulas, we know that
order quantity varies inversely with the square root of carrying cost
(CC). We also know that our average inventory exclusive of safety
stock (AI) is determined by order quantity. Therefore,

$$\sqrt{\frac{CC_1}{CC_2}} = \frac{AI_2}{AI_1}.$$

Substituting,

$$\sqrt{\frac{16}{CC_2}} = \frac{880,000}{1,000,000},$$

and

$$CC_2 = 20.6\%.$$

The new inventory policy can be carried out by using a 20.6 per cent carrying cost in calculating order quantities instead of a 16 per cent cost. The new carrying cost should be used in calculating economic order quantity for all *new* stock items. There is no need to recalculate for items where E.O.Q. was already figured with a carrying cost of 16 per cent. As the calculations above demonstrate, the E.O.Q. for the new carrying cost is 80 per cent of that for the old.

Weaknesses of E.O.Q. Formulas

Many E.O.Q. formulas have been devised and thousands of hours have been invested in research to improve them. Nevertheless, few companies depend entirely on E.O.Q. formulas to determine order quantities, and some very successful firms don't use them at all. The formulas discussed can be extremely useful when used properly, but they also have serious limitations, due to:

1. *Erratic Usages.* The formulas we have used assume that usage of material is both predictable and evenly distributed. When this is not the case, the formulas are useless. Different, far more complex formulas can be developed for wide swings in usage, so long as those swings can be predicted. But if usage varies unpredictably, as it often does, no formula will work well.

2. *Faulty Basic Information.* Economic order quantity calculations are only as accurate as the order-cost and carrying-cost information on which they are based. It is no easy job to calculate average order cost, and in practice the actual order cost varies from commodity to commodity.[8] Carrying cost, as we have seen, can vary with the company's opportunity cost for capital. Both carrying-cost and order-cost calculations include elements of fixed and nonvariable costs that would be incurred over the short term regardless of the procurement actions taken.[9]

Consideration of fixed and nonvariable costs can result in two different economic order quantities, one for short-term inventory management and another for long term. The former takes account only of cash-out-of-pocket costs in calculating costs of possession and acquisition. The later includes fixed and nonvariable costs. For example, a company's total cost of ordering may be $10 and total carrying cost may be 24 per cent. But its cash-out-of-pocket costs may be only $2 and 8 per cent respec-

---

[8] An order for an engineered component requiring special handling would, for example, cost far more than an order for an off-the-shelf maintenance item.

[9] For example, included in a $10 order cost might be an allowance of 40 cents for the share of the purchasing agent's salary that would be allocated to that order. Theoretically, if the company can eliminate an order its costs should be 40 cents lower. But, in practice, the purchasing agent's salary would not vary with the number of orders issued; he would be needed even if the company were to reduce its orders (by buying more) 50 per cent to 75 per cent. Therefore, at least 40 cents (plus all other fixed costs) of the $10 order cost is incurred regardless of whether the order is actually placed or not.

tively. Naturally, use of out-of-pocket costs in the formulas gives answers that indicate economic order quantities different from those that result when total costs are used. Which answer is the right one? There is no general agreement on this. However, many cost accountants would say that total costs should be used when one is developing an over-all, long-term inventory control program, while out-of-pocket costs give a more realistic economic order quantity when the formulas are being applied to individual purchases on a short-term or one-shot basis.

3. Costly Calculations. It is no easy job to estimate accurately cost of acquisition and cost of possession. It requires hours of work by skilled cost accountants. Unfortunately, each major commodity group requires a different study, since the acquisition and possession costs of various commodities can vary widely. Actual calculation of economic order quantities can be time-consuming even when the simple formulas for steady usage (discussed earlier) are used.[10] More elaborate formulas are even more expensive. In many cases, the cost of estimating cost of possession and acquisition and calculating economic order quantity greatly exceeds the savings made by buying the E.O.Q. Also, savings often are reduced because the company cannot buy the exact economic order quantity. If the E.O.Q. is 176 units, for example, it may have to buy the closest round lot—e.g., 2 gross, or 288 units.

Applications of E.O.Q.

Despite their weaknesses, economic order quantities can be applied to at least part of the purchases of almost every organization. They are particularly useful in companies equipped with electronic data-processing equipment, which can eliminate much of the burden of calculations and also enables the use of more complex formulas.

E.O.Q. formulas are particularly suitable for materials that have:

1. Reasonably Steady and Predictable Usage. For example, a large insurance company with a stable work force and work load could profitably use E.O.Q. formulas to buy supplies. But E.O.Q. formulas would not be too useful in ordering materials for which demand is erratic.

2. Relatively Low Cost. A manufacturer might profitably use E.O.Q. for thousands of different supply and maintenance items, which, in the aggregate, account for 10 or 15 per cent of his purchases. But he would almost never use it for one or two key raw materials that might account for 50 per cent of purchase volume. The high-volume items would get individual attention daily, and order quantities would reflect not only objective information (existing inventories, balances on order, etc.) but also subjective opinions on market sentiment, price expectations, and the like. Also, if a material is purchased in large quantities, it often is

---

[10] If a company's inventory records are kept on a computer, cost of computing economic order quantity can be reduced drastically. However, detailed study is still needed to determine carrying cost and order cost.

best controlled if regarded as a flow of material rather than as a series of separate order transactions. It thus becomes suitable for a periodic ordering system. The E.O.Q. approach does not apply, since with periodic ordering the order quantity varies while the review period between orders is kept constant.

3. Short Lead Time. E.O.Q. formulas are best applied when there is little uncertainty about delivery promises. When lead time is long and delivery is less certain, the order quantity should be adjusted to reflect the materials manager's evaluation of the situation. For example, a company might wish to use E.O.Q. formulas in ordering steel from a local warehouse that offers overnight delivery. But few companies would use E.O.Q. formulas in ordering large quantities of steel directly from mills with a lead time of two to three months.

DETERMINING SAFETY STOCK

Average inventory levels are affected almost as much by safety stock as they are by order quantity. Safety stocks are necessary because it is not always possible to predict usages and lead times perfectly.

Figure 10–2 shows a year's usage for a typical item. Total usage for

Demand By Weeks for a Purchased Inventory Item

Week	Demand	Week	Demand	Week	Demand	Week	Demand
1	7	14	6	27	7	40	12
2	16	15	8	28	10	41	10
3	5	16	7	29	11	42	9
4	9	17	5	30	4	43	11
5	13	18	9	31	9	44	14
6	8	19	11	32	7	45	6
7	9	20	6	33	10	46	10
8	1	21	10	34	8	47	12
9	10	22	7	35	11	48	7
10	7	23	11	36	6	49	13
11	8	24	13	37	12	50	11
12	5	25	8	38	8	51	6
13	9	26	9	39	14	52	13

FIG. 10–2.

the year was 468 units, or an average of 9 units per week. Actual weekly usage ranged erratically from a low of 1 unit per week during the eighth week of the year to a peak of 14 units during the 44th week.

Lead time for this item is five weeks, so the order point would be 45 units (the average usage during the lead time) were there no safety stock.

With a safety stock of 8 units, the order point would be 53 units. With this safety stock, as Figure 10–3 shows, there may have been one stockout during the year.

Applying Probability Theory

Probability of future stockouts with given safety stocks can be determined by analyzing usage history. The first step is to convert the number of weeks' usage into percentages, that is, one week's usage is about 2 per cent of a year's usage, two weeks' is about 4 per cent, three weeks' is 6 per cent, and so on. The next step is to make a chart in which one axis represents the demand in units and the other axis the per cent of weeks in which there was this demand.

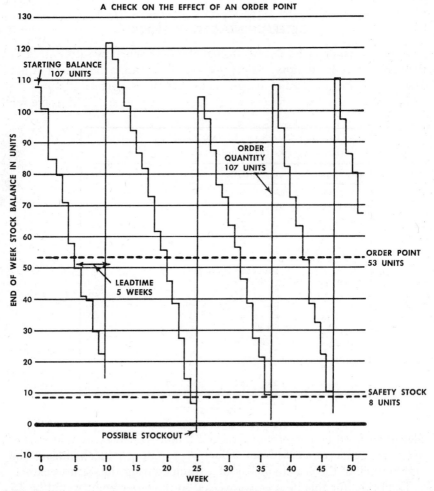

FIG. 10–3. Inventory history of an item with the usage shown in Fig. 10–2, a lead time of five weeks, an order point of 53 units, and a safety stock of 8 units.

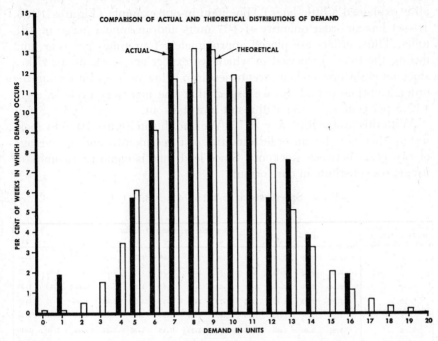

FIG. 10–4. Comparison of actual distribution of demand for an item having the usage history illustrated in Fig. 10–2 with theoretical distribution based on Poisson distribution.

Figure 10–4 shows a chart for the data listed in Figure 10–3. Since one unit of usage occurred during a single week of the year, the chart shows, for example, one unit being used for 2 per cent of the year. When the actual data is plotted like this, the result closely resembles a Poisson distribution,[11] which also is illustrated in Figure 10–4. If we assume that the demand can be measured by the theoretical Poisson curve, we then can accurately determine the probability of stockout with various safety stocks from statistical tables. We use the following formula:

$$\text{Safety stock} = K\sqrt{\text{Average demand during lead time}}$$

All factors in the formula except K are obvious. We get K from various standard tables of normal distribution. Figure 10–5 illustrates K values for most situations.

Using the Poisson Distribution. Let us assume that we are willing to run out of stock once every two years (why we want to take any risk at

---

[11] Since this is not a text on statistics or statistical inventory control, the reader without formal training in these subjects will have to use the tables and formulas presented in this chapter without fully understanding them. Those who have studied statistics can determine how the formulas and tables are derived by referring to E. C. Molina's *Poisson's Exponential Binomial Limit* (New York: D. Van Nostrand, 1942) as well as tables of normal distribution in any standard book of statistical tables.

all is explained a little later). The item in our example (Figures 10–3, 10–4) has an order quantity of 107 units and an annual usage of 468 units. Thus, orders are placed approximately four times per year, and during the two-year period in which we expect one stockout we risk a stockout eight times when inventories drop below order point during the order lead-time period. So we expect that one inventory cycle in eight (12.5 per cent, or .125) will result in a stockout.

With this probability, $K = 1.15$. We find this in Figure 10–5 by looking up the value for an order quantity of three months and an average of two years between stockouts. Since lead time is equal to 45 units of usage, we substitute in our formula

$$\text{Safety stock} = 1.15\sqrt{45} = 8.$$

Acceptable Average Number of Years Between Stockouts	ORDER QUANTITY IN MONTHS' SUPPLY											
	1	2	3	4	5	6	7	8	9	10	11	12
20	2.64	2.39	2.24	2.13	2.04	1.96	1.89	1.83	1.78	1.73	1.69	1.64
15	2.54	2.29	2.13	2.01	1.92	1.83	1.76	1.70	1.64	1.59	1.55	1.50
12	2.46	2.20	2.04	1.92	1.82	1.73	1.66	1.59	1.53	1.48	1.43	1.38
10	2.39	2.13	1.96	1.83	1.73	1.64	1.57	1.50	1.44	1.38	1.33	1.28
9	2.36	2.09	1.92	1.79	1.68	1.59	1.52	1.45	1.38	1.33	1.27	1.22
8	2.31	2.04	1.86	1.73	1.63	1.53	1.45	1.38	1.32	1.26	1.20	1.15
7	2.26	1.98	1.80	1.67	1.56	1.47	1.38	1.31	1.24	1.18	1.12	1.07
6	2.20	1.92	1.73	1.59	1.48	1.38	1.30	1.22	1.15	1.09	1.02	0.97
5	2.13	1.83	1.64	1.50	1.38	1.28	1.19	1.11	1.04	0.97	0.90	0.84
4	2.04	1.73	1.53	1.38	1.26	1.15	1.05	0.97	0.89	0.81	0.74	0.67
3	1.92	1.59	1.38	1.22	1.09	0.97	0.86	0.76	0.67	0.59	0.51	0.43
2	1.73	1.38	1.15	0.97	0.81	0.67	0.55	0.43	0.32	0.21	0.10	0
1	1.38	0.97	0.67	0.43	0.21	0	0	0	0	0	0	0

FIG. 10–5. *K factors used to calculate the safety stock needed to provide various levels of protection against stockout for items whose usage pattern is similar to a Poisson distribution.*

With a safety stock of 8 units, our order point becomes 45 + 8, or 53 units.

Cost of a Stockout. Whether or not 8 units is really the correct safety stock depends on whether or not we can afford to run out of stock once every two years. To find this out, we must determine the cost of the safety stock. If each unit is worth $100, then our safety stock increases inventory by $800. If carrying cost is 24 per cent, the safety stock costs $192 per year to maintain. We could, by similar calculations, determine the protection against stockout and cost of other safety stocks. For example, we could reduce probability of stockouts to one in every twenty years with a safety stock of 15 units. This would cost $350 a year to maintain.

Which is the right safety stock? It depends on the cost of the stockout, and that in turn depends on both intangible and tangible factors. Each company must study the variables and calculate its own costs. If a stock-out costs only a few hours of expediting time to persuade a supplier to shorten lead time by a few days, it obviously pays to keep safety stocks low. If, on the other hand, it means loss of business on an important contract, it may pay to carry very high safety stocks. Materials managers should also consider the profitability of the item and its effect on over-all production and customer good will when they estimate their willingness to risk a stockout.

In general, managements tend to overprotect themselves against stock-outs. All too often they are unwilling to accept the idea that if they want tight inventory control they must be willing to risk an occasional stock-out. It takes a courageous materials manager to risk running out of stock when he knows it pays to take the risk. When the stockout does occur, his boss is all too likely to think only of the immediate loss and forget the enormous gains that come from low safety stocks and close control.

Application to ABC Control

Probability theory can be applied to ABC systems of control. Representative "A," "B," and "C" items are selected. Then cost of various levels of protection can be calculated, using our formula for safety stock, the table of K factors in Figure 10–5, the value of the item, and the carrying cost. Costs of each item can be averaged to get a representative cost of a certain level of protection for the inventory class. Each calculation is then plotted and the final result is a chart resembling that in Figure 10–6, which is based on a carrying cost of 24 per cent.

Note in Figure 10–6 that if management decides it is willing to risk a stockout once every five years on all items in inventory, it incurs the following costs:

STOCKOUT ONCE EVERY FIVE YEARS

	Investment in Safety Stock	Carrying Cost of Safety Stock
"A" items	$ 620,000	$148,800
"B" items	450,000	108,000
"C" items	320,000	76,800
Total	$1,390,000	$333,600

With the ABC approach it is possible to get both greater over-all protection against stockouts and lower carrying costs. For example, suppose that management is willing to accept the risk of a stockout once a year on "A" items, once every five years on "B" items, and once every ten years on "C" items. Using Figure 10–6, we see that the following costs will be incurred:

	Probable Interval between Stockouts	*Investment in Safety Stock*	*Carrying Cost of Safety Stock*
"A" items........... 1 year(s)		$ 250,000	$ 60,000
"B" items........... 5		450,000	108,000
"C" items...........10		390,000	93,600
Total......................		$1,090,000	$261,600

In this case, the ABC approach permits inventories to be reduced by $300,000 (from $1,390,000 to $1,090,000) and carrying costs are cut by $72,000 per year. Risk of stockout also is reduced. Protection on

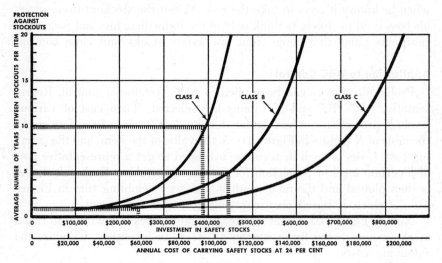

FIG. 10–6.

"C" items, which comprise 70 per cent of the number of items in inventory, is doubled. Protection on "B" items is unchanged. Only the "A" items, comprising 10 per cent of the total, are more vulnerable to stockout. Since these items get close control anyway—because they require 70 per cent of the inventory investment—their low safety stocks need not pose insurmountable problems.

FORECASTING DEMAND

As has been pointed out, safety stocks are needed because of errors in forecasting demand during the lead time. If forecasts were perfect, there would be no need for safety stocks. Consequently one effective way of cutting inventories and safety stocks is by improving forecasts of demand. With conventional order-point systems of inventory control, demand is usually determined by analyzing past usage. This was done, for example, when it was found that the usage during the lead time of the item in Figure 10–3 was 45 units.

This approach works well provided there are no significant changes in usage during the lead time. But, as we saw in Chapter 9, this system of determining demand is inflexible. If there is a major change in usage, the result is either a series of stockouts or excess inventories.

There has been considerable research in statistical techniques to make inventory control systems more responsive to changes in demand.[12] These techniques are becoming more widely used as computers and other data-processing equipment take over the job of making the long, tedious arithmetical calculations that they require. The two most widely used techniques of adjusting order-point quantities to reflect changes in demand are moving averages and exponential smoothing.

The Moving Average

Moving averages permit usage figures to be brought up to date at regular intervals so that order quantities will reflect the latest changes in demand. For example, a company might use a four-week moving average to measure demand. Each week a new average demand is calculated as follows:

Week No.	Usage	4-Week Average
1	10	
2	11	
3	12	
4	11	11
5	14	12
6	14	12.75
7	16	13.75

With the moving average, demand gradually changes to reflect current usage. Each week's demand is weighted equally. The weight given current usage depends on the span of the moving average. For example, a four-week moving average is more sensitive to current demand than an eight-week average. On the other hand, an eight-week average is more likely to smooth out short-term random fluctuations that are not significant.

Moving averages always lag behind current usage. In addition, they present programing problems when used with electronic data-processing equipment. For these reasons, many companies have adopted exponential smoothing techniques to measure demand.

Exponential Smoothing

With exponential smoothing, current usage is weighted more heavily than past usage in forecasting demand. Exponential smoothing is easy

---

[12] These techniques are discussed in some detail in Robert G. Brown's *Statistical Forecasting for Inventory Control* (New York: McGraw-Hill Book Co., Inc., 1959).

to apply. One merely updates the previous demand or usage average by a fraction called A. The formula is:

New average = Old average + A (Current demand − Old average).

For example, suppose that we forecast a demand of 80 units for the week and actual usage was 90 units. If we use a value of 0.1 for the constant A, then our new average equals $80 + 0.1 \ (90 − 80) = 81$. If demand drops the following week to 71 units, then the new average equals $81 + 0.1 \ (71 − 81) = 80$ units.

Note that the value of the constant A determines the effect of current demand on the new average. For example, a constant of 0.1 gives results close to those obtained with a nineteen-period moving average, while a constant of 0.5 is the equivalent of a three-period moving average.

Change in Trend.   The exponential smoothing formula used above lags behind actual demand. To correct for lag due to trend, it is necessary first to measure the change in trend. Our formula is: Current trend = New average − Old average. We can use exponential smoothing to measure the average trend just as we did for the demand itself.

New trend = A (Current trend) + $(1 − A)$ Old trend.

Then,

Expected demand = New average + $\dfrac{(1 − A)}{A}$ New trend.

To see how the formulas are applied, let us assume that averages have been increasing by two units per period. In the current period, they have increased by just one unit (from 80 units to 81 units). To calculate the new trend we substitute: New trend = A (Current trend) + $(1 − A)$ Old trend = $0.1 \ (1) + (1 − 0.1) \ 2 = 1.9$ units; and Expected demand = New average + $(1 − A)/A$ (New trend) = $81 + 0.9/0.1 \ (1.9) = 98.1$ units.

To use this forecast of demand to set an order point, we must first project the demand through the lead time. For example, if lead time is four weeks and the expected demand is 98.1 units, then the demand during the lead time will be 4×98.1 units, or 392 units. To take trend into account in the lead-time forecast, we use the following formula:

Lead time expected demand

$$= \frac{\text{Lead time (Lead time} + 1) \ (\text{New trend})}{2} + \text{Expected demand}$$

$$= \frac{4 \times 5}{2} \ (1.9) + 98.1 = 117 \text{ units.}$$

Our actual order point is equal to 117 units plus a safety stock that allows for uncertainties of demand (which may be calculated by applying the Poisson distribution discussed earlier in this chapter).

Limitations. Exponential smoothing is not a perfect technique for forecasting demand. Like other statistical techniques, it is based on past demand and obviously cannot allow for new and unpredicted changes in demand. In addition, it may help increase inventories because, as was demonstrated in our example, small shifts in weekly demand can be magnified into substantial shifts in order points when trend is taken into account. Despite its weaknesses, however, exponential smoothing is an excellent technique, especially when used in conjunction with electronic data processing to control order points of thousands of low-value "C" items.

CONTROL OF PERIODIC ORDERING

Quantitative techniques for controlling periodic ordering systems are similar to those used in order-point systems. Both compare cost of acquisi-

Month	Demand	Month	Demand	Month	Demand
1	6	9	0	17	5
2	2	10	3	18	6
3	4	11	7	19	5
4	6	12	9	20	8
5	12	13	7	21	9
6	5	14	3	22	4
7	6	15	9	23	3
8	8	16	10	24	7

FIG. 10–7. Monthly demand for a typical purchased item controlled with a periodic ordering system.

tion with cost of possession. The major difference is that order-point systems are governed by order quantities while periodic systems are governed by order review periods.

Figure 10–7 shows monthly demand for a purchased inventory item over a two-year period. During this period, total demand was 144 units and average monthly demand was 6 units. If the item were controlled by periodic ordering with a review period of two months and procurement lead time was one month, inventories would fluctuate as shown in Figure 10–8. A month prior to Month 1, we would have ordered 8 units —the requirements for Months 2 and 3. At the beginning of Month 2, we would order for Months 3 and 4, and so on.

Let us assume that the unit price of the item is $20, that our ordering cost is $10, and carrying cost is 24 per cent. Annual ordering cost would then be $60 (six orders per year at $10 an order). Average order quantity is 12 units and average inventory is half that, or 6 units. The value of the average inventory is $120 (6 units at $20 each). Annual cost of carrying this inventory is $28.80 (24 per cent of $120).

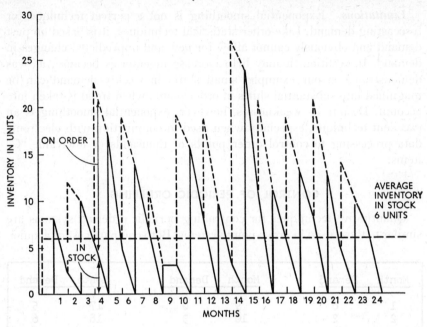

FIG. 10–8. Inventory fluctuations of the item with the demand shown in Fig. 10–7, lead time of one month, and review period of two months.

Total annual cost that would be affected by the review period is equal to the total ordering costs plus the review costs, or $60 + $28.80 = $88.80.

Optimum Review Period. If we calculate order costs and carrying costs for a series of review periods and plot them, we get a chart resembling that in Figure 10–9. Our optimum review period is one with minimum total carrying cost. Figure 10–9 indicates that a review period of three months is ideal for the item in our example. We also can develop a formula to determine optimum review period, which is equal to the minimum value of order cost plus carrying cost. The cost of ordering equals $12\ S/T$ and the cost of carrying inventory equals $TACI/24$ where:

T = Review period (in months).
S = Variable cost of ordering (in dollars).
A = Annual usage (in units).
C = Unit cost (in dollars).
I = Annual carrying cost (as a decimal).

Minimum cost of ordering plus cost of carrying inventory can be determined by differential calculus, resulting in the formula:

$$T = \sqrt{288\ S/ACI}$$

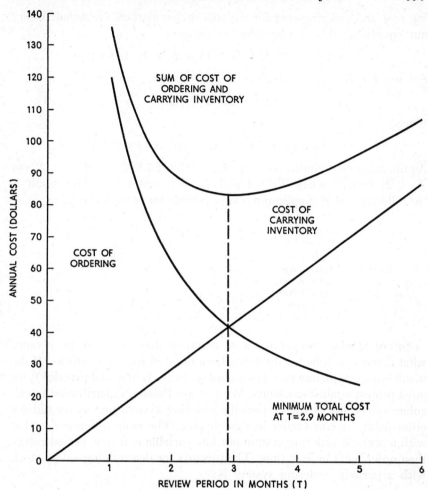

FIG. 10–9. Optimum review period can be determined graphically by plotting total annual cost (purchase cost + ordering cost + carrying cost) for various review periods. It is just under three months for an item with annual usage of 72 units, unit price of $20, ordering cost of $10, and carrying cost of 24 per cent.

Using the data in our example, $S = \$10$, $I = 0.24$, $A = 72$, and $C = \$20$. Therefore $T = (288 \times 10)/(72 \times 20 \times 0.24) = 2.9$ months, which is consistent with our graphic solution.

The optimum review period for an item can change. When sales are high, order quantities will be raised and average inventories will increase. If there is enough change, it may be necessary to reduce the review period between orders so as to have optimum costs. Similarly, the optimum review period is increased when sales fall. The point at which it pays to change can easily be calculated. Let us assume that we have two review periods, T_1 and T_2. The point of change comes when carrying cost and ordering cost for the two review periods are equal. Using our equations, this can be done as follows:

$$12 \ S/T_1 + T_1 \ ACI/24 = 12 \ S/T_2 + T_2 \ ACI/24.$$

Solving for AC, with the data in our example, we get:

$$AC = 288 \ S/T_1 T_2 I.$$

Since

$$S = \$10 \quad \text{and} \quad I = 0.24, \quad \text{then} \quad AC = 12000/T_1 T_2.$$

Again using the data in our example, $AC = \$6,000$ when $T_1 = 1$ and $T_2 = 2$; $\$2,000$ when $T_1 = 2$ and $T_2 = 3$; and so on. The result is the following table of optimum review periods for values of AC:

Value of Annual Use	Review Period
$6,001–Up	1 month(s)
2,001–6,000	2
1,001–2,000	3
601–1,000	4
401–600	5
Up to 400	6

Safety Stocks. So far we have assumed that we know in advance what demand will be, so there has been no need for safety stocks. If demand is uncertain, however (as it almost always is in actual practice), we must protect against stockouts. We can use Poisson's distribution to calculate safety stocks with a periodic ordering system just as we did for order-point systems earlier in this chapter. The main difference is that with a periodic ordering system our key variable is review period rather than order point or lead time. The formula for determining safety stock with a periodic ordering system is:

$$\text{Safety stock} = K \sqrt{\begin{array}{l}\text{Average usage during} \\ \text{lead time} + \\ \text{Review period}\end{array}} \times \text{Average size of demand.}$$

Returning to the example illustrated in Figures 10–7 and 10–8, demand averages six units per month and lead time is one month. If we use a review period of three months, average demand during lead time plus review period is 24 units. From Figure 10–5, we see that K is 1.96 if we want to risk one stockout every 10 years. Then, if all the demands are each one unit, we can substitute in our formula:

$$\text{Safety stock} = 1.96\sqrt{24} \times 1 = 10 \text{ units.}$$

Our order quantity then is equal to the safety stock of 10 units plus the average demand during the lead time plus the review period of 10 units *less* whatever units are available in stock at the time each order is being placed. Figure 10–10 shows how this system would have oper-

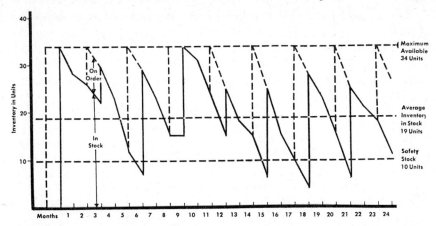

FIG. 10–10. Inventory history of an item with usage history shown in Fig. 10–7, review period of three months, and order quantities equal to 34 units less whatever stock is already on hand when the order is placed.

ated during the past two years, using a maximum of 34 (10 + 24) units.

CASES

CASE 10–1.   QUEENSTOWN CHEMICAL COMPANY (*cont.*)

REDUCING INVENTORIES 15 PER CENT

The inventory-reduction program instituted at Queenstown Chemical (see Case 8–1, p. 150) has been only moderately successful. Nonproduction inventories have been cut to $800,000 and production inventories are down to $5,800,000. Usage continues at the previous level of $100,-000 per month for nonproduction material and $2,000,000 per month for production material.

Both production and nonproduction inventories are controlled with order-point systems. Economic ordering quantity formulas assume reasonably constant usages. They are based on a carrying cost of 15 per cent per annum for production materials and 20 per cent per annum for nonproduction materials. Ordering cost is assumed to be $25 and $10 respectively.

Approximately 30 per cent of the average investment in production and nonproduction materials is represented by safety stocks. There are about 15 stockouts per year with the 7,000 items carried in nonproduction inventories. There were only three stockouts for the 2,700 different items carried in production inventories. John Wilson, Queenstown's controller, estimates that the average marginal cost of a stockout in nonproduction materials is no more than $25, while a stockout of production material may cost $200 or more (depending on the price assigned to lost good will should the stockout delay delivery to a customer).

The marginal carrying cost for production material is probably no more than 7 per cent per year and that for nonproduction material no more than 10 per cent. Marginal ordering cost is probably $5 and $4 respectively. Queenstown's executive committee has asked Mr. Mead, the director of purchases, to cut over-all inventory investment by an additional 15 per cent.

Question

What program can you suggest for Mr. Mead to carry out the executive committee's request?

CASE 10–2.   OWEN ELECTRIC COMPANY

APPLYING FORMULAS TO PERIODIC ORDERING SYSTEMS

Owen Electric (see Case 7–2, page 134) controls inventories of hardware used on its assembly line with periodic ordering. Weekly reports from stock checkers are sent to appropriate buyers, who post them to their records and periodically issue orders to bring stocks up to the required balance.

For example, the company uses about 10,000 pieces of a small screw machine part each month. On the 15th of each month, the buyer looks at his latest stock report and issues an order for a quantity sufficient to bring the inventory balance up to about 15,000 pieces when the order is delivered. Thus, if the stock checker's report indicates an inventory of 12,000 pieces and estimated usage during the 30-day lead time is 10,-000 pieces, the buyer will place an order for 13,000 pieces. Should the next month's inventory rise or the usage forecast drop, he would adjust the order quantity accordingly. For example, he would order only 9,000 pieces with a 30-day usage projection for 8,000 pieces and a current stock of 14,000 pieces.

The unit price of the part purchased in quantities of 5,000 to 10,000 is $.10. But the supplier is willing to cut the price to $.095 if he gets orders that average 20,000 pieces. Owen Electric's controller estimates that it costs $10 to make each purchase and the carrying cost of inventory is 24 per cent.

Questions

1. Should Owen Electric take advantage of the supplier's offer?
2. What is the company's most economic order period if the supplier's price does not vary with order quantity?

Chapter 11

SOURCING: MAKE, BUY, OR LEASE

Theoretically, a company has a choice of three basic decisions in sourcing a new product. It can:

1. Purchase the product complete from a contract manufacturer.
2. Purchase some components and materials, and manufacture and assemble the balance in its own plant.
3. Manufacture the product completely, starting with the extraction of basic raw materials.

In practice, almost no companies can seriously consider the third alternative. Even relatively simple products require an amazing diversity of materials in various stages of fabrication. Even the largest, most highly integrated companies rely on outside suppliers for at least some components and materials.[1] And some companies choose the first alternative and obtain a new product completely from an outside supplier. They usually do this either because they are a merchandising or engineering organization with no manufacturing facilities or because the product is not suited to their facilities. Sears, Roebuck's purchases of its own brands of appliances are a good example of the former; a business-machine maker's purchase and resale to customers of special forms to use in its machines is an example of the latter.

The general rule, however, is that a company will make certain components of its product and buy others. Since few companies make their own raw materials, this becomes a matter of deciding at which stage of fabrication a component should be purchased. The company may buy a component complete from an outside supplier, buy it semifinished, or buy the raw material.

MAKE-OR-BUY CRITERIA

Companies usually prefer to do their own fabricating and buy only raw materials or semifinished parts in cases where the following is true of the finished component:

---

[1] For example, the U.S. Steel Corporation spends about a third of its sales dollar for outside purchases, even though it has completely integrated steel-making facilities and also mines its iron ore, coal, and limestone. The Ford Motor Company makes all major parts of its automobiles and much of the raw materials used in making them, including steel, glass, and so on. Yet Ford spends about half of its sales dollar on outside suppliers—more than twice as much as it spends on wages and salaries.

1. Can be made more cheaply by the company than by outside suppliers, or might require the company to rely on a limited number of vendors for its supply.
2. Is vital to the company's product and requires extremely close quality control.
3. Is readily manufactured with the company's existing facilities and is similar to other items with which the company has had considerable manufacturing experience.
4. Requires extensive investment in facilities that are not already available at supplier plants.
5. Has a demand that is both relatively large and stable.

Companies will usually buy a finished component from an outside supplier when:

1. They do not already have facilities to make it and there are more profitable opportunities for investing company capital.
2. Existing facilities can be used more economically to make other components.
3. The skills of company personnel are not readily adapted to making the component.
4. Patents or other legal barriers prevent the company from making the component.
5. Demand for the component is either temporary or seasonal.

Other Factors. Some companies, by tradition, prefer to make almost every component of their products. Others prefer to buy as much as possible from outside suppliers. In general, an aggressive company in an industry that is expanding very rapidly with many technological changes (e.g., electronics) will prefer to buy many of its components from outside suppliers. In such industries, the company has many opportunities to employ its capital profitably through horizontal diversification—expanding its line of finished products.

A company in a stable or declining industry, on the other hand, has fewer attractive opportunities to invest its capital in expanding sales of its end products. It will be attracted, almost by default, to integration—making a bigger share of its sales dollar in its own manufacturing plants—in order to boost profits.

For example, the major auto companies have steadily increased the percentage of product that they make in their own plants. In most cases, they have been tempted to make themselves the items that yielded high profits to suppliers. In recent years, both the Ford Motor Company and the Chrysler Corporation have built plants to manufacture automobile windshield glass. But it is no coincidence that neither company has shown any intention of building textile mills to make upholstery cloth for cars. Efficient glass producers earn about a 20 per cent return on their investment, while in the highly competitive textile industry even efficient producers consider themselves fortunate if they average a 10 per cent return on their investment.

Cost Comparison. When a company decides to make an item that it has been buying, it always eliminates the supplier's sales expenses and usually eliminates in-bound freight. If its production costs are identical to those of the supplier,[2] it also gains the supplier's profit and usually at least part of the fixed overhead expenses incurred by the supplier.

Suppose a supplier had the following unit costs on a component:

Direct material............................	$.20	
Direct labor................................	.10	
Variable overhead.........................	.12	
Direct cost..............................		$.42
Fixed overhead............................	$.08	
Manufacturing cost......................		.50
Sales expense.............................	$.02	
Administrative expense....................	.01	
Total cost.............................		.53
Profit....................................	$.06	
Supplier's price..........................		.59
In-bound freight..........................	$.01	
Buyer's cost...........................		$.60

If a company were to make this item rather than buy it, it could conceivably reduce its cost from $.60 per unit to $.42. This might be true if the company has idle equipment that could be used to make the part and if its only additional overhead expenses would be covered by the $.12 allowance for variable overhead in the unit-cost estimate. Even if the company had to invest in additional facilities and incur the normal fixed expenses, its cost would presumably be only $.50 per unit if it could use the facilities as economically as a supplier.

Savings Sometimes Illusory. Companies often are confronted with opportunities to make rather than buy that yield theoretical savings comparable to these. In some cases, they try to take advantage of them. But in most cases, they continue to buy the item even though they may be capable of making it. Why? The answer is that it isn't to their advantage to make the item for a number of reasons, including:

(1) The company's direct cost might be substantially higher than the direct costs of the supplier. The supplier presumably is one of the most efficient producers of the item and has achieved his existing costs only after management and labor had acquired considerable experience. And even if the buyer can produce as efficiently as the supplier, his saving will be reduced by start-up cost. No company can immediately produce a new item at peak efficiency; costs on initial production runs are always well above standard.

(2) A company has less flexibility with "make" items. It can easily change suppliers if it wishes to redesign the item so that it makes use

---

[2] Of course, few suppliers will give their customers detailed cost estimates, particularly if they think the buyer plans to use them for a make-or-buy study. However, it sometimes is possible for a buyer to estimate supplier cost quite accurately, using techniques discussed in Chapter 16.

of different materials. This can be expensive if the company has invested in equipment to make the item. Similarly, the company can exploit changes in market conditions on "buy" items and take advantage of lower prices offered by suppliers eager for new business.

(3) Savings in overhead often are illusory. Fixed overhead rarely rises immediately after a company starts using idle facilities to make a part it has previously purchased. But eventually overhead creeps up. When business expands to capacity operations, fixed overhead increases and must be absorbed by each component that is produced. Similarly, if business slumps, fixed overhead is underabsorbed and unit cost rises. For example, the $.08 allowance for fixed overhead in the preceding cost breakdown is valid only for a given volume. If business dropped 50 per cent, the allowance would have to be doubled, to $.16. If the part is purchased from an outside supplier, he also would have difficulty absorbing fixed overhead.[3] But he wouldn't dare to recoup the added unit costs by increasing prices. In fact, competition might become so intense during a slump that he would be forced to cut prices.

(4) There may be better profit opportunities in other areas. Each "make" part requires some investment in facilities, inventories, and top-management time. Even though this investment is profitable, the company may be able to earn even bigger profits by using its resources to expand the business it knows best—its end-product line.

Buy Instead of Make.   Often companies decide to buy items that they have been making. In some cases they even dispose of plant and equipment used to make the item. Such decisions are almost always economic if the supplier's price is lower than the company's direct cash cost of making the part.[4] Sometimes they are worthwhile even if the company has been making substantial profits on the item, for it may be able to use its resources still more profitably on other items.

Similarly, when a company's facilities are temporarily taxed beyond capacity, it may decide to buy part of its needs from an outside supplier. For example, a company with a captive foundry may temporarily buy part of its castings from outside suppliers when business is exceptionally good. Even if the prices of the purchased castings are higher than the company's own costs, the company may not wish to increase its investment in foundry facilities when the need for them may be temporary. When business drops off, the company can return to making all its own castings and need no longer rely on an outside supplier.

Companies that follow this practice may incur the resentment of sup-

---

[3] If the supplier successfully diversifies his business, he might not be badly hurt if customers in a single industry have a bad year. For example, a manufacturer of fasteners might supply dozens of industries. If business from one industry dropped off but other industries suffered no setbacks, the effect on the fastener supplier might be insignificant.

[4] Provided that the supplier's price isn't just a temporary bid to get the business and won't be increased at some later date.

pliers who get orders from them when business is good and they need them least and then lose the orders when business is bad and they need them most. Suppliers may not co-operate when the company wants to subcontract again.[5] In addition, their ill will may have an adverse effect on the company's sales. Either the supplier may also be a customer, or he may "knock" the company and its products to his own suppliers and customers. Ethical materials managers never try to convince suppliers that business is permanent when they know it will move back into the shop as soon as capacity is available to handle it.

Split Items. A company may simultaneously make and buy certain materials and components. For example, the Ford Motor Company makes about half the windshields for Ford cars in its own glass plant and buys the other half from the Pittsburgh Plate Glass Company. When a company does this, it enjoys most of the advantages of making without losing the advantages of buying. Its profits from making the item can be calculated precisely because there is an exact market price from the outside supplier. The company is protected at least partly against strikes at the supplier's plant or other supply failures. It enjoys the benefits of both its own and the supplier's improvements in technology. In addition, when a company has its own facilities to make an item, a supplier may hesitate to increase prices because his costs of production can be precisely estimated and the captive plant stands ready to take a bigger share of the business if it becomes profitable to do so.

A company often can reduce its average costs by buying part of its requirements and making the balance. The captive facility then can operate near capacity almost regardless of business conditions. When business is good, the supplier may make 50 per cent and the captive plant 50 per cent. When business is bad, the captive plant's production remains steady despite the decline in demand and its share may increase to 80 per cent or 90 per cent, while the outside supplier feels the brunt of the business decline. His share drops to 10 or 20 per cent of the business and his actual output drops by an even greater amount. Needless to say, suppliers aren't happy when they are asked to bear more than their share of a business slump, and sometimes they demand a contract providing that the percentage split be fixed regardless of general business conditions.

CONTROLLING CAPTIVE ITEMS

When a company makes and buys the same item, it knows precisely how competitive its manufacturing operations are. Ideally, every com-

---

[5] Apparently this is rarely true in practice. A survey by *Purchasing* ("Does the Trend in Make or Buy Decisions Follow Market Conditions?" December, 1954, p. 71) indicated that 81 per cent of the purchasing agents responding did not believe that making items when business was bad and there was overcapacity had a sufficiently adverse effect on vendor relations to be a handicap when a company's capacity was overtaxed again in the future and its purchasing agent tried to buy the same items once again in a tight "seller's" market.

pany would like the cost of each of its operations to be as low as those
of the most efficient outside producer. The materials manager can render
his company a real service by devoting a substantial amount of effort to
locating shop items whose costs are higher than those of leading suppliers.

Stimulate Improvement. When captive manufacturing operations are
not subjected to outside competition with frequent make-or-buy decisions, they may become complacent and inefficient. Their methods
may not be up to date; they may be lagging in productivity and their
costs may be much higher than those of efficient outside producers. When
this happens, the company's over-all competitive strength can gradually
dwindle.

Suppose, for example, that one company making finished electric refrigerators were to attempt to make all of its components from basic
raw materials while a competitor elected to manufacture parts only when
it could do so at substantially lower cost than it could obtain from outside suppliers. If the captive manufacturing operations of the integrated
company had costs that were higher than the market prices paid for
parts by its competitor, then its total product costs would be correspondingly higher. Its profits would be less despite its greater investment in
facilities that would be needed to make all components.

All well-managed companies try to keep their manufacturing facilities up to date. They also try to keep costs under control with budgets
and the like. But if the component itself is not sold directly to a customer
but is incorporated into one of the company's products, it never really
gets the acid test of market competition. The materials manager can
help manufacturing simulate such competition by periodically reviewing
various items made in captive operations to make certain that their production costs do not exceed market prices.

Decentralized Buying. Big companies go even further. They have decentralized organization structures in which one division may sell all
of its output to one or more of the company's other divisions. For example, the Ford Motor Company's Engine & Foundry Division sells its
auto engines to the Ford Division, which is responsible for assembling
them into all of the company's car and truck models.

In such a decentralized structure, the buying division (which is the
unit responsible for the end product) treats the manufacturing division as
much as possible as an outside supplier, in order to simulate conditions
in a competitive market. In some cases, it can do this rather directly. For
example, if the supplying division makes a product that the using division is also buying from an outside supplier, the market price is
known. Similarly, if the manufacturing division makes something for
which there is a published market price (e.g., steel or crude oil), it is
not difficult to set a realistic market price.

Simulate Competition. A problem arises when the captive operation
makes a product that is unique and for which quotations are not readily

available from outside suppliers. For example, the Fisher Body Division of General Motors makes body stampings that are shared by all GM cars. No outside supplier is equipped to make these bodies in the quantities required by General Motors, nor would GM ever seriously consider buying any major part of its body stamping needs from an outside supplier because of its enormous investment in Fisher Body's facilities.

Under such circumstances, the best the materials manager can do is to simulate market conditions for the captive operation. He can vigorously negotiate with the captive plant to get it to price its output at a level he feels would be competitive if alternate suppliers were available. In negotiating, he uses all of the cost-analysis techniques that will be discussed in succeeding chapters.

Some materials managers spend a great deal of time on intracompany purchases from manufacturing plants. Why do they go to the trouble? After all, if a buying division persuades a supplying division of the same company to reduce its prices by $1, the two divisions are just trading dollars. The buying division's profits go up $1 because of the lower price; the supplying division's profits decline $1. The net effect on overall company profit is nil.

Realistic Profits. One reason big companies go to such trouble is that they feel their manufacturing divisions will be more efficient in the long run if they are subject to as much competitive pressure as it is possible for the materials manager to exert. Another, equally important reason is that a company can calculate realistic profits for an operation only if its output is priced at market levels. If a plant whose prices are competitive doesn't earn adequate profits, either its management is at fault or it is in the wrong business. With realistic profit figures, a company can measure its managers' performance and also can direct new investments into areas that yield maximum profits.

Suppose, for example, that a television manufacturer makes his own cabinets. Each television set costs $135 to make and the company sells them to distributors for $150. Therefore the company makes $15 profit on each TV set, or 10 per cent on sales.

If the company's cost of making each cabinet is $13.50, how much profit is the company earning by making its own cabinets? An amateur accountant might say that since the company is earning a 10 per cent profit on each set it must automatically be earning 10 per cent on each major component. But the fact is that it would be impossible to say whether the company's cabinet operation were profitable or not since the company sells no cabinets. Possibly the company is producing a cabinet worth $30 for a cost of only $13.50. If this is the case, it should expand its cabinet line to supply outside companies and go out of the TV-set business itself. Or, as is more likely, the cabinet that costs $13.50 may be available from a specialist producer for $14.00. In that case, the cabinets, with a return of less than 4 per cent on sales, are eating into the company's profit margin. If the company can dispose of its cabinet plant and invest the proceeds in a more profitable part of the business, it can boost its over-all profit margin.

LEASING

Companies need not always either make or buy their requirements. With capital equipment and facilities, they have a third alternative—leasing. Leasing has grown enormously in popularity in recent years. A survey by *Mill and Factory*[6] showed that 71 per cent of the manufacturers participating leased capital equipment. Respondents also mentioned the types of equipment they leased. Office machines were most popular, with 31 per cent of the mentions. Also mentioned were transportation equipment (23 per cent), materials handling equipment (18 per cent), machine tools (17 per cent), and other machines and equipment (11 per cent).

Companies that lease do so both to avoid the responsibility of ownership and to make capital available for other purposes. They prefer to lease certain highly specialized types of equipment because they needn't worry about its maintenance or possible obsolescence; all they need do is operate the equipment with none of the responsibilities of owning it. In addition, a company gets some tax advantage by leasing. Rent can always be charged entirely as an operating expense and thus is completely deductible from taxable income.[7] On the other hand, if a company owns equipment, it must capitalize its cost. Depreciation charges deductible as operating expense must be spaced over the life of the equipment.

The lessee must pay for these advantages. The rent he pays not only includes an adequate amount to cover probable maintenance, depreciation, taxes, and other expenses, but also includes a healthy profit for the lessor. Typically, a lessor might allow for a 10 per cent return on his investment in calculating his rent. The return would be higher yet on equipment on short-term lease that is subject to high obsolescence, and it would be lower on buildings on very long-term leases.

Why then do most insurance companies and banks prefer to lease electronic data-processing equipment when they are eager to make an investment with a guaranteed return of 5 to 6 per cent? Such institutions rarely want to own this equipment. Its maintenance is much too costly and too highly specialized for them. When equipment is leased, the supplier must fix it if it breaks down. In addition, EDP equipment is sub-

---

[6] "Does Industry Lease Capital Equipment?" July, 1960, pp. 73–74.

[7] In the writer's opinion, many businessmen have been oversold on the tax benefits of leasing equipment. Taxes are lower because profits are lower, since leasing in most cases costs more than owning. It's rarely good business to reduce profits simply because the government gets 52 per cent of them with the corporate income tax.

ject to rapid obsolescence. But this needn't worry the lessee. He doesn't have to worry about getting rid of the old equipment when new models are developed or his needs change.

Companies also lease solely to use capital for other purposes. In some cases, they may even sell and lease back assets to get what amounts to a loan that is not shown as a liability on the balance sheet. For example, a company might sell one of its buildings to an insurance company and then sign a long-term lease for its use. The building becomes the equivalent of collateral on a loan for the insurance company, and the lease includes a rent sufficient to cover depreciation of the property over its life as well as a return on investment. Sale and lease-back is desirable when: (1) The company either cannot raise money more cheaply with a direct loan or does not wish to impair its credit standing by having a loan show on its balance sheet. (2) The company can make a larger profit on the proceeds from the sale of the asset than the return it gives the lessee in rent.

Decisions to make, buy, or lease affect both manufacturing and materials activities. They should not be made without the approval of both the manufacturing manager and the materials manager. Other departments also help shape make-or-buy decisions since they're among the most basic decisions in the management of a business. Once the decision is made to buy, however, the materials manager and his buyers become the dominant factors in selecting the supplier. The next three chapters discuss the buying process in detail.

CASES

CASE 11-1. MIRACLE TOY CORPORATION

MAKE-OR-BUY DECISION ON CORRUGATED CARTONS

The Miracle Toy Corporation is one of the largest manufacturers in its field. It has been consistently profitable since it was founded by Hubert Mack in 1936. The Mack family still owns more than 60 per cent of the company's stock. For this reason, dividend policy has been extremely conservative. A dividend payout averaging no more than 33 per cent of earnings has been more than adequate for the family's needs. The company has been able to finance all of its growth internally, and it currently has the most up-to-date facilities in the industry.

Despite heavy expenditures for plant and equipment, the cash flow from earnings and depreciation has been so great that the company's financial position is very strong (see balance sheet in Table 11–1). In fact, Howard Carlson, the company's treasurer, is becoming concerned lest the U.S. Bureau of Internal Revenue charge that the company has been accumulating cash it doesn't really need by holding back on dividends to wealthy stockholders, who are subject to extremely high surtax rates on their personal income. Carlson feels that it is in the best interests of the company to have available a healthy reserve in cash or marketable securities to protect the company during a business downturn and also for any profitable investments the company might wish to make.

Robert Axelrod, manager of the company's manufacturing engineering department, thinks he may have a solution to the excess cash problem. He proposes that the company invest in a small plant to produce cartons. The company currently spends about $800,000 per year for various

TABLE 11–1

SUMMARY OF CONDENSED FINANCIAL STATEMENTS OF MIRACLE TOY CORPORATION
Balance Sheet, June 30, 1961

ASSETS			LIABILITIES	
Cash................	$3,922,000		Current liabilities.....	$ 3,364,200
U.S. government bonds.	3,265,000		Common stock and	
Accounts and notes			surplus...........	15,846,000
receivable.........	1,910,000		Total........	$19,210,200
Inventories..........	2,050,000			
Current assets.....		$11,147,000		
Plant and equipment...	$9,881,900			
Less: Depreciation...	2,000,700			
		$ 7,881,200		
Land..............		182,000		
Total.........		$19,210,200		

Income Statement for Year Ended June 30

	1957	1958	1959	1960	1961
Sales.............	$18,902,000	$18,786,000	$21,942,000	$23,942,000	$24,020,000
Net profit before					
tax............	2,020,000	1,682,000	2,689,000	2,532,000	2,910,000

types and sizes of cartons. At present, it buys them from three suppliers. Two of these suppliers are divisions of much larger corporations. One, however, is much smaller and depends on Miracle Toy for about 25 per cent of its business. Prices for cartons fluctuate somewhat. When there is excess capacity, they drop; when capacity is tight, they inch upward. Current prices reflect a recovery from a period of price cutting that prevailed during much of the previous year.

Axelrod believes that the company can profitably invest in a plant capable of turning out all but $50,000 of its current annual carton needs. (The plant would not produce the small number of cartons that require special lithographing.) At the start, Miracle Toy would be able to take less than half of the plant's production for its own use in packaging toys; the balance (about $1 million worth of cartons) would be sold to outside customers. As Miracle Toy's business grew, it could rely on the carton plant for its increased needs and cut back on sales to outsiders.

Total investment in facilities would be approximately $1,100,000. This estimate does not include any allowance for land, which the company already owns and which probably is worth $50,000 to $75,000. Nor does it include any allowance for "start-up" costs—i.e., the unusually high operating costs that are almost always incurred when a plant starts producing. Axelrod estimates that these costs will be at least $50,000.

Axelrod estimates that the plant would earn a 10 per cent profit on sales to outside customers and would also save the company about $90,-000 in boxboard costs (see Table 11–2). He believes that sales of the

TABLE 11–2

Miracle Toy Corporation

Estimate of Costs and Revenues on Proposed Carton Plant at Standard Volume

Sales to outside customers.......................		$1,000,000
Reduction in purchases of cartons from outside suppliers..		750,000
		$1,750,000
Cost of purchased paper board..................	$710,000	
Inks, plates, and other factory supplies..............	165,000	
Wages and salaries............................	495,000	
Depreciation, taxes, and other expenses.............	190,000	
		1,560,000
Profit from carton operations................		$ 190,000

extra capacity would be no problem, since most of the company's suppliers purchase cartons. He points out that suppliers should be willing to buy Miracle Toy cartons provided that they were competitive in price and quality. In fact, Miracle Toy is already indirectly buying a substantial number of cartons in addition to those it buys directly to package its end products, since many of Miracle Toy's suppliers use cartons to package the company's purchases.

Question

Suppose you were the materials manager of the Miracle Toy Corporation. How would you react to Axelrod's proposal? State your position and make a detailed analysis of his proposal.

CASE 11–2. ILLINOIS CHEMICAL CORPORATION

Investment in New Facilities

The Illinois Chemical Corporation is a major producer of a diversified line of industrial chemicals. One of its most important products is polystrand,[8] which it sells to plastics fabricators who mold it into a wide va-

---

[8] Names of chemicals are fictitious to prevent identification of the manufacturer who co-operated in furnishing data for this case.

riety of industrial and consumer products. One of the major raw materials in polystrand is trimethylacetate. The company uses 10 million pounds of trimethylacetate per year. It buys from two suppliers, the Blue Chemical Corporation and Gamma Company. Blue Chemical's price is 61.6 cents per pound, and Gamma's price is 62 cents. The business is split evenly between the two sources. Currently Gamma and Blue Chemical are the only producers of the chemical. Their prices have been steady for more than two years despite rising labor and raw-material costs.

Illinois' materials manager, Jim Hartley, estimates that Gamma's capacity is 25 million pounds and Blue Chemical's is about 20 million pounds. Both companies are expanding their capacity, and in the next two years, Hartley estimates, their combined capacity will be 60 million

TABLE 11–3

MANUFACTURING COST SUMMARY

Supplier's Operation

(Ten Million Pounds per Year Trimethylacetate)

	Unit	Unit Cost	Quantity	Annual $M	¢/Lb.
Raw materials:					
Compound X..............	M lb.	$30.00	5,500	$ 165	1.7¢
Compound Y..............	M lb.	17.50	5,380	94	0.9
Others..................	M lb.	10.00	260	3	*
Total..................				$ 262	2.6¢
Wages and salaries:					
Wages...................	Man-year	$5,000	48	$ 240	2.4¢
Salaries.................	Man-year	$7,000	10	70	0.7
Security.................	10% of wages and salaries			31	0.3
Total..................				$ 341	3.4¢
Supplies...................	$1,000/operating employee			$ 48	0.5¢
Utilities:					
Steam....................	M lb.	$ 0.40	45,000	$ 18	0.2¢
Electricity...............	MKWH	10.00	6,000	60	0.6
Cooling Water............	M gal.	0.02	128,000	3	*
Others..................				15	0.2
Total..................				$ 96	1.0¢
Services:					
Technical................	3¢/lb. product			$ 300	3.0¢
General..................	$1,500/employee			87	0.9
Total..................				$ 387	3.9¢
Occupancy:					
Maintenance..............	4% of investment			$ 400	4.0¢
Shops and stores...........	2% of investment			200	2.0
Insurance and taxes........	1% of investment			100	1.0
Depreciation..............	6% of investment			600	6.0
Total..................				$1,300	13.0¢
Total manufacturing cost				$2,434	24.4¢

*Insignificant Amount

pounds. He also understands that they are making improvements in their processes.

Demand for polystrand has mushroomed in recent years, and Illinois estimates that it may double its sales of the plastic in the next five years. Other chemical companies, noting the heavy demand for the material, have been attracted not only to the end product (where competition is growing more intense) but also the major raw material (trimethylacetate). Three other producers have announced plans to enter the trimethylacetate business. If these producers carry out their plans, Hartley estimates that total industry capacity will be well over 100 million pounds per year in the next three years.

Because it expects continued growth in demand for polystrand, Illinois is now considering investment in facilities to produce the key raw material, trimethylacetate. Heretofore, Illinois has preferred to invest its capital primarily in equipment to process end products and has relied on suppliers for raw materials. However, Edward Van de Venter, vice-president in charge of manufacturing, has long been urging the company's executive committee to approve construction of facilities to make raw materials. Van de Venter's staff has prepared an analysis (see Tables 11–3 and 11–4) that indicates that the company can earn a 15 per cent return on invested capital by investing in trimethylacetate manufacturing facilities. This is approximately what the company is currently earn-

TABLE 11–4

SALE PRICE SUMMARY
Supplier's Operation
(Ten Million Pounds per Year Trimethylacetate)

	$M	$/Lb.
Capital investment:		
Fixed investment:		
Battery limits	$10,000	$1.000
Allocated		
Utilities	600	0.060
Services	400	0.040
Shops	200	0.020
Total	$11,200	$1.120
Working capital	$ 490	$0.049
Total capital investment	$11,690	$1.169
Return on total investment (after taxes)	15%	
Annual net profit	$ 1,753	$0.175
Annual income tax	1,753	0.175
Annual gross profit	$ 3,506	$0.350
Annual cost of sales:		
Manufacturing cost	$ 2,434	$0.244
Corporate overhead @ 4%	247	0.024
Total	$ 2,681	$0.268
Annual sales revenue	$ 6,187	$0.618
Selling Price—¢/lb.	61.8¢ lb.	

ing on existing facilities. While the company's bonded indebtedness is already heavy, it could undoubtedly borrow the $11,690,000 it would need for the project—although it would then have to postpone any additional expansion for at least a year or two.

Hartley does not share Van de Venter's enthusiasm for the project. He has asked his administrative assistant, Henry Waterman, to prepare a study in which he considers both the pros and the cons of going into the trimethylacetate business.

Question

What factors should Waterman consider in his study?

Chapter 12

FINDING QUALIFIED SUPPLIERS

The buying process is deceptively simple. Competing suppliers submit bids. If each offers acceptable delivery, quality, and service, a purchase order is issued to the lowest bidder. This is the clerical framework. Within it operates a buying process that requires both extensive knowledge and remarkably keen judgment.

Good buyers never ask a supplier to quote unless they have some knowledge of his qualifications. In fact, they would prefer to solicit quotations only from those suppliers with perfect records for quality, service, and delivery. If they could do this all the time, their jobs would be much easier. All they would need to do is request quotations from three or four such suppliers and then award the business to the low bidder.

Unfortunately, real-life suppliers aren't so perfect. Most buyers aren't completely satisfied with the quality, service, and delivery of even their best and most reliable suppliers. In addition, they must spend a great deal of time looking for new suppliers capable of taking care of their changing needs. No company can stand still. It must continuously be developing new products and processes, which in turn require new suppliers. No supplier can afford to stand still either. Each is looking for new customers, and each must be investigated carefully by the buyer before being trusted with an order.

BUYING ERRORS ARE COSTLY

The costs of mistakes in buying are always substantial; sometimes they are staggering. If buyers pay suppliers higher prices than are justified, a company's profits and competitive position may be undermined. As was pointed out in Chapter 1, in the average company a 2 per cent change in total materials cost brings a 10 per cent change in profits.

If a buyer buys materials of unsatisfactory quality or a vendor fails to deliver, the costs may be enormous. Imagine what would happen if an auto company purchased parts for a critical component like a steering gear or brakes that failed completely after a year's service in the field. Hundreds of thousands of cars would be defective. The company's reputation would certainly suffer. In addition, it would incur losses from lawsuits and from the enormous expense of replacing the defective part in thousands of cars.[1]

Quality failure can be a nightmare when it isn't detected until long after the product is in use. It can also be costly when it is spotted immediately by sharp-eyed inspectors. A shipment of material that doesn't meet minimum quality specifications is the equivalent of no shipment at all. Worse yet, it may mean continued delivery failure until the supplier can correct the defect.

If a supplier fails to deliver an item and the buyer's inventories are exhausted, the costs of the production stoppage that results can be huge. Customers are dissatisfied; sales and profits are lost that can never be recouped. In addition, the direct cost is substantial. A plant employing about 300 persons has fixed costs of several thousand dollars per day, which are incurred whether the plant is operating or not.

If a buyer fails to achieve the fourth buying objective, service,[2] in his dealings with suppliers, the consequences are not nearly so spectacular as with a major quality or delivery failure. But in some cases they can be even more significant economically. Outstanding suppliers sometimes provide their customers with products and ideas that can have tremendous effect on sales and profits for years to come.

CHANNELS OF DISTRIBUTION

Industrial buyers commonly buy materials both directly from producers and through various local distributors. In general, they buy production materials used in fairly large quantities directly from the manufacturer in order to get lowest possible prices. Nonproduction materials and supplies normally come from local mill supply houses or distributors, who buy from the manufacturers in large quantities and then resell to their customers in smaller quantities.

As a general rule, industrial buyers prefer to deal directly with the manufacturer whenever possible. There are no middlemen making extra profits on each purchase, and communication is easier when the buyer has technical problems to discuss with the manufacturer. However, industrial distributors do have a legitimate economic role. When the buyer requires their services, the higher prices they charge are more than

---

[1] Such failures are not theoretical. In recent years several well-known manufacturers have suffered losses because of the failure of some component. For example, several years ago a well-known auto company tried to replace the copper in its radiators with a substitute material. Because of a flood of complaints, it eventually had to replace thousands of customers' radiators without charge at a cost of several million dollars.

[2] The objective of service is comparable to the "favorable supplier relations" objective mentioned in the discussion of primary materials management objectives in Chapter 3.

justified. In fact, when quantities are relatively small, they are usually the most economic form of distribution.

Buying Direct

When a company uses reasonably large quantities of production parts and materials, it almost always pays to buy directly from the manufacturer. Suppliers of standard and semistandard items—steel, chemicals, ball bearings, paper, and so on—sometimes require a minimum factory order on direct purchases.[3] However, all large users buy directly from the factory or mill. Suppliers of parts that are custom-made to the buyer's blueprints and specifications almost always sell direct even if quantities are small.

Full-Time Salesmen. Supplier salesmen are the liaison between their customers and the home office and factory. The salesmen of practically all large and many small companies are full-time employees. They usually are paid a straight salary plus some bonus based on performance and company profits. They may also receive a commission based on sales volume, which may or may not supplement a regular salary.

It is probably to the buyer's advantage to deal with salesmen who are paid a straight salary, since they might be more interested in providing outstanding service to their customers even at the expense of immediate gains in sales volume. However, there is not much a buyer can do to control the way in which a supplier pays his salesmen. Nor, in most cases, can he even find out the method; most suppliers are extremely reluctant to discuss such an intimate detail of their business with customers.

Manufacturers' Representatives. Many smaller firms sell through manufacturers' representatives. They pay a flat commission on sales volume, which ranges from 1 per cent or less on extremely high-volume items to more than 10 per cent on equipment and parts purchased in very small quantities. Typically, each manufacturers' representative serves several noncompeting firms in an area. In most cases, they sell products to the same customers, so the representative often can serve several accounts on a single sales call.

While some buyers complain that the commissions earned by manufacturers' representatives are too high, this method of selling is probably the most economical one for the firms that use it. The company need not maintain sales offices in areas where they wouldn't be economical. Its sales costs are not rigid but vary directly with sales volume.

[3] For example, mills demand a minimum order of 10,000 pounds for most types of sheet steel. Users who want smaller quantities must buy from a steel warehouse firm that specializes in buying mill quantities and then reselling in smaller quantities to users in its area. Warehouse prices usually are at least 25 per cent higher than mill prices. Warehouses earn this premium by offering prompt delivery of small quantities and other services.

On the other hand, a manufacturers' representative usually doesn't give any one company all of his time. Nor can he be expected to know as much about the company's products as a full-time sales representative. As a result, critics say that neither buyer nor seller gets the best service through a manufacturers' representative. When problems arise, the manufacturers' representative often is only an errand boy between the buyer and the supplier. He usually is not empowered to make more than minor decisions for his employer. Some, but by no means all, full-time salesmen, on the other hand, are thoroughly familiar with the details of their product and are able to make many decisions without consulting the home office.

Buying from Distributors

A distributor is a dealer who handles a wide range of products for a number of manufacturers in an area. He may have an exclusive franchise for a manufacturer's products and might not even handle competing brands. In other cases, each distributor in an area handles all major brands. Distributors usually buy materials in fairly large quantities, store them, and then resell in small quantities to customers in their area. About 23 per cent of the typical distributor's sales are drop shipments,[4] where the material is shipped directly from the factory to the user. In such cases, the distributor still takes title to the goods, even though he doesn't handle them physically. But in this case his function is really no different from that of a manufacturers' representative.

Even on drop shipments, however, the manufacturer invoices the distributor, who reinvoices the user of the material. The distributor's profit comes from the difference between the price at which he sells and the price at which he buys. Unlike the manufacturers' representative, the distributor receives no commission and, except where it is prohibited by so-called "fair-trade" laws, is perfectly free to resell at any price he chooses.

Distributor markups vary with the quantity and type of material sold. One study showed that the average gross margin of the distributor was 21.19 per cent of sales.[5] To earn this margin, the distributor anticipates the needs of his customers in his buying, stores the material until there is a demand for it (an average period of three months[6]), and then delivers it to the user.

Role of the Salesman

The modern salesman isn't necessarily a bubbling extrovert. But he almost always has a reasonably pleasant personality, and the fact is that

---

[4] Robert D. Buzzell, *Value Added by Industrial Distributors and Their Productivity* (Columbus: Ohio State University Press, 1959), p. 26.

[5] *Ibid.*, p. 55.

[6] *Ibid.*, p. 71.

many salesmen get business simply because customers enjoy doing business with them. And if all other factors are equal, why shouldn't a buyer deal with someone he likes and trusts? Personality factors are just as important in buyer-seller relations as they are in other phases of business.

But while every buyer is certainly influenced to some extent by the personalities of the salesmen who call on him, he also has more objective reasons for preferring some salesmen to others. A good salesman not only knows his company's products but also knows something about his customer's problems. He is around when the buyer needs him but doesn't make unnecessary calls that waste time for both of them. When the salesman is an able one, there are few problems regarding quality and delivery. The salesman will follow up on most of them himself and thus save the buyer considerable trouble.

Firms with able sales representatives always get more business. And they deserve it, for they offer superior service to their customers. Able salesmen naturally seek out prospective customers. And many a company learns about a supplier only because one of his salesmen happened to call. But the professional buyer doesn't always play such a passive role. He spends a substantial amount of time actively looking for new suppliers who can better serve his needs.

FINDING A SUPPLIER

Buyers most commonly find suppliers for an item either by drawing on their experience with comparable items or by inviting quotations from the same suppliers who made the item on a previous order. Every buyer must often locate new suppliers, however. He wants to stimulate competition on items he regularly buys, and he must also buy new items that present suppliers are not equipped to handle. Buyers usually locate new vendors by checking purchasing directories, catalogue and vendor files, and through personal contacts with supplier salesmen or other buyers.

Directories. There are numerous directories that list potential suppliers both alphabetically and by type of product sold. Probably the most widely used directory is the buyer's local telephone book. In the yellow pages are listed all local suppliers for various merchandise.

Purchasing directories, like Thomas' Register of American Manufacturers, Conover-Mast Purchasing Directory, and MacRae's Blue Book, are widely used by industrial buyers. Each is carefully edited to include only those products that are useful to the industrial buyer, and each lists upwards of a quarter of a million supply sources, both alphabetically and by product. A buyer can quickly locate almost every domestic supplier of an item simply by turning to the product classification in the directory in which he is interested.

Many states publish directories of all industries within their boundaries. Every buyer should have the directory of his home state if there is one. It can be an extremely useful supplement to his general purchasing directory, which might not list all suppliers or commodities in which he might be interested. Trade associations also issue purchasing directories for specialized commodities. The Rubber Red Book is typical of these; it specializes in a very detailed listing and product classifications for rubber-products manufacturers and so is an invaluable reference for a buyer of rubber products. Every buying department should be equipped with all available specialized commodity directories in its fields of interest.

Catalogue Files and Vendor Lists. The typical purchasing department is bombarded with thousands of pieces of direct-mail sales literature every year. Although they discard at least 90 per cent of this mail, most purchasing men carefully review and save any catalogues that might be of use in buying. A big purchasing department may have several thousand different supplier catalogues in its files.

Some purchasing departments try to boost the usefulness of their catalogue files by carefully classifying their contents both by supplier name and by product. For example, they may store the catalogues on shelves or in file cabinets alphabetically by supplier name and then keep a separate card file by type of commodity. Some companies have even developed numerical file cards on which they imitate the Dewey decimal system used in libraries, assigning a code number to each commodity group.

The purchasing department of a manufacturer of office staplers and similar items uses these basic groupings:

1000—Bearings and bushings
2000—Electrical equipment and supplies
3000—Factory equipment
4000—Gears
5000—Mill supplies
6000—Office supplies and equipment
7000—Steel, brass, aluminum, etc.
8000—Taps and drills
9000—Miscellaneous

The third digit in the identifying number indicates the type of material, and the fourth digit classifies it further. For example, in category 7000, 7010 identifies a general steel product, while 7011 is for steel wire, 7012 for steel bars, and so on. Specific catalogues are then identified in numerical sequence with a decimal point after the commodity number. For example, the number 7011.01 might refer to a U.S. Steel catalogue of steel wire, which is the first of several wire catalogues on file. Then 7011.02 might be Republic Steel's wire products catalogue, and so on.

Buyers specializing in high-volume production parts and materials rarely rely on catalogues, since everything they buy is custom-made to company specifications. But they would probably use some sort of vendor list. The simplest of these would be a file of 3 × 5 cards arranged alphabetically by supplier name. On each card would be the supplier's address, telephone number, names of officers and sales representatives, and an indication of the type of work the supplier is equipped to handle. The buyer then can review this list whenever he must buy a new item to see if anyone on it is interested in quoting.

Personal Contacts. Buyers talk to salesmen of potential vendors even when they have no immediate need for the products they sell. When a need does arise, they can refer to the salesman's calling card or "leave-behind" sales literature to see if his company should be considered.

Buyers often get tips on potential suppliers for off-beat items by asking other buyers for assistance. Many of them use their membership in the National Association of Purchasing Agents or some other purchasing organization as a vehicle for becoming acquainted with purchasing personnel in other companies who can be useful sources of information. They also carefully read many trade publications regularly. When they see an ad by a company that might be a potential supplier, they tear it out and file it for future reference.

Similarly, buyers get information about potential new suppliers through regular attendance at trade shows where suppliers have booths and display their products. Some companies take even more direct measures to stimulate sales calls from promising new suppliers. They have displays of their products in their lobbies, so that suppliers will know precisely what they buy. Some companies have even set up (during a defense program, when they had to get many new suppliers in a hurry) exhibits of the items they buy in public halls and invited all potential suppliers to come and look at them.

INVESTIGATION OF SUPPLIERS

No buyer should place orders with a supplier about whom he knows nothing. At best, there is danger of substandard performance in price, quality, delivery, or service. At worst, there is danger of fraud. Almost every buyer occasionally is approached by a sharp operator trying to pass off shoddy merchandise at exorbitant prices. And sometimes the swindler is successful. In a survey of industrial purchasing agents conducted by *Purchasing*, 15 per cent of the respondents admitted that they had been victims of industrial racketeers.[7]

Caveat Emptor. In one of the rackets mentioned in the *Purchasing* article,[8] a pencil salesman[9] calls and claims that his company has printed

---

[7] "Buyers Beware—The Racket Boys Are Back," *Purchasing*, July 18, 1960, p. 72. Since many people, particularly professional buyers, don't like to admit that they have been cheated, presumably more than 15 per cent of the respondents were actually victimized.

[8] *Ibid.*, pp. 71–73.

[9] The racket obviously would work with any item that has the company's name printed on it, including advertising specialties like blotters, calendars, and so on.

the name of the buyer's company on several thousand pencils because of confusion with another customer who has a similar name. If the name of the buyer's company is Universal Screw Machine Corp., for example, the salesman might claim that his firm has accidentally printed this name on pencils ordered by the Universal Screw Products Corp. The salesman appears to be upset over the error and offers the buyer distress prices if he will take the pencils off his hands. The salesman is lying, of course. The company's name is printed on the pencils only after it orders them. And the buyer doesn't get a distress price at all; he pays a high price for the poorest quality of pencils available.

In another, similar racket the salesman claims to be representing a firm that is financially hard pressed. If the buyer will pay in cash, he promises extra concessions. What actually happens is that the buyer winds up with low-quality merchandise worth about half of what he paid. Since it's not economic to sue and the transaction usually is perfectly legal anyway, the buyer is bilked.

Rackets such as these would disappear if every buyer carefully investigated each supplier before placing an order. But everyone likes to get something for nothing, and if the racketeers can convince the buyer that he must move fast, he might forego investigation in his eagerness to exploit what appears to be an opportunity for a bargain. The fact remains that every supplier should be investigated, even those whose morals and ethics are above reproach.

Unfortunately for the buyer, a completely honorable supplier can also cause losses to the buyer's company, for he may be incompetent, a poor manager, and unable to keep promises made in good faith. For this reason, many buyers avoid asking a supplier even to quote on business until they learn something about his facilities, personnel, financial resources, and reputation.

Facilities

Suppliers often are remarkably eager to get orders they are not equipped to handle. From the supplier's point of view, the best way to expand a business is to get the orders first and then worry about buying the needed equipment. The buyer has a somewhat different point of view. He almost always buys best when he deals with suppliers who already have the equipment and skills needed. Costs usually are lower and quality is higher when the supplier performs almost every operation on the product or service himself.

Equipment Lists. The buyer should listen carefully to the salesman's description of the supplier's facilities. If he is buying parts made to his specifications directly from a smaller manufacturer, he should ask for a list of machine tools and equipment. He then can accurately determine if the supplier is actually equipped to do the job. The buyer also can get

Dun & Bradstreet, Inc. **Report** RATING CHANGE

3661
KENT ELECTRONICS

CD 1 OCTOBER 3 1955
MFG. ELEC. ASSEMBLIES

BROOKLYN 19 N.Y.
1246 KENT ROAD

Miles Gross, Partner

Hannah (Mrs. Miles) Gross, Partner

RATING: F 2 1/2 to E 2

STARTED: 1948
NET WORTH: $24,901

PAYMENTS: Discount
SALES: $189,232

SUMMARY
SALES ARE INCREASING AND OPERATIONS ARE PROFITABLE. THE CONDITION IS SOUND.

HISTORY
Style was registered by the partners on April 30, 1948.
This firm was formed April, 1948. Starting capital consisted of $10,500 savings, a $3,500 loan from Teachers Credit Union, and a $3,000 loan from partners' families, making a total of $17,000. Loans have since been repaid.
Miles Gross, 41, native born, and a mechanical engineer. Graduated from Columbia College of Engineering in 1935. Employed as designer by Liggett Electric Co. and by Ray Products Co. until this business was started.
Hannah (Mrs. Miles) Gross is 36. She was a New York school teacher prior to formation of this firm.

OPERATION-LOCATION
Manufactures parts and component assemblies for radio and television receivers (U.S.S.I.C. #3661), against confirmed orders (95%) and own account (5%). Sales to set manufacturers (95%) and mail order to repair shops (5%). Terms 2%, 15 prox, net 60 days. Both partners active, three employed. Equipment includes 6 Cleveland Automatic bench lathes, 4 Salisbury 1" drill presses, 2 Norden stamping machines (19" capacity), and assorted specially-designed jigs, dies, and hand tools. Rents first floor of a two-story building in good condition. Plant measures about 120 x 50 feet. Located in long-established light industry zone.

FINANCIAL INFORMATION
A financial statement at June 30, 1955-cents omitted:-

ASSETS		LIABILITIES	
Cash	$ 6,304	Accts Pay	$ 13,724
Rec	17,872		
Merchandise	4,450		
Total Current	28,626	Total Current	13,724
Fixt & Equip	9,913		
Deposits	86	NET WORTH	24,901
Total Assets	38,625	Total	38,625

NET SALES from July 1, 1954 to June 30, 1955 $189,232; gross profit $39,181; salaries and drawings of partners $6,732; net profit over and above salaries and drawings of partners $3,467. Monthly rent $150. Lease expires 1958.
Signed;September 20, 1955 KENT ELECTRONICS by Miles Gross, Partner
Received by mail.
Accountant: J. C. Harris, C.P.A.
Gross has established a good reputation for quality and adherence to delivery schedules, with the result that both sales and profits of this business have mounted steadily. Part of earnings have been reinvested in the business to finance its steady growth.

PAYMENTS
AUG 20 1955

HC	OWE	P DUE	TERMS			
4431	3927		10th of MO	Disc	Sold 3 yrs to date	
2340	2230		2-10 N30	Disc	Sold 1949 to 3-54	
2250	2049		2-10	Disc	Sold 4 yrs	
1136	1136		2-10 Prox	Disc	Sold yrs to date	
575	480		2-10 EOM	Disc		
115			30	Ppt	Sold 1-49 to 12-53	
10-3-55	(241 29)	Five				

PLEASE NOTE WHETHER NAME, BUSINESS AND STREET ADDRESS CORRESPOND WITH YOUR INQUIRY.
The foregoing report is furnished, at your request, under your Subscription Contract, in STRICT CONFIDENCE, by DUN & BRADSTREET, Inc. as your agents and employees, for your exclusive use as an aid in determining the advisability of granting credit or insurance, and for no other purpose 9R2-4 (23078)

FIG. 12–1. Although they are most often used to check a customer's credit, Dun & Bradstreet reports are also good sources of information about potential suppliers' facilities and finances.

useful descriptions of a supplier's facilities from a Dun & Bradstreet report (see Figure 12–1) or from the current issue of *Moody's Industrials*.

If the supplier is located nearby, the buyer should always arrange to see his facilities. If the contract is sufficiently important, the buyer should visit the supplier's plant even if it is hundreds of miles away. And he may wish to bring along product, process, or quality control engineers from his own company to assist him in evaluating the supplier's facilities.

A buyer's tour of a distributor's facilities can be more superficial than one of a supplier's manufacturing plant. The distributor should certainly be adequately stocked. Equally important to the buyer are the distributor's employees. If their morale is high, if they seem alert and intelligent, the buyer has a reasonably good chance of getting prompt service with a minimum of errors. The distributor's housekeeping also may be significant. The buyer usually has good reason to expect sloppy service from sloppy-looking facilities.

Plant Visits. A manufacturing plant usually is much more complex than a distribution facility and takes much more skill to evaluate. Every buyer who has ever been conducted through a supplier plant has heard the salesman boast of its modern facilities and equipment. If the buyer is an expert in the supplier's industry, it won't take him long to see if the salesman's praise is justified.

If the buyer is not thoroughly familiar with the industry, he can still get clues as to the quality of the facilities by getting answers to these questions:

1. Is the equipment up to date? If the equipment looks new and modern (and doesn't just have a fresh coat of paint on it), the buyer usually can assume that it is reasonably efficient and in good condition. In some cases, he might bluntly ask the supplier when the equipment was purchased. If he notices a number of machines shut down for repairs, he may conclude that the equipment is older than it looks.
2. Is there effective material control? If the supplier has in-process inventory piled haphazardly throughout the plant, his production scheduling may be defective or equipment breakdowns may be creating production bottlenecks.
3. Are working conditions good? The buyer is more likely to get the quality and output he wants from a plant that is well lighted and well ventilated, and that has guards on machines to prevent accidents.
4. Are facilities well maintained? If a supplier skimps on maintenance in obvious areas, he may also skimp in the less obvious ones that cause shutdowns.
5. What are the supplier's fire-protection facilities? If the plant has its own water tower and sprinkler, fires will cause less damage and will be less likely to hold up work on the buyer's orders.
6. Is the work pace fast but unhurried? A well-operated plant doesn't have idle workers in one area and harried workers in another.
7. Does the supplier have the equipment to handle the buyer's order? The buyer should ask to see the equipment that is to be used on his orders. He should ask about the approximate capacity of each machine to make certain that his needs can be accommodated. He may also wish to make note of each machine's model number and specifications so that he can review the supplier's facilities with experts at his own plant.
8. Does the supplier have efficient receiving and shipping facilities? The buyer should note particularly whether the supplier can ship his order by the most economical type of carrier. If the buyer's traffic manager would prefer shipment by rail, for example, the supplier can't ship at low cost unless he has his own siding.

9. Is the supplier currently making products similar to those in which the buyer is interested? If the buyer's order will be different from the supplier's usual line, there might be problems. If it is similar, the buyer can get a good idea of how his order will be handled by watching work on similar orders.

Many companies require buyers to make out detailed reports each time they visit a supplier plant. These reports are filed and can be referred to by other buyers interested in doing business with that supplier. However, a company shouldn't use one report as a guide indefinitely. Follow-up visits are essential to keep up to date on changes the supplier may have made. A series of reports can then be analyzed for trend. A company naturally is more willing to place business with a supplier who is progressively improving than with one who is standing still or even slipping behind.

Personnel

Although buyers should do their best to evaluate a supplier's facilities objectively, this is sometimes difficult and occasionally almost impossible.[10] This is not the case with the supplier's management.

Regardless of their products and processes, all companies depend heavily on the caliber of their managers. A good supplier always has good managers. The buyer is particularly qualified to evaluate the supplier's materials manager. He should insist on meeting him. The buyer should also meet other company executives. He may also, if the contract is an important one, arrange for these executives to meet their counterparts in his own company. If each of the supplier's department heads knows his job thoroughly, the buyer has less to worry about when he places the order.

If the contract is a major one, the buyer should not confine his study of the supplier's personnel to the top managers. He should meet lower-level supervisors as well. The supplier's key men should be backed up by bright, alert subordinates who are being trained to take over in the future.

The supplier's labor relations also should interest the buyer. Do the workers appear contented and reasonably interested in their jobs? Or are they sullen and obviously doing work they hate simply because they must eat? In the latter case, the buyer shouldn't be too surprised if he sometimes gets substandard workmanship on his orders. The buyer should bluntly ask the supplier to show him records on strikes and work stoppages. If they have been frequent, the buyer can expect both an en-

---

[10] Some facilities simply don't lend themselves to the type of superficial appraisal that a buyer can give them on a plant tour. For example, both efficient and inefficient chemical plants look like a maze of pipes and storage tanks to the casual observer.

vironment leading to poor quality and frequent failures to meet delivery promises.

Financial Resources

Why should a company be interested in the financial strength of its suppliers? It need not rely on their credit, nor is it making an investment in them. The answer is that the best suppliers are financially strong and are making healthy profits.

Advantages of Strong Suppliers. In general, it is sound to prefer an extremely profitable vendor to a less profitable one—all other factors being equal. The company with big profits is in a much better position to reduce prices (if it can be persuaded to do so). Its methods and management usually are superior. It also is more likely to be a better source of new products and techniques than its more marginal competitors.

Certainly no buyer wants to give important purchase orders to a weak supplier and then have him suddenly go bankrupt. Also, a supplier who is making adequate profits and is strong financially can take temporary losses if he underbids or has trouble with an order. The buyer needn't worry about such a supplier's coming back after he has accepted an order and demanding extra payments to complete it, financial advances, and so on.

If the company is large and publicly owned, the buyer should ask its sales representative for a copy of the latest annual report to stockholders. Such reports often contain interesting descriptions of company operations as well as basic financial data. If the company doesn't widely distribute its financial reports to stockholders, the buyer has other sources of financial information. He often can get balance sheet and income data and similar basic information from the latest edition of *Moody's Industrials*. Or, if the supplier is too small to be listed in *Moody's*, the buyer can get a Dun & Bradstreet report. The D & B report will usually include a financial statement. In addition, it will indicate the company's credit standing with its suppliers and the over-all credit rating assigned it by Dun & Bradstreet.

Financial Analysis. The buyer, or better yet, a financial analyst on the materials manager's staff, should periodically review the latest balance sheet and income statement of each major supplier. If the balance sheet shows that the supplier's business is deteriorating, the buyer should investigate; he may want to change suppliers before the company's financial condition becomes critical.

The buyer should also be particularly interested in the trend of the company's profits. If profit margins are widening, he may have a legitimate basis for asking the supplier to reduce prices. And certainly he should complain vigorously if such a supplier should increase prices. If the profit margin is narrowing, this may mean that the supplier is gradually becoming less efficient and less competitive. Or it could mean that his prices are too low and the buyer can expect pressure for price increases.

No buyer or materials manager is expected to be an expert financial analyst. But he should be sufficiently familiar with balance sheets and income statements to make intelligent comparisons of competing suppliers and spot individual strengths and weaknesses.

TABLE 12–1

CONDENSED FINANCIAL STATEMENT—ABC COMPANY

Balance Sheet as of December 31, 196?

ASSETS			LIABILITIES		
Cash		$100,000	Accounts payable	$ 50,000	
Accounts receivable		200,000	Wages payable	50,000	
Inventories		200,000	Accrued taxes	100,000	
Current Assets	$ 500,000		Current Liabilities		$ 200,000
Land	$ 50,000		Long-term debt		100,000
Plant and			Common stock	$100,000	
equipment	$500,000		Capital surplus	100,000	
Less: Depre-			Earned surplus	500,000	
ciation	100,000				700,000
	$400,000				
Fixed assets		$ 450,000			
Good will, etc.		50,000			
Total Current Assets		$1,000,000	Total Current Liabilities	$1,000,000	

Income Statement—Year Ended December 31, 196?

Net Sales		$2,000,000
Less:		
Purchases	$1,000,000	
Payrolls	500,000	
Other expenses	200,000	
Operating costs	$1,700,000	
Less: Sales and adminis-		
trative expense	100,000	
Total costs		1,800,000
Operating profit		200,000
Less: Taxes		100,000
Net Profit		$ 100,000

The financial statements of a hypothetical supplier are illustrated in Table 12–1. How would a financial analyst go about reviewing them? One of the best approaches is to calculate various financial ratios for the supplier and compare them with ratios for competing suppliers.[11] The following ratios are particularly significant:

1. The Current Ratio. This is the ratio of current assets to current liabilities. It indicates the ability of the company to pay its immediate

[11] Each year, Dun & Bradstreet publishes 14 important financial ratios for 72 different industries. The title of their publication varies from year to year. Businessmen can get complimentary copies by writing to Dun & Bradstreet, 99 Church Street, New York 8, N.Y.

obligations. In the ABC Company (Table 12–1) this ratio is 2.5 ($500,-000/$200,000). Most analysts agree that it should be at least 2.5 and that when it gets below 1.0 the company usually is on the brink of default on its obligations. The ratio of cash plus accounts receivable to current liabilities ($100,000 + $200,000/$200,000 = 1.5 for ABC Company) is an even better measure of liquidity. Inventories cannot be quickly converted into cash, so they are excluded from current assets. If a manufacturing company is in good financial condition, this "quick" ratio or "acid test" should be at least 1.5.

2. *Profit Ratios.* Profitability can be measured by earnings both as a per cent of sales and as a per cent of net worth. The ABC Company's after-tax earnings are 5 per cent of sales and just over 14 per cent ($100,000/$700,000) of net worth. Average earnings on sales and net worth vary from industry to industry and also from year to year, but they are usually less than those of the ABC Company.[12]

3. *Debt Ratios.* A company that is heavily in debt will have difficulty raising money to invest in improvements. Two ratios measure the extent of a company's indebtedness. The ratio of funded debt to net working capital should rarely exceed 1.0. In the case of the ABC Company, it is 0.33 ($100,000/$300,000). The ratio of current debt to tangible net worth should normally be under 0.75. ABC's is about .28 ($200,000/$700,000).

4. *Inventory Turnover.* Dividing net sales by inventories indicates how rapidly the company is turning over its inventories. This is a barometer of the company's materials management skill. ABC's ratio of 10.0 is probably above average, although the only good way to determine whether the ratio is high or low is to compare it with that of other companies in ABC's industry.

The ratios given above are danger signals. A buyer can successfully deal with a supplier who is financially marginal for years, but he should not do so blindly. Whenever any of the key financial ratios of a supplier are substandard, the buyer should investigate. He may directly ask the supplier to describe his problems, or he may request that his own company's controller make a more detailed analysis of the supplier's financial statements.

Financial Limitations. Regardless of how strong the supplier is financially and how able he is in every other respect, few buyers care to concentrate too great a percentage of their purchase volume on a single supplier. Nor do they care to have the supplier become dependent on them for too great a share of his over-all business. When they place too much business with a single supplier, buyers not only limit competition but they unnecessarily restrict their freedom of action in changing suppliers. No buyer need worry too much about taking a small order away

---

[12] Detailed industry sales and earnings statistics are available in the *Quarterly Financial Report for Manufacturing Corporations* published by the Securities and Exchange Commission and the Federal Trade Commission.

from one supplier and giving it to a competitor. But only a cold-blooded ogre would cancel orders on short notice when they are almost the sole source of the supplier's income and hundreds of workers (sometimes entire communities) depend on the orders for their livelihood.

Suppliers who have staked too much on a single corporation have lived to regret it, too. For example, at one time the Murray Corporation of America depended on the Ford Motor Company for as much as 30 to 40 per cent of its sales. Then Ford decided to make almost all of its own auto body stampings. Murray was hit with a sharp drop in business from which it has never really recovered fully. The Chrysler Corporation had an even closer relationship with the Briggs Manufacturing Company, which depended on it for practically all of its automobile business. When Chrysler decided to make its own automobile bodies, Briggs' only solution was to go out of the auto body business completely and sell its facilities to Chrysler.

There are no hard and fast rules as to how much business can be safely concentrated on a single supplier. But few companies want to use more than 10 per cent of a supplier's capacity unless there is some special reason for doing so.

Reputation

If a potential supplier has a bad reputation, one should clearly avoid doing business with him. Credit reports often provide clues to a supplier's reputation. They describe the backgrounds of the principals and also mention any outstanding litigation. The buyer should also ask a new supplier for a list of his major customers and vendors. Chances are that he may be acquainted with at least a few of the executives of these firms who can give him an unprejudiced view of the potential supplier's reputation. If the buyer belongs to a group like the National Association of Purchasing Agents, he may get tips on suppliers' reputations from his fellow members.

When he investigates a supplier's reputation, the buyer will be interested not only in conformance to ethical standards but also in experience others have had with the supplier in regard to meeting quality standards and keeping delivery promises.

DEVELOPING NEW SUPPLIERS

Ideally, a supplier should have the equipment, know-how, and financial capacity needed for each order he accepts. But in real life this often is not the case. Buyers may deliberately give business to inexperienced suppliers. Sometimes they have no choice; usually they have good reason for gambling on a new supplier.

New Products. If a buyer is looking for a supplier of something that has never been made before, he must obviously select an inexperienced supplier. Sometimes, of course, the buyer is taking little risk. The latest design of automobile bumper guard may look entirely different from last year's model but last year's suppliers can probably handle it without great difficulty. The products that give the buyer problems are those that are completely different from anything that has been made before. For example, the first buyer who had to find a source for a missile nose cone really had a problem. The product was extremely difficult to make and there wasn't a single producer with experience.

Competition. Buyers go to great pains to develop new and untried suppliers even when there is nothing new or revolutionary about the product and there are several qualified producers. Their usual reason is to stimulate competition in the field.

When there are few producers of an item, competition can be less than vigorous. At worst there may even be collusion among producers on bidding. This results in higher prices for the buyer and occasionally also sloppy service and poor quality.

Sometimes a buyer may wish to develop a new supplier even when his existing sources are doing an excellent job. He may feel there is not enough capacity in the industry to take care of his needs. Or he may wish to develop a supplier in a particular area that is not too convenient for the plants of existing producers.

The Development Process. Regardless of the motive, most good buyers are always in the process of developing at least one or two new suppliers. They cannot always use conventional techniques to locate them, particularly if they are considering introducing a supplier to work that is not presently in his line. Sometimes they develop new sources by suggesting that certain dependable suppliers broaden their product lines. Often they play a more passive role; the supplier suggests to the buyer that he be considered for an order not presently in his line. The more aggressive buyers may even go out and actively solicit bids from potential suppliers with management and equipment that they believe could be adapted to a particular item.

The most important criterion by far in selecting suppliers that are to be developed on new products is management. If the supplier's management is good enough, some buyers are willing to ignore almost all other criteria. In fact, when they want the new supplier badly enough, they will go to great lengths to help him. They may lend him money, equipment, and skilled personnel, and be extremely generous in pricing orders until the new supplier gains experience.

In most cases, of course, buyers are not quite so eager to develop a new supplier. But in order to induce a well-managed firm to enter a particular line, they may be willing to place long-term contracts to make it worthwhile for the supplier to invest in plant and equipment needed to enter the new field.

Buyers usually like to start a new supplier with a small part of their total needs. Then, if the supplier has difficulties, they can still fall back on more experienced suppliers for the majority of their requirements. They naturally prefer to negotiate prices from the new supplier that are lower than those charged by established producers. In many cases they are successful in this, particularly when the supplier is being introduced because the buyer considers prices charged by existing producers excessive. Buyers may be forced to discard accepted criteria in supplier selection when they are developing a new source. But they do this only when there is no other choice. They prefer to use the analytical buying process described in the next chapter for all suppliers, both old and new.

CASES

CASE 12–1. LAWRENCE PLASTICS COMPANY

Dealing with Dishonest Suppliers

The Lawrence Plastics Company is a medium-sized molder of both injection-molded and compression-molded plastics. It makes various toys for a department-store chain, knobs for several manufacturers of television sets, and miscellaneous parts for a number of other manufacturers. The company employs 250 persons and its stock is owned entirely by the Lawrence family and certain key executives. The company's founder, George H. Lawrence, serves as president and chairman of the board, and his son, Walter G. Lawrence, is vice-president and general sales manager. Other members of the company's top management group include a treasurer, a superintendent, a chief engineer, and a purchasing agent.

Albert Harrison, the purchasing agent, has complete responsibility not only for the company's buying but also for inventory control of both raw materials and supplies. To a limited extent, he is also the company's traffic specialist and handles most contacts with carriers. In addition, Harrison is responsible for receiving and shipping, the foremen of these departments reporting to him. He has a secretary who assists him on routine purchases.

Harrison himself conducts all interviews with suppliers, however. This takes about one third of his time. But Harrison is convinced that it is worth all of that—and more. The company has a firm rule that no commitments can be made for purchased materials and services by anyone outside the purchasing department. Operating personnel are permitted to talk to suppliers, but they are expected to make it completely clear that purchases can be authorized only by the purchasing department.

Harrison feels that this rule is workable only if he makes a genuine effort to investigate each supplier thoroughly to see if he has anything at all to offer that will help operating personnel do a better job. If the supplier has something to offer that might be worthwhile, Harrison then asks the appropriate operating executive for his opinion. For example, one supplier recently offered a new type of floor cleaning compound that he claimed was superior. Harrison permitted the supplier to give his presentation to the maintenance foreman, who thought the new product warranted a trial. Harrison got a sample for the foreman to test. The foreman reported that he liked the new compound, so now Harrison buys it.

Two weeks ago, Harrison had a caller by whom he was not impressed. His name was Harold LaPorte, and his card indicated that he was president of the LaPorte Tool Company. LaPorte mentioned that he was a good friend of Howard Lawrence, the brother of the president of Lawrence Plastics. He said that Howard Lawrence (who operates a business in a city 500 miles away) had suggested that he call on Lawrence Plastics because he was certain they would be interested in LaPorte's service. LaPorte claimed he had developed a "metallic revitalization process" that could make old worn tools and dies as good as new. While he refused to discuss the details of his process (he had to keep it secret until he worked out the details of the patent application), he implied that it involved plating or coating the worn tool with some special hard alloy. He supported his presentation with testimonial letters from several satisfied customers in the city where Howard Lawrence's business is located. He said he hoped that Lawrence Plastics would become another satisfied customer so it would recommend LaPorte to other companies in the area.

In order to get Lawrence to try the service, LaPorte proposed that he be given a trial order for demonstration purposes. No fee was mentioned, but Harrison assumed that the first order would be at nominal cost. Nonetheless Harrison was cool to LaPorte's proposal. He had never heard of any of LaPorte's customers, was automatically biased against secret processes, and also reacted unfavorably to LaPorte's personality. He said he would think over LaPorte's proposal, discuss it with other Lawrence executives, and get in touch with him in a few weeks. As soon as LaPorte had left, Harrison requested a credit report on the LaPorte Tool Company.

A few days later, Harrison received the credit report. It was not favorable. Harold LaPorte had operated under two other names at various times in his career. He had been arrested and convicted in 1938 for nonsupport of a child. In 1943 he was arrested, but not convicted, on a charge of violating the regulations of the Office of Price Administration in dealings in scrap metals. In 1949 he was involved in a suit that charged him with selling used cars under misleading circumstances. The report indicated that LaPorte was in the "metal business" but credit investigators could find no record of any facilities or bank accounts and recommended that no credit be granted to LaPorte. The report thus confirmed Harrison's suspicions. He dropped LaPorte from consideration as a supplier under any circumstances and made a mental note to mention

LaPorte at the next meeting of his local purchasing agents' association so that other companies in the area might not be hoodwinked by LaPorte's sales pitch.

A week later, Harrison received an invoice calling for Lawrence Plastics to pay LaPorte $185 for reworking an extrusion mold. The controller had passed it on to Harrison because he had no record of any purchase order being issued for the mold to be reworked. Harrison investigated and discovered that LaPorte had managed to impress the foreman of the tool room with his presentation. The foreman had given the mold to LaPorte so that LaPorte's "engineers could study the mold to see how they could apply the LaPorte process to it."

Harrison now called LaPorte and asked him why he had sent Lawrence an invoice for $185 for just "studying" the mold. LaPorte replied that the bill covered engineering time in developing an application of the process. He said that the process could be applied should Harrison authorize it, and that there would be an additional charge of $185. Harrison replied that he had investigated LaPorte's record and did not want to have any dealings with him, and he asked him to return the mold (which it would cost Lawrence about $2,500 to replace). LaPorte refused to do so until his invoice for engineering time was honored.

Questions
1. What action should Harrison take?
2. What, if anything, could he have done to prevent this problem from arising in the first place?

CASE 12–2. MUSKEGON FURNITURE COMPANY
INVESTIGATING A NEW SUPPLIER

Muskegon Furniture is a medium-sized manufacturer of wooden office furniture. It buys its lumber and most of its hardware. Its manufacturing facilities are devoted primarily to finishing wooden parts and assembling finished products. One of its high-volume purchase parts is a metal drawer pull used in its most popular line. This part, along with all other metal hardware parts, is handled by George Schwartz, one of the company's buyers. Schwartz has purchased the part from the Akron Stamping and Hardware Corporation for a number of years. Akron has never changed its price of 40 cents for the part despite several increases in labor and material costs. Apparently, increased volume (from about 50,000 units a year at the beginning to about 250,000 currently) and various improvements in manufacturing techniques have offset rising costs.

While Schwartz is completely satisfied with Akron's quality and service, he feels that it is about time he got competitive quotations on the drawer pull. So he solicits bids from several of Akron's regular competitors. In addition, he invites Americon Industries to quote. Until a few weeks ago, Schwartz had never heard of Americon. At that time, Americon's president, a Mr. Sloan, called on Schwartz and asked for the opportunity to bid on a job. He showed Schwartz a list of his equipment and also indicated that he was already making a number of small parts for several well-known customers.

Schwartz reviews Americon's sales literature and is impressed enough to mail Sloan blueprints of the drawer pull and to ask him to quote. However, he warns Sloan that he won't necessarily get the job even if he is low bidder, since price is not the only factor that determines Muskegon's buying decisions.

Americon's bid, based on tooling for 250,000 units per year, is 30 cents. It is the only bid Schwartz gets that is below Akron's price of 40 cents. Schwartz checks Americon's bid carefully. While it is obvious that Americon is figuring costs closely and will have to work hard to make a fair profit, Schwartz becomes convinced that the bid is a legitimate one that Americon can live up to. He checks with two of Americon's current customers, whose purchasing agents he knows through his membership in a local purchasing agents' association, and finds that they are thoroughly satisfied with Americon's quality and service.

Schwartz visits Americon's plant and discovers that, while it is a little smaller than he anticipated, it is equipped to make the drawer pull. However, the company has only one press capable of forming the part. As long as there is no breakdown, this press is quite capable of handling all of Muskegon's needs, although Americon might have some difficulty in meeting schedules if Muskegon's requirements increased substantially.

Schwartz then gets a copy of Americon's most recent financial statement. The balance sheet shows total assets of $330,000, including $12,000 in cash, $30,000 in accounts receivable, $125,000 in inventories, and the balance in plant and equipment. Current liabilities are $105,000, there is a mortgage of $95,000, and the balance represents the owners' equity. Last year's sales were $300,000, and profits after taxes were $19,000.

Question

Prepare a report analyzing the pros and cons of buying drawer pulls from Americon and recommend a buying decision.

Chapter 13

THE BUYING PROCESS

The buying process is directly concerned with four basic materials management objectives: low prices, continuity of supply, consistency of quality, and favorable supplier relations. The preceding chapter dealt with the selection of potential suppliers, or, more specifically, with the evaluation of a company's ability to supply. This chapter will discuss the actual process of selecting among a number of qualified potential suppliers. Essential to this process are an understanding of quality and an ability to evaluate prices quoted by competing suppliers for goods that sometimes vary in quality.

QUALITY IS PARAMOUNT

Of the four basic buying objectives, quality may well be the most important. If the buyer does not get the quality of material needed, he really gets nothing of any worth. Price, delivery, and favorable supplier relations become unimportant.

Quality is also the least understood buying objective. The price, delivery, and service objectives are fairly obvious. The quality objective seems obvious—but it isn't. For example, professional buyers are always interested in paying the lowest prices for material and getting the delivery and service they need. But they do not necessarily seek the highest possible quality. On the contrary, they usually are interested in getting the minimum quality necessary for the material to perform its function satisfactorily. For example, for most applications silver is a higher-quality metal than copper. It is easier to draw and has superior electrical conductivity. Yet silver is almost never used to make electrical wire, despite the fact that it is the best metal for this purpose. The reason, of course, is price. Silver is 40 to 50 times more expensive than copper, which does an adequate job.

Quality is usually linked with price. A $5,000 Cadillac automobile is of better quality than a $2,500 Chevrolet. Which car is the better value depends on its function. If the car is to be used for company errands, the Chevrolet is undoubtedly the car to buy. It will serve the function somewhat better than the Cadillac because it is shorter and easier to maneuver. It will last almost as long, be cheaper to operate and maintain, and costs half as much. But if the car is to be used to impress

229

company customers, the Cadillac will probably serve the function more than twice as well as the Chevrolet.

Note that quality is related to function. In one case, the Chevrolet is actually a higher-quality car than the Cadillac. Similarly, a $3 pair of blue jeans can be of higher quality than a $50 pair of fine woolen slacks, if they are to be used as work clothing.

Sell Quality, Not Price. Every salesman tries to convince his prospects that his products are superior in quality to those of competitors. In fact, if a buyer tells a salesman his price is too high, the standard rejoinder is that the quality is high, too. In such cases, the buyer and the salesman may both be right. Then it is up to the buyer to determine if the salesman's company is offering the quality he really needs.

Quality determination is only partly the buyer's responsibility. Also vitally interested are the departments concerned with using and specifying the purchased material. Ideally, the users and specifiers should set objective quality standards for each purchased item. Then the buyer need not concern himself with quality so long as the supplier meets those standards. Unfortunately, for many items this cannot be done in practice. Often it is impossible or impractical to establish standards sufficiently detailed so that the buyer would be assured of satisfactory quality if the supplier met them. Sometimes, the users and specifiers don't really know what standards should be set. They want the "best available at a reasonable price." In some cases each supplier's product is different and performance is the user's only really dependable guide to quality.

Thus quality criteria vary from product to product. No company can use the same criteria to measure the quality of every item it buys. And, regardless of the criteria used, quality is always a problem. Specifications can rarely be so precise that an unscrupulous supplier can't find a way to beat them. "It's amazing," one contracting officer for the U.S. Army once said, "how ingenious contractors are in spotting loopholes in specifications."[1] One supplier once almost succeeded in selling back to the Army canned sweet potatoes that had been sold as surplus because they were spoiled.[2] Other contractors have been more successful in beating Army specifications.

Ethical suppliers won't try to pass off such obviously shoddy goods. But they can and do ship substandard merchandise. The quality of material purchased by a company is only as good as the specifications used to measure it. Every company should try to define quality with good specifications. It can never do a good job if it doesn't know what it wants to buy. There are three basic types of specification commonly used to measure quality: technical, performance, and brand name.

---

[1] Paul V. Farrell and Dean S. Ammer, "The Truth about Military Buying," *Purchasing*, October, 1957, p. 119

[2] *Ibid.*

Technical Specifications. Quality can sometimes be measured objectively and impartially with instruments and gauges. The specifications may be either industry-wide standards or determined by the buyer's engineers. Most raw materials are bought to some industry or professional specifications. For example, the Society of Automotive Engineers, the American Iron and Steel Institute, and other organizations have developed specifications for steel. If a buyer orders one-inch bar stock made of SAE 4320 steel, he can define quality standards with considerable precision by using recognized industry specifications. When the order is delivered, his inspectors can measure the diameter, concentricity, and finish of the bars to see if they conform to standards. The quality laboratory can make an analysis of the steel to see if it contains precisely the right alloys in the right amounts. It also can test the material to make certain that its hardness, yield strength, ductility, and so on all are within the specified tolerances.

Similarly, if a company buys parts, its blueprints can specify the type of material and also the exact dimensions and other characteristics that are desired. For example, if the part is to be machined from the one-inch bars described above, the blueprint would indicate each dimension with its permitted tolerance. One dimension might be .875 inch with a tolerance of .020 inch plus or minus. In some cases much closer tolerances might be needed, but the engineer should never specify a closer tolerance than is really needed if the extra quality contributes nothing to the usefulness of the product.

Performance Specifications. When a company buys a finished product designed by the supplier, it is not particularly interested in a laboratory analysis of the materials or the dimensions of the product's components. Its primary interest is the performance of the product itself. Companies measure quality of such vendor-designed items as machine tools and MRO supplies with performance specifications.

Performance specifications are sometimes combined with technical specifications. For example, one company requires that the aluminum paint used by its maintenance department dry tack-free in two hours and hard in six hours. It also specifies that the paint must not crack when a test panel is "rapidly bent 180° over a ⅜-inch diameter mandrel." Hiding and hardness qualities also are specified. All these are performance specifications. The company determines whether or not they are being met by applying the paint to a test panel and then measuring drying time and other characteristics.

The procedure for determining conformance to technical specifications is a little different. Tests are made on the product itself, not on its application. For example, one technical specification requires that the paint be 13.5 per cent pigment and a minimum of 59 per cent nonvolatiles. Conformance to it can be determined in a laboratory, by heating the paint to boil off volatiles and by other tests.

Approved Brands. In some cases neither performance nor technical specifications can be satisfactorily developed. For example, it would be quite difficult to develop worthwhile specifications for products such as typewriters or standard automobiles. Each manufacturer's brand would be a little different, even though it might be designed to provide almost identical performance at the same prices charged for competing brands. Each manufacturer naturally would claim that his product was the best value. The only objective way the user could evaluate this claim would be to test several brands over a period of years to see if they performed satisfactorily. Careful records of breakdowns, repair bills, and user preference would eventually provide objective evidence of quality.

However, the buyer can still make errors with such records. Manufacturers sometimes change specifications and qualities, and a manufacturer whose products have a good history may currently be producing a product inferior to those of his competitors. For this reason, many purchasing departments try to keep abreast of quality changes by asking users of equipment to report regularly on the quality of all newly purchased items (see Figure 13–1).

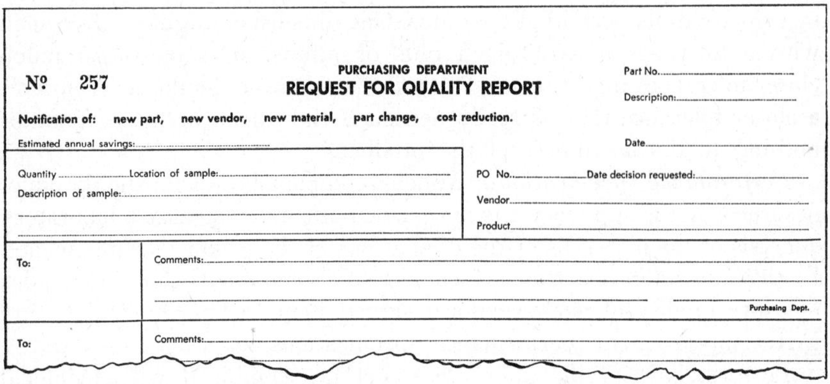
No. 257

PURCHASING DEPARTMENT

REQUEST FOR QUALITY REPORT

Part No.

Description:

Notification of: new part, new vendor, new material, part change, cost reduction.

Estimated annual savings:

Date

Quantity Location of sample:

Description of sample:

PO No. Date decision requested:

Vendor

Product

To: Comments:

Purchasing Dept.

To: Comments:

FIG. 13–1. Sometimes the user's opinion is the buyer's best guide to quality. One purchasing department sends this form to users of material whenever it makes changes in suppliers or specifications.

Whenever possible, the buyer should be given the widest possible choice of competing brands that are equivalent in quality. Most companies test every major brand. The Chrysler Corporation's quality standards for electric typewriters are a good example. All major brands —International Business Machines, Remington Rand, Royal-McBee, Underwood, and Smith-Corona—are approved. Individual characteristics of each brand are analyzed in Chrysler's specifications. The specification then provides that "selection of the models shall be determined by the requirements of the work to be performed." It further provides that "all factors being equal, the selection of the manufacturer, based upon competition, shall remain with Central Purchasing."

Preclusive Specifications. To prevent misunderstandings, specifications should be as clear and explicit as possible. They should be written so as to encourage a maximum number of suppliers to bid. Preclusive specifications that restrict the number of bidders to a few are a problem in almost every company. With them, there is a minimum of competition and buyers find it impossible to do a first-rate job.

Materials personnel can never relent in their efforts to prevent specifications from becoming restrictive. Working against them are almost all of their regular suppliers and many specifiers and users of material in their own company. Every supplier dreams of customer specifications tailored to his products or processes. No longer would he have to fight for business against a number of competitors. Instead, he would automatically get an order whenever a need arose.

Supplier sales efforts are directed at both materials personnel and the engineers who specify the material. Salesmen try to convince engineers in particular that their product and processes are uniquely superior. In some cases, they may succeed in convincing engineers that theirs is the only product that will do the job. When this is the case, the engineer feels obliged to specify the supplier's product in his design or requisition. He may simply include the supplier's brand name in his specification, or he may describe the product with performance or technical specifications that can be met only by one supplier's brand.

If the engineer specifies by brand name, the buyer usually can persuade him to add the phrase "or equal" to his specifications. This permits the buyer to purchase from a number of suppliers equivalent, competing brands. For example, Chrysler's specification for electric typewriters, described above, might read "International Business Machines or equal." The buyer then would be perfectly free to buy from Remington Rand, Underwood, Royal-McBee, or Smith-Corona if he chose to do so, because they are standard, accepted competing brands.

There are more subtle ways in which to make specifications preclusive than convincing engineers that a certain brand is superior. A supplier can achieve the same objective by persuading engineers to incorporate specifications that are unique to his products or processes. Such specifications need not be completely preclusive; all they need do is give the supplier a slight advantage that permits him to underbid competitors without hardship. This is one of the major reasons that suppliers assiduously cultivate engineers and other requisitioners of material.

The more sophisticated suppliers don't necessarily spend much time or effort trying to convince engineers of the intrinsic superiority of their product, particularly when their products are so similar to those of competitors that such a claim would be an insult to the engineers' intelligence. Instead, they have a more positive approach: they assist the engineers in product development. As a result of their help, the specifications either become at least partly preclusive or the supplier gets such a head start on his competitors that he gains the equivalent of restrictive specifications.

This is the best selling approach of all, since both seller and buyer may gain from it. The seller gets an edge on his competitors and so does not have to compete quite so vigorously on price. The buyer gets the benefit of the seller's technical know-how. The only problem, from the buyer's viewpoint, is that the loss of competition resulting from his giving an advantage to one supplier may more than offset the benefits of the supplier's assistance. Buyers try to overcome this drawback by retaining complete control over which suppliers are chosen to give technical assistance and by working to keep the specifications developed as nonrestrictive as possible.

The least restrictive specifications are those that impartially measure technical characteristics or performance. The system of approving certain brands is inherently more restrictive, since such tests can never be completely objective. No set of specifications is foolproof, however. Each inevitably freezes out at least some potential suppliers, but so long as an adequate number remain who are eager to bid, the buyer needn't worry too much.

SECURING QUOTATIONS

When the buyer has reviewed specifications to make certain that they are as unrestrictive as possible, he is ready to solicit quotations from potential suppliers. With new items, buyers try to get at least three competitive quotations (provided the item is not proprietary). For major purchases, six to eight quotations are not uncommon, and, when the buyer has difficulty in finding a supplier, he may issue as many as a hundred quotation requests.

While buyers should not hesitate to permit any qualified supplier to bid, they obviously cannot permit every possible supplier to quote for every projected purchase. They simply don't have the time or the clerical help to prepare that many quotation requests. Many buyers methodically rotate their lists of potential suppliers in requesting quotations. If a supplier is high bidder on several quotations, his name is temporarily dropped from the list. Suppliers who already have a substantial amount of the buying company's business may also be dropped temporarily if the buyer wants to avoid taking too great a percentage of their capacity.

Buyers often are too generous with quotation requests. It is pointless, for example, to go to the trouble of formally requesting a quotation from a supplier who consistently refuses to sell at prices different from those shown in his catalogue or published price lists.[3] Nor should a

---

[3] The buyer should not automatically assume, however, that a supplier will not offer concessions on published prices if he is requested to do so by the buyer or is required to do so by competitive forces.

buyer ever request a quotation from a supplier with whom he has no intention of doing business. Quotations are expensive to prepare, and it is unethical to ask suppliers to prepare them when they won't get an order regardless of what price they quote. In general, price should be the only unknown about the supplier at the time the quotation is requested. The buyer should already have investigated the supplier's potential quality, delivery, and service capabilities (although sometimes it isn't worthwhile to make a really intensive investigation until the supplier submits a favorable quotation).

Exceptions to Quotations

The quotation request should include complete specifications for the material, the quantities required, and a tentative delivery schedule. In addition, most purchasing departments indicate a deadline for submission of quotations; some, including almost all government buying offices, refuse to consider late bids. Some companies also print their purchase terms and conditions on their quotation requests.

If suppliers return quotations with all the information requested and take no exception to any terms or conditions, the buyer is ready to analyze his quotes and select the supplier. However, this is frequently not the case. More often suppliers propose changes in specifications, delivery schedules, and purchase terms, and they also may make errors.

Exceptions to Specifications. On production parts, suppliers frequently take exception to specifications. They usually suggest minor changes that will permit them to make the part more economically. Occasionally, they may even propose a complete redesign. Most companies try to encourage such suggestions, since they frequently reduce the cost of the item. Some companies even go so far as to include a statement in their quotation request that suggestions are welcomed. For example, Ford Motor Company quotation requests include this statement:

We will welcome suggestions regarding design changes that you believe will facilitate the tooling or fabrication of the part or both. However, all such changes must have the approval of our Engineering Department and arrangements must be made to incorporate such changes on our blueprints because our purchase orders will specify delivery as per our blueprint.

As the Ford statement indicates, the purchasing department must submit all proposed changes to the engineering department for approval. Most large companies have routine procedures to handle such changes and use forms similar to that in Figure 2–3 (page 24). The buyer can do nothing with the supplier's quotation until engineering approves or rejects the proposed change. If the change is approved, he usually will get new quotations from other bidders.

Changes in Schedule. If a supplier cannot deliver material when it is needed, he is automatically disqualified. But sometimes suppliers propose delivery changes that aren't so clear-cut. The delivery date requested by the buyer may be unrealistic and the supplier simply must be given more time to fill the order. In this case, the buyer may have to propose a change in schedule to the various managers in his company who are concerned.

Occasionally a supplier may make what amounts to a counterproposal on delivery terms. For example, the buyer may have requested a quotation for 10,000 units of an item with delivery in ten monthly shipments. Suppose a supplier suggests either a single shipment of 10,000 pieces or two shipments of 5,000 pieces each. Obviously that supplier's bid is not comparable to bids that agree to the original plan.

The buyer should request the supplier to requote on the same delivery basis as originally requested. Then he should compare the two bids from the same supplier. If the supplier offers a lower price for different delivery terms, the buyer should analyze them to see if they are really advantageous. Suppose the supplier quotes a price of $1.00 per unit if he can ship in a lot of 10,000 pieces and a price of $1.10 if he must schedule his shipments over a period of ten months at the rate of 1,000 units per month. In effect, the supplier is offering to reduce the total cost of the purchase by $1,000 ($.10 × 10,000) if the buyer will accept the entire order in a single shipment. For this saving the buyer must carry for ten months an average $5,000 inventory instead of a $500 inventory. The buyer can readily determine if this is worthwhile by applying the principles discussed in the chapters on inventory management. If the savings exceed the additional carrying cost (less the saving in procurement cost by processing a single shipment instead of ten separate ones) and possible obsolescence, then the offer to purchase the larger quantity is attractive. The buyer should then go back to the other suppliers who quoted and ask them to requote on the same basis.

Purchase Terms. The buyer should study each supplier's quotation to make certain that all offer comparable terms and conditions. For example, one supplier may quote a firm price, another supplier may insist on some provision for escalation for labor and material costs, and a third may insist on "price in effect at time of delivery." Obviously these quotations are not comparable even if all three suppliers quote identical prices.

The buyer should try to persuade suppliers to revise their bids and accept the terms and conditions he wants. On pricing terms, for example, most buyers prefer fixed-price contracts for short lead-time items, although they will accept escalation on long lead-time contracts in order to prevent suppliers from inflating their bids to allow for possible higher costs.

If the bidder flatly refuses to quote within the terms and conditions desired, the buyer has two choices. He may disqualify the bid, or he may accept it while making allowance for the disadvantageous terms. In the latter case, the buyer may put a price tag on the supplier's terms. Suppose, for example, that a supplier's current price is $1.00 and his terms are "price in effect at time of delivery." The buyer may have to inflate this bid to $1.02 or $1.03 when comparing it to the quotations of suppliers who are willing to guarantee fixed prices.

Errors. The buyer should review each quotation carefully to make certain the supplier made no mistakes in preparing it. He should make sure that the supplier's quotation covers the exact requirements described in his quotation request. If it doesn't, he should return it to the supplier and ask him to requote. The buyer should be particularly wary of bids that are unusually high or low. If a dependable low-cost supplier submits a bid that is substantially higher than those of his competitors, the buyer should return it and have the supplier check it for errors. The buyer should be equally cautious about exceptionally low bids. Only the most inexperienced and naive buyers will quietly accept a bid of 10 cents for an item that is worth at least $1.00. This is not only unethical—it is uneconomic. The supplier eventually will detect the error and will either request a price increase or, if he feels he has been treated unfairly, refuse to do business with the buyer's company.

If a supplier rechecks a bid and insists that no errors were made, the buyer should still be cautious if he is convinced that the bid is unrealistic. If the bidder is not too familiar with the buyer's requirements, the buyer may simply disqualify the bid. But if the bidder is an ex-

16098 REV. 9-61

QUOTATION CHART

Part Name ______ Part No. ______

Specification ______ Model ______

Group

INQUIRY			QUOTATION						
DATE	SOURCE	QUANTITY	DATE REFERENCE	QUANTITY	PRICE	TOOL COST	DELIVERY	F.O.B.	TERMS

PART NO. ______

Courtesy Chrysler Corporation

FIG. 13–2. The Chrysler Corporation uses this form to compare quotations from competing suppliers of production parts. Chrysler buyers keep separate quotation records for each part.

perienced, reliable supplier, the buyer may wish to review the bid in detail with him to make certain that no errors were made. He also may arrange to have the specifications explained to the supplier by product or quality control engineers.

Analysis of Quotations

After exceptions and errors have been taken care of, the buyer is ready to tabulate the quotations on a work sheet for purposes of comparison (see Figure 13–2 on previous page). If there are no special proposals by suppliers, this comparison is not difficult to make. For each supplier, the buyer would list:

1. Net unit prices proposed for various purchase quantities.
2. Terms of payment.
3. Set-up costs and minimum charges, if any.
4. Cost of any special tools to be purchased by buyer for supplier's use.
5. Unit shipping cost if the item is sold on a basis other than F.O.B. buyer's plant.
6. Other charges, if any.

In some cases, the buyer can select the lowest-cost supplier with no more than a glance at his recap sheet. If the low bidder is satisfactory in all other respects, he gets the order. Many buying decisions, particularly important ones, cannot be made so easily. Quotations must be recalculated to make them comparable, quotations may not be for identical items, or all bids may be too high.

Bids Comparable Economically. Quotations from suppliers frequently cannot be compared until the buyer adjusts them to make them comparable. For example, suppose a buyer gets two bids[4] for a part weighing one pound, having a usage of 10,000 units per year, and requiring an investment in special tools. Shipment is to be made in lots of 1,000 pieces.

Supplier A quotes a unit price of $1.00 F.O.B. buyer's plant with a $2,500 charge for special tools and a special set-up charge of $10 for each 1,000-piece lot. His payment terms are 2/10, net 30. Supplier B quotes a unit price of $.95 F.O.B. shipping point with a $3,500 tool charge and no set-up charges. His payment terms are net 30 days, and the LTL freight rate from his plant to the buyer's plant for 1,000-pound shipments is 70 cents per cwt.

It is not immediately obvious which of the two bids is the lower. The buyer must tabulate them for comparison. He would immediately make the following adjustments in the quotations:

---

[4] The reader should note that only rarely would a buyer limit himself to two bids if the purchase were at all important. Usually he would get at least three bids, and he might get half a dozen or more if he had as many qualified suppliers willing to quote.

	Supplier A	Supplier B
Unit price quoted	$1.00	$.95
Unit freight cost paid by buyer (1 lb. × $.007/lb.)	—	.007
Unit cost of set-up charge for 1,000-pc. lots	.01	—
Adjusted unit price	$1.01	$.957
Tool cost	$2,500	$3,500
Payment terms	2/10, net 30	net 30

The table above shows that the adjusted unit price of Supplier B is $.053 lower but his tool charge is $1,000 higher. Therefore, B must ship 18,867 pieces ($1,000/0.53) before his lower unit price more than offsets his higher tool charge. This would take almost 22 months with a usage of 10,000 pieces per year.

In practice, the buyer would want to be reasonably certain that the part will stay in production for at least two years before he would give the order to Supplier B. There are two reasons for the buyer to make the "break-even point" between A and B more than 22 months' usage:

(1) The higher tooling cost for B requires an immediate cash outlay. Cash in hand is always worth more than cash derived from savings made in the future. The cash itself is worth some interest rate during the period. In addition, if the buyer's calculations are incorrect and the part becomes obsolete immediately, there is less loss.

(2) Supplier A offers a 2 per cent discount if bills are paid within 10 days; Supplier B does not. If the buyer's accounting department pays bills within 10 days as a matter of routine, Supplier A's discount is a clear saving of $200 per year and the piece-cost saving by buying from B is reduced from $612 per year to $412 per year. The 2 per cent discount is a definite "plus" for Supplier A even if the buyer's accounting department ordinarily takes 30 days to pay bills. The 2 per cent discount is earned, in effect, if the bill is paid 20 days earlier; this is equal to an annual interest rate of 36 per cent. There are few solvent companies that are so strapped for cash that they can afford to overlook such a profitable short-term investment opportunity. In fact, for most purchases any difference in payment terms between suppliers can be considered a direct difference in price.

If the buyer knows precisely how many pieces he will buy over the life of the tooling, he can compare quotations with precision. If the part in our example were to have a life of precisely two years (or a total usage of 20,000 pieces), then the buyer could make the following comparison between Suppliers A and B:

	Supplier A	Supplier B
Total piece cost (20,000 pieces at adjusted prices)	$20,200	$19,140
Tool cost	2,500	3,500
Total cost	$22,700	$22,640
Savings buying from Supplier B		$60
Discount earned on payment terms	$454	—
Net advantage buying from Supplier A (including payment terms)	$394	

The bids above are so close that it's a toss-up whether the buyer would give the order to A or B. However, there is no doubt that A offers a slightly better deal when payment terms are considered. The buyer, however, would not necessarily give A the order after making the comparison. He might ask Supplier B why he did not offer better payment terms if they were normal in his industry.[5] Or he might suggest to Supplier B that he review his tooling cost to make certain he had gotten the lowest possible quotation from the tooling shops he contacted.[6] While it is unethical to disclose competitors' bids, some negotiation of this sort is normal before an order is placed.

Bids for Nonidentical Items. The example above is applicable primarily to production parts made to the buyer's specifications. An entirely different problem is encountered in evaluating supplier-designed items. In such cases, bidders usually are quoting on performance specifications. They may be bidding on a machine tool to do a given job or sometimes a component to perform a given function. In each case the supplier is selling both his design efforts and his manufacturing skills. Since each supplier's design is unique, bids are not comparable. Technical evaluation is necessary.

In such cases, engineers carefully review each supplier's proposal. They indicate not only which proposals they prefer but which are acceptable. Suppliers whose bids are not acceptable may be asked by the buyer to requote, especially if their proposed prices are attractive.

The final buying decision is based on both the buyer's evaluation of the economic factors of the bid and the engineer's evaluation of the technical factors (see Figure 13–3). Some companies evaluate bids on a point basis. Engineers assign preference ratings to each bid, which reflect their technical evaluation of the supplier's product. They list their preferences in sequence—1, 2, 3, 4,—and also indicate separately bids that are unacceptable to them. The buyer lists his preferences in sequence. If a bidder gets a top rating from both the buyer and the engineer, there obviously is no problem. But what if a bidder rated only second or third by an engineer is rated tops by the buyer? In such cases, the buyer and engineer usually meet and try to resolve their differences. In many instances the buyer's preference will prevail if the engineer agrees that the third-best bid is still technically acceptable. In some instances, buyer

---

[5] On price-fixed items, many buyers get around fair-trade laws by persuading suppliers to offer better-than-usual terms of payment. The supplier is willing to do so to get business from a competitor because the margin of profit on such items is more than ample. Payment terms of 7%–10 days are not unheard of; they are, of course, a thinly disguised trade discount, since the buyer theoretically earns a return of 126 per cent on his money by paying in 10 days instead of in 30 days.

[6] Many suppliers quote on the basis of rather careless estimates of tool costs—made, in many cases, before they have even obtained quotations from tool shops. Thus, they are sometimes willing to reduce tool quotations after they have studied their needs in greater detail.

November 5, 19____

MEMO TO: Chief Engineer
          cc: Plant Manager
               Project Engineer
               Plant Purchasing Agent
               Asst. Director of Purchasing

FROM.   Purchasing Engineer

SUBJECT: QUOTATION ANALYSIS - ELECTROLYTIC CELL - LITHIUM HYDRIDE EXPANSION

The following are the vendors and prices quoted for a fabricated steel electrolytic cell for the Lithium Hydride expansion:

VENDOR		DELIVERY	F.O.B. POINT	TOTAL PRICE
A_____	Welding Co.	3 Weeks	Exton, Pa.	$ 835.00 *
F_____	Welding Shop	1 Week	Exton, Pa.	864.00
N_____	Steel Co.	6-8 weeks	Nazareth, Pa.	1,127.00
B & M Co.		3 weeks	Phila., Pa.	1,780.00
A. J. S & Co.		3 weeks	Exton, Pa.	840.00
P - P Co.		4 weeks	Exton, Pa.	1,235.00

When A__, the low bidder, was contacted and advised of the special requirements as to soundness of weld, they advised that this would require a different method of welding and the cost increase would be approximately $100.00. We had also asked if they could bend two of the corners, instead of welding them, thereby eliminating about 25% of possible trouble area in the wetted section and they advised that they did not have the equipment to bend that heavy plate. A. J. S, being the next lowest bidder, were asked the same question and they advised that they had anticipated the importance of these welds and had provided for it in their original quotation of $840.00 and they also advised that they could bend two of the corners, thereby reducing the welding, with no change in price.

On the basis of price, delivery and quality workmanship, we recommended that this cell be fabricated by A. J. S & Company. S has advised that they will put a code welder on this job and make every effort to produce the very best welding possible.

W. H. Snell

FIG. 13-3. Quotations on capital equipment must be carefully analyzed. Not only are prices and terms different for various suppliers, but so are the products themselves, since each supplier quotes on his own design.

and engineer may compromise and accept a bid that is second-best to both but that still fulfills their objectives.

All Bids High. Good buyers don't necessarily accept the low bid even if they are sure it is made by a first-rate supplier and is comparable to competitors' bids. They may even reject all bids if they feel the lowest acceptable quotation is too high.

Buyers don't reject bids arbitrarily, however. They rely as much as possible on objective price data to assist them in negotiation. Even if the buyer is satisfied, there usually still is some need for negotiation. Packaging, freight rates, supplier inventories, split shipments, and so on may be discussed. (Negotiating techniques are discussed in detail in Chapter 17.)

SELECTING THE SUPPLIER

Buyers naturally prefer to award business to the bidder quoting the lowest prices. However, they don't always do so. If a bidder quoting a higher price offers better quality, delivery, or service, he may get the order. As we will see in the next chapter, reciprocity and other factors also influence the selection of suppliers. In general, however, the buyer is on the defensive if the low bidder doesn't get the job. Many companies require buyers to enter detailed explanations in their records when this is the case, and some buyers prefer to make an explanation even when it is not required in order to protect themselves against charges of collusion.

Companies may have as many as four or five suppliers for a given item simultaneously. But, in most cases, buyers rely on a single supplier for all of their requirements for a particular item. If the item does not become obsolete, they will solicit bids from other suppliers from time to time to make sure that their supplier is still competitive. In addition, they make use of learning-curve analysis[7] and other techniques to make certain that their supplier is passing on the benefits of productivity improvements by reducing prices periodically.

Advantages of a Single Source. By buying all requirements of a particular item from a single source, buyers can gain several advantages:

1. They make maximum use of their buying power. They concentrate all requirements for a certain item on a single supplier and thereby get the largest possible quantity discount.
2. There is less administrative work for the buyer's entire organization, since it is necessary to issue purchase orders, receiving reports, inspection reports, checks, and so on to only one supplier per item.
3. Suppliers often offer special price concessions if they can make 100 per cent of the requirements of a given item, since they then can set up their production in the most economic manner and invest in more efficient tooling.
4. Less investment in special tooling is usually needed. One supplier generally needs only one set of tools; two suppliers need at least two sets.
5. Suppliers have more incentive to aid in methods improvement. If a supplier is the sole source for an item, he is more likely to regard himself as a partner in the company's product, particularly if he is manufacturing the item under a long-term contract. As a result, he will be more likely to devote part of his research and development efforts to improvements.

Advantages of Multiple Sources. Despite these advantages, many companies do their utmost to avoid relying on a single source for all but the most unimportant items. They try to have at least two suppliers for each item and sometimes they have three or four. For doing so they have one or more of the following reasons:

---

[7] This is discussed in Chapter 16.

1. With several sources, there is less risk of interruption of supply due to quality problems, strikes, fires, and so on. If one supplier fails, the other supplier(s) can take up the slack.
2. With two or more suppliers for one item, a healthy competitive spirit can develop in which each vies to improve methods and reduce costs in order to get a greater share of the business. With a single source, the supplier may become so well versed in making the item that he gets a virtual monopoly of its manufacture and, sometimes, no competitor brought in at a later date can meet his prices.
3. Many items either require little or no tooling or are used in such large quantities that duplicate tooling is necessary anyway. In these cases, there is no cost premium for tooling a second source.
4. The unit price of the item is no higher with more than one source than it would be if all requirements were concentrated on a single source.
5. The buyer has found a new supplier with low prices whom he would like to introduce to the item but with whom he is not yet familiar enough to trust with 100 per cent of the business.

PLACEMENT AND DELIVERY

When the buyer concludes negotiations and finally settles on a supplier, he places the order. He may simply mail a purchase order with the agreed-on terms and conditions to the supplier. Or, if he wants the supplier to start on the order immediately, he may telephone or wire him that he has been awarded the contract. The purchase order then is sent in a few days.

The buyer's job ends with the placement of the order only on minor, short lead-time items for which there is no immediate need. In such cases, the supplier ships when he receives the order and the transaction is complete. No buyer, however, would dare place an important order for parts, material, or equipment and then forget about it. He always would make some sort of routine follow-up even if there were no problems.

Acknowledgment of Orders. Routine follow-up may start with acknowledgment of the order. A copy of the purchase order is kept in a separate file of unacknowledged open orders until an acknowledgment is received. If the supplier does not acknowledge within a week after he should have received the order, a buyer or expediter either phones or sends him a written reminder.

Some companies persistently follow up for acknowledgments of orders until they finally get them from suppliers. They know that in most cases the supplier is legally committed to the terms and conditions of the order only after he has formally acknowledged or actually filled the order. Also, when there is no follow-up for acknowledgments, there theoretically can be serious problems if the order should have been mislaid or lost in the mail. The company might suddenly discover a few days before the material was needed for production that the supplier had no record of the order. The result would certainly be a critical shortage, and possibly even a shutdown.

Nevertheless, many companies do not bother to follow up except when they are required to do so by government regulations, as on defense contracts. They maintain that such follow-up is expensive and never is worth the trouble or the expense it causes. The rare order that goes astray need not cause any trouble, either. In most cases, the vendor would have already been notified of the order by telephone or letter of commitment, and he would inquire if he did not receive a formal purchase order. In other cases, companies would discover that an order had gone astray through routine follow-up or when a supplier sales representative called to discuss his business prospects.

A company that insists that orders not be acknowledged can occasionally avoid disputes over purchase terms and contracts. This problem arises when the seller takes exception to the terms and conditions of the buyer's purchase order. If both buyer and seller are completely inflexible on the terms and conditions they will accept, the result is a deadlock. Legally the order is not binding on either party. The problem is solved in most cases by ignoring it. Both buyer and seller assume they have a valid contract (each on his own terms) and eventually the buyer gets the material he ordered. This is bad practice, but sometimes it is the only way two giant corporations with inflexible procedures can successfully deal with each other.

Although such legally vague contracts rarely create problems, some buyers attempt to circumvent a deadlock over terms and conditions by simply mailing the supplier an order and refusing an acknowledgment. For example, the Magnetic Research Corporation of Hawthorne, California, uses this clause as a substitute for an acknowledgment copy of the order:

Delivery is a major condition of this order. If for any reason you cannot meet the terms of this Purchase Order you must reply within 72 hours indicating any deviations. The absence of a reply will constitute an acceptance of this order and an agreement to meet the terms and conditions as specified above and on the reverse side hereof.

Routine Progress Follow-up.   Regardless of whether or not they worry about acknowledgments of purchase orders, most purchasing departments do make routine checks on suppliers' progress on orders. The frequency of follow-up depends on the importance and urgency of the item. Minor items may get no follow-up as long as inventories are ample. Most of the more important items get at least one progress check, which is most often made a week or two before the promised delivery date.

The procedure for handling such a check need not be complicated. One of the more popular procedures involves keeping copies of the purchase orders in file folders marked with the date for which follow-up is scheduled. Each morning (or once a week), a secretary gives the buyer the file folder of orders to be checked that day.

Often the follow-up process is entirely automatic and the buyer doesn't get into the act at all if there are no problems. A clerk sends a postcard requesting progress information on each order a week or ten days before shipment is promised (see Figure 13–4). The buyer is consulted only if the vendor advises that he cannot meet his original delivery promise.

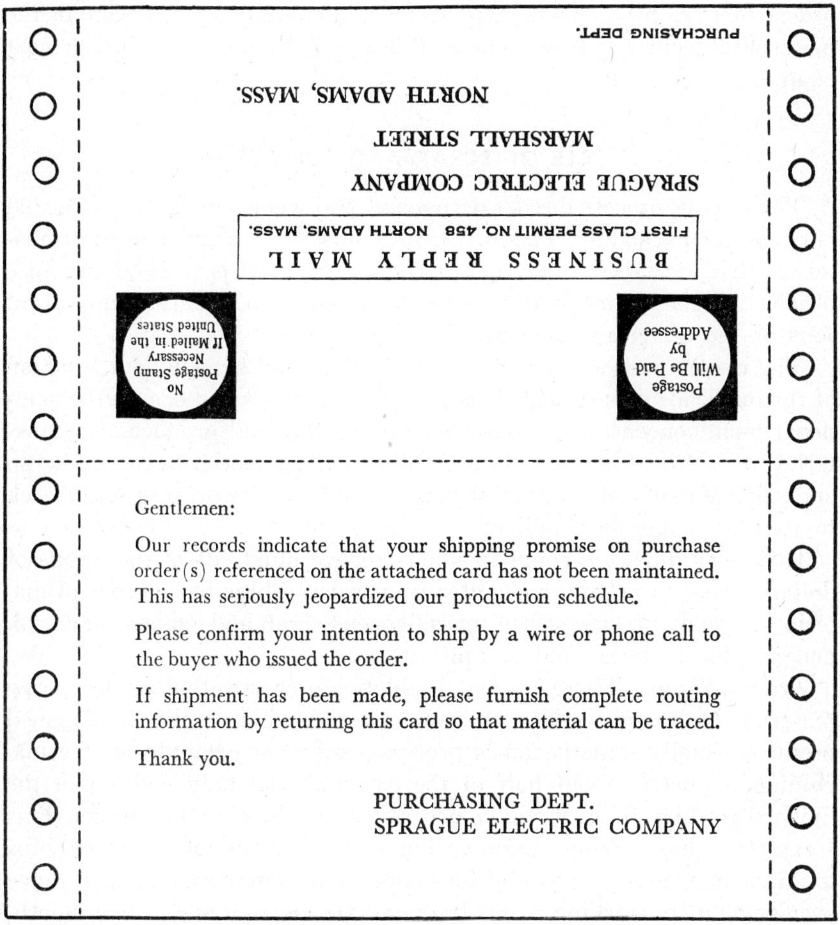

PURCHASING DEPT.

NORTH ADAMS, MASS.

MARSHALL STREET

SPRAGUE ELECTRIC COMPANY

BUSINESS REPLY MAIL
FIRST CLASS PERMIT NO. 458 NORTH ADAMS, MASS.

No Postage Stamp Necessary If Mailed in the United States

Postage Will Be Paid by Addressee

Gentlemen:

Our records indicate that your shipping promise on purchase order(s) referenced on the attached card has not been maintained. This has seriously jeopardized our production schedule.

Please confirm your intention to ship by a wire or phone call to the buyer who issued the order.

If shipment has been made, please furnish complete routing information by returning this card so that material can be traced.

Thank you.

PURCHASING DEPT.
SPRAGUE ELECTRIC COMPANY

Courtesy Sprague Electric Co.

FIG. 13–4. Many companies use double postcards for routine follow-up. One card (directly above) advises the supplier that he is behind schedule. The supplier then returns the second card to the buyer with his shipping promise noted on it.

More complex follow-up systems are used for major production parts and equipment. The buyer estimates what progress the supplier should have made on the order at various dates if he is to complete it on schedule. For example, he might check progress on an order for a production part when completion of tooling is scheduled, when tools are to be tried out, and when initial production is scheduled. If everything is going according to plan on each of these and other critical dates, he is reasonably certain that actual production shipments will be made on schedule.

In the typical purchasing department, more than 99 per cent of all orders can be handled with little or no follow-up. Routine progress checks are insurance against failure, but they aren't really necessary except in a few cases. This is fortunate, since the less than 1 per cent of all orders that are problems manage to take an enormous percentage of the materials executive's time. These orders will be discussed in the next chapter.

SALE OF SCRAP AND SURPLUS

The buying process doesn't necessarily end when satisfactory material is received on schedule. The buyers also must sell surplus and scrap materials that are inevitably generated when material is used or becomes obsolete. This is one of the incidental but by no means unimportant jobs of the materials department.

The reader may wonder why selling scrap and surplus is a function of the materials department. It is so in most companies because the sales department concentrates its efforts on marketing end products. The materials department is much more familiar with potential buyers of scrap and salvage materials; in fact, it may sell much of its process scrap back to its raw materials suppliers.

Even medium-sized companies may realize hundreds of thousands of dollars a year through scrap and surplus sales. Three basic types of material are sold: process scrap; miscellaneous scrap and salvage material; and surplus material and equipment.

Process Scrap. There are few production processes that waste no raw material. Only rarely does all raw material wind up in the finished product; usually some becomes process scrap. For example, in the machining of metal, about half of the raw material may end up in the finished product; the rest will be process scrap, chips, and turnings. This scrap metal has a value ranging from about $30 per ton for steel chips to 25 cents or more per pound for copper and more costly metals. Since even small metalworking plants frequently use tons of metal each month, process scrap sales are an important source of revenue for them.

Miscellaneous Scrap and Salvage. Every plant must dispose of tons of material each year because it is usable neither in finished products nor as process scrap. Cartons, pallets, and boxes are among the most important miscellaneous items. In most areas there is a ready market for scrap paper and lumber for plants that do not find ways to reuse such materials themselves.

Surplus Material and Equipment. As we saw in Chapter 9, no company should carry inventories it doesn't need. Surplus materials should be sold as soon as it becomes reasonably certain that there is no immediate need for them. Obsolete equipment should also be sold as soon as no immediate use can be foreseen for it.

Segregation.   Scrap and surplus have value to a buyer only if they can be used. For this reason, companies are almost as careful in handling them as they are in handling newly purchased materials. It is particularly important to keep scrap segregated. In some cases, a scrap material will have no value at all if it is mixed in with other materials. In every case it will have more value if it is reasonably clean and free from impurities. Many companies employ a color system for scrap collection and segregation. For example, red barrels at strategic locations in the plant might be used only for aluminum turnings while yellow barrels were used only for stainless steel.

Processing.   As in selling any other product, top prices on scrap sales go only to those who deliver top-quality materials. Many companies invest in processing equipment both to facilitate handling of scrap and to improve its quality. For example, they may buy equipment to dry out and clean metal turnings that are soaked with oil. They may bale both metal and paper scrap to get a higher price and to make them easier to handle. They may even wind up with equipment to reprocess the scrap into usable end products. For example, several large corporations have invested in plants to convert their scrap paper into corrugated paper for new cartons.

Sale.   Scrap is normally sold by asking a number of scrap brokers or dealers to bid (see Figure 13–5, page 248), on either a specific quantity or a year's needs of some commodity. Some companies sell to all comers on a cash basis; others will deal only with reputable brokers and dealers with established credit. In either case, the high bidder always gets the material. Published market prices are available for many scrap materials, and it is common practice to use these prices as the basis for long-term contracts on scrap sales. Variations in the quality of scrap sometimes forbid this, however. Regardless of the pricing technique used, the seller always can get a somewhat better price if he exercises his ingenuity. A buyer who is selling scrap looks for buyers with the same thoroughness with which he recruits suppliers when he is buying material. For example, the Aeroquip Corporation of Jackson, Michigan, increased its return on surplus oleum spirits 500 per cent by locating a small local buyer with a specialized use for the material.[8]

Disputes over quality are prevented by permitting each interested bidder to inspect the material physically in advance. Occasionally disputes arise over weights—often because the weight has changed in transit between buyer and seller because of material drying out on being exposed to the hot sun, and so on. Companies prevent such disputes by insisting that the weight shown on their scales determine the buyer's

---

[8] H. B. Ferguson, "There's Money in That Scrap Pile," *Purchasing*, December, 1956, p. 75.

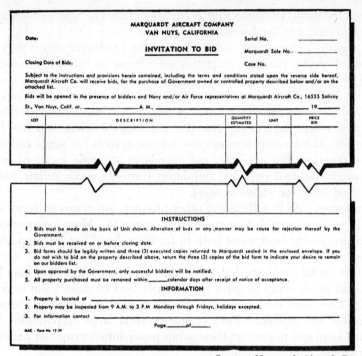

FIG. 13–5. The form used to solicit bids on scrap and surplus material that a company has for sale is not much different from the form used to solicit bids for material it wishes to buy.

payment or by using some local public scale where the weighmaster's certificate is the basis for payment.

CASES

CASE 13–1.   GREAT LAKES AUTO SUPPLY COMPANY

SELECTING THE RIGHT SUPPLIER

Although the Great Lakes Auto Supply Company does some manufacturing, it is primarily a distributor. It buys auto parts from independent manufacturers and resells them to thousands of service stations and repair shops. The parts that Great Lakes buys are almost identical with those distributed by the service departments of the auto manufacturers themselves. Great Lakes is successful because it is willing to undersell the original equipment manufacturers on service parts. For example, the manufacturer purchases mufflers at a unit price of $2.32 for one of the nation's most popular brands of car. It resells them to its dealers for $6.80, and they in turn sell them to the ultimate consumer for $10.50 plus a charge for installation labor. Great Lakes buys almost the same muffler from one of its suppliers for $2.78 (it buys in smaller quantities than the original equipment manufacturer and so must pay a higher price). It resells the muffler for $3.75 and the gas station charges the ultimate consumer $7.50 plus installation labor.

The auto manufacturers and their franchised dealers refer to Great Lakes and its suppliers as "gyp" manufacturers. They point out that the gyps do no engineering but simply copy the parts of the auto manufacturers. They claim that the gyps produce parts of inferior quality. Consumers, attracted by the lower prices charged by the gyps, obviously don't accept the auto companies' charges. Yet the charge that the gyps copy their designs is certainly true.

For example, Walter Norris, Great Lakes' vice-president in charge of purchases, recently secured quotations on replacement floor mats for 1960 Blue Motors sedans. Suppliers got no specifications; instead, they were asked to quote on the basis of "original equipment quality." Norris got the following bids for 10,000 mats:

Supplier	Price	F.O.B.	Tools	Terms
Western Rubber Products....	$3.32	Shipping point	$45	2/10, net 30
Alexander Corporation.......	$3.25	Great Lakes' plant	$110	net 20th prox.
Roberts Rubber Company....	$3.44	Great Lakes' plant	$65	1/10, net 30
Wartly Rubber, Inc.........	$2.84	Shipping point	$50	net 30 days

The mat used as original equipment on Blue Motors cars weighs 9.2 pounds, and Norris assumes that the suppliers will give him a mat of the same weight. Norris understands from one of his suppliers that Blue Motors pays an average of $2.75 for the mat. Thus Norris is not the least bit surprised that none of his bids is that low, since Blue uses an average of 2,000 mats per day from each of its suppliers. In fact, he suspects that Blue's price may be even lower than this.

Norris has made an analysis in which he compares the Blue Motors mat with mats he has purchased for various other auto models. He concludes that a fair price for the Blue mat is probably between $3.10 and $3.25. He passes this on to Western and Roberts and asks them if they would be interested in requoting. Both suppliers reply that their costs have gone up since they quoted last and Norris' estimate of a fair price for the mat is out of date. Western and Roberts are currently supplying other mats to Great Lakes. Alexander and Wartly make mats for other auto parts distributors but have never been Great Lakes suppliers. Norris has some doubts as to whether or not Wartly can supply the desired quality although they have had considerable experience in producing mats for the "gyp" trade.

Questions

1. Which supplier should Norris choose? Support your recommendations with an analysis, making assumptions where necessary.
2. What special studies might be called for in this case?

CASE 13–2.   ST. LOUIS OFFICE FURNITURE COMPANY

A PROBLEM IN USER BRAND PREFERENCE

The St. Louis Office Furniture Company is a medium-sized company that specializes in steel desks and filing cabinets. It buys steel from several mills, forms it in its press shops, welds it into desks and cabinets, and then finishes and paints the completed products. The finishing operation is necessary because the metal is rough where it has been welded and worked in presses and must be sanded down to a smooth finish before painting. It is an extremely dirty and disagreeable job. Workers run abrasive wheels against the semifinished cabinets until they are smooth. Not only is this physically hard to do and requires some skill, but the job is extremely unpleasant. The wheels are noisy, the abrasive grit fills the air and settles into the workers' clothes, and the workers are invariably hot and uncomfortable. They must wear masks to prevent their lungs from being contaminated with dust, and the friction of the abrasive generates heat, which is almost unbearable in the hot summer months.

Because their job is so unpleasant, the metal finishers are extremely well paid. They average about $1.00 per hour more than the average worker at St. Louis Furniture. Despite the high pay, good metal finishers are scarce, and they tend to be extremely independent. Absences and tardiness among them are far more frequent than among other workers. The scarcity of metal finishers and their high pay gives management a double incentive to do everything it can to raise their productivity. The company's materials manager, Edward Kellogg, has been working for the past few months with Reynolds Abrasive, a major supplier, on a new abrasive that will cut at least 25 per cent faster and last 10 per cent longer than the abrasive currently used. Although the new product is much more expensive than the current one, if it works it will raise the productivity of the metal finishers by enough so that the cost premium will be offset many times over.

Kellogg naturally has kept the plant superintendent and others informed of his work on the abrasive. When he gets his first test shipment, he and the superintendent arrange for a test on Sunday, when the plant is shut down. The foreman of the metal finishing line and one of the company's time-study men participate in the tests. The foreman, a former metal finisher himself, uses the abrasive on a few cabinets while the time-study man makes observations. The time studies confirm the supplier's claims: the abrasive is 25 per cent faster. The foreman, however, says he doesn't like the new abrasive. He says it just doesn't feel right, although he doesn't dispute the time study's indication that it is faster. He says he is sure the men won't like the new abrasive. The others are reluctant to see such a big saving evaporate simply because the abrasive doesn't "feel right." They decide that the best thing to do is to change the brand of abrasive quietly and see how the men react. Then, after the workers get used to the feel of the new product, they can make new time studies and raise the standard.

The workers arrive on Monday morning and almost immediately notice the change in abrasive. They ask the foreman what is going on and are told that the company has decided to purchase a higher-quality abrasive that will work faster. No mention is made of any future changes in work standards. The men grumble that the new abrasive isn't as good as the old. After giving the new product a few minutes' trial, they accuse the company of trying to slip in a cheaper new product that requires them to work harder. They flatly refuse to work until they are given the old abrasive again. The foreman gives them the old abrasive to keep production going and advises Kellogg that he had better keep on buying the old product because the men won't accept any changes.

Questions

1. Should Kellogg follow the foreman's advice?
2. What can be done to get the men to adopt the new product and accept a new time study?
3. Did Kellogg handle this problem correctly from the beginning? What mistakes did he make?

Chapter 14

PROBLEMS IN SUPPLIER RELATIONS

One of the basic objectives of materials management is favorable relations with outside suppliers. This is not too difficult to achieve when: (1) Suppliers perform outstandingly well on quality and delivery after they accept orders at competitive prices. (2) A strictly businesslike buyer-seller relationship prevails.

Unfortunately, suppliers do fail to keep delivery promises and don't always meet quality standards. Sometimes they are responsible for the failure; sometimes others are responsible. Buyer-seller relations also are subject to numerous pressures. Some of these pressures reflect the character of the buyers and sellers themselves; others are exerted by outside influences.

DELIVERY FAILURE

The most basic supplier failure is failure to deliver. There are many reasons why a supplier might not deliver on schedule. These include manufacturing difficulties, shortages of raw materials, labor trouble, transportation tie-ups, and just plain bad management.

Meeting the Shortage. The buyer's skill is tested when a supplier fails to deliver. The buyer immediately must find out the cause of the failure and then develop a plan to cope with it. If he moves fast, he sometimes can avoid a costly shutdown resulting from lack of material.

As soon as he learns that a supplier may fail to deliver, the buyer should get the following information:

1. When and how much the supplier can deliver.
2. Current inventories and probable requirements. (Possibly stocks are more than adequate and there is no need for the supplier to ship in the near future anyway.)
3. Cause of the delivery failure.
4. Availability of alternate sources of supply.

From this data, the buyer must develop a plan to cope with the shortage. Whenever possible, he tries to prevent production from being disrupted. But the buyer always should be realistic. If the shortage is so serious that some curtailment of output is inevitable, he should allow for this in his plan. A shutdown that is planned in advance is almost always less costly than one that comes as a complete surprise.

In some cases the buyer may be able to use his imagination and find some way to prevent a production shutdown even when the situation seems almost hopeless. Suppose, for example, that a key supplier of production parts[1] is shut down because of a strike (see Figure 14–1). The buyer tries to estimate how long the strike will last. Then he checks current stocks, both on hand and in transit, and tries to figure out ways to

FORD DIVISION FORD MOTOR COMPANY						DATE
		STRIKE REPORT				
VENDOR'S NAME		VENDOR'S ADDRESS		AFFECTED PLANT		
		NATURE OF ACTUAL OR INDICATED INTERRUPTION OF SUPPLY				
NAME OF LOCAL	NO.	UNION AFFILIATION OF LOCAL	LOCAL PRESIDENT'S NAME	NO. PERSONNEL INVOLVED	TIME & DATE OF STRIKE	
PART NO. AND DESCRIPTION		VEHICLE MODELS AFFECTED		SUPPLY CONDITION		
		STATUS OF BUYING DEPT. ACTION				
					PURCHASING AGENT OR DEPT. MANAGER	

Courtesy Ford Motor Co.

FIG. 14–1. When a strike stops production at a supplier plant, the buyer should immediately advise all departments concerned with a strike report and develop a plan to cope with the materials shortage that the strike will probably cause.

cope with the shortage. Perhaps it can be licked by immediately starting a second supplier on the item, or by making the item in the buyer's plant. Perhaps, although not very likely, surplus stocks can be purchased from some other user. Perhaps defective or used items can be reworked to make them acceptable. Perhaps a substitute can be found. Perhaps extra stock can be "discovered" by shortening supply lines. For example, if a part goes into a subassembly that in turn is assembled into something else, the shortage might not be so serious as it first appears. All the in-process stock can be used before assembly of the end product is delayed.

Field Expediting. Sometimes delivery failure is only partial. A supplier cannot produce desired quantities because of manufacturing prob-

---

[1] Delivery failure is rarely a serious problem for most nonproduction supplies, since in most cases it is fairly easy to buy identical materials from another supplier on short notice. However, this is usually not true for purchases of equipment and machinery or for construction contracts, where delivery failures can seriously affect a company's sales and profits.

lems. Or, in many cases, the supplier isn't even responsible for the delivery failure. Demand for material has increased and the supplier is called on to exceed his original delivery promises.

In such cases, if the shortage is really critical, a buyer or expediter may spend all his waking hours in the supplier's plant until the shortage is licked. Many suppliers privately regard their customers' expediters as a first-class nuisance. In their opinion, they accomplish nothing; if anything, they get in the way at a time when the supplier has enough problems. However, suppliers seldom dare protest openly against the use of expediters, since their customers can retort that the expediters wouldn't be needed if the supplier had delivered promptly.

Why do companies use expediters even when they are fairly certain that the supplier is doing everything he can to cope with the shortage? There are at least four reasons:

(1) The presence of the expediter may stimulate supplier personnel to greater efforts to beat the shortage. If a customer is interested enough in getting prompt delivery to dispatch a field expediter to the supplier's plant, supplier personnel will be more impressed with the need for delivery.

(2) The expediter can make certain that the supplier is actually doing everything possible to overcome the shortage. If a supplier has half a dozen customers pressing him for delivery, some customers are going to be served more promptly than others. An expediter insures that his company is getting high priority.

(3) The expediter can keep the buyer up to date with reliable, first-hand information on current delivery status. Daily telephone reports can keep the buyer posted as to whether the shortage is going to get worse or become less critical.

(4) The expediter can sometimes assist the supplier. If the supplier can be helped with changes in specifications or quality control procedures, the expediter can relay this information to his home office. Sometimes he needs technical help or raw materials. The expediter can arrange for the loan of his company's personnel and also get the buyer to help in obtaining raw materials. The supplier may be willing to work his plant overtime only if the buyer is willing to pay the extra costs that will be incurred. A field expediter can evaluate the need for overtime and secure approval for the cost from his home office.

QUALITY FAILURE

In many industries, the greatest single cause of delivery failure is quality failure. Quality problems begin with a complaint by either the user or the quality control department that a purchased item is of substandard quality. In the case of items purchased by brand or on the basis of performance specifications, the user may complain that the item does not perform as it should. In such cases, the buyer contacts the supplier and advises him of the problem.

The rejection process is somewhat more complex in the case of parts and materials purchased to technical specifications. In such cases quality is determined at least partly by inspection procedures. For example, suppose a company buying a part insists that one dimension be 2.000 inches with a tolerance of plus or minus .005 inch. This theoretically would mean that the company will reject all parts where the dimension does not measure between 1.995 and 2.005 inches. In practice, it would not reject every part not meeting this requirement. Regardless of the inspection method used, the company always tacitly agrees to accept some parts that lie outside its specifications. The reason is that no inspection is 100 per cent foolproof. For example, if an inspector carefully measures each piece to make sure its dimension is between 1.995 and 2.005 inches, it is statistically certain that a percentage of defective pieces will be accepted.[2]

Quality control engineers are realistic about the fact that some defective pieces will be accepted. They try to control the number that slip through inspection undetected by setting an "acceptable quality level" (AQL) for each part. Their AQL's are based on the theory of probability. For example, an AQL might permit four rejections when 100 pieces are inspected out of a shipment of 10,000 pieces. Statistical tables might indicate that with this procedure, at least 96 per cent of the pieces might be of acceptable quality in most cases, and almost never would it be possible to have a shipment that is less than 90 per cent acceptable when only 4 per cent of the sample is found defective.

Conflicting Quality Standards. Specifications rarely indicate what level of quality is acceptable. The engineers who write them would like to have 100 per cent of the vendor's shipments fall within tolerances even though they know that this will never be the case. In fact, some companies refuse to disclose to suppliers precisely what their acceptable quality level is because they are afraid that by doing so they will encourage them to reduce standards to the minimum needed to pass inspection. As a result, many inexperienced vendors may find shipments rejected simply because they underestimated the buyer's quality standards.

For example, if a supplier manufactured and inspected his product so that 95 per cent of the pieces were within tolerances and the buyer's inspectors worked to an AQL requiring a 96 per cent record, practically all of the supplier's shipments would be rejected. A supplier might get occasional rejections even if his quality standards were identical to those

---

[2] The reader who is interested in more than a superficial explanation of statistical quality control is referred to texts on this subject, such as Dudley J. Cowden, *Statistical Methods in Quality Control* (New York: Prentice-Hall, Inc., 1957).

of the buyer. For example, while the supplier might check a small sample and find it within tolerances, the buyer might check an entirely different sample from the same shipment and find it exceeded acceptable tolerances. In practice, many suppliers find they must manufacture to quality standards slightly higher than those required by their customers in order to eliminate occasional rejections of this sort and also to provide themselves with a little leeway on quality before it becomes a problem.

Quality Certification. If a supplier's quality level is either exactly equal to or falls short of the buyer's inspection standards, occasional disputes are almost inevitable. On the other hand, if the supplier's quality is higher than required, costs are usually higher than necessary and there is waste. One solution to this dilemma is quality certification by the supplier. With this approach, the buyer specifies in considerable detail precisely what tolerances must be maintained, the AQL for each dimension, and the inspection and sampling procedures to be used. The supplier then certifies that he meets these requirements on each shipment. The buyer need only make occasional spot checks of shipments to make certain that the supplier isn't getting lax.

With quality certification, much duplicate inspection is avoided, since for most shipments the buyer's receiving inspection can be quite superficial. This can reduce costs substantially, especially for precision parts with many dimensions that must be held within close tolerances. Certification also has boosted quality for most companies that have tried it. Supplier responsibility is clearly specified, and most suppliers take pride in having their quality level certified by their customers.

Companies with quality certification programs are careful, however, to limit their use to suppliers of proved reliability. They rarely have so much faith in a new supplier that they will accept shipments without a thorough inspection.

Dealing with Suppliers. When a shipment is found defective, the buyer first investigates to make sure that the supplier is really responsible for the defects. He may discover that the rejection was due to changes in specifications, inspection procedures, and so on, that were not incorporated into the purchase agreement. If this is the case, the supplier is not responsible for the rejection.

In most cases, however, the rejection is either wholly or partly the supplier's responsibility. The usual procedure is for the buyer to review the inspection report and pass it on to the supplier. If the supplier agrees that the shipment should be rejected and accepts responsibility for the defects, he will indicate how he wishes to dispose of the shipment. (This is often covered by a standing agreement.) The supplier may want to have the shipment returned to him, scrapped, or salvaged by the buyer. If it is scrapped or salvaged, there must, of course, be agreement concerning scrap credits to the supplier (if the buyer sells it to a scrap dealer) or on charges to the supplier for the buyer's salvage work. Should the supplier deny responsibility for the rejection, the buyer must thoroughly investigate and try to reach an amicable agreement with the supplier that still protects his own company's interests.

Regardless of who is responsible for the quality problem, the buyer should do everything he can to prevent a recurrence. He should make certain that the supplier is taking all possible measures to boost quality. If the supplier persists in shipping merchandise that doesn't pass inspection, the buyer may have to switch suppliers.

Poor quality creates the worst possible type of delivery failure. Unlike other supply failures, there is no advance warning before the material is actually received. Nor is the problem necessarily solved if the supplier succeeds in making a shipment to replace the rejected one, for that shipment may also be rejected. Fortunately for many a buyer of precision parts, quality control departments often relax standards and accept shipments with minor defects when there will be a critical shortage if they are rejected. But this does not by any means take the pressure off the buyer to get suppliers who can consistently meet quality standards.

PROBLEMS IN SOURCE SELECTION

Even if a buyer succeeds in getting suppliers who offer outstanding quality, delivery, and service at rock-bottom prices, his selection of sources won't satisfy everyone in his company. In fact, in many cases there are strong forces pushing business toward suppliers who don't necessarily measure up to these basic but tough economic criteria. The environment in which a buyer and his company operate also influences selection of suppliers. Relations with customers, top executives within a company, and the community in which the company operates may dictate selection of suppliers on other than strictly economic terms.

Reciprocity

When a company makes a point of buying from its customers, it is practicing reciprocity. For example, an oil company may buy its pipe only from those steel companies that use its industrial lubricants. Or a chemical company may sell one raw material to another chemical company and buy a second material from that company.

Such reciprocity is more widespread in American industry than many business executives care to admit. One survey showed that 84 per cent of all purchasing executives consciously favor their company's customers when selecting suppliers.[3] One purchasing executive for a chemical company (who prefers to remain anonymous) was able to increase his

---

[3] "Should We Accept Reciprocity As A Business Policy?" *Purchasing*, April, 1954, p. 76.

company's sales by $3,516,000 in a single year by calling on his 50 largest suppliers and asking them to become better customers of his company if they wished to continue as important suppliers. On his travels, the purchasing agent was armed with statistics indicating precisely how much his company sold to each supplier and how much it purchased from him.

Many company salesmen travel from customer to customer equipped with similar statistics. Usually it is considered fair and ethical to deal reciprocally on a proportionate basis—as long as quantities purchased are reasonably great. For example, if a chemical company bought 10 per cent of its bags from a paper company, it might reasonably expect to get 10 per cent of the paper company's chemical purchases (provided, of course, that the chemical company made the chemicals needed for making paper).

Problems in Reciprocity. Proponents of reciprocity maintain that it is simply an application of the Golden Rule: "Do unto your customers as you would have them do unto you." Actually, reciprocity is a vicious practice that saps the efficiency of the economy. When firms can sell on some basis other than the price, quality, and delivery of their product, their efforts are unavoidably misdirected. There is bound to be some waste.

In some cases, the waste is obvious. For example, if all firms could secure business only on the basis of the price and quality of their products, the efficient, low-cost firms would get the business and the marginal producers would disappear. When reciprocity permits an inefficient firm to stay in business and prevents the efficient producer from getting the business he deserves, the real costs of the over-all economy are slightly higher and its productivity is reduced. This happens every time a purchasing agent accepts slightly higher prices or slightly inferior quality from a supplier because of reciprocity considerations.

It also happens—although much less obviously—when reciprocity is the basis for selecting among suppliers who offer identical prices and almost identical quality, service, and delivery. Even in the tightest oligopoly there is usually a faint flicker of competition. Reciprocity reduces constructive competition even further. The result inevitably is slighter higher costs and less efficiency, which can't be detected because low-cost producers make little or no effort to undercut their less efficient collaborators in the oligopoly.

Effect on Firm. Few economists would deny that reciprocity reduces the efficiency and productivity of the economy as a whole, but few business executives are economists. The businessman's job is to manage his firm, not the economy as a whole. And the plain fact is that reciprocity need not hurt an individual company. On the contrary, reciprocity is so widespread that many firms' sales and profits would be hurt if they did not practice it.

Suppose a company has a choice of buying materials from two competing suppliers who charge identical prices. One supplier is a customer; the other is not. Should the company offend a good customer by buying from his competitor? The only excuse for doing so would be if it could make the competing supplier a customer, too. So the only "right" decision from the viewpoint of the business executive is one that is based on reciprocity.

The situation is only a little different when the customer and would-be supplier offers to sell goods that are either slightly more expensive or inferior in quality to those of other suppliers. In such cases, the company is paying a definite price for reciprocity. Whether or not it accepts the deal depends on whether or not the premium is worth the benefit that is gained. Most companies refuse to pay higher prices to suppliers who are also customers. They usually find it more profitable to buy from the more efficient suppliers and bluntly demand that these suppliers reciprocate by becoming customers. Sometimes, of course, this is not possible. For various reasons the more efficient supplier may not be able to use the company's products. In that case the price premium paid to hold a customer by making him a supplier should be regarded as an indirect price reduction on the products sold to that supplier.

Reciprocity is a significant problem only in industries selling goods to other industries. Few consumer-goods manufacturers can push reciprocity on their suppliers, nor would it be worth the trouble to do so. For example, not only would the R. J. Reynolds Toabcco Company have a hard time trying to force all employees of its suppliers to smoke Camels or Winstons, but the effect on sales would be negligible if it did succeed in doing so. Not so with a company that both makes and buys products of industrial consumers. For example, a typical chemical company's major purchases are chemical raw materials, and as much as 50 per cent of its sales go to other chemical companies. Every major chemical company is both buyer of and seller to a number of other major chemical companies. Under these circumstances, reciprocity is inevitable.

Back-Door Selling

When a salesman deliberately bypasses the purchasing department and makes a sales call on personnel in the department using his product, he is engaging in "back-door" selling. Most companies frown on back-door selling. One survey showed that 62 per cent of the companies responding had regulations requiring supplier salesmen to center their sales efforts on the purchasing department.[4] Many companies go so far as to require supplier salesmen to get written permission from the purchasing department before they may call on engineering or manufacturing personnel. (A salesman's interview permit is shown in Figure 14–2.)

---

[4] "Can Back-Door Selling Be Controlled?" *Purchasing*, December, 1953, p. 75.

COPY

SALESMAN'S INTERVIEW PERMIT

Issued to _____ _____ Date_____

Company _____ Time_____

Permission is hereby given to the above Salesman to interview

Mr. _____ at _____

with the understanding that he will not initiate contact with any other person or department unless authorized by the undersigned; No purchase commitment or change in an existing order is to be made unless authorized by the Purchasing Dept.; All proposals for Materials or Services must be submitted to the attention of the Purchasing Dept.

PURCHASING DEPARTMENT

By_____

THIS PERMIT GOOD ONLY ON DATE ISSUED AND MUST BE RETURNED TO THE PURCHASING DEPT. BY THE SALESMAN ON DEPARTURE, BEARING THE SIGNATURE OF THE PERSON INTERVIEWED.

Interviewed By_____

FIG. 14–2. This interview permit is designed to regulate "back-door" selling. The purchasing department uses it to control supplier sales calls on operating personnel.

Discouraging Back-Door Selling. Companies try to prevent suppliers from making sales calls on operating personnel for at least four reasons:

(1) To increase efficiency. They simply don't want salesmen to waste the time of operating personnel. The company's purchasing personnel get paid to interview supplier salesmen; operating personnel are supposed to concern themselves with their own operations.

(2) To control purchase commitments. If personnel outside of purchasing have dealings with suppliers, they may innocently commit the company to purchases that have not been properly authorized. Expenditures can be closely controlled only if the authority to commit the company is limited.

(3) To maintain competition. If a supplier persuades the user of a material that his product is the only one that will do the job, the purchasing department may be handicapped in its efforts to reduce costs. If it is forced to buy one brand exclusively, it cannot get bids from competing suppliers. Sometimes a supplier can gain a tremendous advantage by working with the user of the material even if he does not succeed in getting preclusive specifications tailored to his products. He can become more familiar with the operating problems in the buyer's plant and can more easily locate applications for his products. This, of course, is to the buyer's advantage, but not if it is done at the cost of freezing out all of the supplier's competitors.

(4) To maintain security. Many companies, even those not engaged in defense work with security regulations, do not like to have outsiders

strolling around almost at will in their plants and offices. They don't want their new product plans and other advance efforts to become widely known.[5] Since supplier salesmen usually call on the company's competitors as well and often are not averse to gossip, better security is maintained by restricting them to the purchasing department except under special circumstances.

Need for Calls. Despite the efforts to discourage them, most salesmen make as many calls on operating personnel as they do on purchasing personnel. Many salesmen get more business by calling on the engineers who specify material and the factory superintendents who use it than they do from the purchasing personnel who theoretically buy it. If engineers or superintendents can be sold on a supplier's brand, sometimes the salesman's job is done. The brand is specified on the requisition and the buyer buys it. Most companies permit their buyers to ignore a brand name on a requisition so they can get quotations from manufacturers of competing brands. But some buyers will go to great lengths to avoid offending the requisitioner, and most buyers will try to give some consideration to the requisitioner's preferences.

Thus back-door selling is effective. Consequently it is not surprising that one survey showed that 53 per cent of the salesmen responding bypassed the purchasing department on 20 per cent of their calls, and about 25 per cent of them avoided the purchasing department on half of their calls.[6] On many other calls, salesmen first call on the purchasing department and then are referred to one or more operating departments to explain their product.

While back-door selling definitely is a bad practice, few would deny that there is a real need for contact between suppliers and operating personnel. Materials managers and buyers cannot be experts on every product. In most cases, they can't hope to know as much about the details of the product as the engineer who specifies it or the manufacturing supervisor who uses it. This is particularly true when the product is designed partly or wholly by the supplier. In such cases some exchange of information between supplier and user is essential and should be encouraged.

The question is—when does an innocent exchange of information become back-door selling? This varies with the product and the personnel involved. Well-managed materials departments are careful to devise procedures that prevent unauthorized purchases from being made and

---

[5] Some companies making civilian products are so fussy about internal security that they classify various documents just as the military do, and are even equipped with paper shredders to foil anyone who might try to discover company secrets by going through wastebaskets. The Ford Motor Company even has a little booklet, "Safeguarding Confidential Information," to instruct its employees in security procedures.

[6] James K. Blake, "Sales and Purchasing: Here's How They Look to Each Other," *Duns Review and Modern Industry*, June, 1955, p. 45.

brand preferences from creeping into specifications. However, rules and regulations will do only half the job. The other half can be done only when there is good will between the materials department and the departments it serves. Good purchasing executives do their best to cultivate good interdepartmental relations. Some even go so far as to hold seminars for operating personnel in which they explain their objectives and why it is to the company's best interest to have purchases made by professional buyers rather than by persons who use or specify the material purchased.

Personal Purchases

Many purchasing departments use one hand trying to avoid being bypassed through back-door selling while with the other they try to be bypassed on personal purchases. It is safe to say that personal purchases are a problem in every company. Should the company use its buying power to purchase things for employees at a discount or shouldn't it? In general, companies have one of three policies on personal purchases:

(1) They explicitly forbid them. In this case, a buyer may ignore the rules for his personal friends by informally lining them up with suppliers who, he knows, are willing to sell at a discount. But this would have to be a clandestine procedure and would occur only occasionally.

(2) They permit suggesting sources of supply. Most companies permit buyers to suggest sources of supply to company personnel if they have the time and desire to do so. In such cases, the buyer will often make a deal with a supplier whereby any employee of the company can get a discount if he is sent by the buyer.

(3) They encourage personal purchases. Some companies will cooperate on personal purchases to the extent of issuing company purchase orders for the material and then reinvoicing the employee. With this approach, the employee can buy at the same price as the company. Most companies restrict issuing of purchase orders for personal purchases to top executives. Some are less strict, and a few firms even operate company stores.[7]

Policies on personal purchases vary not only from company to company, but with rank within a company. Generally, top executives and purchasing personnel themselves make far more extensive use of the company's buying power on personal purchases than others in the organization.

A lenient policy on personal purchases helps boost employee morale. It also can increase employees' effective purchasing power, particularly in areas where there are no "discount houses" and there is little price competition among retailers. On the other hand, personal purchases are

---

[7] For example, oil companies operating in remote areas of the Middle East are almost forced to assist employees with personal purchases through operating company stores that sell at relatively low prices.

expensive for a company.[8] Valuable purchasing department time is wasted on trivial purchases. Vendor good will can be endangered by nuisance purchases for employees. If the company uses its purchase orders to make them, personal purchases can take accounting department time, and there also is the problem of collecting an invoice rendered to an employee. Community relations also can become a problem. Local merchants resent a company that uses its buying power to help employees purchase at a discount from out-of-town suppliers.

Local Purchases

If all other factors are equal, it is to the buyer's advantage to buy from a local supplier. He usually can get prompter service, and his lead time will be shorter. In addition, it makes for good community relations when a company spends its money locally whenever possible. This is particularly true of a franchised monopoly like a public utility, which must maintain the good will of the community and is also trying to stimulate business in its service area.

Municipal and state purchasing agents usually encounter strong pressure to buy within the boundaries they serve. The money they spend comes from taxes collected within the state or city, so it is reasonable that they should make some effort to spend it on businesses in the same area. However, public purchasing agents should not subsidize local industry with tax money if they can buy more cheaply elsewhere—unless they are forced to do so by statute. Federal government agencies, for example, can lawfully buy from a foreign supplier only if his delivered price is more than 25 per cent below that of the lowest-cost domestic supplier. This "Buy American" Act has resulted in millions of dollars of hidden subsidies to higher-cost domestic producers.

ETHICS

Ethics is perhaps the only problem in purchasing and materials management that receives widespread publicity. A big-city newspaper can count on at least three or four big stories a year concerning purchasing ethics. A top federal government official accepts entertainment from a major defense contractor; a city purchasing official favors a supplier who is a close personal friend; the president of a large corporation is part-owner of a firm that is a major supplier. These are typical stories that make the front page periodically.

On the average, professional buyers and materials managers probably

---

[8] Sometimes the cost can be staggering when compared with the results achieved. A number of years ago, the writer was asked to get some bolts for the general manager of the firm in which he was employed. He spent about one hour of his time plus $2 for a long-distance phone call to get bolts directly from the manufacturer that could have been bought retail for 30 or 40 cents at any hardware store.

have higher moral standards than most of their fellow citizens. But they also are subjected to more temptations. Buyers spend millions of dollars of their company's money each year. As a result, they wield tremendous economic power and are the objects of considerable attention from suppliers. They are in an excellent position to be dishonest if they want to be. Buyers can bluntly demand kickbacks and other favors from suppliers. Sometimes they can almost make themselves millionaires before they are caught.[9] For this reason, materials managers are careful to select buyers with strong character and high moral standards, as well as to devise procedures and controls to prevent them from giving in to temptation.[10]

Gifts and Entertainment

Even though they may be completely honest, buyers and top management executives will often receive many wholly unsolicited favors from suppliers. These range from an occasional lunch or entertainment at a convention to Christmas gifts, theater or football tickets, and other favors.

The Advertising Specialty Association once estimated that business gift-giving is almost a billion-dollar industry.[11] A survey of industrial sales managers indicated that 51.7 per cent of their companies purchased Christmas gifts for their customers.[12] About 76 per cent of them said they would like to see gift-giving eliminated entirely. But they feared to do so. About 36 per cent considered gifts an established custom; 34 per cent frankly feared an unfavorable reaction if they discontinued the practice; and the rest thought the good will was worth the expense.

What should the buyer's attitude be if a supplier or potential supplier offers him a gift or other favor? Under no circumstance should he accept anything from a supplier if it will tend to obligate him directly or indirectly to favor that supplier. There is no general agreement on what a buyer can ethically accept from a supplier. Some believe the buyer should refuse anything except gifts of nominal value used for advertising and

---

[9] One buyer for a subsidiary of Sears, Roebuck got kickbacks amounting to more than $250,000 before he was caught in 1952. He had $124,000 in bonds and cash in 27 different banks; his home, most of his furniture, and his personal belongings all were paid for by suppliers (see "A Classic Case of Kickbacks," *Purchasing*, Sept. 1, 1958, p. 59).

[10] Needless to say, corruption is less likely when there is a strict policy against back-door selling. In fact, many of the scandals that have been exposed didn't involve materials personnel, but developed from improper relations between operating executives and suppliers. One case that received widespread publicity involved William C. Newberg, president of the Chrysler Corporation, and Chrysler suppliers in which Newberg was a silent partner.

[11] Dean S. Ammer, "Who'll Shoot Santa Claus—the Salesman or the P.A.?" *Purchasing*, December, 1957, p. 75.

[12] *Ibid.*, p. 77.

sales promotion purposes. Most managements have a somewhat more lenient attitude.

No Gifts. A few companies and most government agencies have written policies forbidding any employee to accept any favors from suppliers. When a buyer receives an unsolicited gift, he is expected to return it with a letter advising the supplier of the no-gift policy. The top procurement official often goes even further and warns the supplier that he will lose business if he continues to send unsolicited gifts. When a company receives gifts that are perishable and can't be returned (e.g., food, flowers, and so on), it may donate them to some charitable institution. The only gifts that are acceptable are advertising novelties such as ballpoint pens with the supplier's name on them, calendars, and the like, which are often passed out at conventions and trade shows by the exhibitors.

Gifts of Nominal Value Only. In the course of normal business relations, certain amenities are both accepted and customary. Buyers and sellers often conduct business over cocktails and lunch or on the golf course at the local country club. In such cases, either may pick up the check. Many completely honorable buyers and sellers remember each other with a gift at Christmas. In many cases, their frequent business dealings have led to friendships that endure even after they are no longer active in business. They naturally would resent any implication that such gifts were unethical. However, there is no doubt that there have been some misguided applications of the Christmas spirit in the business world.

Ethical Behavior

A buyer can be completely honest, resolutely refusing all favors from suppliers, and still be guilty of unethical behavior. In fact, it is extremely difficult for the best-intentioned buyer to be wholly ethical at all times. To do so he must always be completely equitable and honest in his dealings with all suppliers. This is not easy in an atmosphere in which each supplier is vying for the buyer's favor. The buyer is bound to be attracted to the personalities of some supplier salesmen and repelled by others. But this should not influence his buying decisions.[13]

Although a buyer is expected to work hard to negotiate the best possible purchase for his company, he should never stoop to unethical techniques for achieving this goal. If he does, he will eventually develop a reputation for underhanded dealing and suppliers will no longer trust him. Among the practices in which no ethical buyer indulges are:

---

[13] This is admittedly idealistic. Since buyers are human beings, they are bound to be influenced by the personalities of the people with whom they deal. The best buyers, however, can subordinate their personal feelings with respect to suppliers and make fairly objective buying decisions that bring maximum benefit to their company, even if this involves awarding business to suppliers whom they personally dislike and not awarding it to individuals they like.

(1) Permitting a favored supplier to examine the quotations of his competitors. All quotations submitted to a buyer are confidential and should not be shown to any outsider. Nor should a buyer disclose to competitors any information he might have about a supplier's costs, processes, new products, or the like unless he has the supplier's explicit permission to do so.

(2) Giving the supplier misleading information to get him to reduce his prices. The buyer with scruples never asks a supplier to meet a lower bid that exists only in the buyer's imagination. Nor does he give the supplier fictitious information regarding planned production schedules, etc., so that the supplier will be encouraged to grant bigger discounts or other benefits.

(3) Using his company's buying power to force suppliers to sell at prices well below cost. This is not only unethical but uneconomic, since only a reasonably prosperous supplier can be useful for future contracts. For both ethical and economic reasons, good buyers scrupulously avoid taking such a big percentage of a given supplier's output that he becomes too dependent on them for business.

(4) Asking suppliers for quotations when they have no chance of

---

PRINCIPLES AND STANDARDS OF PURCHASING PRACTICE

1. To consider, first, the interest of his company in all transactions and to carry out and believe in its established policies.
2. To be receptive to competent counsel from his colleagues and to be guided by such counsel without impairing the dignity and responsibility of his office.
3. To buy without prejudice, seeking to obtain the maximum ultimate value for each dollar of expenditure.
4. To strive consistently for knowledge of the materials and processes of manufacture and to establish practical methods for the conduct of his office.
5. To subscribe and work for honesty and truth in buying and selling and to denounce all forms and manifestations of commercial bribery.
6. To accord a prompt and courteous reception, so far as conditions will permit, to all who call upon a legitimate business mission.
7. To respect his obligations and to require that obligations to him and to his concern be respected, consistent with good business practice.
8. To avoid sharp practice.
9. To counsel and assist fellow purchasing agents in the performance of their duties, whenever occasion permits.
10. To cooperate with all organizations and individuals engaged in activities designed to enhance the development and standing of purchasing.

FIG. 14–3. This code of ethics was developed by the National Association of Purchasing Agents to guide the conduct of its 18,000 members.

getting the business. It often is convenient for a buyer to use quotations from an outside supplier to check up on an established supplier or to compare with shop costs. The quote is used only to negotiate a price reduction from the established supplier or stimulate a cost-reduction drive in the buyer's manufacturing plant. The supplier who quotes has absolutely no chance of getting the business regardless of his quotation. Since quotations are expensive to prepare, the buyer who requests them under false pretenses is, in effect, guilty of stealing from the supplier.

(5) Having a financial interest in any company that is a supplier. In such cases, there is an obvious conflict of interest. Most companies do permit buyers to own stock in suppliers who are so large or diversified that the buyer's actions would have no significant effect on sales or profits. For example, few would object if a buyer of utility services owned a few shares of American Telephone & Telegraph. A.T.&T. is so big that no buyer could significantly affect its profits; it also is a monopoly in its service areas, so the buyer would not have an alternate source of supply anyway.

Few business executives would deny that industrial purchasing ethics today are higher than they have ever been. Scandals make news because they are relatively rare. One reason for this is the work of the National Association of Purchasing Agents in boosting the stature and recognition of purchasing. The N.A.P.A.'s code of good practice, to which its members subscribe, is illustrated in Figure 14–3.

PROMOTING SUPPLIER GOOD WILL

Supplier relations are a problem even when both buyer and seller have the highest possible ethical standards. A supplier who doesn't get business may sometimes wonder if the buyer isn't unjustly favoring some "pet" supplier.

Buyers try to promote supplier good will as much as possible. Salesmen never are left waiting in the lobby for more than a few minutes without some explanation. If a buyer is busy, he will usually try to arrange for the salesman to see another buyer if he wishes. If the salesman is from out of town, buyers often will make a prearranged appointment to make certain they are not busy when he calls.

Buyers always will listen sympathetically to the salesman's presentation, even though they may not have any foreseeable need for the product. Seasoned buyers also have mastered the art of ending an interview. If they are busy and the salesman has nothing new to say, they know how to rise, thank the salesman for calling, and conclude the interview in a tactful way. They want the salesman to like them and to like the company, and they do their best to make his visit a pleasant experience.

Large companies even publish purchasing directories to help their suppliers. In them they list the major commodities they buy and a break-

CONTENTS

Courtesy General Electric Co.

FIG. 14–4. Many companies have "welcome" booklets in which they describe their purchasing policies, organization, and products to suppliers. Shown here is the table of contents of *Selling to General Electric.*

down of their purchasing organization, so that the visiting salesman can readily locate the buyer specializing in his product line. They also try to explain company purchasing policies and procedures so that there will be no misunderstandings. Figure 14–4 illustrates the contents page of the booklet, *Selling to General Electric*, which was prepared to help the 45,000 firms that sell to that company.

Many companies go still further to bolster supplier relations. They arrange hotel and transportation reservations for visiting salesmen. Most firms permit purchasing personnel to buy lunches for suppliers and extend other courtesies. A few firms even remember suppliers with a Christmas gift of nominal value.

Why do they go to the trouble? Suppliers not only can use a company's products but they also may become some of the company's biggest boosters if they are sold on the company as a customer. More important, suppliers can be an important source of cost-reduction ideas. This aspect will be discussed in detail in the chapters on price negotiation and cost reduction.

CASES

Case 14–1.   COLONIAL LAUNDRY EQUIPMENT COMPANY
Coping with Supplier Labor Trouble

Production will be shut down at the Colonial Laundry Equipment Company's main plant in Louisville, Kentucky, unless the company's purchasing director, Kenneth Caldwell, can achieve "the impossible." Colonial makes coin-operated washing machines for use in apartment buildings and stores. The transmission housing in its product is made from a gray iron casting that the company buys from the Allied Foundry Company.

Allied has now been shut down by a strike. Its union, the United Foundry Workers, is demanding a 50-cent-per-hour wage increase for its members. Allied insists that it can't afford any increase at all and cites its shrinking profit margins and the price cutting currently prevalent in the industry as evidence. Caldwell believes that the strike may be a long one, not only because the company and union are so far apart on a wage settlement but also because Allied's labor relations have never been too placid. The UFW local at Allied is unusually belligerent, according to Allied's management. In addition, Caldwell suspects that the company's labor relations policies have been a little heavy handed.

Allied has suffered from a series of one-day walkouts over the past year. In addition, its quality has suffered; apparently some of its workmen no longer take any pride in their work. For these reasons, Colonial's inventories of castings are somewhat lower than they would otherwise be. Although Caldwell was aware of the fact that the company's union contract expired on June 30 and that a strike was likely on July 1, he was unable to accumulate more than one week's inventory of castings. He had hoped to get at least three weeks ahead, which would take up all available storage space at the Colonial plant.

Because Allied has definitely been slipping on both quality and delivery, Colonial had already solicited bids from other foundries:

Supplier	Price	Cost of Patterns	Delivery Promise after Receipt of Order
Consolidated Gray Iron..........$2.65		$1,950	8 weeks
Archer Foundry................. 3.10		1,800	6
Young Industries.............. 2.40		2,200	6

Colonial is currently paying Allied $2.20 per casting. Allied's price and its competitors' bids all are based on shipment of approximately 4,000 castings per month in lots of 1,000, and each supplier would be willing to quote the same price for a volume as low as 2,000 castings per month. Caldwell has hesitated to switch sources previously because he was unable to find a supplier who could meet Allied's price. He hoped that Allied would straighten out its problems without a price increase. Now he doubts that Allied will be able to hold to the $2.20 price, since the settlement of its strike will be too costly to permit it to do so. Caldwell expects a price increase of at least ten cents after Allied settles with the union.

Of course, Caldwell has no idea when the settlement will be made, but he doubts that Allied's workers will still be on strike in six weeks, when he can get his first castings from Archer or Young if he places an order with them now. This isn't Caldwell's only alternative, however. The patterns that Allied uses were paid for by Colonial. If Caldwell can get them from the Allied plant, he can cut the lead time needed to start up a new source by at least several weeks.

None of the other foundries can give Caldwell a firm promise as to when it can start production with Allied's patterns, since none of them has ever seen the patterns. It might be possible to use them without any rework at all, or it might be necessary to make substantial changes. Nor can the other vendors be held to the prices they have quoted if they use Allied's patterns. Their quotations are based on patterns of their own design. But Caldwell doubts that there would be more than a small price increase were Archer, Young, or Consolidated to use Allied's patterns.

However, Caldwell does have another problem, even if he can get the patterns out and they can be used. If Archer, Young, or Consolidated work hard to deliver castings as promptly as possible during Allied's strike, they naturally expect some reward in the form of future business. They believe it would be unfair to extend themselves to help Colonial in an emergency and then promptly lose the business once Allied settled its strike. On the other hand, Allied has been supplying Colonial for several years, and except for occasional difficulties resulting from its poor labor relations, it has been a dependable, low-cost supplier. Also, it is possible that Allied's competitors may likewise be faced with labor problems and higher costs in the next six months when their union contracts expire.

Questions

1. What course of action do you recommend that Caldwell follow to cope with the shortage of castings?
2. What should he do after Allied's strike has been settled?
3. What, if anything, could he have done to prevent these difficulties from arising?

CASE 14–2. GNU STEEL CORPORATION

A PROBLEM IN RECIPROCITY

The GNU Steel Corporation is an integrated steel producer with mills strategically located in several cities on the Great Lakes. Its products include carbon sheet steel, strip, plate, and bars, in addition to a broad line of alloy and stainless steels. Reciprocity has always been a problem for GNU because the company both buys from and sells to thousands of different companies.

The company's director of purchases, W. H. Arnold, tries to award business on a reciprocal basis as long as by doing so he suffers no penalty in price, quality, or delivery. His decisions are based on a master book that shows exactly how much GNU both bought from and sold to its suppliers and customers the previous year.

Arnold tries to split his business as equitably as possible among competing customers. For example, last year GNU sold $35 million worth of steel products to automobile manufacturers. The Blue Motors Corporation was the company's single biggest customer, taking $18 million worth of steel. Central Motors bought $8 million worth, and the Acme Automobile Company spent $9 million with GNU. Arnold allocated his purchases of automobiles accordingly. This year he purchased 65 new passenger cars and 135 trucks. Acme makes no trucks, so Arnold bought all of his passenger cars (except for three cars used by salesmen calling on Central and Blue Motors) from Acme. He then purchased 100 trucks from Blue Motors and 35 from Central Motors, which was roughly in proportion to their importance as customers. The auto companies know that GNU divides its auto business as fairly as possible on the basis of the proportion of steel business they give GNU, and they have never complained.

GNU also spends substantial amounts for chemicals and gases. It is a particularly large user of oxygen and divides its business 50–50 between the two largest domestic producers, the Midwest Chemical Corporation and Allied Air Products. Both of these companies are part of very large chemical corporations, both of which are over-all big steel users. They are approximately equal in importance as GNU customers, each taking about $2.5 million worth of steel per year. GNU in turn buys about $5 million worth of oxygen from each of them.

Arnold has recently been approached by the Zibitsu Chemical Corporation, Ltd., of Kyoto, Japan. Zibitsu has excess oxygen capacity and is offering it at a laid-down cost to GNU that is 25 per cent less than the prices charged by Midwest and Allied. Zibitsu is not able to handle all of GNU's requirements but can guarantee delivery for 20 per cent of its needs. Arnold investigates Zibitsu and finds it has an excellent reputation for living up to its agreements.

Knowing the reciprocity problem concerning oxygen, Arnold presents his proposal to Kevin Roberts, GNU's vice-president in charge of sales. Roberts agrees that Zibitsu's offer is tempting but points out that both Midwest and Allied will be unhappy if Arnold accepts it. Arnold then presents the problem quite frankly to his two suppliers. Roberts' guess was correct: both companies threaten to cut back their steel purchases from GNU if Arnold accepts Zibitsu's bid. They admit, however, that Arnold must consider Zibitsu's price attractive and finally offer (Midwest makes the offer and Allied says it will adjust prices to remain competitive with Midwest) to cut prices 10 per cent to keep Zibitsu from making inroads on the domestic market. They also point out that Zibitsu is trying to get rid of excess capacity and may, sometime in the future, raise its price when capacity gets tight again. They also observe that while their purchasing departments know that Belgian and German steel producers will sell pipe more cheaply than American producers such as GNU, they have continued to buy American steel because they feel that mills like GNU are more reliable. They suggest that they may be forced to change their minds if business gets tough enough and they lose a major customer like GNU.

Questions

1. Should GNU accept Zibitsu's offer?
2. What factors should be considered in making the decision?
3. What executives are involved, and who should make the final decision?

CASE 14–3. JOHNSON INSTRUMENT COMPANY

GIFTS AND ENTERTAINMENT FROM SUPPLIERS

The Johnson Instrument Company manufactures a line of precision instruments that have both civilian and military applications. Because of its defense business, the company is especially careful to keep its relations with suppliers "as clean as a hound's tooth." It takes great pains to get competitive bids on every order. When a contract is not placed with the low bidder, an explanation is written into the purchase record so that government contract auditors will know there has been no collusion.

Naturally, the company has a firm policy prohibiting any of its employees to accept gifts or gratuities from suppliers. The only exceptions to this rule are business lunches and advertising novelties of nominal value. Johnson Instrument doesn't even like to have its suppliers pay for all lunches. Its materials executives have expense accounts and are expected to pick up their fair share of the checks.

George Browning is one of the company's buyers. He handles a wide variety of maintenance, repair and, operating supplies, including all of the lumber used by the plant. One of his major suppliers is the Warren Lumber Company, a well-known local firm with a deserved reputation for integrity and dependability. Browning is a dedicated baseball fan, and Ned Warren, the young sales manager of Warren Lumber, knows it. Warren is also familiar with Johnson's policy on gifts and has never offered Browning any gift of more than nominal value at Christmas.

Two days before the World Series, Browning receives two box seat tickets for a week-end game with this note:

DEAR GEORGE:
I intended to use these myself. Unfortunately, I had forgotten that my brother and sister-in-law are coming to stay with us for the week end. They're not interested in baseball, and at this late date I don't think I could get tickets for them anyway. So it looks as if I'm going to miss the game. I know how crazy you are about baseball. Why don't you use them?

Cordially,
NED

Needless to say, Browning would very much like to go to the game. But there is no doubt that the tickets are of more than nominal value. The list price is $10 each, and they're actually worth more, since scalpers are selling them for as much as $20. Not only would it be against the company's policy for him to accept the tickets, but Browning is honest enough to admit to himself that while Warren may have sent him the tickets as a gesture of friendship he will undoubtedly regard them as a legitimate deduction for "sales expense" and not as a personal gift.

On the other hand, Browning is equally certain that the gift is not going to influence his buying decisions in any way. Warren is his lowest-cost lumber supplier (in fact, he's the only major lumber supplier in the area), and Browning will not buy any more lumber than what the plant requires regardless of how much he likes Warren. In addition, Browning can say with complete objectivity that he wouldn't think of jeopardizing his reputation or integrity for the sake of $20 worth of baseball tickets. If he returns the tickets to Warren, he is saying in effect, "This $20 gift will corrupt me." Also, he is by implication insulting Warren, since he is then tacitly accusing Warren of trying to bribe him when, in fact,

Warren might have no such intention. So, in returning the tickets, Browning might well jeopardize what has been an excellent business relationship between Warren and himself.

Questions

1. What should Browning do?
2. If Warren should offer to let Browning and/or other employees of Johnson's purchasing department make personal purchases of lumber and other supplies at the same wholesale prices paid by the company, would it be ethical for Browning to accept this offer? Should Browning attempt to solicit such a discount for personal purchases?

Chapter 15

BUYING TRANSPORTATION SERVICES

American industry spends more than $35 billion a year for transportation services.[1] About two thirds of this amount is spent for the services of common carriers regulated by the Interstate Commerce Commission and other government agencies. The balance is spent for the services of intrastate or chartered carriers not subject to federal regulation.

Traffic management is a big job in most industries. In the typical manufacturing company, transportation services are the third most important expenditure; only purchased materials and labor are more important. For example, the Koppers Company spends 13.75 per cent of its sales dollar on transportation.[2]

Most companies have a separate traffic department. The traffic manager is a major executive; in some cases he reports directly to the president of the company.[3] Even when he doesn't, he generally is only one echelon lower in the organization, reporting to the manager of manufacturing, purchasing, or sales.

THE TRAFFIC JOB

The traffic department is responsible for problems related to the purchase of transportation services, including the selection of mode of transport and of carrier, negotiation of rates, tracing and expediting of shipments, filing and negotiation of claims for lost or damaged shipments, and audit of freight bills. In addition, as the company's experts on transportation, traffic personnel are involved in many special studies designed to minimize transportation costs or to advise management about the

---

[1] According to a *Fortune* study (Gilbert Burck, "The Great U.S. Freight Cartel," January, 1957, p. 104), American industry spent $27.2 billion for the services of regulated and nonregulated carriers in 1956. Because of price increases and general growth of the economy, these expenditures should have risen to at least $35 billion since 1956.

[2] James F. Haley, "Research and Development—A New Approach in the Traffic Function," *Toward the Factory of the Future*, Special Report No. 28 (New York: American Management Association, 1957), p. 35.

[3] According to an American Management Association survey, the traffic manager reported directly to the president in 13 of 100 large companies (Ernest Dale, *Planning and Developing the Company Organization*, A.M.A. Research Report No. 20 [New York: American Management Association, 1952]), but the proportion would undoubtedly be even greater in smaller firms.

effect of various decisions (such as plant location or product distribution) on transportation cost.

The typical traffic department also has a number of miscellaneous functions, including the handling of all passenger reservations for employees traveling on company business and the moving of household effects of employees transferred from one company plant to another. Sometimes the traffic manager also is responsible for the operation of all company-owned vehicles; even if he is not, he should always be consulted prior to their purchase.

Traffic also is concerned with packaging material. The heavier the package, the higher the freight costs to ship the product. On the other hand, lightweight packaging is more liable to damage in shipment. For this reason, many tariffs are based on shipments being made in certain types of packaging.

Traffic usually is concerned with both in-bound and out-bound shipments of materials and finished products. Although many traffic departments become intimately involved with charter carriers or company-owned trucks, traffic departments normally have most of their dealings with various common carriers, including railroads, trucks, pipelines, and water carriers.

As Figure 15–1 shows, railroads are by far the most important common carriers in terms of tonnage handled (nearly half the total). Trucks are second in both dollar volume and tonnage (see Figure 15–2 for the dollar volume of the various carriers). Oil pipelines handle almost as much tonnage as trucks but get only a small fraction of their revenue. The reason for the discrepancies between shares of tonnage and revenue of the various carriers is obvious: the rate per ton-mile for all commodities is not the same. A trucker who hauls a ton of household goods for one mile may get 100 times as much as a pipeline gets for moving a ton of crude oil the same distance.

PICKING THE CARRIER

A company should buy transportation services just as it buys any other commodity—on the basis of quality, price, and service. It should try to direct its business to carriers that provide prompt delivery with a minimum of lost or damaged shipments, co-operate readily in tracing and rerouting shipments, make a minimum of errors in invoicing, and so on. These are sound criteria for selecting among like types of carrier (who charge identical rates when they are subject to regulation).

The transportation buyer must also select among various types of transportation service. His two basic criteria should be price and service. Carriers that give fast service charge relatively higher tariffs and those charging the lowest rate usually provide the slowest service. Figure 15–3 (pages 280–81) illustrates a chart used by North American Avia-

INTERCITY TON-MILES, PUBLIC AND PRIVATE, BY KINDS OF TRANSPORTATION, 1939–1958

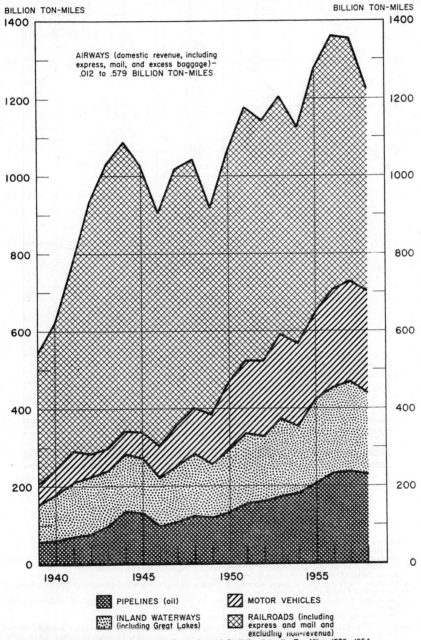

BILLION TON-MILES

BILLION TON-MILES

AIRWAYS (domestic revenue, including express, mail, and excess baggage)– .012 to .579 BILLION TON-MILES

PIPELINES (oil)

MOTOR VEHICLES

INLAND WATERWAYS (including Great Lakes)

RAILROADS (including express and mail and excluding non-revenue)

Source: 1939-1954, I.C.C., Bureau of Transport Economics and Statistics, Intercity Ton-Miles, 1939–1954, Statement No. 568; 1955-1957, 70th and 71st Annual Reports of the Interstate Commerce Commission; 1958, staff estimates

FIG. 15–1.

OPERATING REVENUES,[1] BY TRANSPORT AGENCY
1947 — 1958

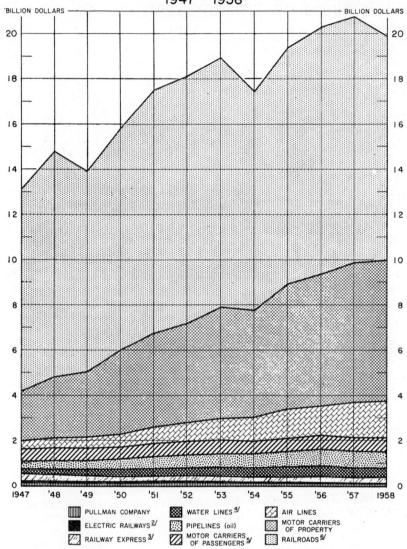

Footnotes for Chart, Operating Revenues, by Transport Agency, 1947–1958:
  [1] Partly estimated.
  [2] Shifts of carriers from the electric railway to the railroad group during the period
have resulted in an overstatement of declines by an undetermined amount.
  [3] After deducting payments to others for express privileges.
  [4] Includes only revenues from domestic traffic of carriers subject to the jurisdiction of
the Interstate Commerce Commission.
  [5] Does not include motor carrier revenues of electric railways, included under electric
railways.
  [6] Includes switching and terminal companies.
Sources: 1947–57, Annual Reports of the Interstate Commerce Commission; revised motor
  carrier revenues, 1947–1956, I.C.C., Bureau of Transport Economics and Statistics,
  Statistics of Class I, II, and III Motor Carriers, 1939–1956, Statement No. 589; and
  1958, staff estimates.   Air data from Civil Aeronautics Board; data cover operating
  revenues in domestic revenue operations only, not including Alaskan or oversea, but do
  include the local Hawaiian line within those islands.

FIG. 15–2.

tion, Inc., as a general guide to the services and relative costs of various types of carrier.

Rail Freight

Although their relative importance has declined substantially in the last 30 years, the railroads still are the most important carriers. Rail freight rates in carload lots are always lower than air freight, parcel post, and rates charged by freight forwarders. For many commodities they are cheaper than truck rates and sometimes they are competitive with barge and ship rates. They rarely are cheaper than pipeline rates, however.

The most economic type of rail transportation is in full cars between two points equipped with rail sidings. When a company does not have a siding, it must transfer its shipment from the railroad box car to a truck. This creates extra transport and handling expenses, which usually make it more economic to ship 100 per cent by truck, or may even force a company to relocate near a siding if its costs are to remain competitive.

Truck Freight

Almost every factory is equipped with a dock to receive truck shipments; in fact, truck lines are the most important common carrier for many types of manufactured goods. Truck rates often are as low as those charged by railroads for finished manufactured products, and service usually is faster. Trucks are especially competitive on shorter hauls. They often offer overnight service between cities that are only a few hundred miles apart. Both interstate truck and rail rates are regulated by the Interstate Commerce Commission. The ICC tries to set rates that permit fair competition between the two carriers. In recent years, trucks have substantially increased their share of traffic at the expense of the railroads.

Shipment by Air

Air cargo shipments have increased at a fantastic rate since the end of World War II. In 1947, air shipments totaled less than 100 million ton-miles. By 1963, they may reach 1 billion ton-miles. Although rates have become progressively more attractive in relation to surface transportation, air freight still is very expensive. Tariffs are two to three times higher than those charged by railroads and truck lines.

If rates are so high, how have air shipments managed to grow so fast? Obviously because for some shipments, speed is the only important factor and the shipment must be made in the fastest possible manner almost regardless of the cost. There are at least two other reasons for the rapid growth of air shipments. First, air tariffs are not as high as they appear. In most cases, it is possible to use much lighter containers when shipping by air, and sometimes no packaging at all is needed. Thus the total weight paid for when shipping by air is often less than it would

BUYER'S TRANSPORTATION CHART

Transp. Media	Description	Application	Can Be Traced
Carload and Truckload	Full rail car or trailer.	Where quantity is sufficient to warrant. (Differs with product.)	Yes
Truck	Motor Truck	For all shipments over 50 lbs. not requiring emergency Air Service.	Yes
Freight Forwarder	Truck pick-up for assembly into carloads, includes truck del'y at destination.	For all shipments over 50 lbs. not requiring emergency Air Service. Forwarder usually on long haul.	Yes
Railway Express	Freight handled by Express Company on passenger trains. Includes pickup and delivery.	To or from out-of-way points. Also between large cities when expedited service is required.	Very Difficult
Air Freight	No. 1 Regular passenger airlines which also handle air freight up to a limited size and weight.	Rush shipments over 20 lbs. Usually as fast as Air Express.	Yes
	No. 2 Cargo air carriers handling freight only.	Rush shipments over 20 lbs. Usually as fast as Air Express.	Yes
Air Express	Complete pickup and delivery service using all commercial airlines on shipments of limited size and weight.	Extreme emergency only! Of little value to and from points not on a scheduled airline.	Very Difficult
Air Freight Forwarder	Brokerage service using all commercial airlines and surface transportation when necessary.	Extreme emergency only!	Yes
Parcel Post	4th class regular mail.	Up to 20 lbs. when transit time is not important. 40 lbs. up to 150 miles.	No
	4th class airmail.	Very small rush shipments!	No

Courtesy North American Aviation, Inc.

FIG. 15–3. Buyers at North American Aviation's Columbus, Ohio plant use this chart as a guide to the relative merits of various types of transportation service.

be if shipment were made by surface transportation. This reduces the premium paid for air shipment. For certain extremely fragile shipments that would require especially heavy packaging if shipped by surface freight, it may actually be cheaper to ship by air. Air shipments also

BUYER'S TRANSPORTATION CHART (cont.)

Can Be Expedited	Cost Comparison	Remarks
Yes (in advance)	Cheapest Method	Total charges depend upon minimum weight required, routing used, and many other factors. CONTACT TRAFFIC DEPARTMENT for best method.
Yes (in advance)	Most economical method of shipping over 50 lbs.	Recommend truck routings when single-line service is available.
Yes (in advance)	Most economical method of shipping over 50 lbs.	Superior to motor truck service in many specific cases. Should never be used on shipments over 10,000 lbs. without consulting Traffic Department.
Difficult	Generally cheapest under 50 lbs.	Inferior to truck service in many cases.(CONTACT TRAFFIC DEPARTMENT)
Yes (in advance)	2 1/2 to 3 times more costly than truck or freight forwarder. Cheaper than Railway Express in many cases.(Check with Traffic Department.)	In rare cases may be delayed to give priority to mail or Air Express.
Yes (in advance)	2 1/2 to 3 times more costly than truck or freight forwarder. Cheaper than Railway Express in many cases. (Check with Traffic Department.)	Good service between major cities; only one flight daily into Columbus.
Difficult	3 to 4 times more costly than Air Freight generally.	We have no choice of airlines used or routings chosen by Express Company. Air Freight service is comparable in most cases. (CONTACT TRAFFIC DEPARTMENT)
Yes (in advance)	Usually more costly than Air Express (except over 100 lbs.) ALWAYS MORE COSTLY THAN AIR FREIGHT.	Cost is prohibitive except in cases when a few hours' transit time differential is vital. (CONTACT TRAFFIC DEPARTMENT)
No	Cheaper than Railway Express.	Generally not advisable except on very small packages on which delivery is not urgent.
No	Approximate to Air Express up to 5 lbs.	Generally not advisable except on very small packages on which delivery is not urgent.

permit buyers to carry lower inventories. If they can get overnight shipment, they need not carry an item in inventory. For this reason, air shipment is quite commonly used for repair parts for machinery.

The cheapest type of air shipment is air freight. The shipper delivers the goods to his local airport and they are handled by a regularly scheduled passenger airline or air cargo carrier. For a substantial premium (usually about 200 to 300 per cent), the shipper can get faster, more complete service with air express or by using an air freight forwarder. The tariff for such shipments includes pickup and delivery by truck, and routing over the best available commercial air routes.

Barge and Pipeline

Shippers of bulky, relatively inexpensive raw materials try to ship by water or pipeline whenever possible in order to keep transportation costs at a minimum. In fact, chemical, aluminum, steel, and power plants often are intentionally located at deep-water ports or on inland waterways in order to reduce the cost of in-bound raw materials. Water shipment is slow but the rates always are low. Also, when railroads or trucks are faced with competition from water carriers, they are more prone to offer rate reductions.

Only fluids can be shipped through pipelines,[4] and pipeline shipment often is more expensive than water shipment. However, the pipeline is the most economic vehicle for shipping natural gas, oil products, and similar materials to inland points. For this reason, its use has increased enormously in the last decade.

Piggyback and Fishyback

Sometimes the most efficient way to ship is by using two carriers—truck trailer and either railroad or ship. "Piggyback" shipments are made by loading truck trailers aboard railroad flat cars for shipments between cities. The trailer is delivered from the shipper's plant to the flat car by truck, which also moves it to the customer's plant. "Fishyback" shipments are made by loading the truck trailers on a barge or ship. After the water shipment, the trailers can be towed by truck to their final destination.

Piggyback and fishyback shipments combine many of the advantages of shipping by rail, barge, or ship with those of shipping by truck. The advantages include:

1. *Reduced Handling Expense.* Material need be handled only when it is loaded into the truck trailer and when it is unloaded at the final destination.

2. *Lower Rates.* Shipment between points not on rail sidings often is cheaper by piggyback than by motor freight, since the long intercity haul can be made by rail.[5] With fishyback, it is possible to eliminate

---

[4] With one exception so far: coal. The Consolidation Coal Company is shipping coal by pipeline from one of its Ohio mines to a generating plant of the Cleveland Electric Illuminating Company. It does it by grinding up the coal and mixing it with water to form a slurry, which is pumped through the pipeline.

[5] For example, the Savage Arms Company of Chicopee Falls, Massachusetts, pays $2.48 per cwt. for piggyback on certain shipments to Chicago. Were it to ship LCL (less-than-carload-lot) by rail in comparable quantities, the rate would be $4.60, according to the company's director of purchases, R. J. Stuart.

extra handling and packaging for export by loading the truck trailer directly onto the ship.

3. Faster Service. Since they minimize handling and enable shipments to be routed by the best service available, piggyback and fishyback usually permit quicker deliveries than the conventional approaches to surface transportation.

Combination Rail Trailer. A new type of carrier that is a combination truck trailer and railroad box car promises further improvement over piggyback. The carrier has two sets of wheels—one for rails and the other for highways. It travels between terminals by rail. Then its highway wheels can be dropped into position and it can be pulled from

TABLE 15–1

ROUTINGS AND RATES—CLEVELAND TO AKRON
Iron and Steel Articles

Weight (lbs.)	Rate (per cwt.)	Carrier
0–2,160	$.91	Allmen Transfer Co.
2,160–5,450	.51	Allmen Transfer Co.
5,451–11,200	.26½	Allmen Transfer Co. Lake Erie Cartage Co. Kaplan Trucking
11,201–26,290	.17½	Allmen Transfer Co. Modern Motor Express Kaplan Trucking
26,291 and over	.12	Lake Erie Cartage Co. Kaplan Trucking Glenn Cartage
40,000 and over	.13	Erie R.R.
80,000 and over	.12	B & 0 R.R. Penn. R.R.

Source: *Purchasing Manual*, B. F. Goodrich Co.

the rail terminal to its ultimate destination over highways. It promises to be cheaper than piggyback, which requires separate truck trailers and railroad flat cars, and also more efficient, since little handling is needed when the trailer is switched from railroad track to road.

Small Shipments

Railroads and trucks offer the lowest rates when the shipper uses a complete box car or full truckload. Barge and pipeline shipments are made in even larger quantities. Every common carrier has minimum rates that are charged regardless of how small a shipment is. Railroads and trucks always charge for 100 pounds even when a shipment weighs much less. In addition, they charge premiums for LCL (less-than-carload) and LTL (less-than-truckload) shipments. Table 15–1 shows rates for various shipments of iron and steel articles between Cleveland and Akron. Note how rates go up enormously for small shipments. For example, it costs 91 cents per cwt. to ship 2,000 pounds but only 12 cents per cwt. when the shipment weighs more than 26,290 pounds.

If the shipment is small enough, it no longer pays to ship by truck or rail. For example, the minimum charge for a Class 100 shipment by truck from Baltimore, Maryland, to Syracuse, New York, is $4.16. A 20-pound package can be shipped parcel post for just $1.21 and a 5-pound package costs only 44 cents.[6] Shipping these packages by Railway Express costs $2.40 and $3.32 respectively, and air express costs only $3.50 for either weight. Even air freight forwarded ($6.02 for 5 pounds and $7.92 for 20 pounds) or air parcel post ($2.52 and $9.72) look reasonable compared to the truck minimum charge in this case.

Commercial freight forwarders are another possibility for somewhat heavier shipments. They consolidate small shipments from a number of customers into carload and truckload quantities. Their rates often are lower than those of Railway Express, but their service sometimes is not as fast. Forwarders also handle shipments from overseas points; in routing a shipment, they may make use of almost every means of transportation.

When the package is fairly small and prompt delivery is desired, intercity bus service shouldn't be overlooked. Charges are fairly high (although they usually are much lower than air shipment), but service can be extremely fast provided that points of origin and destination are on the bus line's route.

TARIFFS OF COMMON CARRIERS

Like other prices, the tariffs charged by common carriers are influenced by supply, demand, and cost of production. They also are influenced by peculiar variables of their own. Unlike most other sellers of goods and services, common carriers are not free to set their own rates. Nor can they operate wherever and whenever they please.[7] Each carrier must have a franchise to operate at all, and, as a condition of the franchise, almost every phase of the carrier's business is subject to regulation.

The Interstate Commerce Commission is the most important regulatory agency for interstate railroads, motor carriers, and barge line operators. The Federal Power Commission regulates pipelines. Intrastate shipments are regulated by various state agencies.

---

[6] One company carefully studied parcel post rates and regulations. It concluded that parcel post was ideal for all shipments weighing less than 25 pounds. Other means of shipment were considered for heavier shipments, which were usually too bulky for parcel post.

[7] Carriers are not even free to cease operations without getting approval from one or more regulatory agencies.

Economics of Rate Structures

Regulatory agencies try to set rates that both are fair to shippers and permit carriers to earn an adequate return on their investment. This is not an easy job. It is almost impossible to determine the cost of handling a particular type of shipment. In addition, regulatory agencies are subject to considerable noneconomic pressures.

Cost Determination. Each carrier ships thousands of different items between thousands of different terminals. A big railroad, for example, is available to carry any type of shipment from any terminal on its own or another railroad's line to any other station. It would be a difficult enough job to determine the cost of an individual shipment if all costs were direct. Unfortunately, most costs do not vary directly either with the type of shipment or with the distance it is carried. They are fixed, or nonvariable.

For example, railroads must spend prodigious sums on maintenance of their roadbed. Most such expenditures are necessary regardless of whether the road handles one train a minute or one train a year. How, then, does one calculate the wear and tear on the road from an LCL shipment of shirts from the factory in Troy, New York, to a department store in Memphis, Tennessee? The shipment may move over several railroads and chances are that several alternate routes are available. The expenses of each road involved will be almost exactly the same regardless of whether or not the shirts are shipped.

It is impossible for a carrier to determine the real cost of any single shipment or even any group of shipments. About the best it can do is determine the average cost per ton-mile for all shipments by dividing total ton-miles shipped by total costs. It also can calculate the average cost per shipment by dividing total number of shipments by total costs. Special studies also can yield valuable information concerning the relative costs of handling various types of shipment. But when it comes to determining what the costs and rates should be for transporting a particular commodity, such as shirts, from one point to another, arbitrary assumptions must be made.

Pressures on Rates. Tariffs are influenced by both political and economic forces. Since a company in a given community can compete more effectively if it has favorable freight rates, regulatory bodies often are pressed by local communities and industries to set low rates. In fact, much of the original pressure for regulation of carriers came from farmers and small businessmen who believed that the railroads were getting too big a share of their output by charging high tariffs to ship their goods to market.

Even today, rates are almost always lower when carriers have competition. For example, on coast-to-coast shipments, railroads are conscious of competition from ships using the Panama Canal. This sometimes makes the coast-to-coast rate lower than rates charged for shipping identical commodities to inland points. Competition from barge traffic on the Mississippi and Ohio rivers keeps rail rates low in those areas. Recently, railroads in the Great Lakes area have been forced to reduce some rates because of competition from ships using the St. Lawrence Seaway.

Even if a carrier has little effective competition, it cannot afford to charge too high a tariff. If it does, the traffic may simply disappear. A rock quarry, for example, will go out of business if it can't negotiate a competitive freight rate. The major cost of the rock delivered to the user is freight. The lower the freight rate, the greater the distance from the quarry can the rock be shipped and still remain competitive with rock from other quarries.

In general, most tariffs are based on "whatever the traffic will bear." If the product has an extremely high value per pound, freight cost is relatively unimportant to the shipper. For example, a freight cost of $5 would have an almost insignificant effect on the cost of a very fine chair designed to sell for $400. But it would be quite significant in a cheap chair intended to sell for $40. Whenever possible, carriers try to distinguish between cheap products and expensive ones in order to charge what the traffic will bear. Usually only part of the premium paid to ship the higher-cost commodity is justified by the greater cost of damage claims and other costs that characterize the more expensive item.

To add to the confusion, the rate isn't necessarily identical in both directions. For example, the lowest rate at which one could ship a truckload of "printed matter" from Boston to Philadelphia is 87 cents per cwt. But one could ship a truckload of the same printed matter from Philadelphia to Boston for only 72 cents per cwt. The rates should be identical. Why do they differ by more than 20 per cent? The most likely explanation is that shippers of printed matter from Philadelphia to Boston were more successful in negotiating with carriers and arguing the validity of a lower rate before the Interstate Commerce Commission than shippers in the opposite direction were. Or possibly there is more southbound traffic, so that trucks sometimes must travel partly loaded or empty northward from Philadelphia to Boston. The northbound traffic simply won't take as high a tariff as the southbound traffic, so the carriers established a differential designed to encourage more northbound shipments.

The density of the product also is important in determining tariffs. A carload of lightweight, bulky material costs almost as much to transport as a carload of very heavy materials. The carrier naturally must charge a higher rate per hundredweight for the low-density material in order to recoup his costs. For example, the *National Motor Freight Classification*[8]

[8] The *National Motor Freight Classification*, published by the American Trucking Association, 1424 16th Street, N.W., Washington, D.C., provides up-

indicates the following rates per cwt. on LTL (less-than-truckload) shipments from Washington, D.C., to Atlanta, Georgia:

Density (per cu. ft.)	*Rate (per cwt.)*
Less than 6 lbs.	$7.31
6–12 lbs.	3.79
More than 12 lbs.	3.26

Class and Commodity Rates

So complex are rate structures that it is even possible to pay two different rates for identical shipments with identical origins and destinations. For example, the tariff for shipping a carload of steel from Baltimore to San Francisco can be either $3.98/cwt. or $2.43/cwt. The higher is the "class" rate; the lower is the "commodity" rate.

Carriers have class rates for almost everything. As the term implies, the rates are created by dividing goods into classes (or classifications) and setting rates for each class. An occasional shipper of a commodity will check first to see if there is a commodity rate for the shipment he wishes to make. If there isn't, he will always find a class rate.

A frequent shipper of a commodity between two points is foolish to pay a class rate. When no commodity rate is available, he negotiates one with the carrier. The proposed rate is reviewed by the ICC and hearings are held. At these hearings, the shipper's competitors may object if they feel the proposed rate is too low and gives him an "unfair" competitive advantage. Competing carriers also may protest if they feel the rate is too low and will cause them to lose traffic. The final commodity rate[9] usually represents a compromise among the conflicting interests of the shipper, his carrier (or carriers), competitors of the shipper, and competing carriers. However, in every case the commodity rate is lower than the class rate, so it is well worth a big shipper's trouble to obtain commodity rates for all key commodities he handles.

COST-REDUCTION OPPORTUNITIES

Because rate structures are so complex, there are many opportunities for traffic experts to make tremendous savings in buying transportation. They often can save their companies millions of dollars by finding "loopholes" that permit shipments to be made at lower tariffs and also by spotting errors that carriers make in computing charges. For example, North American Aviation, Inc., was able to reduce its $2,929,400 an-

to-date information on truck rates. Its counterpart for rail rates is the *Uniform Freight Classification*, available from the Tariff Publishing Office, 202 Union Station, Chicago, Illinois.

[9] The reader should note that there is a separate rate for each commodity and each point of origin and destination. Thus, a traffic department in a large corporation may be working with hundreds of thousands of rates, each of which must be approved by the ICC.

nual freight bill by $597,344 in a traffic cost-reduction program.[10] More than $180,000 of the savings came from overpayments detected in audit of freight bills that had already been paid. The balance came from more economical shipping methods. More than $143,000 was saved by making increased use of pool car shipments. Savings of more than $230,000 came from consolidation of service from air cargo carriers, use of company-owned trucks returning empty from deliveries, special fixtures in freight cars, and so on.

Auditing Freight Bills

Of the savings made by the North American Aviation traffic department, the most surprising to the student may well be the huge sum recouped by auditing freight bills to detect overcharges. It might appear that North American had been extremely inefficient to accept such overcharges in the first place or that its carriers were either inefficient or dishonest. Neither is true.

Every well-managed company audits its freight bills and makes enormous savings as a result. The rate structure is so complex that errors are inevitable. Moreover, when two different rates apply to the same commodity (and there is always the problem of classifying the shipment), who is to blame the carrier if it charges the higher of the two rates? Many such mistakes are the shipper's fault. The carrier's rate clerk never sees the shipment and must rely on the shipper's description of the material. If the description is incomplete, he naturally applies the higher rate. Class ratings[11] vary substantially with the completeness of the shipping order description. For example:

If you ship:	And describe them as:	They will be rated:	They should be rated:
Cotton work shirts	Cotton shirts	Class 100	Class 77½
Crude sulfate of soda	Chemicals	Class 100	Class 50
Wooden forks or spoons	Woodenware	Class 100	Class 50
Portable phonographs	Phonographs	Class 125	Class 110
Solid toy blocks	Toy blocks	Class 85	Class 70
Cotter pins, iron or steel	Hardware	Class 70	Class 50

Even after freight bills have been audited once, it is still possible for a skilled auditor to detect errors. For this reason, almost every big corporation sends bills that its own auditors have checked to an independent auditing firm for a second review. Such firms find it profitable to check clients' bills for a commission of 30 to 60 per cent on the errors they

---

[10] "How North American Saved $600,000 on Its Traffic Bill," *Purchasing,* Jan. 20, 1958, p. 91.

[11] The lower the class number, the lower the rate. In other words, a Class 77½ rating carries a lower tariff than a Class 100 rating.

detect. They will also provide complete traffic management service for smaller companies.

Not every freight bill is incorrect, of course. In fact, more than 99 per cent usually are not challenged. Monsanto Chemical's experience[12] is not untypical. It limits its audit to invoices that exceed $100; even then it must check about 600 of them a day. About 20 of these are "pickups," that is, bills picked up for further investigation because of some discrepancy. On about half of the pickups there is a discrepancy between the rate charged by the carrier and the rate Monsanto feels should be paid. The balance of the pickups result from errors in computation. Monsanto's experience in auditing freight invoices is typical of most large companies with first-rate traffic departments.

Charter Truck

Switching from common carriers to private chartered truck has been a sure-fire cost-reduction technique for many traffic departments. For example, Montgomery Ward cut its transportation costs by $2,500,000 a year with a company-operated fleet of 280 trucks.[13] Big savings result mainly because charter rates are not regulated. A company can carry the "cream" of its traffic in its own trucks and ship the balance by common carrier. It saves enormous amounts in this way because common carriers charge rates much higher than their true cost for some shipments in order to offset losses on other shipments.[14]

Many companies even find it profitable to use chartered trucks to ship to customers and then return empty to the plant. Naturally, traffic managers try to route their trucks so that they expend a maximum amount of time traveling with payloads. One way to do this is to use the trucks to pick up materials from suppliers after they have made deliveries to customers in the same area. One New York-based manufacturer of steel laboratory furniture uses a charter truck to make weekly deliveries to customers in the Milwaukee and Chicago area. The truck returns with steel purchased from Chicago mills. In this particular case, the company's choice of steel suppliers is influenced by the fact that many of its customers are in the Chicago area. Were the company to buy its steel from mills nearer New York—in Bethlehem, Pennsylvania, or Sparrows Point, Maryland, for example—it would have to ship by common carrier since it does not have many customers in these areas.[15]

---

[12] "Traffic Know-How Keeps Costs Down," *Purchasing*, April 14, 1958, p. 77.

[13] "Captive Carriers," *Wall Street Journal*, Aug. 18, 1960, p. 1.

[14] For example, almost all common carriers lose money on LTL and LCL shipments while carload and truckload rates for most finished manufactured goods are extremely profitable, especially when shipment is between two points on the carrier's main line.

[15] Close co-operation between purchasing and traffic is essential to take advantage of deals like these. This is obviously much easier to effect when the two functions are grouped together in a unified materials organization similar to those discussed in Chapter 5.

Not only do charter trucks sometimes reduce the direct cost per hundredweight of shipping goods, but they also have other advantages, including tighter scheduling, better packaging and materials handling, promotion, and convenience.

Tighter Scheduling. When a shipper controls his own fleet, he can more easily regulate relative priority of various shipments. Sometimes he also can offer prompter service to customers or reduce his in-transit inventories. For example, the Admiral Corporation reduced its average time to ship TV sets from its Hillsdale, Illinois plant to its New York distributor from 50 hours to 30 hours when it started using chartered trucks.[16]

Packaging and Materials Handling. It often is practical to equip chartered or company trucks with special racks or other materials handling devices to cut packaging and materials handling costs. Comparable savings often can be made by leasing specially equipped railroad cars from common carriers. Even when special racks won't eliminate packaging, it still is possible to cut packaging costs by using company trucks. Since carriers are responsible for damage to goods in transit, they naturally insist that shipments be securely packaged. In some cases, it is possible to ship in lighter, cheaper containers with little increase in damage. For example, the Douglas Furniture Company cut packaging costs $25,000 per year because it was able to use 150-pound test cartons in its own trucks instead of the 200-pound test cartons required by common carriers.[17] In addition, it cut its damage losses 80 per cent because merchandise was handled more gently in company-operated trucks.

Good Will and Convenience. A company-owned truck with the company name and trade-mark emblazoned on its side is a rolling advertisement. In addition, customers are more likely to be impressed when delivery is made by company truck instead of by common carrier. There is good reason for this. A company often can give better service with its own trucks, and it is almost always more convenient to dispatch a company-owned vehicle than to call on a common carrier.

Despite their advantages, however, there is no doubt that charter trucks would not be used so widely today were it not for the rate structure and antiquated regulations governing common carriers. Few manufacturers or distributors can operate truck lines as efficiently as common carriers. And most would not want to do so were it not so advantageous.

Other Cost-Reduction Techniques

Sometimes a company can get common carriers to reduce rates simply by threatening to charter its own trucks. The process is an involved one, because the carrier cannot cut rates unless it has approval to do so from

---

[16] "Captive Carriers," *op. cit.*
[17] *Ibid.*

the ICC or some other regulatory body. The carrier's competitors will often resist its request for rate reduction. Competitors of the shipper benefiting from the reduction also may protest.

Classification Change. An easier route to rate reduction sometimes lies in creating a brand-new rate classification for the item. The shipper must convince the carrier and the regulatory body that his product is unique and should get a lower rate because it either costs less to ship or is worth less than other products in the same rate class. For example, the *National Motor Freight Classification* shows the following classifications for a simple item like a garment hanger:

Hangers, garment, aluminum, aluminum alloy, magnesium
  metal, or magnesium metal alloy, NOI, in boxes . . . . Class 100

Hangers, garment, plastic, or plastic and metal combined,
  in boxes . . . . Class 100

Hangers, garment, NOI, in barrels, boxes, or crates . . . . Class 100

Hangers, skirt or trouser, cast aluminum, in boxes . . . . Class 85

Hangers, garment, wire, or wire and paper combined, in
  barrels, boxes, or crates . . . . Class 70

Hangers, garment, wood, or wood and wire combined, in
  barrels, boxes, or crates . . . . Class 70

Hangers, garment, pulpboard, printed or not printed, in
  barrels, boxes or crates . . . . Class 55

The lower the class number, the lower the tariff that will apply. Thus the cheapest hanger to ship is one that is "garment, pulpboard, printed or not printed, in barrels, boxes, or crates." The most expensive is the first one listed. If a company should develop a new type of garment hanger—one of molded Fiberglas, for example—how does it determine what rate class should apply? Of course, it always can ship the product as "hangers," but then the carrier would apply the highest tariff. Or it could describe the item in terms of the rate class that best fitted it. Fiberglas hangers presumably would be considered "hangers, garment, plastic, or plastic and metal combined, in boxes." In this case they would be shipped as Class 100.

If there were any legitimate basis for doing so, the traffic manager would try to get the Fiberglas hangers assigned to a lower class than the plastic hangers. He might claim, for example, that Fiberglas hangers had a higher density, were of lower value, or less subject to damage than ordinary plastic hangers, and therefore they were entitled to a lower rate class. In this particular case, he probably would not be successful, since Fiberglas would probably be considered a superior form of plastic.

Needless to say, shippers should be extremely careful in describing shipments. To earn a lower rate, the shipment not only must fit the specifications of that rate but must be described as such.

Reducing Demurrage Charges. Railroads allow 48 hours to unload a boxcar. If the car is held beyond this free time, they make a penalty charge called "demurrage." The traffic department is responsible for keeping demurrage charges low. It makes periodic studies to analyze charges and recommend changes in procedure that will reduce them.

Many plants simply pay a demurrage charge for each day they keep a car beyond the free period. Large plants that receive many cars make an "Average Agreement." If they unload a car within 24 hours after receiving it, they earn a "credit," which offsets a "debit" charged for each 24 hours a car is held after the free period. The unit charge for net debits in any 30-day period is $4; if credits offset debits, there is no charge.

Periodic studies show whether or not cars are being handled in the most economical fashion. They must take account not only of demurrage charges but also of unloading and storage costs. Sometimes it pays to incur extra demurrage charges; for example, it may be cheaper to pay demurrage than to have an unloading crew work overtime at premium rates. Also, many companies prefer to pay demurrage during peak production periods rather than invest in the additional storage space that would be required to eliminate it. In many cases, materials managers can reduce demurrage charges substantially by carefully scheduling shipments so that unloading facilities are never overtaxed.

Special Projects

The traffic department always should have at least one or two special cost-reduction studies underway. Particularly promising for cost reduction are changes in packaging specifications, various pool car arrangements, and various facilities studies.

Packaging. Although it may not be directly responsible for package design, the traffic department should be concerned with packaging specifications. It can analyze damage claims. If there is almost no damage because of poor packaging, perhaps a less expensive package can be used. If damage claims are high, more costly packaging might be worthwhile. Figure 15–4 shows the relative costs of various types of nonreturnable containers per pound of contained product. Needless to say, traffic men prefer to select the lightest possible package. A shipper must pay freight not only for the product but also for the package that holds it. In some cases, costs can be reduced by selecting a container that weighs less even though it may cost slightly more.

Pool Cars. Shippers try to avoid paying high LCL and LTL rates whenever possible. One way to do this is to pool a number of small shipments headed in the same direction. For example, many Eastern manufacturers load orders for a number of West Coast customers in a single car. Thus a manufacturer may load orders for distributors located in a number of California cities in a boxcar with a San Francisco destination. When the car arrives, the orders are separated and carried by company-owned truck or by some other conveyance to their separate destinations.

NON-RETURNABLE CONTAINER COSTS PER POUND OF CONTAINED PRODUCT

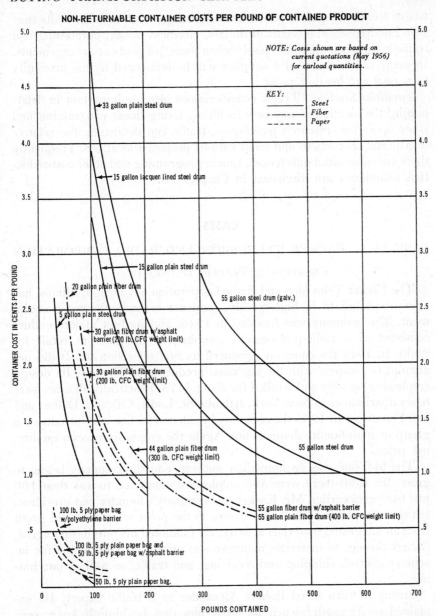

FIG. 15—4. The ideal container is both cheap and can survive shipment with minimum damage to its contents. This chart is a guide to the relative costs of various types of container.

Pool cars also can be used for purchased materials. In this case the company pools all shipments from suppliers in a given area. For example, an auto company with a Los Angeles assembly plant might arrange for pool cars to leave at regular intervals from all cities in which it has a number of parts suppliers. Suppliers then deliver to the loading point, where a carloading firm pools their shipments. Such arrangements may save hundreds of thousands of dollars. Needless to say, purchasing and traffic must work together closely when there are pool car arrangements. In many cases, choice of a supplier will be influenced by his proximity to a pool car loading point.

Facilities Studies. Traffic considerations also are important in determining the location of any new facilities. Using linear programing and other operations-research techniques, traffic can determine the relative transportation costs to and from various proposed locations. Frequently there are substantial differences. Linear programing and other cost-reduction techniques are discussed in Chapter 18.

CASES

CASE 15–1. EACKER TELEVISION AND RADIO CORPORATION

CREATING A TRAFFIC DEPARTMENT

The Eacker Television and Radio Corporation of Chicago, Illinois, has always specialized in high-quality, semicustom-made electronic equipment. The company was founded in 1946, and its first major product consisted of a radio-phonograph combination designed to retail for $900. In 1949 the company produced its first television set. It did not attempt to compete with the big mass producers of TV sets. Its design emphasized quality and retailed for about $475. Practically all sales went to six distributors in New York, Atlanta, St. Louis, Chicago, Dallas, and San Francisco. In 1955 the company broadened its line and introduced a group of high-fidelity components. Again the emphasis was on quality, not price.

The hi-fi line was an immediate success, and the company began to grow. By 1960 there were 500 employees, compared to less than 100 just five years earlier. Mr. Eacker, the company's founder and president, felt that the company had now grown to the point where it could profit from an integrated materials activity. He promoted his purchasing agent, Robert Strong, to materials manager and made him responsible for inventory control, shipping and receiving, and traffic, as well as purchasing.

Strong in turn hired Robert Alexander as a traffic expert. He explained to Alexander when he hired him that he himself knew very little about traffic management but was certain that substantial savings could be made, since the company was currently spending nearly $550,-000 per year on transportation services.

Prior to the creation of the independent materials department, traffic had been something of a stepchild in the Eacker organization. The sales department was responsible for all out-bound shipments. Practically all shipments were made either by parcel post or by the Great Lakes Trucking Company, a leading Midwestern trucking firm. If the shipment was directed to a destination outside of Great Lakes' territory, the Great Lakes traffic manager routed it through other trucking firms.

In-bound shipments were the responsibility of the purchasing department. As Strong puts it: "I buy from suppliers within a 300-mile radius of Chicago and require all vendors to quote F.O.B. our plant. This makes it easier to compare bids of competing suppliers and makes the vendor responsible for delivery to our plant on the date we request it. It also gives the vendor an incentive to combine shipments in one geographical area and thus keep his costs down."

While Strong is convinced that this approach may have been the most economic one while the Eacker Company was small, he is open to any suggestions that Alexander may have for improvement.

Questions

1. Prepare a program of traffic management for the Eacker Television and Radio Corporation.
2. What should Alexander's duties and responsibilities as traffic manager be?
3. Suggest specific areas of investigation to reduce the company's transportation costs.

CASE 15–2. MOHAWK ALUMINUM AND CHEMICAL CORPORATION

FREIGHT RATE NEGOTIATION

The Mohawk Aluminum and Chemical Corporation ships bauxite from its mines in the Caribbean to a tidewater plant in Louisiana, where it converts the bauxite into alumina. Currently, it is shipping 400,000 tons of alumina to a reduction plant on the Ohio River, where the alumina is converted into aluminum. The Ohio River facility is strategically located for several reasons. First, it is reasonably close to most of the major aluminum fabricators in the East and Midwest. Second, it can get favorable rates from huge steam power plants located close to the West Virginia coal fields. Third, it can get alumina by both barge and rail.

Currently, Mohawk gets all of its alumina by rail. The current rate is $6.10 per ton. Mohawk's traffic manager, Herbert Reynolds, has been working hard to get the railroads to reduce this rate. He warns the carriers that they must be competitive with barges if they are going to continue to haul Mohawk's alumina. He says that he believes he could get water carriers to transport alumina for as little as $5 per ton and suggests that the railroads try to meet this rate.

The railroads point out that it isn't fair to compare their rates with those charged by barge companies. Their service is faster. In addition, Mohawk cannot handle barge transportation until it invests in terminal facilities. Reynolds is fully aware of this, of course, and has already gotten an estimate on the cost of constructing such facilities. Mohawk's investment would have to be at least $4 million.

Reynolds believes that his position would be strengthened for negotiation with the railroads if he actually had river terminal facilities to handle barge shipments. But, on the other hand, $4 million is a lot of money to spend for bargaining power. His guess is that the railroads have an out-of-pocket cost of $4.00 to $4.50 per ton for hauling alumina. If they had to, he is quite certain that they would be willing to cut rates to as little as $4.75 per ton in order to hold the traffic. He believes that the best barge rate he could negotiate would be between $5.00 and $5.25 per ton—after having invested $4 million in terminal facilities.

Recently, Reynolds called in top railroad officials and bluntly informed them that Mohawk would go ahead with construction of barge terminal facilities if it were not possible to get a more favorable rate on alumina. He pointed out that the traffic currently was worth more than $2,400,-000 to the railroads, and in the future it would be worth a lot more since demand for aluminum was steadily increasing. He said he preferred the faster rail service to barge. But, in most cases, Mohawk isn't in a hurry to get material anyway, since it carries large inventories of alumina at its Ohio River plant.

Questions

1. What is the highest rate Reynolds can afford to accept from the railroads before he seriously proposes construction of terminal facilities to his company's finance committee?
2. Has Reynolds exhausted every possibility for rate negotiation other than actually going ahead with building terminal facilities?

Chapter **16**

PURCHASE PRICE ANALYSIS

The most basic materials management objective is low prices. It has a more direct effect on profits than any other objective. In Chapter 1, we saw that if the average manufacturing company can reduce materials costs by just 2 per cent it can boost its profits by 10 per cent.

The cost structure of a typical 500 T/D superphosphate fertilizer plant provides an extreme example of the effect of changes in materials costs on profits. The principal raw materials for the plant—phosphate rock and sulfuric acid—together cost $12.15 per ton of fertilizer, or slightly more than 82 per cent of the $14.79 per ton total manufacturing cost.[1] The cost of sulfuric acid alone is $8.46 per ton of fertilizer, or 57 per cent of the total production cost. Figure 16–1 shows the effect of changes in sulfuric acid prices on net profits. When sulfuric acid costs $1.17 per pound, the plant makes a profit of $.50 per ton of super-phosphate (based on a price of $16.00 per ton). When the price of sulfuric acid goes up to $1.25 per pound, the break-even point is crossed and the plant is unprofitable. A difference of only $.08 per pound in the price of sulfuric acid therefore signifies the difference between satisfactory profits and loss.

THE PRICING PROCESS

It is no wonder, therefore, that materials managers devote a great deal of their time to price negotiation and cost reduction. Their actions can have considerable effect on the prices they pay for purchased materials. For, contrary to what some students learn in elementary economics courses, the prices of most commodities are *not* determined by impersonal interaction of supply and demand forces in "pure" competition. Instead, they are what economists call "administered" prices, determined by a process of "imperfect" competition. When there is relatively little competition among producers, the administered price usually is high enough to yield handsome profits. When there are many producers and competition is keen, profits shrink even though an individual producer theoretically is free to charge any price he pleases.

Administered prices are quite different from prices determined by "pure" competition (discussed in Chapter 7). "Pure" competition pre-

<hr>

[1] W. L. Hardy, "Fertilizer Plant Costs," *Industrial and Engineering Chemistry*, November, 1956, p. 41A.

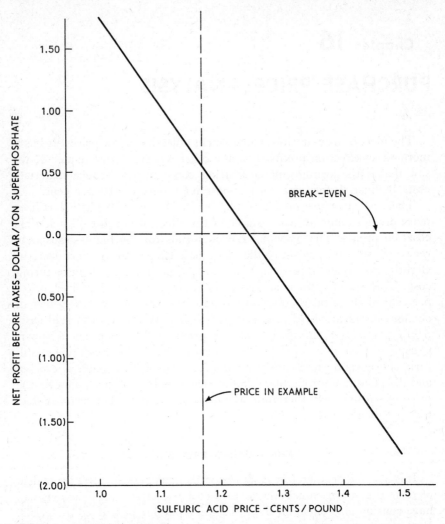

FIG. 16–1. Superphosphate fertilizer is a classic example of the effect of relatively minor changes in purchased material prices on product profits. When its key ingredient, sulfuric acid, costs $1.25/lb., the fertilizer plant breaks even. When it costs $1.40/lb., the plant loses more than $1.00 on each ton of fertilizer it produces.

vails only when there are a large number of buyers and sellers and the product is homogeneous. One seller's product is as good as that of any other seller, and no single buyer or seller can influence prices. Everyone must do business at the prevailing market price, which is determined by the collective action of all buyers and sellers.

Imperfect Competition

When reasonably pure competition prevails, as it does for most materials traded on commodity exchanges, materials management is primarily concerned with price forecasting and timing of purchases. When imperfect competition prevails, as it does for 99 per cent of the items that a typical company buys, the scope of the materials management job is far broader. It is intimately concerned with the pricing process and product quality.

Product Differentiation. The outstanding feature of imperfect competition is product differentiation. No longer are the products of the producers homogeneous. Each is unique. For example, Ford and Chevrolet are competing brands of automobile, but they are completely different; only a few components are interchangeable. Unlike commodities whose prices are determined by pure competition, the prices of a Ford and a Chevrolet are not identical. The differential presumably is justified by higher cost of production or higher quality.

Product differentiation creates tremendous opportunities for sellers. If a company can successfully convince its customers that its product is substantially different from those of its competitors, it can charge slightly higher prices and earn much greater profits. For example, the Polaroid camera is a unique product that is protected from imitation by patents. The prices and profits of Polaroid reflect this position. At the other extreme, prices of textiles also are determined by imperfect competition, but there is little product differentiation among producers. Quality standards are almost identical, there are a large number of competing producers, and it is relatively easy to go into the textile business should it look profitable to any would-be producer. As a result, price competition in the textile industry is extremely keen and profits of producers are very low.

Manufacturers know that profits are almost always higher when they can convince buyers that their product is unique. They do this through advertising and sales efforts. In some cases they are successful in establishing product differentiation for products that are almost identical with those sold by competitors. This is true of both consumer and industrial products. A consumer pays $.79 for a bottle of brand-name aspirin tablets that are identical with and may even have been made by the same chemical company as those sold for $.12 a bottle. An industrial buyer may pay a premium for a brand-name cleaning fluid when the identical material is available at a lower price directly from the manufacturer of the basic chemical ingredient.

Industrial buyers aren't nearly so naive as consumers. And, in most cases, they can use their skill to negotiate lower prices. Only relatively few items have rigid, inflexible prices. There often is genuine product differentiation on these items. Or there are a limited number of producers who control the market and can arbitrarily set prices and make them stick regardless of the buyer's skill or the state of the market.

The Buyer's Economic Role. In most cases the supplier doesn't have the last word on prices. Able buyers can exert tremendous leverage if they really understand how prices are set and don't hesitate to use their skills. In doing so, they are doing a service not only to their own company but also to the supplier and to the economy as a whole.

When competition is imperfect and prices are not regulated impersonally by market forces, some other regulatory force is needed. In a totalitarian economy, the force is exerted arbitrarily by government bureaucrats. In a free economy, it is exerted by negotiation between buyer and seller. Every time a buyer challenges a vendor's bid, he forces the vendor to recheck his costs and review ways in which productivity can be increased. He becomes a substitute for the impersonal competitive market forces that determine the prices of materials. In this role, buyers are collectively a tremendous force in the over-all economy. When they award business to the efficient, low-cost producers and force the high-cost producers either to mend their ways or to go out of business, they help make the over-all economy wealthier and more productive.

Suppliers also benefit when buyers challenge their prices, although few suppliers are aware of the benefit and even fewer would admit it. Pressure from buyers stimulates improvements and prevents complacency. Although sloppy purchasing will certainly permit a supplier to boost profits temporarily, the day of reckoning comes eventually. Only the supplier who is really efficient can hope to earn high profits indefinitely.

Administered Prices

Pricing can be a real problem when there is imperfect competition. The supplier can't simply sell at some market price because there is no market. Nor, in most cases, can he set a price that will yield the highest possible return. Instead, he must grope for a price that is high enough to be profitable but not so high that a buyer will turn to a competitor's product.

In many cases, the supplier's estimate of what the "right" price should be isn't much better than the buyer's estimate. Few suppliers will admit this, of course. But the reasons become obvious when we examine the supplier's pricing process on items where imperfect competition prevails and prices must be administered. In such cases, prices are determined by each producer on the basis of:

1. Probable demand at various prices.
2. Selling prices of similar products by competitors.
3. Profit objectives.
4. Cost of production at various levels of output.

Establishing an administered price is as much an art as it is a science. Each of the four factors above must be considered in making the final pricing decision. The desired profits often are not achieved because of high costs, lower prices of competitors, or changes in demand.

Effect of Demand.   When a supplier gets an inquiry from a buyer, he knows what the immediate demand is. But he may not know what the ultimate demand from that buyer will be. In most cases, the buyer doesn't know either; he can only guess what his company's future prospects are. But he should pass on to the supplier any information on future demand that isn't confidential in order to help him in negotiating the most realistic price.

The buyer also should try to determine what demand, if any, buyers in other companies will have for the supplier's products. He won't necessarily get accurate information from the supplier; he may have to base his estimate on his own general knowledge of the market. In general, the stronger the demand for the supplier's products and services, the higher the price the supplier can seek. It is the buyer's job to undermine this demand by finding numerous alternate supply sources that are eager, able, and available.

Competitors' Selling Prices.   Every company's sales department tries to keep up to date on the selling prices of competitors. With some products this is easy. Published prices are readily available, and producers actually sell at the published prices. For other products the job is not so easy. In fact, in many cases neither buyer nor seller is fully informed about the selling prices of all possible competitors. The buyer often is better informed than the seller since he can always solicit bids from a number of suppliers. But many suppliers are better informed than some buyers give them credit for being. Only a foolish (and unethical) buyer will deliberately mislead suppliers as to their competitors' selling prices. But, on the other hand, a buyer need not go out of his way to tip off a supplier when his competitors are raising their prices.

Profit Objectives.   Well-managed companies almost always set specific targets for profits both in relation to sales and in relation to net worth. For example, a company might seek to earn 15 per cent before taxes on sales and 25 per cent on net worth or invested capital. One of the easiest ways to achieve this objective is to set selling prices high enough so that they virtually guarantee success. Almost every supplier will do this if demand, competitors' selling prices, and customer acceptance of his prices permit it. And no smart buyer seriously objects if a supplier achieves his profit objectives. But he prefers to have it done through lower costs and increased efficiency rather than through high prices.

Cost of Production.   No supplier is eager to sell below his total costs and any supplier would be extremely foolish to sell for less than his cash-out-of-pocket cost. Cost of production is the single most important factor in price determination, since it sets the minimum level below which prices drop only on rare occasions. The supplier's pricing theoretically rests firmly on his estimates of cost of production. To this cost estimate he adds a profit that reflects his profit objectives moderated by his estimate of competitors' selling prices and demand.

For example, if a supplier calculates that unit costs will total $1.00 for an item and his profit objective is a 20 per cent return on sales, his bid would be $1.25. Up to this point, the estimate may well be made by a junior employee in the cost estimating department. But before the bid is submitted to the customer, a top executive—the sales manager, general manager, or president—will study it. The price will then be modified to reflect over-all demand and competitors' selling prices. Usually the senior executive will reduce the bid. Strong competition or a weak market prevent the desired profit markup from being added in full to the estimated cost. When business is booming, the senior executive may raise the bid and shoot for a higher-than-standard profit. No executive ever was fired for making too much profit for his company.

SUPPLIERS' COST ESTIMATES

The vendor pricing process is much less exact than we have shown so far. The supplier doesn't work with a rigid estimate of costs to which he adds a profit that is flexible and determined by market conditions. Instead, his whole cost estimate is quite flexible. The reason for this is that costs can never be calculated exactly until after they have actually been incurred.[2] And a supplier's price quotation is, of necessity, based on estimated future costs that he thinks will be incurred if he gets the business. Such estimates are no more than educated guesses, regardless of the proficiency of the estimators. This is true regardless of the cost estimating system that is used. Most systems break costs into four major components: direct material cost, direct labor cost, manufacturing overhead, and administrative expenses. Each component is estimated separately.

Direct Material Cost

This usually is the easiest component to estimate. Direct material includes any purchased part or material that is used directly in the product. Some cost accountants even consider paint, packaging, and plating materials direct material, although there is no universal agreement on this. Cost accountants do not regard materials consumed in the production process (such as cutting oils) as direct material. All other maintenance, repair, and operating supplies are considered indirect material and are part of the manufacturing overhead, since they are not incorporated directly into the product.

---

[2] And sometimes they can never really be determined. One major problem is that of joint costs chargeable to several products. For example, if a mining company recovers several minerals from the same ore, how does it allocate the cost of digging the ore to the finished minerals? Or how does a company allocate the salary of its chief executive to its various products? By the amount of time he spends on each product, by sales volume, by gross profit on each product, or by some other means? Regardless of the method used, the allocation is arbitrary, as any student of cost accounting knows.

Usually the cost estimator determines the cost of direct material simply by asking the purchasing department for the price. He then calculates usage and multiplies by the unit price. It is not necessarily an easy job to estimate materials usage. The estimate of the stainless steel molding in Table 16–1 is a case in point. The estimator must be able to calculate the initial blank size of stainless steel needed from the blue-

TABLE 16–1

Cost Estimate—Automobile Door Molding

Material cost:

SAE 51430 stainless steel
.018″ × 1.6125″ × 42.32″ = .3470 lbs.
.3470 lbs. × $.4456/lb..$.1546
Packaging material...0080

Labor cost:

Equipment	Operation	Minutes	Labor Rate per Minute	Cost
Roll form	Load coil, form, sweep & cut-off	.063	$.035	$.0022
Light press (2 stage die)	Open flange, notch, trim end to shape	.165	.033	.0054
Light press	Form end, close flange	.165	.033	.0054
Light press (2 stage die)	Open flange, notch	.132	.033	.0044
Light press (2 stage die)	Form end, turn down flange	.132	.033	.0044
Automatic polish	Load & unload—3 at a time, 2 men	.088	.038	.0033
Hand polish	Polish formed ends	.165	.038	.0063
————	Package	.110	.032	.0035

Total labor cost..	.0349
Manufacturing overhead..	.0698
Total manufacturing cost..	$.2673
Commercial and Administrative expense................................	.0133
Total cost...	$.2810
Profit..	.0420
Price...	$.3230

Note: Suppliers try to estimate each cost element as accurately as possible. Their pricing process usually is less exact. It takes account not only of cost, but also of profit objectives and market factors.

print of the finished molding. Once he knows the blank size, the job is not too difficult. He calculates the weight and then multiplies by the price per pound to get the cost. Sometimes estimates of material cost are wrong because the unit price changes. The most common error, however, is a bad estimate of usage. Either the estimator's calculations are incorrect or he fails to make the proper allowance for process scrap and shrinkage.

Direct Labor Cost

Errors are made even more frequently in estimating labor costs. Direct labor includes all work performed directly on the product—assembly, machine operations, and so on. It does not include work that is indirectly performed on it—inspection, materials handling, maintenance, supervision, and so on. The estimator first decides what operations are needed and estimates the time required to perform each of them. He then calculates the cost by multiplying the time by the wages that must be paid. This is illustrated in Table 16–1.

Errors rarely are made in estimating wages, since the estimator knows what average wages are for each job skill. Actual labor costs differ from estimates mostly because of variations in the time required to perform various operations. In calculating the time, the estimator must be able to visualize an operation and, in effect, make a mental time study. To the actual standard, the estimator then adds an allowance (usually about 10 per cent) for delays, rest periods, and other inefficiencies. Even if the estimator makes no errors, his estimate will be unrealistic if the workers don't perform up to his standard.

Overhead

Manufacturing overhead and sales and administrative expenses both are overhead. One is overhead associated with the factory—MRO supplies, indirect labor, depreciation, and so on. The other is overhead associated with the office—clerical and executive salaries, office supplies and rent, and the like. A cost estimator has little difficulty in estimating overhead. For example, note how easy it is to calculate the overhead in the estimate in Table 16–1. The estimator assumes that manufacturing overhead is 200 per cent of direct labor and that administrative overhead is 5 per cent of total manufacturing cost.

These calculations are deceptively simple. Allocation of overhead is essentially arbitrary and usually has little relation to the direct costs of making the product. The reason for this is the nature of overhead, which includes all costs other than direct labor and direct material costs. Overhead must be charged in some way to the product in order to be recouped. In calculating overhead, accountants try to include all miscellaneous costs directly associated with the product or its manufacturing operations. But in many cases this is not feasible. Important expenses —depreciation and maintenance of the building, part of the payroll, and expenditures for various supplies—cannot be traced directly to any one product or operation. Allocation must be made on some arbitrary basis, usually as a percentage of the direct labor cost or total cost.

Types of Overhead. There are three types of manufacturing overhead: fixed, nonvariable, and variable.

Fixed overhead means exactly what the term implies. It includes costs that are incurred regardless of how much the plant produces. Real estate taxes, certain insurance premiums, depreciation on buildings and some equipment, salaries of certain personnel, like watchmen, and so on, all cost the same regardless of whether the plant is operating at 100 per cent capacity or at only 10 per cent.

Nonvariable overhead is not quite so rigid as fixed overhead. It will vary slightly with changes in production volume but will not vary in direct proportion to such changes. For example, when a plant is producing near capacity, there might be a need for two receiving department foremen, one on the first shift and one on the second shift. When the plant is operating at 75 per cent capacity, these foremen are still needed and nonvariable overhead remains unchanged. But when operations are cut back to 40 per cent capacity, it is possible to get along with a single receiving department foreman and the "nonvariable" overhead varies.

TABLE 16–2

Costs, Profits, and Prices at Two Production Levels

	100,000 Units Production		110,000 Units Production	
	Total Cost	*Unit Cost*	*Total Cost*	*Unit Cost*
Direct material................	$ 15,000	$ .15	$ 16,500	$ .15
Direct labor....................	20,000	.20	22,000	.20
Fixed overhead.................	25,000	.25	25,000	.225
Nonvariable overhead...........	10,000	.10	10,500	.096
Variable overhead..............	15,000	.15	16,500	.15
Sales & administrative expense....	5,000	.05	5,250	.048
Total operating cost.........	$ 90,000	$ .90	$ 95,750	$ .869
Profit.......................	10,000	.10	14,250	.131
Sales (selling price).........	$100,000	$1.00	$110,000	$1.00
Profit (as per cent of sales)........	10.0%		13.0%	

Note: This table shows the effect of an increase in production volume on unit cost. When volume goes up, fixed overhead is overabsorbed and unit costs decline, opening opportunities for buyers to negotiate price reductions.

Sales and administrative expense (i.e., the cost of operating the "front office") usually behaves very much as nonvariable manufacturing overhead. It is relatively unresponsive to small changes in sales or production volume, but when there are major changes in sales it will increase or decrease.

Variable overhead is similar to direct labor and direct material costs in that it varies in direct proportion to production volume. If production volume doubles, variable overhead also doubles. Examples of variable overhead include the cost of most public utility services, perishable tools, various operating supplies, and depreciation that is calculated on the basis of machine hours.

Cost-Volume Relationship

It is the fixed and nonvariable types of overhead that create the real problem in pricing. Table 16–2 shows why this is true. One column shows costs for a hypothetical manufacturer whose production volume is 100,000 units of an item that he sells for $1.00. At this volume, his unit profit is 10 cents. A total profit of $10,000 or 10 per cent on sales permits him to achieve his desired return on investment.

Now let us suppose that this manufacturer is able to boost his sales by 10 per cent, to 110,000 units. Note that his costs do not go up proportionately. They increase by only $5,750—from $90,000 to $95,750. In other words, the additional 10,000 units produced cost only 57½ cents each ($5,750/10,000). If the manufacturer can maintain his selling price of $1 each for the extra volume, he can boost his profits 42½ per cent (from $10,000 to $14,250) with only a 10 per cent increase in sales. The reason for this, of course, is that fixed and nonvariable costs do not increase proportionately as output expands. These costs are what accountants call "overabsorbed"—i.e., already paid for by being allocated over a lower level of output.

Of course, if the company could plan on a production of 110,000 units it could cut prices and still achieve its profit objective. If we assume that a $10,000 profit provides an adequate return on investment, then a unit profit of just over 9 cents would be required if production were 110,000 units. With costs of $.869 at this level of output (see Table 16–2) the price could be cut from $1.00 to about $.96.

The Break-Even Chart. If a series of cost-volume relationships is calculated and plotted, the result is a break-even chart. Figure 16–2 illustrates such a chart for the data in Table 16–2. The break-even chart is invaluable for pricing decisions. With it, the supplier can determine the precise effect of any change in volume on costs and profits. He also can use the break-even chart to predict costs and profits from his sales forecast.

The break-even chart graphically illustrates the effect of relatively small changes in volume on costs and profits. It proves that there is nothing sacred about a supplier's cost estimate regardless of how ably it is made. Unit costs of a given product are affected not only by the proficiency with which the product is made but also by the supplier's over-all efficiency and by the amount of business he succeeds in getting from other customers. So no buyer need feel restrained from asking a supplier to reduce a bid.

Despite the buyer's best efforts, suppliers usually succeed in avoiding price cuts when costs decline because of an over-all increase in sales. During these periods, demand is strong and markets are tight. The result is sharply higher profits. On the other hand, when sales drop off during a business downturn, suppliers will study their break-even charts. They may decide that it pays to sell below cost if necessary in order to keep plants operating at levels sufficient to absorb overhead costs.

Using the Chart. Suppose a supplier with a break-even chart like that in Figure 16–2 is operating at 50 per cent capacity. He is producing

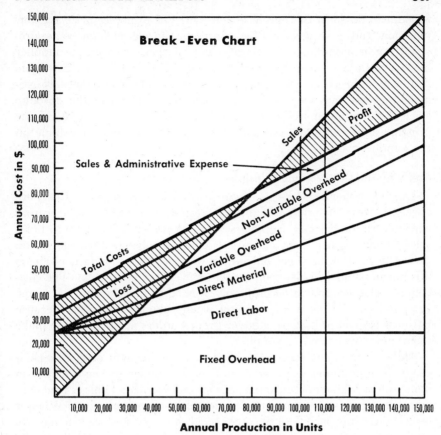

FIG. 16–2. The break-even chart is an excellent guide for profit planning and forecasting of costs. It shows what costs will be at any level of production.

50,000 units and his price is $1.00 per unit. A mail-order house offers him a contract to produce 20,000 units for 70 cents. Can the supplier afford to take the order? He looks at his break-even chart. With present volume, he is losing $13,000. With the additional order, his revenues rise by $14,000, but the break-even chart shows that his costs only rise by $11,000, from $63,000 to $74,000. Obviously it pays the supplier to take the order (provided that his other customers don't insist on price cuts) even though the business is not theoretically "profitable."

USING COST DATA

So far in this chapter, we have discussed pricing primarily from the supplier's point of view. The buyer also can make use of his knowledge of supplier pricing. In some cases, the supplier may be quite willing to give the buyer access to his cost estimates and records. The buyer definitely has the right to examine the supplier's costs if there is provision for him to do so in the purchase contract. For example, price redetermination and cost-plus-fixed-fee contracts always include some provision for an audit of costs. If there is no provision, however, the supplier has every right to keep his costs to himself. In many cases, this is no handicap to the skilled purchase analyst or buyer. He can accurately estimate the costs anyway. When it is difficult to estimate the absolute level of the supplier's costs, the buyer can still apply the cost-volume principle and accurately estimate the effect of a change in volume on the supplier's cost.

Applying the Cost-Volume Principle

Every supplier's cost curve resembles that in Figure 16–2. Costs are always lowest and profit margins greatest when the plant is operating near maximum capacity. Suppliers always have extra incentive to build sales volume when their plants are operating below their optimum. As we have seen, they not only stand to make their standard profit on this business but will also gain increased overhead absorption. The cost-volume relationship can be profitably applied to make-or-buy decisions. It should also be taken into account when volume rises either because business is good or because a buyer groups orders of like items to make them more attractive to a supplier.

Make or Buy. It sometimes pays to make an item even though it can be bought more cheaply from an outside supplier. When it makes an item a plant is able to absorb part of its fixed overhead. This is true only when the plant is operating at a fraction of its normal capacity. When it is operating at capacity, on the other hand, it sometimes is economical to buy items from an outside supplier even though they theoretically can be made at lower costs in the buyer's plant. The reason for this is that costs can soar over standard when a plant is operated beyond its normal capacity. Expansion may not always be a solution, since additional capacity increases the fixed and nonvariable costs that must be absorbed.

Grouping Orders. Many buyers get spectacular cost reductions by offering suppliers a "package" of business for all requirements of a group of similar items. Both buyer and seller benefit, since it is possible to process like items in large quantities at lower costs. Production is greater and unit overhead is lower. As is obvious from the figures in Table 16–2, a supplier making 100,000 units of an item often is willing to offer price concessions if he can get a customer to take an extra 10,000 units. His costs justify a price reduction and his profits will be greater if he offers a price cut less than his actual reduction in costs.

Exploiting Sales Gains. When business is good, companies buy more from their suppliers. Since the extra volume helps reduce costs, smart buyers don't hesitate to ask their suppliers to pass on the benefits by cutting prices. If suppliers know that no one else will sell the item at lower prices, they usually will refuse to cut prices. (Needless to say, they're usually less candid about the real reason they decline to reduce prices; generally they insist that costs have gone up.) Even when costs have gone up, the buyer's efforts may not have been in vain. In some cases he can persuade the supplier to absorb increases in wages and materials costs that are almost inevitable when business is good.

Buyer Cost Estimates

A buyer usually can estimate the direct material cost of a purchased part as accurately as the supplier's estimator can. He can readily calculate the amount of material that will be used, and he usually knows the price of the raw material. The buyer should also be able to estimate the approximate labor cost. He is familiar with his supplier's equipment and processes, and he should be able to estimate how fast they will operate. He easily can find out what wage rates are in the supplier's area from employers' associations or from his own industrial relations department. The buyer normally can get burden rates for various types of manufacturing operation from his own company's cost department.

Thus, the buyer has all the raw material to make a reasonably good cost estimate. And, in fact, many skilled buyers can estimate costs with at least 95 per cent accuracy. Some of them follow the same procedure as the accountant, estimating labor, material, and overhead separately. Others do just as well by comparing the new item with similar items and by drawing on their past experience.

The buyer's estimate becomes a useful target price. If the buyer calculates that the price of an item should be $1.00, then he will certainly think twice before he accepts a bid of either $.50 or $2.00. In either case he will probably ask the supplier to double-check his quotation for errors. He may, provided the supplier is willing, compare his cost estimate with that of the supplier.

While many buyers can prepare reasonably accurate cost estimates, they are not professionals. Some large companies have expert cost estimators working on purchased parts. Their estimates are used to budget costs, negotiate purchase prices, and measure the performance of purchasing personnel. Table 16–3 illustrates an estimate of an automobile-engine air cleaner that was used for this purpose. The estimator believes that a price of $2.54 would provide the supplier with an adequate 10 per cent profit on the air cleaner. The actual price is $2.65.

The 11-cent difference between the estimator's target price and the actual price is a target for the buyer in negotiation. The buyer can ask the supplier why he cannot produce the cleaner for $2.54. This may result in a detailed comparison of the buyer's estimate with the supplier's estimate. If the buyer's estimator is competent, the supplier may be hard put to justify the 11-cent price difference.

Detailed buyer cost estimates normally are used only for major items that are made by highly specialized suppliers. Since they are expensive to prepare, it is pointless to do so unless expenditures for the item are substantial. It also is pointless to make them if the normal process of soliciting competitive bids brings prices down to the level of the estimates. However, for many components there is not that much competition. Some are so complicated that only a few suppliers can produce them. Others, like the automotive air cleaner in Table 16–3, are not complicated, but one or two suppliers have become so adept at making them that their costs are much lower than those of any other potential producer. Their know-how gives these suppliers an advantage that effectively eliminates most potential competitors. In this case, the buyer's cost estimate is a substitute for a more competitive market.

TABLE 16–3

PURCHASED PART PRICE OBJECTIVE
14″ Air Cleaner & Silencer Ass'y—Dry Type—8 Cyl.

Objective price $2.5400
Current price . . . . 2.6500 Eff. Job #1, 1961
    Current price (over) under objective . . . . . . $(.11) × S.V. $45,371.92

Comments:

Material cost of make parts—steel.	$ .6343
Purchase cost of element ass'y, incl. freight.	.4850
Purchase parts cost incl. paint and carton.	.2415
Labor cost @ $.0346/min.	.2488
Burden cost.	.5476
Total mfg. cost—painted and packaged.	$2.1572
Prod. dev. eng'g. @ 3% of mfg. cost.	.0647
Adjusted mfg. cost.	$2.2219
A & C @ 5%.	.1111
Total cost with A & C.	$2.3330
Profit on element ass'y @ 5% of total cost.	.0262
Profit on remainder of ass'y @ 10% of total cost.	.1808
Estimated selling price—painted and packaged.	$2.5400

Source: Courtesy Ford Motor Co.
Note: Some companies make detailed cost estimates of key purchased parts and use them as targets in negotiating prices with suppliers.

The Learning Curve

Every supplier selling a custom-made product is to some extent a monopolist. Competition is restricted because: (1) The supplier has unique experience with the item that makes his production costs inherently lower than those of an inexperienced producer. (2) It is both costly and troublesome for the buyer to change suppliers. Often new tooling must be made. Quality and delivery problems develop. Sheer inertia makes it easier to continue doing business with the existing supplier.

If the purchased part or assembly is extremely complicated and order quantities are small, it won't do the buyer much good to negotiate strictly on the basis of cost of production. The supplier's skills will increase so much with experience that past costs are not a good guide to future costs unless the supplier's experience is taken into account. The solution in such cases is the "learning curve" approach, which is widely used in the aircraft and missile industries where order quantities are quite small, parts are extremely complex, and labor input per unit is very high.

The principle behind the learning curve is quite simple: each job is performed more efficiently as it is repeated. In the aircraft industry, studies show that a supplier cuts his labor costs about 20 per cent every time he doubles production. This is the 80 per cent learning curve. It means that if one unit of an item takes 100 hours of labor, two units

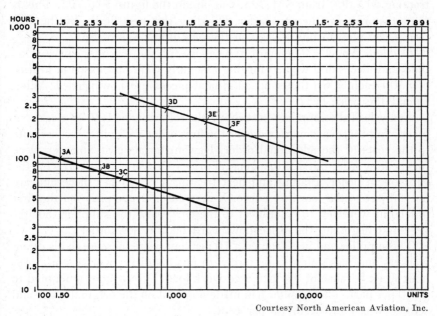

Courtesy North American Aviation, Inc.

FIG. 16–3. The learning curve is based on the principle that the number of man-hours needed to produce an item declines as the supplier gains experience. This 80 per cent learning curve is used by North American Aviation for certain aircraft parts.

will take 80 hours each, four units 64 hours each, eight units 51.2 hours, and so on.

Buyers plot learning curves for various levels of operating efficiency on log-log paper. For example, Figure 16–3 shows an 80 per cent learning curve used by North American Aviation, Inc. The vertical scale indicates the vendor's direct labor costs and the horizontal scale shows units of output. The curve slopes downward because as the vendor gains experience he is able to make the product with fewer and fewer labor hours.

The learning curve is an excellent negotiating tool. Here are two typical applications.[3]

---

[3] Courtesy of Rulon Nagely, director of material, North American Aviation, Inc., Los Angeles, California.

Problem No. 1. 150 pieces of a special machined forging were purchased from Company A for $100 each. You now want 300 more pieces. What should you pay?

Plot (see Figure 16–3) point 3A at $100 and 150 units. Plot point 3B at double the quantity and 80 per cent of the price. These two points establish the 80 per cent slope. At point 3C, which represents the sum of the old and new quantities (450), the total cumulative average price is $70.50. By multiplying the total quantity of 450 pieces by this figure, you arrive at a total price for both orders of $31,725. The total price of the old order (150 pieces × $100 each) equals $15,000. By subtracting $15,000 from $31,725, you obtain the figure $16,725. This is the total price for the new order. Dividing this new figure by the 300 pieces you plan to buy gives you the new unit price of $55.75.

Problem No. 2. The most typical use of the learning curve. One thousand pieces of a welded forging assembly were purchased at a price of $300 each. Two thousand additional pieces are now needed. What should the price be?

Analysis of the supplier's cost shows the following: $10,000 was spent for tooling that was amortized over the first order and will not contribute to the costs of the additional order. Raw materials cost $65 per piece for the first order but due to a general price increase will cost $70 for the subsequent order. Plating and heat treating cost $5 per piece and are not subject to the learning curve. X-rays cost $2 per piece on the first order but were felt to be subject to the curve and the supplier thought he could negotiate the price downward on the new order.

The supplier had just granted a 10 per cent wage increase to his direct workers and was going to be forced to put his direct workers on a 48-hour week because of the increased work load. Direct labor amounted to $100 per part. The supplier had made no profit on the original order and felt he was entitled to 10 per cent.

The computation is as follows:

Original price...		$300.00 ea.
Less: Tooling, $10,000, for 1,000 pieces		
equals $10 ea......................................		10.00 ea.
		$290.00 ea.
Less: Items not subject to curve:		
Material.............................	$65.00 ea.	
Plating and heat treating..............	5.00 ea.	
	$70.00 ea.	70.00 ea.
		$220.00 ea.
Plus:		
10% wage increase....................	$10.00	
Overtime cost.......................	8.80	
	$18.80	18.80
Adjusted costs subject to learning curve..........		$238.80

Plot (Figure 16–3) point 3D at 1,000 units and $238.80. Then plot point 3E at double the quantity (2,000) and 80 per cent of the price

($191.04) to establish the 80 per cent curve. Then read at point 3E the new cumulative average price at the total quantity of the old and new orders, 3,000 units at $167 each:

```
           3,000 pcs. @ $167.00...........$501,000.00
  Less: 1,000 pcs. @ $238.80........... 238,800.00
               Total price of new order......$262,200.00
```

By dividing the total price ($262,200) by the number of pieces, you arrive at $131.10 as the new unit price of the cost elements that are subject to the curve. Then add the items not subject to the curve that were previously subtracted:

```
Unit price.........................................$131.10
Raw material ($65 previously subtracted and
  $5 increased cost)............................... 70.00
Plating and heat treating (previously subtracted)....... 5.00
        Net price before profit......................$206.10
```

By adjusting this price to give a 10 per cent profit, you establish the new selling price of $229.00.

Limitations. One major problem in using the learning curve is change in purchase quantity. Only rarely is the second order for the same quantity as the first order. In some cases, the change in quantity is more significant in pricing than the supplier's experience. A company can determine the effect of change in quantity and experience on various types of item only by studying cost changes on a number of items. North American Aviation's materials department made such a study. It believes that an 80 per cent learning curve with various changes in purchase quantity results in the following relationships:

Per Cent Increase in Quantity (New Order Divided by Old Orders)	Per Cent of Old Price That Should Be Paid for New Order
10%	67%
50	63
100	60
150	57
200	55
500	47
1000	41
1500	37

The learning curve has other limitations. The most obvious one is that buyer and supplier often will not agree on which learning curve should be applied.[4] Such disagreements can best be resolved by comparison of the cost experiences of a number of companies making similar products.

The learning curve should be used carefully. It can't be applied to

---

[4] The differences in the prices that result from using various learning curves can be enormous. With a 90 per cent curve, prices on succeeding orders would run 100, 90, 81, 72, etc. With a 70 per cent curve, the decline would be much steeper: 100, 70, 49, 35, etc.

standard items for which a supplier has already reached optimum efficiency. Nor can it be applied to a cost estimate. If there are errors in the estimated price for the first order, the errors won't be magically eliminated by applying the learning curve to determine the price for the second order. Nor can one curve be applied universally to all items. The 80 per cent curve works for certain types of aircraft parts; it won't work for everything. Each company must devise its own learning curves after making a study of the effect of production experience on the costs of various items. Success in using the curve also depends on the buyer's success in persuading suppliers that the curve actually works. Negotiating techniques will be discussed in the next chapter.

CASES

CASE 16–1. BLUE MOTORS CORPORATION

SUBMISSION OF IDENTICAL BIDS

The Blue Motors Corporation (whose periodic ordering system was discussed in Case 9–3, p. 169) makes both passenger cars and light trucks. It has a central purchasing department headed by John Stone, vice-president in charge of purchasing. Stone puts constant pressure on his staff to reduce costs. Blue Motors is not nearly so integrated as its major competitors and spends 64 per cent of its sales dollar on purchased parts and materials. As a result, its competitive position depends heavily on how successfully it can control prices charged by suppliers.

Stone sets cost-reduction quotas for each of his buying supervisors, and their year-end bonus is based partly on their success in meeting these quotas. Stone's electrical buying section is headed by Walter Karney, who was recently transferred to the purchasing department from the electrical components section of the company's engineering department. Karney is especially eager to meet his cost-reduction quota, since he wants to make good on his new job.

One of the items that attracts Karney's attention is the parking and tail-light light bulb that the company will be using on its new model cars, coming out the following autumn. Usage of this light bulb is quite heavy (more than one million units annually), and even a modest reduction in unit price will bring a substantial yearly saving. Traditionally, Blue Motors has divided its business equally among all four producers of the bulb, since there was no incentive to concentrate business with any of them. On the new bulb, Karney got the following quotations from the company's suppliers:

    Alpha Electric..............................$4.8117/C
    Consolidated Electronics..................... 4.8117
    California Lamp Corporation.................. 4.8117
    Donaldson Lighting Company................. 4.8117

Karney simply can't understand how four competing suppliers can quote independently and come up with prices that are identical to four decimal places. Naturally, he suspects collusion, and he decides to talk to each of the suppliers' sales representatives separately.

Roger Alpert of Alpha Electric says, "Our prices are carefully calculated in our estimating department and reflect not only our cost of production but also the extensive research program we have for developing new types of electrical items." Alpert denies having prior knowledge that his competitors would charge the identical price but agrees that "competitive forces" often result in identical prices from competing producers on identical products.

George Watson of Consolidated Electronics also emphatically denies having had any advance knowledge of what his competitors would charge. He points out that, although its price may be the same, Consolidated offers better quality and service than its competitors because it is the largest producer in the industry.

Charles Sincere of California Lamp observes that prices of competing producers must be identical, although he denies that there has been collusion. The reason for this is the Robinson-Patman Act, which requires that identical prices be charged to like customers. Blue Motors' competitors will also be using the new type of lamp in their new models, so California had to quote the same price to Blue Motors that it quoted to its competitors.

Joseph Allison of Donaldson Lighting, the smallest producer in the industry, points out that his firm is a licensee of patents vital to the process, which are owned by Alpha Electric and Consolidated Electronics. While Alpha and Consolidated make no attempt to dictate the prices to be charged, they have exercised a traditional role of price leadership in the industry.

Karney is reasonably certain that his suppliers haven't violated any of the antitrust laws in their pricing. But he is equally convinced that competition among them isn't as vigorous as it might be. He also suspects that the company's prices on the bulbs will yield substantial profits.

Question

How can Karney stimulate price competition among his light-bulb suppliers?

CASE 16–2. NUCLEONICS CORPORATION

USE OF THE LEARNING CURVE IN NEGOTIATION

The Nucleonics Corporation of America is the prime contractor for the U.S. Air Force's Greyhound missile. The company has relied heavily on subcontractors in the development and manufacture of the missile, and about 65 per cent of the sales dollar is for purchased components. In the early stages of the missile's development, when Nucleonics had an Air Force research and development contract, the company did a great deal of contracting on a cost-plus-fixed-fee basis. These contracts were converted to price redetermination as soon as suppliers knew enough about specifications to quote reasonably realistic prices.

Now many suppliers have had sufficient experience to be willing to quote on a fixed-price basis, and the materials manager, Mr. Swinbourne, buys a number of small components at fixed prices. However, he prefers to continue to buy the more complex items on a basis that permits prices to be redetermined periodically by either party. He believes these items are so specialized and his suppliers now have so much experience with them that no competitor could successfully produce them at lower cost. As a result, if suppliers were awarded fixed-price contracts after competitive bidding, they could easily charge prices high enough to earn rather exorbitant profits.

This is true even of some relatively simple parts. For example, Boston Electronics makes a special resistor used in the missile's guidance system. Tolerances on this resistor are extremely tight, and at first the company had a fantastically high scrap rate. At least 100 resistors were rejected for every one accepted. The company accepted its first order for 2,000 resistors at $6.00 each, with price redetermination. After it completed half of this order, the company submitted the following cost breakdown and requested a new price:

Material	$ .92
Labor	1.22
Manufacturing overhead	9.24
Total manufacturing cost	$11.38
Sales and administrative expenses	.56
Total cost	$11.94

Nucleonics' materials manager was particularly shocked at Boston's enormous overhead charge. Boston's sales manager explained that these charges included the cost of scrap that had been run. After substantial negotiation, Nucleonics finally agreed to pay Boston $11.94 for the second batch of 1,000 resistors provided that Boston would stick to a price of $6.00 for the first batch. Boston agreed, since it believed it had found a way to reduce its scrap substantially.

While Boston was completing this order, Nucleonics got an extension of its prime contract from the Air Force. It placed an order with Boston for an additional 4,000 resistors. The order was priced at $6.00 with a redetermination clause. Calculating that Boston should be gaining additional experience and should be reducing costs, Nucleonics' materials manager decided to invoke the redetermination clause and reopen price negotiations on the second order.

In accordance with the provisions of the clause, Boston submits the following unit cost breakdown for the final lot of 1,000 pieces made on the initial production order:

Material....................................	$ .87
Labor......................................	1.05
Manufacturing overhead.....................	2.25
Total manufacturing cost.................	$ 4.17
Sales and administrative expenses.............	.21
Total cost..........................	$ 4.38

Boston suggests that since the second order will be manufactured in lots of 2,000, it can afford to reduce its price to $4.85 and still make a 10 per cent profit on sales. It regrets that it cannot make any further price reduction because its suppliers are increasing prices and so materials costs will rise by two cents per resistor. In addition, Boston recently negotiated a new two-year contract with its union that called for wage increases of 15 cents per hour. Boston's current average wage is $2.65 per hour.

Questions

1. Should Nucleonics accept Boston's offer of a $4.85 price?
2. What price would be reasonable based on Boston's current costs, its projected increases in cost, and the experience it has gained based on an 80 per cent learning curve?

Chapter **17**

NEGOTIATION WITH SUPPLIERS

Negotiation is one of the most interesting phases of buying.[1] It may be limited to a three-minute telephone conversation about the details of a purchase or it may consist of several all-day sessions involving top executives in both the buyer's and the supplier's organizations. If the purchase is a minor one, the buyer may not negotiate at all; he may simply get a bid and place the order. It's pointless to make any effort to negotiate the purchase of a low-value, nonrecurrent item. Negotiation may be unnecessary even for fairly high-value purchases. If the supplier's proposal is entirely satisfactory, the buyer may simply place the order.

The buyer should concentrate his efforts on negotiating the high-dollar-volume items for which some phase of the supplier's bid is not entirely satisfactory. Particularly suitable for negotiation are purchases with one or both of the following characteristics: (1) Competition is so limited that the buyer feels all bidders are quoting excessive prices or offering unsatisfactory delivery terms. (2) Prices are fixed (because of patents, collusion, fair trade, or trade custom) but it is possible to wangle "fringe" concessions from the supplier.

Negotiation with Low Bidder

Experienced buyers don't automatically award business to the lowest qualified bidder. The low bidder may be disqualified if the buyer feels his bid is too low and reflects lack of familiarity with the specifications. Nor will he necessarily get the job if the buyer feels that the item is worth less than the low bid. In the latter case, the buyer may bluntly inform all bidders that he considers their bids too high and ask them to requote. Or he may deal only with the low bidder or the bidder to whom he would like to award the contract.[2]

Possibly minor changes in specifications can be made that will reduce

---

[1] This chapter is primarily concerned with negotiation of parts and materials prices. But the principles developed in this chapter can be adapted to negotiation of freight rates. Regulated interstate rates can be treated not unlike price-fixed purchased materials, while nonregulated rates can be negotiated just like any other commodities whose prices are determined by imperfect competition.

[2] Such favoritism need not indicate collusion. A buyer may feel it is advantageous to give preference to a certain supplier for a number of legitimate reasons, including reciprocity, proximity of the supplier's plant, a history of favorable relations with a particular supplier, or the belief that a particular supplier will, in the long run, be the lowest-cost producer and the greatest contributor to the buyer's cost-reduction program, new product efforts, and so on.

costs. Sometimes the supplier will permit the buyer to compare the details of his cost estimate with the buyer's own estimate. When this is done, differences often can be resolved. For example, a supplier may have included a certain manufacturing or inspection operation not considered necessary by the buyer. The buyer's quality control or product engineers can be called on to clarify specifications and ascertain if the operation is really needed.

The buyer doesn't necessarily give up even if the low bidder flatly refuses to reduce his quotation. If the buyer still is convinced that the supplier's price is too high after he has unsuccessfully attempted to negotiate a price reduction, he may take one of several courses of action:

(1) He may solicit bids from new, untried suppliers. When he doesn't have time to do this because of delivery pressures, the buyer may be forced to accept the existing supplier's bid. But he should then go to work to locate new suppliers. He may wish to warn his existing supplier that he is looking for a new source. This will put some pressure on the supplier to reduce his costs.

(2) He may suggest to his company's manufacturing or engineering department that the item be made in the plant rather than bought from an outside supplier. The threat of an adverse make-or-buy decision may put pressure on the supplier to reduce his costs and prices. Examples of this were discussed in both Chapter 9 and Chapter 15. In Chapter 11, it was brought out that automobile companies invested in glass-making facilities primarily because they were not satisfied with prices charged by their suppliers for windshield glass. The case of the Mohawk Aluminum & Chemical Corporation in Chapter 15 is a good example of how this technique can be applied to transportation charges. Mohawk uses a threat to build dock facilities to handle barge shipments as a lever to negotiate a substantial reduction in rail freight rates for alumina.

(3) The buyer may propose that a high-priced item be designed out of the product if this is at all feasible. For example, the fact that steel prices have advanced more than twice as fast as other industrial prices in the last ten years is causing industrial buyers some concern. Although steel still is a low-cost material, engineers in many industries have been hard at work looking for alternate materials that look more and more attractive with each steel price rise. There have been hundreds of substitutions of aluminum and plastics for steel in various industrial applications. In the construction trade, architects have made greater use of concrete and less of structural steel.

The measures above are fairly drastic. The buyer need not go to such trouble until he is certain that he really has negotiated the best possible price with his supplier. He should continue negotiations until all possibilities for reducing prices have been exhausted. In many cases, the supplier will be willing to cut prices if the buyer in turn makes certain concessions. The buyer can offer:

(1) A long-term contract for the item. With such a contract, the supplier may feel secure enough to invest in additional specialized equipment that will reduce his costs. He may also be persuaded to regard the contract as "bread-and-butter" business that will pay his overhead and permit him to make profits on his standard line. The mail-order houses buy in this way. They offer long-term contracts provided that the supplier will quote rock-bottom prices. A review of the break-even chart illustrated in Chapter 16 shows why this approach is successful for both buyer and seller.

(2) Changes in specifications or design that permit the item to be adapted to the supplier's manufacturing processes. In many cases, minor changes bring substantial savings. Both buyers and engineers should be alert to such changes; in many cases the value-analysis techniques that will be discussed in Chapter 18 help stimulate suggestions for change.

(3) Additional business on similar items to permit grouping of shipments and production runs in order to cut costs. This technique can be applied to any material or service. For example, a buyer may be able to get price concessions if he offers to buy all his office supplies from a single vendor. The same approach may work with production parts and materials (although here the buyer may not want to become too dependent on a single supplier). Even if the buyer gets no price concession, order grouping will almost always reduce both administrative and freight costs. Fewer shipments weigh more, and lower rates are charged per pound; they also cut administrative costs for both buyer and seller.

(4) Contracyclical buying. Some industries are seasonal or cyclical. Suppliers in these industries will make major price concessions during their slack season. A good example of this is the electrical equipment industry. Although the demand for electric power increases each year and is relatively unaffected by the business cycle, equipment demand is quite unstable. Utilities tend to be either in a rush for equipment or not the least bit interested in it. As a result, the equipment manufacturers either are operating at full capacity with an enormous order backlog or their plants are almost idle because of lack of business. In return for price concessions, the purchasing department of the Tennessee Valley Authority is now doing much of its buying during the slack season. Other utilities have not been as farsighted—or they have hesitated to tie up their money in equipment until there is a definite need for it.

Some purchasing departments deliberately negotiate long-term contracts during the industry's slack season. Suppliers in such industries know that depressed business during this period is normal. Theoretically, they should have no more reason to offer a price concession on a long-term contract when business is temporarily slow than at any other time of the year. But suppliers are human. An almost empty factory has a psychological effect on a businessman even though he knows the condition is temporary. He is more likely to be inclined to cut prices than he would be during the busy season—even though delivery dates on the orders are identical.

One purchasing agent in a small Midwestern city claims that he cut costs by nearly 5 per cent by negotiating all of his contracts for mill supplies during the month of August. His suppliers are in a one-industry area, and during August the industry is almost completely idle. The purchasing agent solicits quotations for the following year during August. Although suppliers are fully aware that they will be delivering against the purchase order throughout the year, the purchasing agent claims that psychologically they feel less secure during this slack month and will quote slightly lower prices.

Fixed-Price Items

If the purchased material is industry priced, the buyer usually is wasting his time if he tries to negotiate a price reduction, particularly if the buyer is not a significant user of the item. In such cases the supplier often is selling the identical item to many customers, and in some cases other sellers also are selling the identical item. It is both illegal (according to the Robinson-Patman Act) and unethical for a supplier to discriminate among customers. If a supplier cuts the price for one customer, he must cut it for all customers. This makes price cuts extremely expensive and very difficult to negotiate. In some cases, if the item is legally price-fixed by "fair-trade" laws, it even may be illegal for the seller to reduce the price under any conditions.

Even such rigid pricing leaves the buyer plenty of room to negotiate lower prices. He often has the opportunity to:

1. Become a "Unique" User. Sometimes it is possible to become a "unique" user of a material with changes in specifications. When this is the case, buyer and seller can negotiate any price they please. Then, if the supplier reduces his price, he need not reduce prices of similar items sold to other customers. This is one of the reasons large mail-order houses use private brands. For example, the Whirlpool Corporation makes refrigerators and home-laundry equipment both under its own brand name and under Sears, Roebuck's Kenmore brand. Whirlpool presumably charges Sears less for equipment carrying the Kenmore brand name than it charges its own wholesalers for almost identical merchandise carrying the Whirlpool name. Were Sears to attempt to get similar prices on the Whirlpool brand, it would almost certainly run afoul of the Robinson-Patman Act (see Chapter 6).

When a company succeeds in becoming a unique user of an item that would otherwise be price-fixed, the resulting price structure is sometimes weird. Auto companies, for example, pay less for exhaust tail pipes than they would have to pay for the steel tubing from which the tail pipes are made. The tail pipes are designed to fit each model of car, and their prices are negotiated by the auto company and its suppliers.

The tubing from which the pipe is made is a standard commodity, sold at identical fixed prices by all producers. Tubing prices cannot be reduced through negotiation but tail pipe prices can. As a result, auto companies use their buying power to get low prices from tail pipe fabricators, whose costs are low because they have their own tubing mills to convert steel strip into the tubing that is made into finished tail pipes.

2. Negotiate Payment Terms. Although the price of a material may be fixed, individual sellers of the material often have different payment terms. For example, mill supply houses have been known to offer thinly disguised reductions on price-fixed items by offering unusually generous payment terms. The standard discount for paying an invoice within ten days is either 1 or 2 per cent. But some buyers get trade discounts as high as 7 per cent from distributors. Obviously this is a concealed price cut, not just a concession to get the buyer to pay his bill promptly. A price reduction of 7 per cent for paying a bill in ten days instead of thirty days is the equivalent of paying interest at the rate of approximately 150 per cent per annum. Needless to say, few distributors are so hard pressed for cash that they will pay such an interest rate; most can borrow from a bank at 6 per cent per annum or less.

3. Use Concealed Discounts. When a company buys both price-fixed and nonprice-fixed items from the same supplier (as is often the case in buying from mill supply distributors), it is not difficult to negotiate discounts on the price-fixed items. The buyer simply lists both price-fixed and nonprice-fixed items on the same purchase order. By previous agreement he deducts his negotiated discount on the price-fixed items from the prices of the nonprice-fixed items.

4. Use Vendor Inventory. As we saw in Chapters 9 and 10, inventories are expensive to maintain. If a buyer can get a supplier to carry part of his inventories for him, he is getting the equivalent of a reduction in purchase price. For example, a buyer may negotiate an agreement whereby the vendor guarantees that a 60- to 90-day stock will be maintained exclusively for the buyer's requirements. The buyer then can operate on a hand-to-mouth basis with no fear of stockouts. He buys small quantities from the vendor, who periodically replenishes his stock when it drops to some predetermined level.

5. Obtain Quantity Discounts. Sometimes a buyer can persuade a supplier to give him a quantity discount even though he is not actually buying the quantities required for such a concession. For example, suppose a supplier's price schedule provides for an extra 10 per cent discount on purchases of more than 1,000 units. If the buyer uses only 100 units per month, he certainly would not want to buy a ten-month supply to earn the discount. But he might be able to persuade the supplier to give him the discount anyway. His gimmick: a purchase order for 1,000 units that doesn't call for immediate delivery but permits the buyer to draw on material as he needs it. Then the buyer can get 100 units each month as he requires and still gets the discount for buying the larger quantity.

Companies with several plants often can persuade suppliers to consider company-wide volume when calculating quantity discounts even though each plant may order its needs separately. For example, the Cleveland Graphite Bronze Company negotiated a combined discount of 36 per cent on lamps for all of its plants.[3] Formerly, some plants were paying the net price and only one plant was getting the 36 per cent discount.

6. Adjust Packaging and Shipping. There is almost no limit to the number of ways an imaginative buyer can find to reduce costs—even when the prices of the items he buys are theoretically fixed. Various packaging and shipping arrangements offer numerous possibilities. The simple act of buying "F.O.B. our plant" instead of "F.O.B. shipping point" can in itself bring substantial savings. Packaging and palletizing arrangements also can cut costs. For example, one company has persuaded its vendors to ship in cartons that it can reuse for shipments to its own customers.

NEGOTIATING PRICE INCREASES

During the past twenty years, the prices of finished and semifinished materials have advanced steadily despite the best efforts of buyers. The reason is that rising wages have increased both manufacturing costs and materials costs.[4] When demand for their products is weak, suppliers usually are forced to absorb wage increases from profits, and occasionally they are even forced to cut prices in the face of rising costs. When demand is strong, however, the shoe is on the other foot: suppliers not only can pass on the full costs of wage hikes to their customers but sometimes can also boost prices to more than offset the cost of future wage and materials increases. The result has been that prices have gone up when business is booming but have not declined substantially when business has dropped off. This has meant an average rise in prices of about 3 per cent a year.

When demand is strong, no materials manager can expect consistently to avoid compensating suppliers for increases in cost. But often he can prevent suppliers from getting price increases in excess of cost increases.

Suppose a materials manager gets a letter from a supplier saying that "effective immediately, the prices of our products are hereby increased 5 per cent." What does he do? His course of action depends on the nature of the commodity. If it is one that is standard and sold to a number of users, he has much less flexibility and bargaining power than if the commodity is made to order for the materials manager's company.

---

[3] "Purchase Analysis Program Saves $113,000 First Year," *Purchasing*, September, 1957, p. 121.

[4] Wage increases naturally drive a supplier's materials costs up because the supplier's suppliers also are confronted with higher costs that they pass on through price increases.

For example, if there is an industry-wide price adjustment on a standard commodity like steel, it would be a waste of time for an individual buyer to try to persuade the United States Steel Corporation that this increase should not be applied to him. The best he can do is to look for a lower-cost supplier or for a substitute material. The buyer is not so restricted on items made to his company's specifications, where the price is determined by negotiation between buyer and seller. When a supplier increases the price of these items, he must give the buyer a good reason for doing so. The usual reason is "higher costs," and few would deny that both labor and raw materials costs have progressively crept higher and higher during the last 25 years.

Justifying the Increase

No buyer worth his salt will accept a price increase on a purchased component with the simple explanation of "higher costs." He will insist on substantiation from the supplier that costs really have risen. Sometimes the supplier will furnish a breakdown of his costs (and, in fact, such a breakdown may be provided for in the purchase order terms and conditions). In any case he should be willing to furnish some quantitative evidence.

If the price increase is caused by higher labor costs, the supplier normally will tell the buyer what his average increase is in cents per hour. He also should be willing to indicate either the number of standard hours of direct and indirect labor used in making each part or the total old and new labor cost in dollars per unit. If the price increase is caused by higher materials costs, the supplier should be willing to disclose his materials costs, materials specifications, and the precise materials usage per unit.

Needless to say, the documentation offered by a supplier will always "prove" that his price increase is completely valid. This does not mean that the buyer should accept the "proof," however. The fact is that many suppliers have never attempted to calculate closely the unit costs of the items they produce. When over-all costs rise, they simply add enough to the price of each item to achieve their profit objective. Often the individual price increases represent the sales manager's best estimate of "what the traffic will bear." Some parts are increased by less than the amount of the cost increase because the supplier feels his competitive position on these items is weak; others are increased by much more. Thus the buyer should never be reluctant to ask for substantiation (or feel that he is challenging the supplier's integrity by doing so).

Cost Analysis

Since the "evidence" submitted will always "prove" the increase justified, how does the buyer determine whether or not he should accept it? The skilled buyer can determine with amazing accuracy precisely how much a supplier's costs have increased if he is given a little data to work with. Suppose, for example, that a supplier wishes to increase the unit price of a part by 5 per cent, from $1.00 to $1.05, on account of higher labor and materials costs. The supplier submits the following cost breakdown to prove that his increase is justified by higher cost of production:

	Old Cost	*New Cost*
Materials cost: 0.5 lbs. brass bar stock		
@ 62¢/lb...........................	$ .31	@ 66¢/lb. = $ .33
Labor cost...........................	.20	.21
Overhead (@ 200%)..................	.40	.42
Total cost.......................	$ .91	$ .96
Profit................................	.09	.09
Price.......................	$1.00	$1.05

Before the buyer should even bother analyzing the supplier's cost breakdown, he should ask himself these questions:

1. Is the supplier's proposed new price still competitive with that of other qualified producers?
2. Do purchase order terms and conditions permit price escalation?
3. Are other producers in the supplier's industry also confronted with these higher costs, and are they succeeding in passing them on to their customers?
4. Has the supplier passed on, in the form of price reductions, the benefits of increased productivity or other changes that have cut his costs?

If the answer to any of these questions is, "No," then the buyer has a basis for negotiation with the supplier other than cost of production. In such a case, he might possibly be able to convince the supplier that he should forego his price increase without making any analysis of cost.

But let us assume that the buyer must analyze costs. He does this most easily by analyzing each basic component: material, labor, overhead, and profit.

Material. This is the easiest component to analyze. Most raw material costs are readily available, and it doesn't take too much study to verify the weight of material used by the supplier. In the example cited, which is a part made of brass bar stock, the buyer would check the supplier's old and new costs per pound against price lists available from the major brass mills. These price lists would include also the weight of each diameter bar per linear foot. Thus it would be simple to verify the supplier's estimate of unit weight.

When the buyer is reviewing a price increase charged to higher materials costs, he should be sure to check also for a change in the value of scrap material. Usually when the price of the finished raw material goes up, so does the price of scrap. If the material has a relatively high value, the value of process scrap can become significant. This is true particularly if the design of the part generates a great deal of scrap. For example, some finished brass screw machine parts weigh only about half as much as the bar stock from which they are machined. Since brass is a relatively expensive metal, this scrap is valuable. If its price goes up, the price the buyer pays for the finished part should be reduced.

Labor. In the example given, the supplier indicated that his direct labor cost per unit had increased by 5 per cent, from $.20 to $.21. The buyer should ask the supplier what the wage increase is in cents per hour and also what the new average wage is. Naturally, these figures should indicate a 5 per cent increase. The buyer should then compare the supplier's wage figures with over-all wage averages issued by the Bureau of Labor Statistics for the supplier's industry and his area. In addition, the buyer also can often get excellent wage statistics from his local Chamber of Commerce or manufacturers' association. In most cases, the buyer won't have to get such data firsthand; his own industrial relations department often has excellent statistics on average wages and is also familiar with the pattern of wage increases. Needless to say, the supplier's indicated wages and wage increases should not be too far out of line with industry and area averages. If they are, the buyer has a point for negotiation.

Overhead. As all students of cost accounting soon learn, all labor is not "direct" labor. Wages paid to employees who are not directly concerned with making the product are an "indirect" labor expense and are charged to various overhead (or burden) accounts. Indirect labor in most manufacturing companies is by no means an insignificant expense. Typically it amounts to between 60 and 75 per cent of direct labor costs. In highly automated plants, of course, the ratio is much higher.[5]

In any event, overhead consists of many costs in addition to indirect labor. Therefore, in no case does a 5 per cent increase in wages automatically increase a supplier's overhead costs by exactly 5 per cent (from $.40 to $.42) as it does in the example given. The buyer thus has a negotiating point even if the 5 per cent wage increase is completely justified.

Frequently buyers and suppliers will disagree about the total labor cost content of a given part. The supplier's estimate of direct and indirect labor cost as a percentage of selling price usually will be higher than the buyer's. Smart buyers try to accumulate as much comparative data as possible. They try to get estimates from their own cost department of what relative costs should be on the type of work the supplier is performing. They also build up files of comparative data from competing suppliers.[6] Experienced buyers eventually are able to estimate a supplier's cost structure with considerable accuracy.

---

[5] In a completely automated plant (i.e., with no production workers), the ratio of indirect labor cost to direct labor would be infinite. In such a case, the cost accounting convention of separating direct labor cost from overhead would be meaningless, since there would be no direct labor costs and buyers would concern themselves only with changes in direct materials and overhead costs.

[6] Buyers should always remember, however, that cost data they get from suppliers are nearly always confidential. They should never show such data to a

Profit. The example given shows that the supplier theoretically is not increasing his unit profit of $.09 with the price increase. This may mean that the supplier feels his competitive position is such that he cannot hope to boost profits when he raises prices. Or—and far more likely —it means that the supplier has made up a cost breakdown especially designed to please the buyer and convince him that higher prices don't mean higher profits.

One of the major objectives in setting administered prices is an adequate return on investment. Many companies try to achieve this objective by setting as a target a given percentage of profit on sales. Naturally, when costs and prices go up, profits go up proportionately. Most suppliers follow this accounting convention. Therefore a buyer can assume, regardless of what the supplier's cost breakdown shows, that a request for a price increase includes a request for added profit. If competitive conditions warrant it, the buyer should not be outraged at such a request. And in fact he should hesitate to use his buying power (if he has enough) to push down the price of an item so far that there is no profit in it for the supplier.

Need for Pressure. In our example, cost analysis has opened up several areas for negotiation of the supplier's price increase. The buyer could: (1) Ask for a credit against the increase in materials cost because the scrap being generated also had a higher value. (2) Claim that the supplier's wage increase was being applied to his entire overhead even though indirect labor was probably less than half of total overhead.

The supplier, of course, can always flatly refuse to reduce the amount of the price increase. Or, as is far more likely, he can attempt to work up new figures to "prove" that the increase is really justified and that only the original "justification" was in error. Sometimes the supplier will cheerfully reduce the amount of the increase. In this case, it is quite possible that he has anticipated the buyer's attempts at price reduction and has deliberately padded his estimates so that he will end up with what he actually wants after he has made substantial concessions in negotiation with the buyer.

Error in Supplier Pricing

So far we have discussed only price increases that result from higher wages or raw material costs. These are the most common price increases. But buyers sometimes encounter suppliers who accept an order at a certain price and then find they cannot meet this price. There has been no change in basic wages and materials costs. The supplier's problem is that he finds he's using either more material or more direct labor hours than he had anticipated.

---

competing supplier without the express permission of the supplier from whom they obtained the information. Nor should they attempt to play off one supplier against another by implying they have data that they actually don't have.

Unless the purchase order terms permit price redetermination (see Chapter 5), the buyer should normally treat such requests unsympathetically. No supplier can be right all the time. And the best supplier will sometimes be too optimistic when he is making the cost estimate on which he bases his quotation. But this will be offset by the jobs on which the supplier's profits are higher than expected. If a buyer permits suppliers to charge higher prices every time they bid too low on a job, his competitive bidding process will become a farce. Suppose, for example, that a supplier bid $100 on a job and the next lowest bid was $105. If the supplier later requests a higher price, the buyer might well have been better off if he had given the order to the competitor who bid $105.

Unfortunately, the buyer's bargaining position may be weak when a supplier exerts strong pressure for a price increase. Suppose, for example, that the buyer places an order with a supplier in June for delivery in December. If manufacturing lead time is six months, what does the buyer do if in November the supplier refuses to ship unless he is awarded a general price increase? In practice, the buyer probably would settle with the supplier. If he wanted to, he could refuse to adjust the contract and attempt to enforce it with legal action. However, this is rarely done by industrial buyers, whose supplier relations seldom deteriorate to the point where even a threat of legal action is necessary.

A far more common problem in industrial purchasing is the supplier who comes to the buyer and says: "We bid too low on this job. We just didn't anticipate the difficulties we've had. Costs have been so high that we cannot continue to produce on the job unless we get some sort of price relief." The buyer investigates and discovers that costs have indeed been so high and the job has actually been more difficult than either he or any of the suppliers who quoted on the job probably could anticipate.

Even then the buyer may insist that the supplier deliver at the purchase order price. Buyers for government agencies have no other choice. If their purchase order does not specifically call for price redetermination or escalation, they can do nothing. Industrial buyers usually can be more flexible. If they feel that specifications were misleading or that the supplier might be useful for future contracts, they may wish to renegotiate the contract even though they are under no obligation to do so.

In such a case they normally would insist on a detailed substantiation of costs. They might even call on their own company's internal auditors for help in checking the supplier's cost records. Then they would try to negotiate a price that was somewhere between the original price and the supplier's actual cost.

PRINCIPLES OF NEGOTIATION

The word "negotiation" carries many connotations that are not consistent with modern industrial buying practices. To some, negotiation means the haggling that might take place in a public market in the Eastern Hemisphere. Buyer and seller carry on an animated conversation, exchanging either insults or compliments. The buyer starts negotiation by offering a price well below that which he knows he ultimately must pay. The seller's demands are equally outrageous; his first offer may be two or three times what the merchandise is actually worth. After some time spent in haggling, buyer and seller finally agree on a price that is close to what each could have predicted before negotiation was begun.

Some buyers use a rather crude version of this basic approach to negotiation. They are never satisfied with any quotation, regardless of how low it is. Some of the more obnoxious buyers try to browbeat suppliers into submitting lower quotations. Their negotiating techniques are pretty much limited to pounding on the table and demanding concessions. Such buyers are quite rightly called chiselers by their suppliers. In most cases, the price reductions they negotiate are illusory. Suppliers who know them for what they are simply quote higher than normal and then make "concessions" when the buyer figuratively—and, occasionally, literally—pounds on the table and demands them.

Successful buyers have a more sophisticated approach to negotiation. They know that they can negotiate nothing but what suppliers are willing to concede. So they concentrate on creating an environment conducive to voluntary concessions by suppliers. Some of the principles applied by successful negotiators include:

1. Put Yourself in the Supplier's Shoes. One of the most basic principles of successful selling is to think in terms of the customer's requirements. When a buyer is trying to wangle concessions from a supplier, the shoe is on the other foot: he is trying to sell the supplier. So he should think in terms of the supplier's objectives, not his own. For example, he might say to the supplier: "If you offer me a price concession, I will try to work you in as a supplier of some new products that we currently have in the development stages." He would *not* say: "If you cut prices, you will help me meet my quota on cost reduction." If you were the seller, which approach would appeal to you—the one where the buyer in effect says, "Let me help you," or where he says, "Help me."

2. Let the Supplier Do Most of the Talking. The vice-president in charge of purchases of a large electrical equipment manufacturer once said: "Supplier salesmen can't stand silence. They'll talk just to fill the vacuum, and in the process they often talk themselves into making just the concessions you want." This is the exact opposite of the approach used by "old-school" buyers who try to browbeat suppliers into making concessions, and it is infinitely more effective. After all, salesmen are professional persuaders. They consider overcoming customer resistance to be the greatest test of their skill. If a buyer challenges the price or quality of their product, they're ready with arguments to sell him. But what if the buyer says almost nothing? In this atmosphere, the salesman is at a disadvantage and may well end up making concessions that he never intended to make at the outset.

3. Let the Supplier Save Face. The buyer should at all costs avoid a showdown. He never wants to force the supplier into a position where he says, "Here are my terms—take them or leave them." Once the supplier does this, he must lose face if he makes further concessions. Similarly, a buyer should never imply, directly or indirectly, that cost breakdowns or similar data submitted by a supplier are false or misleading. Such breakdowns always justify the supplier's position. When the buyer analyzes them and finds they are incorrect, he should point out the "errors" or "misinterpretations" in them. But under no circumstances should he imply that the data were created solely for use as a sales tool by the supplier.

4. Satisfy the Supplier's Needs. Most suppliers have two outstanding characteristics. They genuinely like selling, and they feel somewhat insecure. Smart buyers cater to these characteristics. They give the supplier a chance to sell them. Thus a good buyer provides a test for the supplier's skills that is both stimulating and satisfying. The buyer should also remember that many of his suppliers are in businesses that are subject to violent ups and downs. Suppliers inevitably are attracted to buyers who make them feel secure, who do not unnecessarily increase their insecurity so long as their terms are competitive. They often will offer better terms to such buyers simply because their emotional needs are partly fulfilled.

5. Talk to the Proper Person. Some buyers make the mistake of trying to negotiate with the wrong person in the supplier's organization. When they do, they are simply wasting their time. For example, most supplier sales representatives have limited powers to negotiate purchase terms and conditions. Sometimes they have no authority at all. Most suppliers give their salesmen a little leeway. For example, they may be instructed to quote a price of $100 for an item, which they can cut to $95 without consulting the home office if they are forced to do so in negotiation. In such a case, the buyer should try to estimate in advance approximately what concessions the supplier is willing to make. If he's satisfied with these concessions, he can conclude negotiations shortly with the salesman. If he's not satisfied, he should negotiate with higher-level officials in the supplier organization. If the purchase is an extremely important one for both buyer and seller, the top management of both companies may become involved before negotiations are concluded. Minor purchases, on the other hand, rarely involve much negotiation. If an agreement cannot be reached with the supplier sales representative, the buyer will either accept the supplier's terms or start looking for another supplier.

The Negotiating Session

Major purchases of equipment or parts almost always require formal negotiating sessions. Usually they are held in the purchasing agent's office. The vendor generally will send a top sales official to assist the local sales representative. He may also send his controller, chief engineer, or manufacturing superintendent if the discussion involves their specialties. The purchasing executives also may draw on other departments for technical assistance, especially on quality control and engineering.

The participants in a negotiating session accomplish more if the session is planned in advance, with an agenda indicating what is to be discussed. Purchasing should be prepared to discuss price and delivery terms. Engineering and quality control experts may be called upon to discuss the proposed purchase in terms of their specialties. Shrewd purchasing executives never go into a negotiating session unprepared. They try to anticipate what the supplier will propose so they can be ready with a counterproposal. Some go so far as to conduct prenegotiating sessions in which all the participants except the supplier's representatives meet to plan the real session. Good planning pays off. In some cases, the supplier can be caught off guard, and the result is a greater concession than he had originally planned to grant. In every case, good planning reduces the probability that some important area for negotiation will be neglected.

Negotiating sessions take varying amounts of time. Two hours may be adequate for many rather important purchases. Sometimes a full day or longer must be allowed, particularly if there are a great many engineering details to review. In any event, the atmosphere should be calm and unhurried. Some purchasing executives even believe in spending the first few minutes of the session in discussing completely irrelevant subjects—such as who won yesterday's ball game—in order to create the proper atmosphere.

Every effort should be made to prevent the participants from becoming the least bit emotional. When there is sharp disagreement, the chairman should make note of it and pass on to the next topic on the agenda. Perhaps the disagreement can be resolved at another session, or one party may concede to the other rather than see negotiations broken off. When every point has been covered, the chairman should summarize all points of agreement—and disagreement—and conclude the meeting. Many materials executives follow up such meetings with a written summary of the minutes in order to prevent any possible misunderstanding.

CASES

CASE 17–1. BLUE MOTORS CORPORATION

Negotiating a Supplier Price Increase

Blue Motors (see previous histories, Cases 9–3 and 16–1 on pages 169 and 314) spends about $10 million a year on "chrome" moldings used to decorate the sides of its various automobile models. The moldings are made from a relatively low-cost type of stainless steel. There are three basic steps in the process. First the stainless steel is run through a series of rollers to form the desired cross section. Then the rolled molding is cut to length, and notches and holes are pierced in a press operation. Finally, the completed moldings are inspected for scratches, polished if necessary, and packaged for shipment. Most suppliers perform the two basic operations—rolling and forming—on a single machine. Occasionally, supplementary press operations are required. Inspection and buffing out of scratches are always necessary.

All together, Blue Motors buys about 40 different moldings. But it uses only two different cross sections. Most of the differences between parts come at the press stage rather than at the rolling stage. For example, a four-door car might have four different moldings running along each side—on the front fender, the front door, the rear door, and the rear quarter panel. The moldings are almost identical (in fact, to the casual observer they would blend together to look like a single molding running the length of the car); the only differences are in length, holes, and the forming of the ends.

Blue Motors buys its moldings from three suppliers: Detroit Molding Corporation, Galway Corporation, and Stainless Forming Company. In addition, there are two other suppliers of moldings to the auto industry, Great Lakes Molding Company and Albertson Corporation. Blue Motors has done business with Great Lakes and Albertson in the past. But it prefers to limit itself to three suppliers, and these two firms were not competitive when the last buy was made.

The technology of the stainless steel molding is far from complex. Almost anyone who has a quarter of a million dollars to invest could go into the business. The equipment is standard throughout the industry, and relatively little know-how is required to operate it. There is just one big problem: making a profit at the prices the auto companies are willing to pay. Although there are only five producers, competition among them is so keen that four of them have been forced to move their plants from the Detroit and Cleveland areas to the South, where wages are 50 per cent lower.

The lowest-cost producer in the industry is the Galway Corporation, which has always been located in South Carolina. Until 1955, the company was exclusively a manufacturer of eave's trough and similar rolled products used in construction. At that time, Blue Motors' assistant purchasing agent, Edwin Barnes, felt that there was not enough competition in stainless steel moldings, and he decided that he would try to persuade new producers to enter the field. The ideal new producer, Barnes reasoned, would already be familiar with the techniques of forming metal by rolling and would have the necessary equipment. He also would be in an industry that was price-conscious and in an area where labor costs were relatively low.

Barnes was looking for a supplier with a completely fresh approach, one who had never done any business with the auto industry. He particularly wanted a supplier located in the South. Not only did the lower labor cost in that area appeal to him, but there also might be some savings in transportation costs with a Southern supplier for 15 to 20 per cent of the total requirements. In 1955 Blue Motors was shipping moldings from Detroit and Cleveland suppliers to all 18 of its automobile assembly plants. A Southern supplier would have a definite freight advantage on shipments to Blue Motors' Memphis, Houston, Norfolk, and Savannah plants.

After several trips to the South for visiting supplier plants and discussing the possibilities of their doing business with Blue Motors, Barnes finally met Joseph Galway of the Galway Corporation. Galway was eager to diversify. His company looked efficient and well managed to Barnes. The workers were capable, conscientious, and well trained. Since Joseph Galway was the sole stockholder and had no need for dividends, finances were remarkably strong for a company of Galway's size (sales about $10 million in 1955). Galway was an excellent manager. There was only one problem. As in so many companies with a strong owner-manager, Galway Corporation was a one-man show. No one but Galway himself made any but minor decisions.

Barnes broke the market for stainless steel moldings when he brought Galway in as a supplier. Galway's original prices were nearly 20 per cent lower than those charged by the Northern companies. Galway had no difficulty in increasing its share of Blue Motors' business to 33 per cent of total requirements, and it later got substantial contracts from Blue Motors' competitors. The Northern companies simply couldn't compete. They tried to get their employees to either take wage cuts or boost their productivity. They were unsuccessful on both counts. To stay in business, they moved their plants South to get a more placid and lower-cost labor supply. By 1961, they had managed to get their new plants operating efficiently and were making modest profits at prices that averaged about 5 per cent above those charged by Galway.

Although materials and wage costs have climbed more than 20 per cent since 1955, Blue Motors calculates that its prices for moldings are slightly lower than they were six years ago. This is only an estimate, of course. A direct comparison is not possible, since new moldings appear on almost every new model of car.

Blue Motors recently negotiated prices for the moldings for its 1962 models. Despite slightly higher labor costs, it was successful in persuading suppliers to forego price increases. But it met strong resistance when it tried to negotiate price reductions, and it wound up with no change in price. In 1962, as in 1961, Galway would again be Barnes' lowest-cost molding supplier, with prices averaging 5 per cent below those of its competitors.

On June 10, 1961, Barnes received a letter from Galway requesting a 10 per cent general price increase for the 1962 moldings. The letter said that the reason for the increase was higher costs of labor and materials. Barnes wrote Joseph Galway and asked him to substantiate the increase since he knew of no increase in wage and materials costs since the contracts for the 1962 moldings were negotiated three months earlier.

The following week Galway arrived at Barnes' office in Detroit accompanied by his Detroit sales representative, controller, and general sales manager. Galway had work sheets on which he had broken down what he claimed were the actual manufacturing costs of each molding based on the most recent production run. Typical is the breakdown of part CF-101172, the right rear quarter panel molding for Blue Motors' "Stardust" sedan:

```
.32 lb. of stainless steel @ 46¢/lb.............$.1472
Labor.......................................    .1600
Overhead....................................    .4900
        Total manufacturing cost.............. $.7972
Sales and administrative expense.............   .0797
        Total cost............................ $.8769
Loss........................................   (.0269)
        Price................................. $.8500
```

Barnes was ready to talk to Galway. His purchase analyst, Roger Spade, had prepared detailed cost estimates of the moldings. His breakdown of part CF-101172 was as follows:

```
.30 lb. of stainless steel @ 46¢/lb.............$.1380
Labor—2.1 minutes @ 6.5¢/minute...........    .1365
Burden @ 250%...........................       .3413
        Total manufacturing cost.............. $.6158
Sales and administrative expense.............   .0300
        Total cost............................ $.6458
Profit......................................    .0720
                                               $.7178
        Estimated Price..................... $.7180
```

After exchanging pleasantries, Barnes said to Galway, "I'm glad you're up in Detroit to discuss molding prices again. We have made a detailed cost analysis, and frankly we think there's still plenty of room for price reduction."

Galway replied, "That isn't what my records show. I know we're the lowest-cost producer in the business—and you know it, too—and we just can't make out at these prices. Here are my records to prove it."

Galway's controller then produced detailed records of actual direct labor and overhead costs for Spade and Barnes to examine. Spade immediately asked if he might study the records for a few days. Galway refused. He said that his costs were actually nobody's business but his own, and he didn't intend to let these detailed records out of his sight. Spade then made a superficial examination of the records in the presence of the others. He concluded that the records supported Galway's statement that he was losing money on Blue Motors' molding orders.

Spade and Barnes now pointed out that their orders were not issued on a cost-plus basis. They said their estimates showed that an efficient producer should be able to cut prices and still make money on Blue Motors orders. Galway asked them if they could support their claim. Spade then showed Galway his own detailed estimates.

"That estimate looks mighty fine on paper," Galway declared, "but you've never had any experience running a molding factory."

Spade replied that he had spent some time in almost every molding plant in the country, including Galway's own, and that these figures were based on efficient operation of modern equipment not unlike that he had seen in the Galway plant.

The group then proceeded to compare estimates. The difference of .02 lb. in stainless steel usage was readily resolved. It turned out that Galway's costs were based on a size he had purchased some months before to protect himself against a steel strike. He agreed that his materials cost would drop to the $.1380 shown in Spade's estimate as soon as he started using stainless strip of exactly the right size.

The difference in labor cost between Galway's and Spade's estimates was all but resolved. Spade agreed that he had neglected to include all of the hand polishing operations that Galway insisted were necessary to meet Blue Motors' inspection standards. But he claimed that total labor cost, including the polishing costs, should not exceed $.15. Galway finally agreed that $.15 was a good target provided that Barnes would get Blue Motors' quality control manager to visit the Galway plant and agree to accept parts with the polishing labor possible with a $.15 direct labor allowance.

Galway and Spade found it impossible to reconcile their differences on overhead and administrative expense. Spade claimed that these costs depended heavily on volume of production and that Blue Motors could not be held responsible for Galway's underabsorbence of overhead. Spade suggested that the reason that Galway's overhead was high was because his sales volume was off from the previous year. Galway had lost part of the business it had previously enjoyed from one of Blue Motors' competitors. Over-all auto sales were off from the year before and auto manufacturers were using less molding on each car because of the increased popularity of "compact" cars, which had less "chrome" decoration.

Galway declared that the breakdown showed his actual costs, and that he knew full well he was the most efficient producer in the industry. He told Barnes that no "young punk" (meaning Spade) was going to tell him what his costs should be and how his business should be run. He said he expected an answer from Barnes when he returned to Detroit the following week.

Barnes knew that if he awarded any increase to Galway his other molding suppliers would undoubtedly hear of it and also ask for price adjustments. Negotiation with the others would be particularly difficult if Barnes were forced to give Galway a price increase that eliminated the differential between Galway and his competitors. Since Blue Motors had already announced that it planned no increase in auto prices on the 1962 models, any increase in costs would be a direct charge to profit.

Question

How should Barnes and Spade plan negotiations with Galway and the other molding suppliers?

Chapter 18

COST-REDUCTION TECHNIQUES

The best-managed materials departments have continuing cost-reduction programs. They would have them even if it were possible to negotiate the lowest possible prices for every purchased item. Price negotiation is only one of many contributions the materials department can make to reduce costs. Others include:

1. Design or specification changes that permit suppliers to manufacture at lower cost.
2. Materials substitution, either to reduce the cost of material or to secure a superior material with no change in cost.
3. Reduction of the number of items carried in inventory through standardization or through weeding out obsolescent material.
4. Application of analytical operations-research techniques that sometimes permit costs to be reduced with no change whatever in prices paid for materials or transportation services.
5. Purchase of materials and equipment that reduce labor costs or boost efficiency of the buyer's operations in other ways.

Almost every company has some sort of informal cost-reduction program, and for purchased materials many have formal programs. One survey showed that 49 per cent of the companies responding had formal cost-reduction programs. They reported savings averaging 5 to 10 per cent on successful cost-reduction projects.[1]

VALUE ANALYSIS

One of the most widely accepted cost-reduction techniques is "value analysis." The term was coined by L. D. Miles, manager of value-analysis services at the General Electric Company in 1946. Other companies use the terms "purchase analysis" or "purchasing research" to describe cost-reduction activities that are substantially the same as Miles' value analysis.

There are almost as many specific definitions of value analysis as there are value analysts. But few would quarrel with this general definition:

Value analysis is the study of the relationship of design, function, and cost of any product, material or service with the object of reducing its cost through modification of design or material specification, manufacture by a more ef-

---

[1] "What Is Purchasing Doing on Cost Reduction?" *Purchasing*, February, 1957, p. 75.

ficient process, change in source of supply (external or internal), or possible elimination or incorporation into a related item.[2]

The objective of value analysis is to get more value from an item in terms of function. As the examples in Figure 18–1 graphically show,

This push button was made as a screw machine part. Research among suppliers turned up one who could cold head the part from aluminum wire. Cost of the item dropped from 19¢ to 2¢.

Readily available zinc die cast nuts were successfully substituted for acorn brass nuts turned out on screw machines. Use of a standard reduced cost from $12.24/M to $5.76/M.

 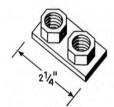

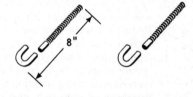

This machined clamp bar cost 32¢. The design was changed so that the item could be made from a stamping with two nuts resistance welded on. New cost: 8¢, plus $350 for tools.

A rolled thread specialist studied this steel J-bolt—suggested the words "cut thread" be removed from the drawing. The part is bought now for 1.5¢ as against 11.7¢—an $80,000 saving.

Courtesy General Electric Co.

FIG. 18–1. Examples of value analysis.

the value analyst seeks to perform a function at lower cost. The function of the J-bolt in Figure 18–1, for example, is performed equally well whether the threads are rolled or cut. But there is an enormous difference in cost between the two processes; switching from cut threads to rolled threads reduces cost by nearly 90 per cent.

Organizing for Value Analysis

While every firm can benefit from value analysis, only the bigger companies can afford full-time value analysts. At present, no more than a few hundred companies have them; some of these, however, are fairly small companies. For example, the A. C. Gilbert Company of New Haven, Connecticut, has a value analyst in its purchasing department even though it spends only $6 million a year for purchased parts and materials. In some cases, it may be economic to hire a value analyst in a

[2] Dean Ammer, "What Value Analysis Is All About," *Purchasing*, May, 1957, p. 38.

company with a volume of purchases as small as $2 million to $3 million, provided that the company buys many parts and has frequent design changes.

According to General Electric's Miles, a full-time analyst should be able to save more than eight times his salary even in a smaller company. Even so, only very large companies in the process industries tend to have full-time analysts. One reason for this is that opportunities for savings are limited to nonproduction materials. There are no production parts in the process industries and it is difficult to save through value analysis on basic raw materials.

The Staff Function.   Anyone can apply value-analysis principles: buyers, manufacturing engineers, design engineers, and others. But some special training is necessary before one becomes really proficient at value analysis, and it is best carried on by someone who is free from the distractions of other duties. For these reasons, value analysis is normally organized as a separate staff activity[3] except in the small firms that can't afford to hire a full-time analyst. Typically, the chief analyst reports directly to the director of purchases or the materials manager. The value analysts usually work on value-analysis projects of their own and also co-ordinate value-analysis activities of other materials personnel.

The typical value analyst has several projects of his own to work on at all times. He periodically reports his progress on existing projects and also suggests new projects. In addition, he might instruct other materials personnel in value-analysis techniques and assist in getting their ideas approved by all the departments involved.

When a value-analysis project is completed, a written report usually is submitted to all interested parties. Figure 18–2 shows a typical value-analysis report. The Celanese Corporation saved $1,490.25 by changing its specification for cresylic acid. Before the change was approved, it was analyzed by the Celanese laboratory, and the accounting department audited the savings estimate to make certain it was realistic.

Value-Analysis Committees.   The committee approach to value analysis is particularly well suited to the small company that can't afford a full-time analyst. The typical value-analysis committee includes members from the purchasing, production, product engineering, manufacturing engineering, and cost departments. It might meet once or twice a month. Specific projects—for example, a commodity group such as steel stampings or specific products—are selected for analysis at each meeting. Each member of the group studies the project in advance of the meeting. The combined and varied skills of the group frequently lead to ideas that cut costs.

The committee form of organization works well in value analysis. It

---

[3] For example, the "research specialist" shown in the organization chart in Figure 4–10 on page 69 could be responsible for value analysis.

COMPLETED COST REDUCTION PROJECT
PURCHASING DEPT.   GEN-1479 (4-58)

COMMODITY

Cresylic Acid (meta para feed)

TYPE OF REDUCTION	PROJECT STARTED	PROJECT COMPLETED	LOCATION	PROJECT NUMBER
☒ A ☐ B	Nov., 1958	March, 1959	Point Pleasant Plant	12

DESCRIPTION OF COST REDUCTION

By special arrangement with Productol Company samples of certain mixtures
were obtained and evaluated in the plant laboratory. It was found that
certain blends would result in a feed equal to that which normally would
be priced to us at $1.15 per gal. and that components would be priced so
that a savings would be realized. Therefore, 26,000 gals. was purchased
for blending and it is hoped this can be repeated once each quarter in the
future.

```
20,392 gals.  Grade 25A (MP) @ $1.15/gal less freight equalization  $20,163.73
 5,961 gals.  Grade 2876 (special xyl) @ $0.90/gal less freight
                                                    equalization        4,413.28
26,353 gals.  Blend equal to Grade 25 (MP) delivered for              $24,577.01
Normal cost @ $1.15/gal. less $4,238.69 (freight equalization)
                                          would have been              26,067.26

                              One time saving                         $ 1,490.25
```

No extra handling occurred since materials could be mixed either in feed
or product tanks.

	AMOUNT OF SAVINGS		
ONE TIME SAVINGS		RECURRING SAVINGS	
	ANNUAL VOLUME	UNIT SAVING	ESTIMATED ANNUAL SAVINGS
$1,490.25	:	:	: $6,000.00

	OFFSETTING COSTS		
CAPITAL	EXPENSE	INVENTORY LOSS	TOTAL OFFSETTING COSTS
$	$	$	$ None

DEPARTMENT AFFECTED	OTHER PARTICIPATING DEPARTMENTS
Production	Plant Manager. Laboratory, Central Purchasing, Operations Control (NYO),

AUDITED BY: *Accounting*   *βBℓ*   *OEA.*
                        DEPARTMENT   INDIVIDUAL

SUBMITTED BY: *H.O.Columbus,* Mgr.   Operations Service Dept.   4/22/59
                        INDIVIDUAL   TITLE   DATE

Courtesy Celanese Corp. of America

FIG. 18–2. Many companies have standard forms for reporting value-analysis projects. This
report of the Celanese Corporation of America is typical.

helps generate ideas that no individual member of the group could probably come up with on his own. However, after the committee meets,
someone must see that these ideas are thoroughly investigated and if
possible applied. If a company has full-time value analysts, they can
handle the necessary follow-through. Otherwise, the chairman of the
committee must administer the program to make certain that the committee's recommendations are acted on.

Value-analysis projects often take months to bring to a successful con-
clusion. In some cases, almost every major department in the company
must approve suggestions before they are incorporated. As a result, committee members can't simply meet, dream up new ideas, and then go

back to their regular jobs and forget all about value analysis until the next meeting. Someone must follow through ideas if anything is to be accomplished.

Value-Analysis Techniques

Tests for Value. One of the simplest—and sometimes one of the most effective—value-analysis techniques was developed by the General Electric Company. Each part being analyzed is subjected to "Ten Tests for Value." The value analyst asks himself these questions as he studies the part:

1. Does its use contribute value?
2. Is its cost proportionate to its usefulness?
3. Does it need all of its features?
4. Is there anything better for the intended use?
5. Can a usable part be made by a lower-cost method?
6. Can a standard product be found that will be usable?
7. Is it made on proper tooling, considering the quantities used?
8. Do material, reasonable labor, overhead, and profit total its cost?
9. Will another dependable supplier provide it for less?
10. Is anyone buying it for less?

If a part "flunks" any of these tests, the analyst makes a more detailed investigation. For example, the high-cost design of each part in Figure 18–1 would flunk one or more value tests. The push-button fails tests 2, 4, 5, and 9, and the acorn nut fails tests 2, 5, and 6. What tests would the clamp bar and J-bolt fail?

As the tests for value imply, the value analyst believes in creative skepticism. He is never satisfied that any item has the ideal design and is being produced at the ideal cost. An item that may pass all the tests for value today may fail one of them tomorrow as lower-cost processes and designs are discovered. The value analyst must keep abreast of all new developments. He must also be versed in cost estimating in order to evaluate the effect of new developments on the cost of the items he analyzes.

Comparative Analysis. Sometimes the analyst can get more leads on potential savings by making comparative analyses of similar items rather than by applying tests of value individually to each item. For example, the analyst might review all of the die castings his company buys. Simple comparison might give him some clues. Castings should get progressively more expensive as their weight increases, special features such as inserts are added, usage decreases, and so on. Whenever there is an inconsistency, the analyst investigates.

Some analysts plot the weight of like parts against their cost per pound. As indicated in Figure 18–3, the price per pound should progressively decrease as weight increases. Parts that don't follow the curve (for example, part no. 7 in Figure 18–3) are not necessarily poor values, since they may have special features that justify a cost premium. But they should be in-

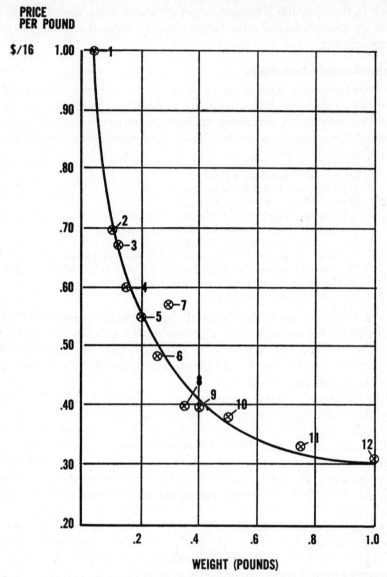

FIG. 18–3. Weight analysis is a widely used value-analysis technique for comparing like items. As weight increases, cost per pound should decrease. Parts that do not follow the pattern (such as No. 7 above) are analyzed in more detail.

vestigated, and in many cases they are good prospects for a detailed individual analysis.

Even if the cost curve doesn't locate any good prospects for value analysis, it still may be useful. The curve can be used to make quick cost estimates of new items. Suppose that a new part weighs 0.8 pound and is similar to the parts in Figure 18–3. A glance at the chart shows that this part should cost about 31 cents per pound, so the unit price must be about 25 cents (0.8 lb. × 31¢/lb.).

Cost of Each Property. Another basic technique of value analysis is to determine the cost of each property of the item. For example, if the purpose of the item is to cover something, its cost per square foot might be calculated and compared with the cost per quare foot of other materials. If the item does some other job, it might be analyzed in terms of the properties needed. For example, light bulbs can be analyzed on the basis of their cost per watt-hour of life, electrical capacitators on the basis of their capacitance, and so on.

A variation of this approach is to evaluate an item on the basis of its cost per function. This approach would work well with the machined clamp bar in Figure 18–1. This bar performs the function of holding two bolts or studs. The cost of this function with the old design is 32 cents. This cost is high, since ordinary nuts will hold studs or bolts for a cost of only a penny or two each. This approach would naturally lead the analyst to look for a way in which nuts could perform the function at lower cost. The result: the 8-cent design that uses two standard nuts fastened to a little plate.

Brainstorming. The advertising industry originated brainstorming as a technique to stimulate creative thinking on advertising copy. Its applications broadened after Alex Osborne of the big advertising firm of Batten, Barton, Durstine & Osborne popularized the technique with his book, *Your Creative Power.*[4]

Brainstorming is a group activity in which four to ten persons participate. Each participant applies his imagination to a single problem and is encouraged to propose any idea that occurs to him, no matter how ridiculous it may seem. Every idea is duly noted by the chairman; none is criticized during the meeting lest this inhibit the creative power of the participants. The hope is that one idea, even though it may be ridiculous, will touch off other suggestions, which ultimately will lead to a genuinely original and workable solution to the problem.

Brainstorming is as useful in value analysis as it is in creating advertising copy. Value-analysis ideas often are inhibited by preconceived notions and prejudices. The value analyst gets used to being told, "Why change, we've been doing it this way for twenty years," "It just won't work," and the like. He often gets results only if he can remove all preconceived ideas about how a product should be made and concentrates on the function of the item. Brainstorming can provide an ideal environment to shake out old prejudices and look at a problem in a new light. If some of the ideas proposed are a little wild, they can readily be discarded in the evaluation stage following the brainstorming session. Most sessions last no more than a couple of hours (the participants gen-

---

[4] New York: Charles Scribner's Sons, 1948.

erally are exhausted by then), and usually dozens of ideas are generated —and most often only one good one is needed to solve the problem in question.

Supplier Seminars. Even small companies often have thousands of suppliers, and each supplier usually knows far more about his specialty than any of his customers do. One of the most profitable value-analysis techniques is to draw on this huge pool of supplier know-how for cost-reduction ideas. Buyers try to do this in their day-to-day contacts with suppliers. Some companies go further: they organize supplier seminars to which they invite top executives from all the companies with which they deal.

The seminars are usually held at the buyer's plant or at a nearby hotel. They almost always feature a luncheon or dinner at which company executives introduce new products, outline corporate objectives, and discuss future plans and their effect on suppliers. But the real purpose of the meeting is to permit suppliers to tour the company's facilities and study its products in detail.

Some companies make up special product displays in which they have every detail part of their product spread out on a table or attached to a display board. Suggestions for improvement are solicited from suppliers, even for items that the supplier doesn't manufacture. The results can be amazing. For example, a few years ago the Whirlpool Corporation held a supplier seminar at its home laundry plant in St. Joseph, Michigan. Suppliers made more than three hundred suggestions for improvements. About a dozen of these were acceptable, and they resulted in unit savings of more than 90 cents on every combination washer-dryer made by the company.

Some companies that have held successful supplier seminars try to stimulate supplier suggestions on a continuing basis. They do this with permanent product displays in which they show all of the major components of their product. One of the "Big Three" auto companies goes even further: its product display room has components of not only its own cars but competitors' products as well.

Selling Value Analysis

Value analysis is a staff activity. The value analyst can accomplish nothing without the help and co-operation of those with whom he must work—buyers, engineers, suppliers, and others. A considerable part of his time must be spent in arousing enthusiasm for cost reduction and value analysis in everyone he contacts.

To Suppliers. Seminars do a lot to stimulate supplier interest in value analysis. But some companies do even more. For example, many companies have published booklets in which they explain their problems to suppliers. Others go in for gimmicks like that used by Aerosol Techniques, Inc., shown in Figure 18–4. The International Minerals & Chemi-

Courtesy Aerosol Techniques, Inc.

FIG. 18–4. Aerosol Techniques, Inc., uses this simulated theater ticket to stimulate supplier cost-reduction ideas. "Tickets" were mailed to all suppliers and also were available in the reception room of the company offices. They have space on the back for the supplier to note his ideas.

cals Corporation of Skokie, Illinois, puts to good use a blackboard in the room where suppliers wait to see the company's buyers. On the board is lettered a "Dear Mr. Supplier" message. One such message read: "What have you contributed to IMC's Purchasing for Profit Program this year? Be prepared to give a definite written answer by July 1."

Many companies have had considerable success with Vendor Value Awards (see Figure 18–5). If a supplier has been consistently helpful with cost reduction, he gets a certificate in recognition of his achievement. Suppliers like to receive the certificates both because they like to know that their efforts are appreciated and because they can use the certificates as a selling tool. What better advertising is there than the written testimony of satisfied customers?

Within the Company. The value analyst must not only sell value analysis to others in his company; he must also sell himself. Almost all of the value analyst's proposals will mean stepping on someone's toes. The value analyst's forte is change. This means, in effect, proving that what is being done now is not too good. If the value analyst doesn't tread carefully, his ideas will inevitably be taken as implied criticism of those responsible for the older, higher-cost approach.

Value analysts sell themselves and their ideas with talks and presentations in which they explain value-analysis concepts to others in the organization. Value news bulletins are another means of doing this (see Figure 18–6). Their objective is to stimulate enthusiasm for value analysis. They review the cost-reduction progress that has been made to date and also single out individuals who have made outstanding contributions to value analysis. The full-time analysts usually try to give all the credit for successful projects to others. That way they get better cooperation on future projects.

Some companies do more than just congratulate those who come up with cost-reduction ideas. They give awards. For example, the Bearings Company of America, in Lancaster, Pennsylvania, has a "man-of-the-

An Award of

VENDOR VALUE

conferred upon

ABC Supply Company

In recognition of consistently helpful service and cooperation
in the field of cost reduction.

The Purchasing Department of

John Manufacturing Company

makes this award in conformance with the principles appearing below.

"The Vendor's Know-How is the Buyer's Greatest Asset".

Jan. 2, 1961   *Richard Roe*
Date   Purchasing Agent

The tests of a

VENDOR'S VALUE

1. He knows precisely how the customer uses his product.
2. He makes every effort to help the customer with standardization.
3. He tries to help customers cut costs by eliminating unnecessary features in his products.
4. He knows all his own capabilities and how they can help the customer.
5. He stays informed on — and tries to top — features of competitive products.
6. He tries to simplify his products before he's forced into it by the customer.
7. He stays informed on new processes and materials, and discusses them with the customer.
8. He tries to package his products in the cheapest and most efficient way.
9. He promotes the idea of blanket orders and other devices to help the customer cut costs.
10. He tries to give each customer the best possible price on his product.

Copyright 1957, Purchasing Magazine

FIG. 18–5. Some companies present vendor value awards to suppliers who have made outstanding contributions to their value-analysis programs. Suppliers like the awards because they can use them as a selling tool with new prospects.

month" program to recognize performance in its plant-wide value-analysis program. The person selected is photographed. One print of the photo is prominently displayed on the plant bulletin board; the other goes to his wife. Consistent winners also are remembered at the end of the year when salary adjustments are being considered.

Purchasing Cost Reduction ₷ News Letter

CENTRAL PURCHASING DEPARTMENT • CHARLOTTE, N. C.

July 1, 1959   No. 59-3

At the halfway mark in 1959, our "buying for value" policy has resulted in
a savings of almost $200,000 in purchased materials. This indicates the
responsibility each of us feels to contribute to Corporate profits. For
the second half of the year, it is the considered opinion of most economists
that we are facing a period when prices will be firmer and higher and an
increased demand will be evident in some lines. This may make cost reductions
more difficult to accomplish and will call for greater effort on our part to
do the best buying job possible.

COST REDUCTION

Cost Reductions for the first six (6) months of this year are running at a
rate well ahead of our target level with a notable increase in savings during
the second quarter. Number of projects completed together with total savings
compare with target as shown below:

	1st Qtr. 1959	2nd Qtr. 1959	Total 1st 6 Mos. 1959	1st 6 Mos. Target-1959
Projects Completed	66	63	129	---
Savings	$74,933	$123,797	$198,730	$157,000

As shown on the Detail Sheet (attached) the increase in activity, as measured
by the number of projects completed, during the months of May and June is
particularly creditable in view of the heavy buying load currently being
experienced at all locations.

Courtesy Celanese Corp. of America

FIG. 18–6. A few companies keep interest in value analysis at high pitch by publishing cost-reduction newsletters in which they report progress and discuss value-analysis techniques.

STANDARDIZATION

Value-analysis programs are usually designed to reduce the cost of an item. Standardization programs may eliminate the item entirely. For example, Figure 18–7 illustrates what happened as a result of a standardization program at the Bryant Electric Company, Bridgeport, Connecticut.[5] The company reviewed 1,447 items carried in stock and found it could eliminate 794 of them. Unit costs were reduced because fewer items were bought in larger quantities; carrying costs were reduced because of a net reduction in inventories. Total savings are estimated at $102,000 in the two years since the program was started.

Bryant's experience with standardization is not unique. For example, before it set standards, one large Cleveland auto-parts manufacturer stocked several hundred different types of oils and other lubricants in its plants. Each production supervisor requisitioned the precise type of

---

[5] Gerald L. Swartwood, "How Standardization Helps Everybody," *Purchasing*, July 4, 1960, pp. 54–58.

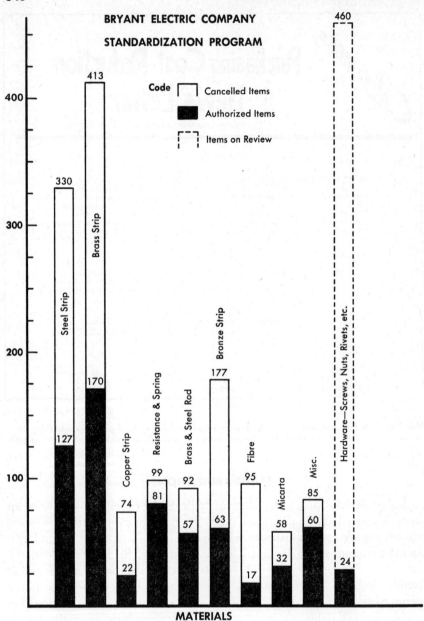

FIG. 18–7. The standardization program of Bryant Electric Co. was an outstanding success. In two years the number of items stocked was reduced by more than 50 per cent and savings totaled $102,000.

oil he thought would best serve his needs. A standardization study showed that less than 50 different types of oil were needed to do every possible lubrication job in the company's factories. As a result, the company uses 80 per cent fewer types of lubricant than before. Inventories are lower, and prices have also been reduced because the company can buy each type of lubricant in larger quantities.

The Standardization Program

The examples cited above are dramatic, but they illustrate why standardization is important in industry. Standardization is essential to a modern mass-production economy. Almost every major industry has standards to classify its products. The American Standards Association co-ordinates and promotes standardization of thousands of products for the 122 technical societies and trade associations and the 2,000 companies that are its members.

A standard is defined as "that which has been established as a model to which an object or an action may be compared."[6] The purpose of a standard is to provide a criterion for judgment. Companies are concerned with standards both for the products they design and for the materials designed by their suppliers. In the former case, the company's engineer may create his own standards or work to the standards of an industry. For example, when an engineer in an office-furniture factory designs a drawer, he may work within industry standards for strength, shape, durability, and so on. But his final design is unique—although it may become one of the company's own standards for drawer pulls. The materials the company buys usually are in accord with the supplier's industry standards. For example, the engineer may specify that the drawer be made of steel specified in an American Iron & Steel Institute standard.

Company-Wide Standards. Although industry standards help prevent unnecessary variation in specifications, the needs of our economy are so great that each industry usually offers many more standard products than any single consumer can possibly use. In addition, many industries try to sell by brand name rather than by industry standards. For this reason, many companies establish their own standards, not only for products they design for themselves but also for products designed by their suppliers. For example, the Chrysler Corporation has set its own standards for the carbide tool inserts it buys (see Figure 18–8) by specifying the exact dimensions and grades it requires. If Chrysler did not go to the trouble to do this, it would soon find itself using far more different types of carbide insert than it does at present.

When there are no written standards, each user of material has carte blanche to specify what he needs. For example, note that Chrysler has

---

[6] *Industrial Standardization—Company Programs and Practices*, Studies in Business Policy, No. 85 (New York: National Industrial Conference Board, 1957), p. 7.

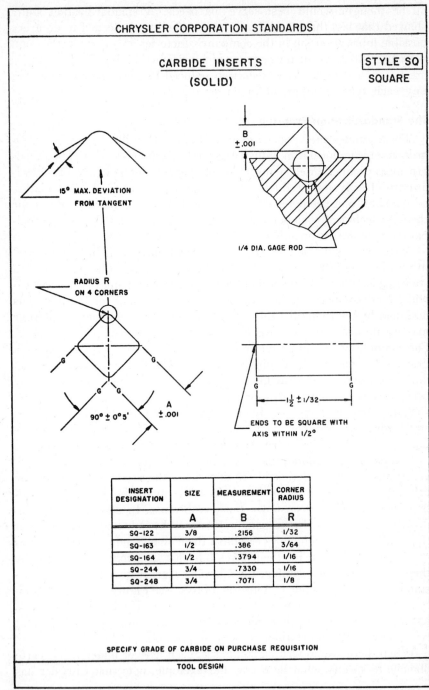

CHRYSLER CORPORATION STANDARDS

CARBIDE INSERTS
(SOLID)

| STYLE SQ |
| SQUARE |

15° MAX. DEVIATION
FROM TANGENT

RADIUS R
ON 4 CORNERS

B
± .001

1/4 DIA. GAGE ROD

90° ± 0° 5'   A
                    ± .001

G   G

1½ ± 1/32

ENDS TO BE SQUARE WITH
AXIS WITHIN 1/2°

INSERT DESIGNATION	SIZE	MEASUREMENT	CORNER RADIUS
	A	B	R
SQ-122	3/8	.2156	1/32
SQ-163	1/2	.386	3/64
SQ-164	1/2	.3794	1/16
SQ-244	3/4	.7330	1/16
SQ-248	3/4	.7071	1/8

SPECIFY GRADE OF CARBIDE ON PURCHASE REQUISITION

TOOL DESIGN

Courtesy Chrysler Corp.

FIG. 18–8. A company can limit the number of items it stocks by developing its own specifications. For example, this standard indicated that Chrysler Corporation uses only five sizes of square carbide insert.

five different types of square carbide insert. No. SQ-122 has a ⅜" square cross section with .2156" clearance and 1/32" corner radius. The comparable dimensions for the next size, SQ-163, are ½", .386", and 3/64" respectively. If one size is too small, the next size is used. But what would happen if there were no standards? Each user would calculate the dimensions that most closely suited his needs. Eventually Chrysler would wind up buying and stocking several dozen different sizes of insert with dimensions intermediate between those of SQ-122 and SQ-163.

The experiences of Bryant Electric, the auto parts company, and numerous other companies prove that there is a natural tendency for companies to stock more and more different items to do the same job. Each user likes to get the item that is *exactly* what he wants and will not settle for the nearest standard item if he can help it. As a result, standardization is a continuing process. Periodic reviews of every item are essential to root out the items that are no longer needed.

How to Standardize

Bryant Electric's standardization program is fairly typical. Decisions were made by a committee that included representatives from every major department. The chairman was the company's standards engineer. The first step in the program was to list all inventory items in detail on large (14" × 24") accounting sheets. (Figure 18–9 shows a part of

							Material Substitution		
BRYANT MATERIAL STANDARDIZATION PROGRAM									
Material Description Thk Width Length PDS	Ann. Act.	Part No.	Dwg. No.	Part Desc.	Cat. No.	Dwg. No.	Thk Width Length PDS		Remarks
016x5/32xC Brass 2676-6	570	E27214 E27844	14514C 15207C	Bracket Bracket	FS40 FS40	14526A 14540C	016x5/32 Brass 2676-6 Bracket width 5/32 required		
016x255xC Brass 2676-6	100	E21236 E21237	9922C 9921B	Contact Contact	20 20	9920L 9920L	016x1/4 Brass 2676-6 1/4 width o.k.		
016x255xC Brass 2676-10	360	E29438 E29439 E29440 E20654 E21287 E21679 E24024	15914D 15913D 8030C 8979C 10015B 10213C 8979C	Brush Brush Contact Contact Brush Contact Contact	207 204 200 4013 5128 310 15	8051L 8014L 15455L B01076 10012A 14141A Cat. card	016x1/4 Brass 2676-10 Ex. Hd. Temper required		
016x255xC Brass 2676-4	48	E28254	15600C	Strap	5269	15599A	016x1/4 Brass 2676-6 1/2 hd. o.k.		
016x255xC Brass 2676-11	924	E20126	8943C	Brush	706	6294B	016x1/4 Brass 2676-10 -10 o.k. per 6/10 lab rpt.		
016x7/16xC Brass 2676-8	10	E2737	3125A	Washer	392	4957B	Slit from 1" wide-2676-5 1/4 hd. o.k.		
016x13/32xC Brass 2676-10	2376	E2757 E4238 E13064 E16123 E18213 E22163	7671C 6340C 7671C 6180C 6180C 10459C	Contact Contact Contact Contact Contact Contact	70 4229 4190 421 421 337660	1800A 4299A Cat. card 10783B 10783B 4299A	016x13/32 Brass 2676-10 Ex. hd. Temper Required		
016x15/16xC Brass 2676-3	500	E17718	7152C	Housing	746	SK521	016x15/16 Steel 7300-5 Steel o.k.		

Courtesy Bryant Electric Co.

FIG. 18–9. The first step in a standardization program is to list all items stocked. Bryant Electric did this for the brass strip listed above and changed much of the 0.255-inch-wide material to a standard 0.25-inch width.

Bryant's listing of various types of brass strip.) Listed initially for each item was a description of the material, its usage, and how it was used. Potential substitutes for the material were listed later. The committee then reviewed the list to make certain that there were detailed buying specifications for each item. Then possible substitutions were proposed.

Economic Substitution. Even if a substitute is technically feasible, it isn't necessarily economic to use it. But the economics of standardization are not complex. All one need do is to compare cost of acquisition and carrying cost before the substitution was made with costs after it was made.[7] For example, suppose an item costs $.10 and 500 units per year are used. Its substitute, which is also stocked, costs $.105. Let us assume that ordering cost is $10 and carrying cost is 24 per cent. If we substitute the higher-cost item, we increase our purchase cost by $5 per year (500 units × $.005). But, assuming that we used to buy the item once a year, we reduce ordering cost by $10 and carrying cost by $6 (24 per cent of $25).

Items Not Needed. A similar approach can be used for obsolescent items. An item is worth eliminating entirely if the carrying cost, which probably will be incurred before it is used, exceeds the purchase cost less the scrap or salvage value. Many well-managed companies consider an item obsolescent if it has not been used for the past twelve months and there is no immediate need for it. If they can sell the item back to the supplier or to another company that needs it, they do so, even if they must take a 50 per cent loss to make the sale.

Standardization programs are designed primarily to root out unneeded inventories. But they also can bring direct savings on material. Most companies must stock thousands of repair parts for their equipment. Standardization programs can locate duplicate inventories—cases, for example, where a spare fan belt or ball bearing stocked for one manufacturer's machine is identical with a spare part for a different manufacturer's machine. Stocks of such components can be combined by tracing each component back to the standards of the original manufacturer. Once the buyer knows who made the component, he is foolish to pay a premium price for it to the equipment manufacturer. He can buy at much lower cost directly from the original manufacturer's distributor.

The Tennessee Valley Authority made substantial savings in buying spare parts by doing just this. For example, it used to buy replacement V-belts for certain pulverizing equipment from the equipment manufacturer (who, in turn, had purchased it from a V-belt supplier). The price of the special steel-cable V-belts was $12.08 each from the equipment manufacturer. It was reduced to $5.67 by buying directly from

---

[7] These terms and this type of analytical approach were discussed in some detail in Chapter 10.

the V-belt manufacturer. The TVA and numerous private companies have made comparable savings on other items. Most manufacturers can make enormous profits (markups of 400 to 500 per cent are not uncommon) on their service-parts business. Smart buyers often can circumvent the equipment manufacturer and buy at lower prices directly from his supplier.

LINEAR PROGRAMING

Sometimes costs can be reduced without making any changes whatever in design, price, or number of items carried in inventory. A few materials managers are giving their companies a competitive edge with operations-research techniques. So far the only operations-research technique that has been at all widely applied is linear programing. At this writing, the others—game theory, queuing theory, and so on—are still in the experimental stages as far as materials management is concerned.

As the term implies, linear programing can be applied to any problem in which the mathematical relationships are linear (i.e., in algebraic terminology, $a + bx = c$). Typical are problems with these characteristics:

1. One plan of action must be selected from many possible plans. For example, which of 200 parts used in the product should be manufactured and which should be subcontracted?
2. The objective is to maximize or minimize a critical factor, such as to minimize the cost of buying silicon.
3. Relationships in the problem are linear. This means, for example, that it costs ten times as much to buy ten gallons of paint as it does to buy one gallon.
4. The resources you can use in achieving your objective are limited. Perhaps the amount of steel you can buy in any one month is limited by your storage capacity.

In materials management, linear programing can be applied to make-or-buy problems, inventory management and scheduling problems, and transportation problems. To date its most popular application has been in transportation. For example, in the past five years Western Electric has applied linear programing techniques to 39 different items that have a total annual purchase volume of $84,500,000. Its savings with the technique have totaled almost $2,500,000, or 3 per cent, on the items for which it has been used.

The Transportation Problem

Many large companies buy material from several suppliers that is shipped to several plants. In considering how business is to be divided, they must take into account not only the price charged by each supplier but also the cost of shipping the material to each plant.

Take the case of the hypothetical Rocket Chemical Corporation,[8] which has three plants, A, B, and C. Each plant uses a certain chemical that it buys in 100-pound bags. Requirements for the next three months are:

$$
\begin{aligned}
&\text{Plant A}\ldots\ldots\ldots\ldots\ldots\ldots 1{,}200 \text{ bags}\\
&\text{Plant B}\ldots\ldots\ldots\ldots\ldots\ldots 4{,}800 \text{ bags}\\
&\text{Plant C}\ldots\ldots\ldots\ldots\ldots\ldots 3{,}000 \text{ bags}
\end{aligned}
$$

Four vendors, W, X, Y, and Z, have agreed to supply this material. Each has a capacity restriction limiting the total amount he can supply during the next three months. The capacities and selling prices are as follows:

Vendor	Capacity (in Bags)	Price
W.................	5,000	$30
X.................	2,500	25
Y.................	1,200	20
Z.................	1,000	15
Total capacity.....	9,700	

The costs of shipping from each vendor to each plant are:

Vendor	Plant A	Plant B	Plant C
W...........	$10	$5	$6
X...........	4	3	5
Y...........	1	7	6
Z...........	4	9	3

By adding the shipping costs to the selling prices, we can determine the cost per bag of material delivered from each vendor to each plant:

Vendor	Plant A	Plant B	Plant C
W...........	$40	$35	$36
X...........	29	28	30
Y...........	21	27	26
Z...........	19	24	18

The problem is to decide on the quantities to be purchased from each vendor and where they are to be shipped so that the plants' requirements will be met at over-all minimum cost.

If there were no restrictions on the amounts that could be purchased

---

[8] Data in this case is adapted from an article by Spencer B. Smith ("Linear Programming: New Tool for Purchasing Problems," *Purchasing*, November 9, 1959, pp. 68–75).

from each vendor, the problem would be simple. We see that the lowest delivered cost for each plant is obtained by buying from Vendor Z. The solution would call for buying the total requirements from Vendor Z and nothing from the other vendors. Vendor Z, however, cannot supply the total requirement for any one plant, let alone for all plants. Therefore, this plan is not feasible, and we must analyze the problem further.

The First Solution. The first step in solving the problem is to construct a grid like that in Figure 18–10, listing the unit delivered costs from each vendor to each plant and the total requirements of each plant. Note that in addition to Plants A, B, and C we have also listed Plant D. This is a dummy plant that is needed to balance out the problem. Also

PLANT / VENDOR	A	B	C	D	AVAILABLE
W	40	35	36	0	5,000
X	29	28	30	0	2,500
Y	21	27	26	0	1,200
Z	19	24	18	0	1,000
REQUIRED	1,200	4,800	3,000	700	9,700

FIG. 18–10.

note that while we need only 9,000 bags of material, our vendors have the combined capacity to produce 9,700 bags. The extra 700 bags are assigned to the dummy Plant D; the delivered cost to Plant D is 0 since we won't actually be making any shipments to this plant.

To solve the problem, it is essential that each vendor ship his quota and that each plant (including dummy Plant D) get its requirements. The first solution does not give the lowest-cost plan, but it can lead to it. Figure 18–11 illustrates a typical first solution. Each vendor's capacity is allocated to each plant in sequence. Vendor W satisfies all of Plant A's and part of Plant B's requirements; Vendor X satisfies the balance of Plant B's and part of Plant C's needs; and so on. The final 700 units of capacity are assigned by Vendor Z to the dummy Plant D, so the sum of the shipments from each vendor equals the sum of the shipments received by the plants.

VENDOR \ PLANT	A	B	C	D	AVAILABLE
W	40 (1,200)	35 (3,800)	36	0	5,000
X	29	28 (1,000)	30 (1,500)	0	2,500
Y	21	27	26 (1,200)	0	1,200
Z	19	24	18 (300)	0 (700)	1,000
REQUIRED	1,200	4,800	3,000	700	9,700

FIG. 18–11.

Cost of this solution is as follows:

```
Vendor W to Plant A: 1,200 bags @ $40.............$ 48,000
Vendor W to Plant B: 3,800 bags @ $35.............  133,000
Vendor X to Plant B: 1,000 bags @ $28.............   28,000
Vendor X to Plant C: 1,500 bags @ $30.............   45,000
Vendor Y to Plant C: 1,200 bags @ $26.............   31,200
Vendor Z to Plant C: 300 bags @ $18...............    5,400
Vendor Z to Plant D: 700 bags @ $0................        0
      Total cost...................................$290,600
```

Evaluation. Now we must make an evaluation to see if we have the lowest-cost solution to the problem. This can be done by determining the net effect on cost of buying one bag through a vendor-plant combination different from those in our solution. For example, what happens to cost if we have Vendor X ship one bag to Plant A at a cost of $29? To do this, we must deduct from X's shipment to some other plant. If we deduct from B, we cancel one bag worth $28. If we replace the bag for B with a shipment from Vendor W, the cost is $35. To stay within W's capacity, we must cancel a shipment to A costing $40. Since we are considering adding one shipment from X to A, we retain our balance with these changes. The net effect on cost of these changes is equal to the sum of the costs of the shipments that were added less the sum of shipments that were eliminated. This gives $29 − $28 + $35 − $40 = −$4. In other words, by reallocating our shipments we have reduced net costs by $4.

In general, to evaluate an unused route, add the unit cost shown for that route, move horizontally to a circled value in the same row, and deduct the unit cost. From there move vertically to a circled value in the same column and add the unit cost. Move along that row to a circled value and deduct the unit cost. Proceed in this way, alternately moving horizontally and vertically, adding and subtracting, until you are back in the same column as the unused route to be evaluated. Enter the sum of the additions and subtractions in the unused route column.

All the unused routes should be evaluated in this way. If it turns out that all the unused routes have positive values, this means that you already have the lowest-cost plan and using any other routes would only add to the total cost. If, on the other hand, one or more unused routes have negative values, this means that the plan can be improved.

The values for all the unused routes have been entered in Figure 18–12, and several of them are negative. Therefore, we can improve the plan.

PLANT \ VENDOR	A	B	C	D	AVAILABLE
W	40	35	36	0	5,000
W	(1,200)	(3,800)	−1	−19	5,000
X	29	28	30	0	2,500
X	−4	(1,000)	(1,500)	−12	2,500
Y	21	27	26	0	1,200
Y	−8	+3	(1,200)	−8	1,200
Z	19	24	18	0	1,000
Z	−2	+8	(300)	(700)	1,000
REQUIRED	1,200	4,800	3,000	700	9,700

TOTAL COST = $290,600

FIG. 18–12.

Solving the Problem

Figure 18–12 shows that the largest negative value for an unused route is −19 for shipments from Vendor W to Plant D. We would like to change our plan to ship as much as possible by this route, as every bag shipped will save us $19.

To determine how much we can ship by this route without violating the restrictions on requirements and capacities, we proceed as follows. First, trace a path from *WD* horizontally to a circled value in the same row, then vertically to a circled value in the same column, continuing, as we did in evaluating unused routes, until we are back in the same column in which we started. This path will be:

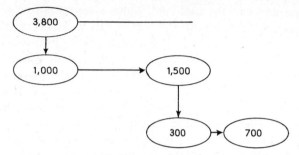

Let the quantity to be shipped by route WD be Q. Then, in order to keep within the restrictions of the problem, the amounts shipped by other routes in the path we have traced must be adjusted in the following way:

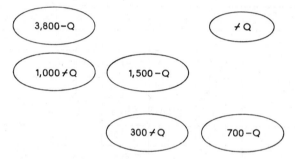

Q will be that amount that will just reduce one or more of the quantities being shipped under the first plan to zero without making any of the quantities negative. In this case Q will be 700, eliminating shipment from Vendor Z to Plant D.

Making the adjustments above, the new solution is shown in Figure 18–13. The total cost associated with this solution is $277,300, obtained in the same way as the total in the first solution. This is $13,300 less than the first plan, which would have cost $290,600.

We determined before that we would obtain a saving of $19 per bag shipped over route WD. As our second plan calls for shipping 700 bags over this route, the saving is 700 × $19, or $13,300, which checks with our calculations above.

Evaluating the unused routes in the second solution, we find that some still have negative values, indicating that we can reduce the total cost further. The largest negative value for an unused route in Figure 18–13 is −8 for shipment from Vendor Y to Plant A. Proceeding as we did in changing the first to the second solution, we find that we can ship 1,200 bags from Vendor Y to Plant A. In adjusting the amounts shipped by other routes, shipments will be eliminated from Y to C and from W to A. The total number of routes used will be reduced from seven to six. In order for us to be able to evaluate the unused routes,

VENDOR \ PLANT	A	B	C	D	AVAILABLE
W	40 / (1,200)	35 / (3,100)	36 / -1	0 / (700)	5,000
X	29 / -4	28 / (1,700)	30 / (800)	0 / +7	2,500
Y	21 / -8	27 / +3	26 / (1,200)	0 / +11	1,200
Z	19 / -2	24 / +8	18 / (1,000)	0 / +19	1,000
REQUIRED	1,200	4,800	3,000	700	9,700

TOTAL COST = $277,300

FIG. 18–13.

however, we need to have a solution that uses a number of routes equal to the number of vendors plus the number of plants less one, or $4 + 4 - 1 = 7$.

To meet this requirement, enter ϵ, meaning a very small quantity, in one of the routes that was eliminated. In Figure 18–14 we have entered it in route WA. In arriving at the final solution, ϵ is treated just like any other quantity being shipped. Once the final solution is achieved, however, ϵ will be ignored.

The largest negative value for an unused route in Figure 18–14 is

VENDOR \ PLANT	A	B	C	D	AVAILABLE
W	40 / (ε)	35 / (4,300)	36 / -1	0 / (700)	5,000
X	29 / -4	28 / (500)	30 / (2,000)	0 / +7	2,500
Y	21 / (1,200)	27 / +11	26 / +8	0 / +19	1,200
Z	19 / -2	24 / +8	18 / (1,000)	0 / +19	1,000
REQUIRED	1,200	4,800	3,000	700	9,700

TOTAL COST = $267,700

FIG. 18–14.

−4 for shipments from X to A. Changing the plan according to our previous methods involves adding ϵ bags to route XA and WB and deducting ϵ bags from routes WA and XB (see Figure 18–15). As ϵ is very small, this does not change the cost of the plan, and the total costs associated with the third and fourth solutions are both $267,700. However, this does help us in finding the final solution, as we see that of the unused routes in Figure 18–15, only one, WC, has a negative value.

The Final Solution. To obtain the fifth solution from the fourth, we add 2,000 bags to routes WC and XB and deduct 2,000 bags from routes WB and XC. This plan has a total cost of $265,700, a saving of $24,900 over the first plan developed. We now find that all unused routes have positive values. No further improvements are possible; we

PLANT / VENDOR	A	B	C	D	AVAILABLE
W	40 / +4	35 / (4,300+ϵ)	36 / −1	0 / (700)	5,000
X	29 / (ϵ)	28 / (500−ϵ)	30 / (2,000)	0 / +7	2,500
Y	21 / (1,200)	27 / +7	26 / +4	0 / +15	1,200
Z	19 / +2	24 / +8	18 / (1,000)	0 / +19	1,000
REQUIRED	1,200	4,800	3,000	700	9,700

TOTAL COST = $267,700

FIG. 18–15.

now have the minimum-total-cost plan. If any of the unused routes had zero values, it would mean that though no better plans were available there was another plan just as good.

The final plan can be transcribed directly from Figure 18–16 by simply ignoring the shipments to the dummy Plant D. The plan is:

1. Buy 4,300 bags from Vendor W and ship 2,300 to Plant B and 2,000 to C.
2. Buy 2,500 bags from Vendor X and ship to Plant B.
3. Buy 1,200 bags from Vendor Y and ship to Plant A.
4. Buy 1,000 bags from Vendor Z and ship to Plant C.

So far, linear programing has limited application to materials management and, as was mentioned before, not more than a handful of companies has attempted to do more than experiment with other operations techniques on materials problems. One of the main reasons that opera-

PLANT VENDOR	A	B	C	D	AVAILABLE
W	40 +4	35 (2,300+ε)	36 (2,000)	0 (700)	5,000
X	29 (ε)	28 (2,500−ε)	30 +1	0 +7	2,500
Y	21 (1,200)	27 +7	26 +5	0 +15	1,200
Z	19 +1	24 +7	18 (1,000)	0 +18	1,000
REQUIRED	1,200	4,800	3,000	700	9,700

TOTAL COST = $265,700

FIG. 18–16.

tions research is not more widely used to cut materials cost is lack of trained personnel. The demand for university graduates skilled in operations-research techniques greatly exceeds the supply.

CAPITAL-EQUIPMENT ANALYSIS

In fact, it is only in the last twenty years that analytical techniques to evaluate investment in capital equipment have become widely used. Unlike other cost-reduction techniques, which result in direct savings, a company spends to save when it buys capital equipment. It makes an immediate outlay in the hope that it will reduce future outlays or gain some intangible benefits. For example, a company may have a choice of buying an item or manufacturing it in its own plant at lower cost if it is willing to invest in the necessary equipment. Or it may have the choice of reducing the cost of making an item provided it is willing to invest in new equipment.

The decision to invest in equipment is made by comparing the reduction in operating cost resulting from use of the new equipment with the investment required. The Machinery & Allied Products Institute has developed numerous formulas to evaluate the profitable purchase of equipment. The application of one such formula by the Norton Company, a leading manufacturer of abrasives, is illustrated in Figure 18–17.

Norton is considering the purchase of a new abrasive grain-handling system. Norton estimates that the new equipment will reduce labor and other costs by $96,000 a year. On the other hand, the older equipment has operating advantages amounting to $14,500 a year because of lower taxes, less power consumption, and less maintenance. Net operating ad-

Sheet 1 of 3 Sheets

1926

NORTON COMPANY
EQUIPMENT REPLACEMENT ANALYSIS

Est. No. _7831_
Date _4/20/54_

Line No.		PRESENT			PROPOSED
1	Description Present Grain Handling System in Plant #2		Description	Pl. #2 Portable Grain Tanks, Bldg. Add.; TBS & Magnorite System	
2	Salvage value	$ 0		Cost installed	$ 689,200
3	Age	40 yrs.		Service life	* 31 yrs.
4	Equipment Number			Est'd. salvage value	$ 0
5	Department	Pr. Whl.-Abr.#2		Salvage ratio	0 %

ADVERSE MINIMUMS

6	Operating inferiority (line 29)	$ 81,500	Total cost installed	$ 689,200	
7	Loss salvage value - next year	0	Chart %	31 %	
8	Interest - salvage value	0	Interest %	10 %	
9	Proration - capital addition 25,000	* 1,670	Total %	%	
10	Interest - capital addition @ 15%	2,500			
11	ADVERSE MINIMUM $ 85,670 (A)		* ADVERSE MINIMUM $ 93,000 (B)		
12	GAIN FROM REPLACEMENT (next year) (A - B)	$ - 7,300			

OPERATING ADVANTAGE (next year)

			PRESENT	PROPOSED
	Income Advantages			
13	X Superiority of product		$	$
14	Increased output			
15	X Other			
	Cost Advantages			
16	Direct labor }			* 75,000
17	Indirect labor }			
18	Fringe benefit cost (20 %)			15,000
19	Maintenance		* 6,000	
20	Supplies Cap Replacement			1,000
21	Tools			
22	Spoilage Reduction in Rejections due to streaks			5,000
23	Down time			
24	X Floor space			
25	Power		500	
26	Property taxes and insurance		* 8,100	
27	X Other			
	(8½ year payback period DCF return on investment 11½%)*			
28			$ 14,500 (C)	$ 96,000 (D)
29	Net Operating Advantage (D - C)		$ 81,500	(to line 6)

Remarks: This analysis has been computed without appraisal of intangible benefits checked above, and discussed in detail on attached sheet. Acceptance of this proposal is tantamount to evaluating all these benefits at a minimum of $7,300 per year. This is considered satisfactory.

Recommendation: Approval recommended.

Signed _C.O.S_

Date _4/20/54_

Approved ....

Date ....

FIG. 18–17. Norton Company uses an analysis technique developed by the Machinery & Allied Products Institute to determine whether or not it pays to replace capital equipment. (Reprinted from "The Procurement Problems in a Multi-Plant Company," *Essentials of Machinery Procurement and Development*, Special Report No. 14 [New York: American Management Association, 1956], p. 29).

vantage of the new equipment thus is $81,500 ($96,000 − $14,500). To this must be added the capital cost (prorated over 15 years) and interest of $25,000 in needed improvements on the old equipment. These capital charges plus the $81,500 adverse operating cost of the old machine total $85,670. This compares with an annual charge of $93,-000 for interest and depreciation on the new equipment. Thus costs are theoretically $7,300 higher if Norton buys the new equipment. Norton decides to buy it anyway because it feels the intangible benefit of improved product quality with the new equipment is worth $7,300.

Note that Norton's profits will actually increase when it buys the new machine. Included in the "cost" is an allowance of 10 per cent for interest. If we assume that Norton buys the equipment with idle cash, its profits increase because the 10 per cent interest charge was included in the cost calculation.

Note also that if Norton were willing to accept a 5 per cent return on capital, the interest cost of the new equipment would drop to $34,460. The "adverse minimum" on the new equipment would be $58,540 per year and the "adverse minimum" on the old equipment (giving effect to an interest rate reduction on the $25,000 investment in improvements) would be $84,420. Thus the company would theoretically save $25,880 per year by investing in the new equipment instead of incurring a $7,300 cost increase to improve quality.

The MAPI formulas are very useful in comparing the relative desirability of investing in various types of equipment. The interest rate can be varied to reflect the company's availability of capital and willingness to invest in a not-too-certain future.

PREPRODUCTION PURCHASE ANALYSIS

The newest and least direct cost-reduction technique is preproduction purchase analysis. All of the cost-reduction techniques discussed so far are designed to reduce the cost of existing parts and materials. Preproduction purchase analysis aims to reduce the cost of an item before it is produced, while it is still being designed. PPA encompasses all value-analysis techniques. It also makes considerable use of the cost-estimating techniques discussed in Chapter 16.

Preproduction purchase analysis was first developed in industries where rapid product obsolescence made value analysis impractical. If a product is never going to be made again, it is pointless to make a detailed value analysis of it. With PPA, materials personnel work closely with product designers and follow every stage in the evolution of a new product, from the point at which ideas are first developed to the point where production drawings are made and purchase orders issued.

The objective of PPA is to steer the designer into concepts that result in maximum value. This may mean suggesting that a product be made of a lower-cost material. More likely, it means that the designer will be guided into components that cost less because they are standard for some other product.[9] This approach works especially well for companies

---

[9] In many cases, this approach results in the designer's specifying a component that theoretically costs more but actually costs less because it is standard with a number of manufacturers. To cite a simple case, suppose the ideal design indicated that a screw should be $127/128''$ long. This screw theoretically would be cheaper than one that is $1''$ long, but naturally the $1''$ screw is standard and is available in large volume at prices that may be a fraction of the cost of a $127/128''$ screw.

making extremely complex and expensive products in small volume—computers, missiles, ships, and so on.

PPA also works well in the mass-production industries. For example, the Ford Motor Company's Ford Division has 180 purchase analysts working on PPA.[10] They start to work on new car models about three years before actual production commences. Their cost estimates guide stylists in preparing preliminary designs. More detailed estimates are made from clay models of the new cars. By the time production blueprints are prepared, which may be a year or two after the design was first proposed, purchase analysts have highly refined estimates that often are accurate within a fraction of a penny.

PPA can stimulate imaginative designs that can reduce costs substantially. For example, in the Ford Falcon station wagon, the top part of the gas tank doubles as a section of the floor pan. This design costs substantially less than the conventional design, which makes use of a separate floor pan and gas tank. The saving would not have been possible to make with the standard value-analysis approach, where a part is reviewed after it has been designed and manufactured. Dies to make automobile gas tanks and floor pans are so expensive and take so long to produce that there would be precious little saving were the change to be made after the more costly design was already in production.

PPA is a new cost-reduction technique. Only a few companies use it at present. But there is no doubt that it will become more popular in the future. It is the best way yet devised to combine the skills of the materials specialist with those of the product engineer in creating a design of optimum quality and value.

CASES

CASE 18–1. CONSOLIDATED ELECTRIC COMPANY[11]

A PROBLEM IN VALUE ANALYSIS

The Consolidated Electric Company has designed a system to measure impurities of gases. It anticipates that this system will have wide application among natural gas pipeline and distribution plants, chemical producers, and others. The system picks up a sample of gas (see Figure 18–18) that is sucked into a chamber where its composition is measured. The sample is then discharged and the process is repeated. During the moment when one sample is being measured, the rotary valve is closed. This causes the gas to force the relief flipper valve up (see Figure

---

[10] Dean Ammer, "The Purchasing Department: Ford's Cost Control Center," *Purchasing*, May 23, 1960, pp. 52–84.

[11] This case study is adapted from one published in *Purchasing*, May 8, 1961, and is based on an actual value-analysis problem encountered by the General Electric Company.

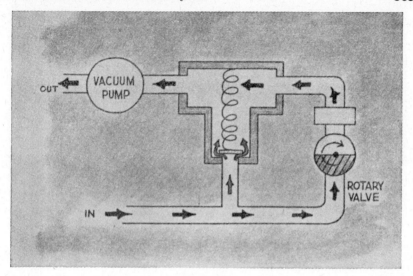

FIG. 18–18.

18–19), providing an alternate and continuous path of flow. As the rotary valve opens for a new sample, the spring closes the flapper and shuts off the alternate path.

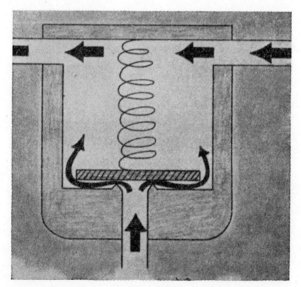

FIG. 18–19.

The Roberts Company, one of Consolidated's regular suppliers of special valves, has designed a relief valve, model no. 3360100, for the system. Stated simply, the function of the relief valve is to provide a continuous flow. Its function is illustrated schematically in Figure 18–19,

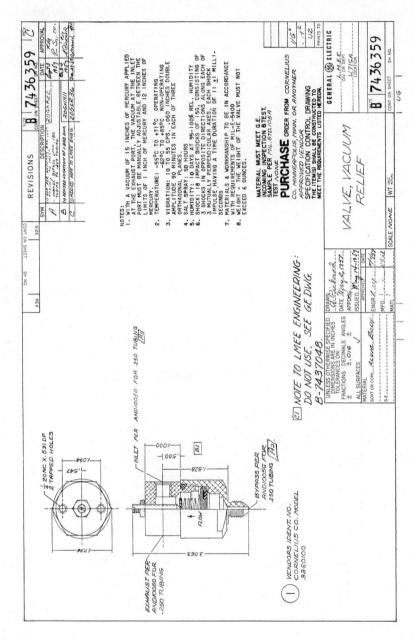

FIG. 18-20.

and engineering details are shown in Consolidated's drawing no. 7436359 (see Figure 18–20).

The valve has an aluminum body (see illustrations in Figures 18–21 and 18–22), and has male and female half sections. It is assembled with mating threads that are made airtight by means of a Neoprene rubber "O" ring. The female body has a male AN (i.e., made to Army-Navy

FIG. 18–21.

standards) air line fitting, while the male body has two threaded holes for accepting AN fittings and two for stud mounting. The female body has two decals, one indicating the direction of flow and the other identifying the supplier. The flapper has a molded Teflon (an extra-tough, chemical-resistant material made by DuPont) surface that seats on a

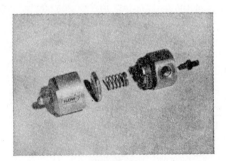

FIG. 18–22.

knife-edge diameter to provide a closed-valve position. It is held in place and can be adjusted with a spring, stud, and locking nut. The assembly contains ten individual parts.

The Roberts Company has quoted a unit price of $73.20 for an order of 546 pieces.

Questions

1. Does Roberts' quote represent good value?
2. How might costs be reduced through value analysis?

CASE 18–2. MID-STATES TELEPHONE COMPANY

Use of Linear Programing

The Mid-States Telephone Company uses large amounts of "K" rural wire to support telephone lines. The wire is stored in five warehouses scattered throughout the company's service area. The company buys the wire from four sources, and because of price, quality, capacity, and other factors, business has been divided among them as follows:

Supplier	No. of Reels of Wire Purchased per Year	% of Purchases
Allen	1,795	40%
Bruce	1,120	25
Carter	1,120	25
Doner	450	10
Total	4,485	100%

The requirements of each warehouse and delivered costs of a reel of wire from each supplier to each destination are as follows:

Destination	No. of Reels Required	Delivered Prices per Reel			
		Allen	Bruce	Carter	Doner
Johnston City	950	$299.50	$304.85	$311.25	$303.70
Kankakee	1,105	307.10	305.90	308.40	312.10
Laramay	770	310.80	310.40	311.60	314.20
Montook	1,080	310.40	311.10	314.80	316.50
Norrisfield	580	321.15	321.85	325.25	326.10
Total	4,485				

Mid-States is presently trying to have the lowest-cost supplier ship to each destination—within the limits of its allocation of business. The current shipping pattern is as follows:

Destination	Supplier				Total No. of Reels
	Allen	Bruce	Carter	Doner	
Johnston City	950				950
Kankakee		1,105			1,105
Laramay		15	755		770
Montook	845		235		1,080
Norrisfield			130	450	580
Total	1,795	1,120	1,120	450	4,485

Question

Using linear programing, determine the lowest-cost shipping pattern from Mid-States' four suppliers to its five warehouses.

CASE 18–3. STANFORD SHIRT COMPANY

Purchase of Capital Equipment

The Stanford Shirt Company has a national reputation as a manufacturer of high-quality shirts. For forty years the company has catered to the executive who likes the very finest ready-made shirts. Until recently, Stanford's cheapest shirt retailed for $7.50. While the company has earned an enviable reputation for quality, its growth has been limited by its pricing policies. Very few men are willing to pay premium prices for shirts. Finally, the company decided to enter the medium-priced shirt field and created its Stanfast line. The brand name chosen was designed to be similar to the Stanford brand name in the hope of trading on the company's reputation but sufficiently different to prevent the two lines from being confused.

The Stanfast line is designed to retail for $4.50. Part of the savings comes from narrowing the dealer's profit margin from nearly 50 per cent to the 30 per cent that is more common on lower-priced shirts. The Stanfast shirts also are made of cheaper cloth and buttons. In the manufacturing operations, the company is able to make only minor savings through the elimination of a few sewing operations. It is difficult to make greater savings because both shirts must be sewed together in approximately the same way.

As a result, the company's profits on the new line have been disappointing. Currently, unit profits are less than five cents per shirt, and everyone in the organization is searching for ways to widen the profit margin without hurting quality. The purchasing director, Frank Adams, believes he may have the answer. Currently, all of the company's shirts are ironed by hand. Finished shirts are conveyed in hampers to women workers who pick them out of the hamper, iron them, and then fold and pack them in boxes. The women work on piece rate, and the company's total labor cost per shirt for these operations is eleven cents. The company controller estimates that the variable overhead applicable to this operation is about six cents.

Laundries have been using semiautomatic shirt ironing machines for years. The freshly laundered shirts are folded over a series of forms, and it is possible to iron and pack a shirt with about 1.2 minutes of direct labor. Ironing machines have never been used much by shirt manufacturers, however. Newly manufactured shirts are much harder to iron, and the laundry equipment won't remove all of the wrinkles. In addition, shirt manufacturers are convinced that their products will sell better if they are ironed perfectly. So far, laundry equipment manufacturers have failed to devise a machine that can approach the quality achieved by a skilled woman equipped with hand iron and ironing board.

Alma Laundry Machine Corporation now thinks it has made a breakthrough. Its M-9 shirt-ironing machine will turn out 60 shirts per hour that are almost wrinkle-free. Purchasing Director Adams arranges to ship a gross of newly manufactured Stanfast shirts to the Alma plant and himself watches the machine iron them. Accompanying him on the trip is Stanford's quality control manager, John Connally. The two men agree that while the M-9 doesn't do a good enough job for the Stanford line, it should be adequate for the Stanfast line.

On checking with the personnel department, Adams discovers that an operator for the machine would probably have to be paid $2.40 per hour. Alma insists that its estimated production rate of 60 shirts per hour includes more than adequate allowances for down-time, delays, rest periods, and so on. The supplier also claims that maintenance expenses on the machine will average less than $500 per year, and that the machine probably has a useful life of at least ten years on three-shift operation. Other operating expenses in connection with the machine total about $0.001 per shirt ironed, exclusive of any allowances for return on investment. The machine costs $20,000 installed, and Stanford can easily make use of at least one machine working two shifts, five days per week. Adams doubts that the scrap value of the hand equipment that the machine would replace is more then $100.

Questions

1. Should the Stanford Shirt Company buy the new machine?
2. Support your conclusions with a MAPI analysis, using the facts presented in this case plus any additional assumptions that are needed.

Chapter 19

CUTTING THE COST OF PAPER WORK

A company with 2,000 employees may have 100 persons working in its various materials activities: purchasing, production control, traffic, and so on. More than 85 per cent of these jobs are predominantly clerical. A fantastic number of man-hours are devoted to filling out thousands of different forms, keeping records, and the like. One company with about 5,000 employees found that its materials personnel filled out more than one million pieces of paper a year.

All surveys show that paper work in materials management is increasing much faster than general business activities. For example, one survey of purchasing agents showed that 91 per cent had experienced increased volume of paper work in their departments in the last five years.[1] The average increase was 25 per cent, but one fifth of the respondents reported increases of 50 per cent or more.

Paper Work Is Costly. The costs of this paper work are obviously substantial. One writer estimated that it costs at least ten cents to fill out each purchase requisition, request for quotation, purchase order, receiving report, inspection report, and accounts payable voucher, and five cents for posting each inventory record and key-punching each tabulating card.[2] Even a small company will issue thousands of purchase requisitions per year. When one considers that each requisition may generate a need for one or more quotation requests, purchase orders, and so on, one can easily understand how clerical costs can mushroom.

Accountants sometimes divide a materials department's total operating costs by the output of some key document such as a purchase order. Such comparisons have limited usefulness as barometers of operating efficiency. But they do sometimes dramatically illustrate the high cost of paper work. For example, the writer once estimated that it cost the purchasing department of the Ford Division of the Ford Motor Company $58 to issue each of its purchase orders.[3] And materials division wages

---

[1] "Too Much Paperwork in Purchasing," *Purchasing*, October, 1956, p. 71.

[2] Ralph R. Tekulve, "A Purchasing Mechanization Primer," *Purchasing*, Oct. 12, 1959, p. 97.

[3] Dean Ammer, "The Purchasing Department: Ford's Cost Control Center," *Purchasing*, May 23, 1960, p. 54. The cost per order was calculated by dividing the Ford purchasing department's estimated annual operating budget by 85,000, the number of purchase orders it issues each year.

and salaries were equal to 2.01 per cent of the value of purchase orders issued by the Los Angeles plants of North American Aviation, Inc.[4]

Need for Paper Work. Is all this paper work necessary? Much of it is. The materials management process inherently involves a lot of detail. A company with only a few hundred employees will have thousands of different items that must be controlled in some fashion, while a big corporation may have hundreds of thousands of items to control. Records must be kept for each item. And if a company is to do a first-rate job of materials management, it must have systems designed to bring any deviation from routine to the attention of the materials managers immediately.

It behooves each materials manager to get the information he needs for making decisions with a minimum of paper work and clerical manpower. In so doing, he helps achieve one of his primary objectives: to manage materials with minimum operating cost. This in itself is adequate motivation for a program to eliminate clerical effort through improved forms and procedures and mechanization. But managers should be interested in reducing the enormous amount of clerical effort required in materials management even if they could persuade clerks to work without pay.

Effect on Organization. The bigger the clerical work force, the more complex the materials organization structure inevitably becomes. As was explained in Chapter 4, each supervisor has a limited span of control. As the work force grows, more supervisors are required; inevitably more levels of organization are needed. The organization becomes progressively more complex. Top materials managers are forced to devote an increasing amount of their time to managing people rather than managing materials. This reduces their efficiency.

In a large, complex organization, procedures for transmitting information to make decisions become cumbersome and time-consuming. All other factors being equal, a small organization can always move faster than a big one. In materials management, speedy transmission of information permits faster materials cycles with lower inventories and less obsolescence.

When clerks are eliminated through improvements in procedures or through mechanization, it isn't just the simpler organization structure that permits faster flow of information. The new methods can speed data transmission directly since they are inherently faster. For example, if a company computes its inventory balance by manually totaling and extending the balances on thousands of record cards, the job will probably take a week or two regardless of how many clerks are assigned to it. On the other hand, if inventory records are kept on the memory drum of an electronic computer, it is possibly to get daily inventory reports.

---

[4] According to the annual report of the Materials Division of North American Aviation, Inc., 1956, p. 31.

Reduction of Errors. Not only do people require far more management effort than machines do, but they also are more prone to make mistakes. If a clerk is posting hundreds of inventory records each day, it is inevitable that he will occasionally make an error. Most such errors can be detected by having the work double checked by another person. But management can be certain that on rare occasions an error will go through undetected regardless of how many different persons try to spot it. A clerk will enter "100" as an inventory balance when he should enter "10," or a form will be mislaid and he will simply overlook an item entirely. If the error isn't detected, the item won't be available when it should be and a costly shutdown may result.

Companies will have problems of this sort as long as they have employees. But they can reduce the chances for error by reducing the number of times basic data must be transcribed by human beings and by giving as much of the job as possible to machines. No machine can actually think, but it can perform repetitive operations without fatigue and with built-in controls that detect any errors that might occur.

SHORT CUTS IN FORMS

In bigger companies, the materials manager may have an administrative assistant (sometimes even an entire staff department) who devotes a major share of his efforts to improving forms and procedures. Periodically, each form and report used should "stand trial for its life." If its existence can't be justified, it should be eliminated. Even in the best-managed departments, such "trials" occasionally uncover paper work that can be done without. Conditions change, but if there is no control the obsolete forms and procedures will continue anyway unless someone does something about them. Periodic reviews are valuable even if they don't reveal any paper work that can be eliminated. They can alert management to savings in clerical time, which can result from such improvements as special ordering procedures, combining of forms, and changes in forms design.

Special Ordering Procedures

Transactions in a materials department vary widely. Consecutively numbered purchase orders may be issued for a $20,000 machine tool, a $2 charge to fix a flat tire on a company truck, and a contract to purchase $100,000 worth of production parts. Different types of order warrant different treatment if they are to get the control they deserve without excessive paper work. This can be done with blanket orders, cash pickup orders, and similar procedures.

Blanket Orders. Items that are used regularly often require a dozen or more purchases a year. Each time inventory drops to the reorder point, the stores department issues a requisition that touches off a complete purchase transaction. A company can cut paper work, of course, by ordering less often and in larger quantities. But this is an expensive solution to the problem. Increased inventory carrying cost may more than offset the savings in paper work. Blanket orders offer a better solution. The buyer issues an order good for a year's requirements to be shipped "as released." Then, whenever stock of material runs low, the buyer simply telephones the supplier and asks him to ship against the blanket order that is outstanding.

Blanket orders help save on repeat items in four ways:

(1) They usually reduce paper work. A single blanket order is substituted for many individual orders. There is some saving in paper work even when the buyer sends written release forms (as is customary on important purchases) to the supplier each time he wants a shipment. In this case the buyer still is relieved of the need to get quotations for each transaction. And in most cases, the releasing procedure is less complex than the ordering procedure.

(2) They save the time of skilled buyers. Once a blanket order is placed, the job of ordering can be transferred from a skilled (and highly paid) buyer to a clerk (or even to a machine, if the company has electronic data-processing equipment). The clerk simply writes out a release against the blanket order and mails it to the supplier.

(3) They facilitate price negotiation. Suppliers often will quote lower prices when they are bidding for a year's requirements rather than for a single order. Multiplant companies can go even further; they can combine requirements for all plants on a single blanket order in order to maximize their buying power.

(4) They permit closer inventory control. Blanket orders help companies operate with shorter lead times and lower inventories. If they can get an order for a year's requirements, suppliers often can be persuaded to stock the material so it is available for immediate delivery. This permits the buyer to operate hand-to-mouth, with almost no safety stock.

Cash Pickup Orders. Few companies can process the paper work necessary for a complete purchase transaction for less than $10,[5] and the supplier who "cannot enter the smallest order at less than $10 cost"[6] also is typical. Small orders are money-losers for both buyer and seller. Yet, of necessity, a substantial percentage of the orders issued (50 per cent in many smaller companies and 25 per cent in big corporations) are

---

[5] Surveys made of the cost of issuing a purchase order have been inconsistent because there is no agreement on what costs should be charged. However, big companies that have made detailed studies usually have found their costs to be much greater than $10 when they consider the cost of the complete materials cycle, from initiation of the requisition to the point where the material is received, stored, and used. However, the *marginal* cost (i.e., the cost of one extra order) is in most cases probably less than $10.

[6] *The Small Order—Asset or Liability?* Studies in Business Policy No. 21, (New York: National Industrial Conference Board, 1956).

for $50 or less. Even though such orders may comprise less than 5 per cent of total expenditures, they can consume a disproportionate share of the total administrative and clerical expenses.

With conventional purchasing procedures, an order for a $5 item will get the same administrative treatment as a major order. Special procedures help short-cut costly administrative controls on small orders. One of the simplest is merely to authorize a supplier to ship and bill on the basis of a telephone order. The only records of the transaction are the requisition and the receiving report. No purchase order is issued; the purchase is cleared by matching the requisition, the receiving report, and the supplier's invoice.

Another short cut eliminates the invoicing process; the buyer pays cash for the order. Typical is the small-order procedure used by Argus Cameras, Inc., Ann Arbor, Michigan, for local purchases (see Figure 19–1). The purchase requisition doubles as a purchase order. When the buyer gets it, he telephones the order to the supplier, fills in the supplier's name and price on the requisition, and makes out a check to pay for the order. When the supplier delivers, the check and one copy of the purchase-order requisition are ready for him in Argus's receiving dock.

Many managers view special small-order procedures with mixed enthusiasm. They like to eliminate paper work, but they are afraid that small orders will encourage unnecessary expenditures, discourage grouping of orders that might reduce costs even more, or stimulate a lax environment where there will be repeated last-minute "emergencies" calling for small orders. Companies that do have small-order procedures maintain extremely close control over them for these and other reasons.

Combining of Forms

Certain data are repeated again and again in materials transactions. Part numbers and names appear on almost every form used in every department in a company. Supplier names appear on buy records and quotation requests, and then are repeated on numerous other forms, including purchase orders, receiving reports, inspection reports, inventory records, and so on. Order quantities and prices similarly are repeated again and again.

Each time information is transcribed, not only is clerical cost incurred but a costly error is risked. Thus, it pays to combine forms to make use of common information whenever possible. This can be done both by making one form do several jobs and by preparing different forms with a single, simultaneous operation. The traveling requisition is a good example of the former; combination purchase-order, receiving-report forms and various duplicating techniques are good examples of the latter.

The Traveling Requisition. With conventional procedures, a separate requisition is filled out to authorize each purchase of an item. This means that common data, such as item number, description of the item,

| ACCOUNT NO. | A/P | REQ. NO. 6502 | WRITTEN BY | DELIVER TO | STD. COST | V/R |
| | | DATE | | | | |

MISCELLANEOUS PURCHASE REQUISITION

1. PREPARE ONLY FOR NON—PRODUCTIVE PURCHASES.
2. FILL IN ALL NECESSARY INFORMATION IN WHITE AREAS OF THE REQUISITION.
3. REMOVE YOUR FOLLOW—UP COPY AND FORWARD TO PURCHASING DEPARTMENT.

PURCHASE ORDER ☐
LOCAL ORDER ☐

No. ▓▓▓▓▓▓

THIS NUMBER MUST APPEAR ON INVOICE AND PACKING SLIP

DATE OF ORDER

SHIP TO
ARGUS CAMERAS
ANN ARBOR, MICHIGAN

VENDOR ADDRESS

DIRECTOR OF PURCHASING

BUYER

FOR MICHIGAN SALES AND/OR USE TAX THIS ORDER IS: TAXABLE ☐ NON—TAXABLE ☐

THIS ORDER IS CONFIRMING: RECEIPT ☐ WIRE ☐ PHONE ☐ SALESMAN ☐ _____ ☐

| TERMS | F.O.B. | SHIP VIA | DELIVERY: |

QUANTITY	UNITS	DESCRIPTION	PRICE

REQUIRED DELIVERY BY:

DEPARTMENTAL AUTHORIZATION

DATE IN PURCHASING

SPECIAL INSTRUCTIONS AND/OR SUGGESTED VENDOR:

PURCHASING FOLLOW-UP

REQ. NO.	AMOUNT

GROSS AMOUNT	
CASH DISCOUNT (3704)	
EXCISE TAX	
SALES TAX	
TOTAL AMOUNT THIS ORDER	

DATE

argus cameras

Division of Sylvania Electric Products Inc.
Ann Arbor, Michigan
CAMERAS AND OPTICAL INSTRUMENTS

74—100/744

No. 13229

PAY TO THE ORDER OF _____

NOT VALID IN EXCESS OF $100.00

PAY EXACTLY _____ DOLLARS _____ CENTS $

AMOUNT

ANN ARBOR BANK
ANN ARBOR, MICH.

00 - 301014 - 3

AUTHORIZED SIGNATURE
PURCHASE ACCOUNT

FIG. 19—1. Argus Cameras, Inc., uses these forms in its small-order procedure. The purchase requisition doubles as a purchase order. The buyer telephones the order to a supplier and makes out a check to pay for it. The supplier gets a copy of the requisition-purchase order and the check when he delivers the order.

and so on, will be copied over and over again in requisitioning frequently used items. The traveling requisition is larger than the conventional requisition form and also is made of heavier paper. A permanent traveling requisition is kept for each item in stock (see Figure 19–2). On it is space for common data and also for data specifically describing a particular purchase.

When stock drops to the reorder point, the stores clerk pulls out the traveling requisition from the file and sends it to the buyer. After the purchase is made, the buyer or his clerk posts the order data to the requisition, which travels back to the stores clerk. He notes that the purchase has been made and then refiles it until it is needed for the next purchase. Since the traveling requisition form provides a complete purchase history, some buyers also use it as a purchase record. Other buyers,

54612 Impeller Assembly, part no. 625 Type 316 Elc Stainless Steel 22" diameter, 3 vane, right hand							ORDER POINT	1
							E.O.Q.	2
							PURCHASE UNIT	ea
							ISSUE UNIT	ea

BY REQUISITIONER				BY PURCHASER				
REQUIRED		CHARGE NO.	P. O. NO.	V E N	PRICE	TERMS	F.O.B.	# VENDOR
DATE	QTY.							1 City Supply Co.
6/4/59	2	16040l	9-16120	1	320⁰⁰	2/10/30	St. Louis	2 ABC Dist.
10/7/59	2	16040l	9-19960	4	318⁰⁰	2/10/30	Baltimore	3 J. Doe & Co.
3/4/60	2	16040l	0-13240	3	300⁰⁰	net	Bartow	4 State Mfg. Co.
								5
								6
								7
								8
								LOCATION 3R4-5
								EQUIPMENT
								For Type 2,
								Model B. Pump

FIG. 19–2. A typical traveling requisition form. The requisitioner fills in data on the left of the card; the purchaser acts on this data and returns the form to the requisitioner, who files it until stocks drop again to the reorder point.

particularly of high-dollar-volume commodities, prefer to keep separate purchase records. They wish to keep a more detailed record than is possible on the traveling requisition, and they often are afraid that stores personnel or others will reveal competitive price data to favored suppliers.

Occasionally, traveling requisitions also double as inventory records. It is not difficult to include space for stores receipts and withdrawals on the form. Most companies prefer to post to a separate stores record, however. Then, if the traveling requisition is lost, there is still a basic record of the item in the stockroom.

Other Combination Forms. With electric typewriters, which can make about ten reasonably clear carbon copies, it is possible to combine physically many forms that use common data. Most common is the purchase order-receiving report, which consists of an 8″ × 10″ copy "snap-out" type of form with one-time carbon paper inserted. The first four or five copies of the form are a conventional purchase order set. The last copies become the receiving report. Since most of the basic purchase order data is also needed for the receiving report, this combination of forms can save a considerable amount of typing.[7]

In similar fashion, many companies have a combined receiving report and inspection report or inspection report-move ticket. The combination can also be achieved with duplicating equipment. For example, a purchase order set might include a duplicate master, which in turn is used with a second master to run off copies of receiving reports and other documents.

Forms Design

The materials department usually does not design its own forms. Most companies have separate "office services" or "procedures" departments (usually as a staff activity reporting to the controller) staffed with forms and procedures experts who serve the entire company. The materials department should naturally make use of any help it can get in designing forms. However, the materials manager should never forget that he—not the manager of the procedures group—is ultimately responsible for every phase of administering his department, including its forms and procedures. Therefore the materials manager should be familiar with the general principles of forms design, since he is responsible for and should approve every form his department uses.

Principles. A good form transmits needed information at minimum cost. The forms designer should observe six principles:

(1) Keep design as simple as possible. The more complex the form, the more difficult (and costly) will be its use. Procedures and forms should be as foolproof as possible.

(2) Allow adequate space. Forms that are tight on space are inefficient. If data is filled in by typewriter, there should be space between lines equal to typewriter double spacing. If the form is filled in with pencil (and this may be preferable because it eliminates the need to type a "finished" copy from a rough, handwritten copy), there should be enough space for rather large handwriting and rather lengthy descriptions.

(3) Keep copies to a minimum. Naturally everyone vitally concerned with a transaction should get a copy of the form. But copies never should go to persons or departments with only occasional interest in the

---

[7] It does not completely eliminate the need for separate receiving reports, however. Many orders are not completed in a single shipment, and, of course, a separate receiving report is needed for each shipment.

transactions. Instead, if anything, such persons should have forms directed through them—that is, they receive the executed form, look at it, and then pass it on to someone who actually uses the information it contains.

(4) "Try each form for its life" at least once a year. Forms and procedures frequently become obsolete, but sometimes they live on simply because no one periodically reviews their application to make certain that there still is good reason for their existence.

(5) Design to reduce the amount of handwritten data to an absolute minimum. Use multiple-choice answers on a form when there are a limited number of alternatives; then all the clerk need do is check the appropriate one. If the information required should change, don't be afraid to scrap existing forms and change the design to accommodate the new data. The cost of the paper and printing is negligible compared to the cost of the time of those who fill out the forms.

(6) Keep data in sequence. Information on a form should be listed in the sequence in which it naturally comes to the person filling in the form. If a form moves from department to department, the first department using the form should fill in the top part of the form, with succeeding departments filling in information in sequence.

Design Criteria. Typewritten forms should be laid out to minimize carriage returns, positioning, and spacing required to type in the data. Each of these has a price in keystrokes:

Carriage return	5 keystrokes
Horizontal space	1 keystroke
Tabular stop	5 keystrokes
Hand positioning	12½ keystrokes
Vertical space	2½ keystrokes

The materials manager can evaluate the forms designs he approves simply by adding the number of keystrokes. The fewer the keystrokes, the lower the clerical cost. If one form requires 1,200 keystrokes and another form doing a similar job requires only 600, the materials manager may well consider requesting that the first form be redesigned since it costs about twice as much to fill out as the second one does.

INTEGRATED DATA PROCESSING

The techniques discussed so far help reduce paper work. But, to be realistic, their impact on the over-all materials job is minor. Even if they are applied intensively, 80 to 90 per cent of the work of materials management will continue to be clerical. Mechanization is more promising: it permits machines to be substituted for people.

Every materials department is mechanized to some extent. It has duplicating equipment, copying machines, dictating machines, electric desk calculators, electric typewriters, and so on. At this stage of mechanization, machines do various jobs but data continues to flow in conventional fashion on conventional forms and records.

Integrated data processing is more advanced. Data moves from operation to operation in a form that permits each machine to operate automatically from the instructions it receives in some "common language." The vehicle of the common language is either punched cards or punched tape. Numbers and letters of the alphabet are coded by changing the position and frequency of holes in cards or tape.

Punched-Tape System. One of the simplest systems of integrated data processing involves the use of a patented Flexowriter machine made by the Commercial Controls Division of Friden, Inc. A typical application of the system starts with a traveling requisition form printed on an envelope. Stored inside the envelope is a punched tape generated the last time the item was bought. On this tape is all the data that was typed on the last purchase order. If the buyer wishes to issue another order to the same supplier at the same price as before, the tape can be fed into the Flexowriter and a new order will be generated almost entirely automatically. The machine types at the rate of 600 characters per minute with no errors. Carriage return and line spacing are also regulated by the punched tape.

Usually the old order tape cannot be used to type out a new order so directly. For example, the buyer may wish to send quotation requests to a number of suppliers. In this case, the old order tape (or the previous quotation request tape) will permit a large part of the job to be done automatically. Information not on the tape is added manually. The machine can be set to stop at predetermined points to permit the typist to enter such variable information as the date of the order, the date delivery is required, price, and so on.

The purchase order tape is saved. It can be used to issue purchase order amendments and also for receiving reports. In either case, most of the needed information is already on the tape. The balance can be typed in manually. Sometimes Flexowriters are used from remote points. For example, the purchasing and receiving departments can have their punched-tape systems linked by wire. When a shipment is received, the receiving clerk pulls the appropriate order tape, inserts it in the Flexowriter, and prepares a receiving report, typing in variable receiving information. Two receiving reports are typed simultaneously. One is typed in receiving on a conventional machine. The other is typed in purchasing on a slave machine connected by wire to the conventional machine. Connection can even be made by leased telephone wire to connect plants that are hundreds of miles apart. This eliminates the day or two lost by mailing receiving reports and thereby shortens purchase lead time and reduces inventory needs.

Punched-Card Systems. Data on punched tapes can be run through tape-to-card converters and automatically transferred to punched cards.

Most mechanized inventory-control systems use punched cards. With them, every transaction that has any effect on inventory is key-punched on the cards. In some cases, this is done automatically when a form is typed; special typewriters are available that can be set to key-punch certain data after it has been typed. In most cases, a key-punch operator must record the data onto the cards in a separate operation.

Punched cards can be used also to automate purchasing operations. Typical is a system used by the Sprague Electric Company, in which the purchase requisition is a punched card (see Figure 19–3). The buyer fills in the variable data—purchase order number, purchase quantity, vendor's promised delivery date, and so on—in pencil, and a key-punch operator punches this information on a new "buy" card. This buy card, along with a deck of cards for the vendor's name and address (see

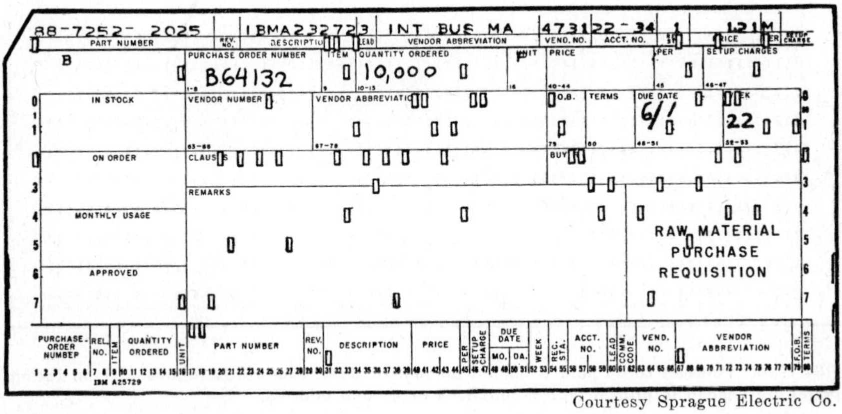

Courtesy Sprague Electric Co.

FIG. 19–3. Sprague Electric Co. uses punched cards as purchase requisitions. Buyers fill in purchasing data, which is then punched on another "buy" card.

Figure 19–4 on next page), is fed into a machine that automatically prints a purchase order (see Figure 19–5 on page 384).

The cards used to print the purchase order are saved until the supplier delivers. They then can be combined with another punched card and used to print a receiving report. They also can be used to print reports on open orders. For example, Sprague Electric makes run-offs of all open orders the week before they are due (see Figure 19–6 on page 384). It also makes separate run-offs of orders where delivery is behind schedule, and uses the same punched cards to print out expediting notices that are mailed to suppliers.

Punched cards have many other uses in materials management. If a card is punched for each materials transaction, it is possible to use the cards to print almost any form used in materials management. In addition, the cards can be combined and recombined to produce a wide variety of reports. Cards for each withdrawal, receival, rejection, and pur-

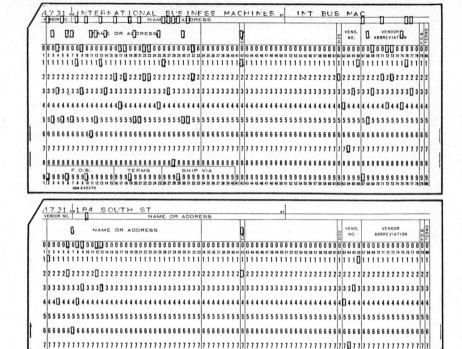

Courtesy Sprague Electric Co.

FIG. 19–4. Punched cards hold a limited amount of data. Four cards (above and on facing page) are needed to print a typical supplier's name and address.

chase can be combined to run off a complete inventory report. The report can be made according to supplier, product, part number, or in almost any other way that may desired.

ELECTRONIC DATA PROCESSING

Punched-card systems are still widely used. But they are gradually being replaced by electronic data-processing systems that rely on computers to do most of the work. Many of these EDP systems continue to use punched cards for input data, but in most cases the cards play almost a minor role. The bulk of the data-processing job is done by the "memory" cells, transistors, and vacuum tubes in complex computers. Contrary to popular belief, the computers won't think, but they can carry out complicated instructions and perform calculations at fantastic speed, as well as store enormous amounts of information in their magnetic memory cells.

Advantages of EDP

Electronic data processing has yet to be adopted by more than a few dozen companies for materials management, and there undoubtedly will continue to be substantial improvements in equipment and techniques. Even so, there is little doubt that its effect will be revolutionary. EDP promises to take over practically the entire clerical phase of materials management. In addition, it will provide managers with data to permit them to manage materials as they have never been managed before.

The computer can analyze data in minutes that would take a small army of clerks weeks to do. As a result, the materials manager can get data for making decisions much faster than before; he also can get more data than would be possible with manual or mechanical techniques. A large computer can store about ten million characters of information (enough to fill about 25 ordinary-size books).[8] In addition, the computer has access in minutes (or even fractions of seconds with some designs) to a number of reels of magnetic tape; each reel will hold about ten million characters of information.

---

[8] John A. Postley, *Computers and People* (New York: McGraw-Hill Book Co., Inc., 1960), p. 29.

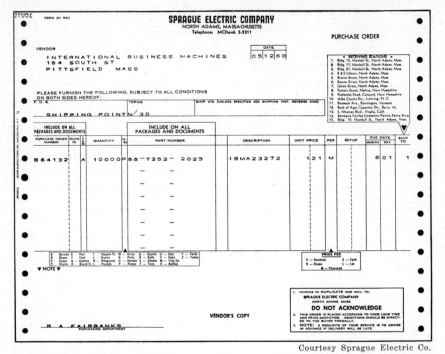

Courtesy Sprague Electric Co.

FIG. 19-5. When the punched "buy" card and the vendor deck are fed into the proper tabulating equipment, a purchase order like the one shown here is printed automatically.

Courtesy Sprague Electric Co.

FIG. 19-6. Punched buy cards can be used also to print various reports. Sprague Electric Co., for example, prints a weekly report of all open orders due the following week.

Materials management by computer normally starts with a magnetic tape that is, in effect, a list of the items to be controlled, and a "program" that tells the computer what to do with this basic list and the variable data fed into it. The "program" is an attempt to simulate a clerk's reaction to data; it permits the computer to regulate itself and make basic operating decisions. This ability to "think," plus its fantastic operating speed, are what make a computer and electronic data processing different from punched-card mechanical processing.

On the basic magnetic tape is more than a simple parts list. Included are not only such basic data as each part number, part name, and product usage, but also such materials management information as safety stock, unit weight, lead time, inventory balance, and inspection requirements.

When a program is devised and desired basic information is on tape, variable information is fed into the system. Every transaction affecting the status of the items controlled is fed into the computer for compilation and analysis. Included would be all receivals and withdrawals from stock, placement of purchase orders, and usage schedules. The usual procedure is to describe each transaction on punched cards[9] and then transfer the information from the punched cards to magnetic tape,[10] which in turn is fed into the computer.

Periodically, usually once or twice a week, the magnetic tape listing transactions is fed into the computer and compared with the permanent data already in the program. The computer compares the two sets of data, and makes necessary calculations. Its conclusions appear on reports made on a high-speed printer to which it is linked.

A well-designed EDP system will handle all routine materials management transactions. It will:

1. *Provide Up-to-Date Reports.* Current inventories of each item can be calculated and printed in detail. In addition, almost any type of inventory summary can readily be compiled for analysis. The computer can also be programed to compile estimates of future inventories based on projected schedules of purchase and usage.

2. *Complete Materials Transaction Records.* Not only the inventory balances but a complete record of each transaction for each item can be compiled and printed automatically.

3. *Compute Economic Order Quantities and Usages.* The computer can automatically analyze previous usage of an item and revise anticipated usages in accordance with some formula. It then can recompute economic order quantity. If there is a need for them, the computer can be programed to use mathematically complex ordering formulas for which a clerk would have neither understanding nor the time to make the necessary calculations.

---

[9] This is virtually the only manual operation in an EDP system. There are various devices that permit cards to be punched automatically as other data is generated, but most EDP systems still require a number of skilled key-punch operators to prepare cards from basic input data.

[10] This additional operation is needed to keep the costly computer working at peak efficiency. It is physically impossible to feed data from punched cards into the computer at a rate much faster than 2,000 characters per second. This is wasteful, since computers normally are capable of handling an input of 1,000,000 characters per second and magnetic tape feeds in data at the rate of about 50,000 characters per second.

4. Make Routine Materials Decisions. The computer can review the lead time and planned usage of each item. When inventory drops to the safety stock level, it can be programed to print automatically a purchase requisition calling for a new buy. If there is no need to get competitive bids, the computer can be programed to print a purchase order instead of a requisition.

When a predetermined lead time has elapsed or when inventories drop to some dangerous level, the computer can be programed to print automatically a notice calling for expediting. The supplier's promised delivery date also can be fed into the computer, and another expediting notice generated if the material is not received before this time. If an item needs expediting for several consecutive buys—or if delivery is consistently early—the computer can analyze the purchase history and calculate a new time.

5. Provide Up-to-Date Cost Data. The computer can easily be programed to multiply purchase quantities and inventory balances by unit prices. This gives the controller current reports on inventory investment and also gives him an accurate estimate of future cash needs to pay for deliveries against open purchase orders.

The computer can also be programed to make a special report on all items where there is a price change; this naturally would facilitate the materials manager's control over purchase prices. It would also be easy to print from data already in the computer special reports showing expenditures by supplier. This information would be useful both for reciprocity and for various reports that prime contractors must make for the armed services on relations with small business, and so on.

Problems with EDP

Although they are revolutionizing business procedures, computers are not a completely unmixed blessing. They are extremely expensive. For example, the big IBM 7080 computer rents for approximately $55,000 a month.[11] The smaller computers aren't cheap, either. At this writing the cheapest is the Monrobot XI, which the Monroe Calculating Machine Company rents for $700 per month.

The cost of developing a program and transferring data from manual records to the computer can also be enormous. One writer estimated that it took between 20,000 and 50,000 man-hours of labor to translate the basic data for an inventory of 6,000 items into "machine language."[12] Many companies that have adopted EDP systems control 20,000 or more items with them. Needless to say, their investment in EDP "start-up" cost is even greater.

---

[11] "Layman's Guide to Computers," *Business Week*, September 10, 1960, p. 172.

[12] Postley, *op. cit.*, p. 66.

Because of these high costs, only a few giant corporations could conceivably afford to use a computer exclusively for materials management. The normal practice is to share the computer among all the major departments of the business. Usually the biggest user is finance, for payroll, general accounting, and cost accounting. The marketing and engineering departments also can be big users of computers.

When a computer is used reasonably close to its effective capacity, it will normally effect savings in clerical costs that will more than offset its high operating costs. To get these savings, management must reduce its clerical work force. This can create personnel relations problems.

There are also problems in programing the computer. Even the most routine clerical job has dozens of minor problems that require decisions. Each problem must be anticipated in programing the computer. A few of them are bound to be overlooked. For example, suppose a company has programed a computer to generate a buy notice if safety stock drops to a given level. Regardless of the reason why the stock drops, the computer faithfully follows instructions and generates the buy notices. This can create problems if other controls are not programed into the computer as well.

Suppose, for example, there are engineering or quality control problems with a given product. Management wants to let stocks run down until the problem is solved. With manual inventory control, the clerks would simply ignore the declining stock balances on the items affected and would write no requisitions until they were told the problem was solved. With automatic control, the computer would flood the buying department with dozens or even hundreds of useless buy notices. If they are not properly regulated, automatic systems can generate so much unnecessary paper work that their usefulness is substantially reduced.

Every company that has attempted to set up an EDP system for materials management has encountered expensive and troublesome "bugs" that must be ironed out before the system works well. However, practically all of them agree that the results are worth the effort and cost.

A Typical Application

The Fairchild Engine and Airplane Corporation of Hagerstown, Maryland, uses an IBM model 650 computer and related equipment for materials management. Basic scheduling data and parts lists are stored on magnetic drums in the "memory" part of the computer. Every materials transaction—schedule changes, purchase orders, receivals, and so on—is recorded on punched cards (see Figure 19–7). Information is then transferred to magnetic tape so it can be fed to the computer at a faster rate.

Nine times per month the tape is fed into the computer along with a predetermined program (i.e., set of instructions that tell the computer what to do). The computer automatically performs the calculations that

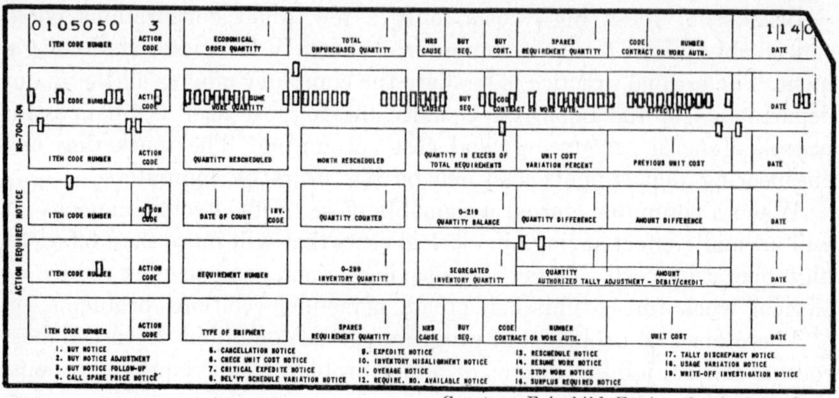

Courtesy Fairchild Engine & Airplane Corp.

FIG. 19–7. Fairchild Engine and Airplane Corp. key-punches every materials transaction on 21,000 components onto cards like this one. The data is then transferred to magnetic tape.

the program directs. Results of these calculations are printed on individual Material Inventory Status Reports for each item controlled. Figure 19–8 shows transactions for a typical active item.

Reports for Action. In addition to status reports for each of 21,000 active items it controls, the computer simultaneously prints orders calling for specific action on items that need it. When stocks of an item drop to the point where they equal probable usage during the lead time plus the safety stock, the computer calculates the economic order quantity and prints a buy notice. Similarly, if stock on hand or on order exceeds foreseeable demand, it prints a cancellation notice. The computer also prints three different types of expediting notice:

1. When there is a variance between the planned delivery schedule and the supplier's actual schedule.
2. When inventory drops to one-half the safety stock.
3. When there is not enough stock for current operations.

If some purchasing action is not taken, the computer is programed to find out why. If an order is not placed after the computer issues a buy notice, the computer asks why when the follow-up time programed into it has expired. For example, the computer might print a buy notice on March 1 requesting that a purchase order for material be placed by March 15. If the order is not placed and recorded on the magnetic tape, the computer may print a notice asking why the order was not placed when the tape is run through it on March 15. If engineering has issued a "hold" on the item requesting that all new commitments for an item be delayed because of possible design changes, the computer is programed to take this into account and refrain from printing new buy notices until the part is taken off the "hold" list.

Quantities calculated by the computer include predetermined contin-

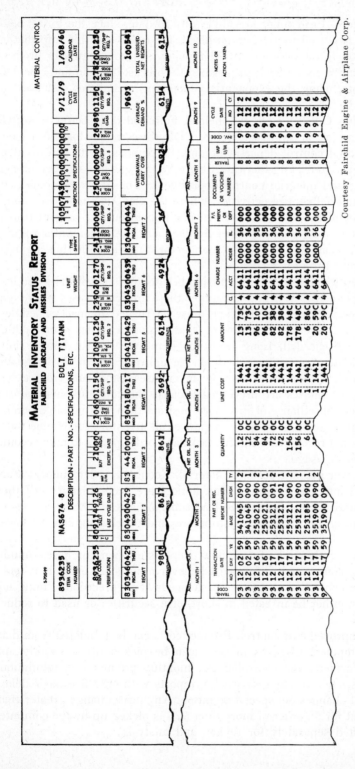

Courtesy Fairchild Engine & Airplane Corp.

FIG. 19–8. Fairchild runs a magnetic tape of all materials transactions through its computer nine times per month. Every transaction for each item is automatically printed on a Material Inventory Status Report.

gency factors. Lead times are always up to date, since the buyer must indicate a new lead time when he places the order and this information is passed on to the computer. Order points also are regularly brought up to date. The computer is programed to forecast demand and calculate order points, using the exponential smoothing techniques discussed in Chapter 10.

Fairchild's Gains. EDP has helped Fairchild do a better materials management job at lower cost. Before EDP, the company had 26 persons in its material control department and 41 persons in its procurement department. After EDP, there were only 38 persons in a new, combined purchasing and material control department. The heavy personnel cut came in material control activities, where the computer took over about 90 per cent of the clerical work. In addition to cutting administrative overhead (most of which is offset by the share of the computer's rental that is chargeable to materials management), Fairchild has enjoyed these benefits through EDP:

(1) Fewer delays in manufacturing because of late deliveries and less expediting expense. With the computer there are fewer cases where material is ordered late and delivery must be rushed to meet schedules.

(2) Lower average inventories. The computer issues a buy notice only when it's needed. Long lead-time items are bought before short lead-time items; material is scheduled for delivery only when it is actually required. This reduces average inventories. Stockouts from excessively low inventories are prevented because the computer maintains a much closer surveillance of inventory position than was possible before. The computer makes a complete review of all inventory items nine times per month and recomputes safety stocks and order points to take account of changes in usage.

(3) Lower average costs of material. Economic order quantities are programed into the computer. Buy notices are accumulated until they are absolutely needed because of lead time. As a result, there are fewer buys and in larger quantities than before, and purchasing can get lower prices.

(4) Better planning of cash flow. Reports of open purchase commitments (the computer is informed whenever a purchase order is issued) permit the controller to project cash needs with precision. Funds not needed can either be invested in short-term securities or used to reduce loans.

(5) Improved cost control. Product costs can be tabulated from data on the computer. Changes in costs can be picked up accurately and rapidly. Formerly the controller got monthly product cost tabulations two weeks late; now he gets weekly reports with only five days' delay. Major cost changes get special attention. Any price change greater than 10 per cent for an order of more than $25 is picked up by the computer and reported separately for review and analysis.

(6) Faster purchasing. Formerly, contract extensions had to be added manually to each material control card before new requirements could be figured. This was a slow, tedious job. Now the change in end-product requirements is put into the computer and all of the detail work is done automatically. Purchasing knows the effect of a contract change almost in a matter of hours. Similarly, when a contract is cut back, purchasing can move faster on cancellations.

Fairchild's Price. All these benefits were not gained without sacrifice. Besides the recurring expense of operating the computer, Fairchild had to make a one-time investment of roughly 5,000 hours of labor, including 1,800 hours at overtime rates, to translate its materials records into a form that could be handled by the computer. Even with the best programing that can be devised, the computer cannot do what the lowliest clerk can do: think. If some data must be handled in a slightly different fashion, a clerk will automatically make allowances. With a computer the problem must be anticipated or there will be trouble.

For example, with conventional programing the computer will not issue a buy notice until the lead time requires it. This is desirable in most cases, of course—but not always. If a certain item is in short supply, a buyer may wish to order as soon as there is a requirement, even if this is months before he would be required to do so by the lead time. A clerk could work from a special list of all such items. A computer can only follow the instructions in its program. Fairchild overcame this particular problem by programing the computer to handle certain items as "buy instant." The computer is programed so that it generates a buy notice for such items as soon as there are requirements.

Other problems haven't been solved that easily. One that took a great deal of time to overcome was minimum buys. Suppose the computer calculates that 12 cotter pins are needed and generates a buy notice to that effect. If the buyer's vendor requires a minimum order of $5, the actual purchase quantity might be 1,000 cotter pins.

When the purchase-order data is fed into the computer the trouble begins. The computer compares a requirement of 12 pieces with a potential inventory of 1,000 pieces and proceeds to take steps to prevent excessive inventories from accumulating by printing a purchase order cancellation notice for 988 pieces. This wasted paper work can be corrected by another special addition to the program that tells the computer to handle minimum order parts in a special way.

The computer won't solve the problem of usage variation, either. It can compute procurement lead times and safety stock by almost any mathematical technique. But if usage varies erratically, eventually the computer will make a mistake: either safety stock will be inadequate and there will actually be a stockout before a new shipment arrives or the safety stock will be so big that inventories will be excessive. Clerks also have trouble with erratic demand fluctuations, but sometimes they manage to do a better job of controlling them than a computer can.

For these and other reasons, Fairchild still has about 1,400 items under manual control. For these items, clerks keep records and relate past usage to future sales. Customer-choice items are also controlled manually; it simply isn't worthwhile to put them into the system since the item is being bought only for one customer's special order.

The Future. Despite the cost and the problems, Fairchild has no intention of ever going back to manual methods of materials management. It believes EDP is here to stay. In fact, it anticipates further improvements that will result in even wider application of EDP. The role of EDP in the materials organization of the future will be discussed in Chapter 21.

CASE

CASE 19–1.   CAROLINA PAPER COMPANY

IMPROVING RECORDS AND ADMINISTRATIVE CONTROLS

The Catawassa mill of the Carolina Paper Company was built in 1910 to take advantage of the ample supplies of timber in the area as well as the almost unlimited water supply available from the Catawassa River. Since 1945, the mill has more than trebled its capacity. Now it has reached a period of consolidation. The entire paper industry is currently suffering from overcapacity. Every producer is hard pressed to preserve profit margins. Carolina is no exception, and it has called in a management consulting firm, Walker, Thompson, and Karen, for advice. One of the changes the consultants recommend is that Carolina adopt a materials-management type of organization. The following year this recommendation is followed, and George Jenkins, from a leading New England paper company, is hired as Carolina's materials manager.

One of Jenkins' first jobs as materials manager is to analyze the procedures and records in his department. He discovers that the company's single most important material, logs for the pulp mill, is controlled almost entirely by the log buyer, Alan White. Logs are purchased from dozens of small lumber mills and are also supplied by the company's own forestry department, which White treats as an outside supplier. White's procedure is to get a copy of the company's pulp mill schedule and to determine from it what the demand for logs will be. He then places orders with his suppliers. The traffic department arranges with the railroad to have cars available to pick up logs from White's suppliers.

White keeps a separate record for each supplier. Whenever he places an order, he posts it to the appropriate supplier's record. When a shipment is received, White gets a copy of the receiving report and credits it against the open order. White also keeps a separate inventory record for hard- and soft-wood logs. As cars come in from the suppliers, he debits this record; as they are unloaded for the logs to be cut into pulp, he credits the record. His inventory is represented by the full cars waiting in the company's switching yard.

Somewhat different systems are used by the company to control other raw materials (mostly chemicals) used in papermaking and for maintenance supplies. Raw materials are stored either in the mill's yard or in a storage shed. Manufacturing makes withdrawals whenever necessary. The buyer knows from experience approximately what usage will be, and he schedules his purchases so that they will approximately equal usage. Occasionally he also makes physical checks of the stock to make certain that there are no drastic fluctuations. When usage is extremely heavy, the mill's general foreman will sometimes warn him that his stock of a particular chemical is getting low. The buyer then gets on the telephone immediately and places a rush order. This is rare, however, since the buyer normally protects himself with a more than adequate safety stock. He readjusts this stock once a year, when the annual inventory is taken. Last year, the inventory indicated that he was carrying $500,000 in chemical inventories, which was an average three months' usage.

Carolina's maintenance storeroom is organized somewhat like a grocery supermarket. Whenever they need material, individual maintenance men walk into the storeroom and help themselves to whatever they need. They record their withdrawals on a stores requisition form. The maintenance men on the day shift simply give the form to the stores clerk, who then posts it to perpetual inventory record cards. The men on the afternoon and evening shifts leave the forms in a box to be posted later by the clerk.

The clerk reorders whenever there is a stockout or when his records show that the stock has dropped to the reorder point. He calculates the reorder point by studying usage history and comparing it with the lead-time estimate he gets from the purchasing department. His reorder point is normally equal to his estimate of usage during the lead time plus a 50 per cent safety allowance. Whenever there is a stockout, however, the clerk increases his safety allowance a little to try to prevent a recurrence. Stockouts do not occur too often even though the annual physical inventory always indicates that there have been more withdrawals from stock than were ever recorded in stores requisitions; the safety stocks are more than adequate to take care of shrinkage.

When stock does drop to the reorder point, the clerk prepares a purchase requisition for the desired purchase quantity. The purchasing department then issues a conventional purchase order for the required material. The stores department gets a copy of this order, which it posts to the perpetual inventory card. In most cases, it then can forget about the order until the material is received and it posts the receiving report and move ticket to the inventory card. If there is a stockout before the material is received, the stores clerk calls purchasing and requests that the purchase be expedited. He also increases the lead time shown on his inventory card to prevent a recurrence of the stockout.

Questions

1. What improvements, if any, can be made in Carolina's materials management procedures?
2. How can control be improved or cost of paper work reduced?

Chapter 20

MEASURING MATERIALS MANAGEMENT PERFORMANCE

There are four basic steps in measuring the performance of any manager or department. They are:

1. Define the limits of the job.
2. Determine the objectives to be achieved within these limits.
3. Develop a program to meet these objectives.
4. Compare progress on the program with the objectives.

The limits of the job are defined by the organization structure and policies and procedures. In previous chapters, we saw that the ideal materials organization embraces all related materials activities: purchasing, traffic, material control, and so on. We also saw that the typical objectives of the materials organization include:

1. Low operating costs (i.e., low costs of acquisition and possession and low payroll costs).
2. Low prices of purchased material.
3. Minimum investment in inventory (i.e., high inventory turnover).
4. Superior supplier performance (i.e., adequate quality of purchased materials, prompt delivery, and generally favorable vendor relations).
5. Development of materials personnel.
6. Good records.

DEVELOPING THE PROGRAM

The third basic step in measuring performance—developing a program to meet objectives—was discussed in Chapter 7. The program normally would include both qualitative and quantitative goals. Among the latter would be a detailed budget to control operating costs and specific cost-reduction and inventory-management performance. Other goals are inherently qualitative, however, including those of better supplier relations, development of personnel, and good records.

The materials manager should have a program for the department to achieve these goals. In addition, he should require each of his key subordinates to develop programs to achieve similar goals. Authority to develop a program should be delegated to the lowest possible level in the organization. In doing this, the materials manager ensures that the efforts of everyone in the organization will be directed toward goals that are consistent with those of the whole department and of the company.

In the plant materials organization described in Chapter 4, each divisional materials manager should develop his own program. Typically, he might submit a plan to the materials manager once a year in which he describes his goals for the coming year. The materials manager would then review and compare the plans submitted by his subordinates. Some of them he might accept without any questions. Others would have to be reviewed in some detail in order to make them consistent with department-wide goals.

In this way, each divisional materials manager is encouraged to exercise his initiative and set standards against which his performance could be measured. He naturally would set goals for cost reduction and inventory turnover. In addition, he would be encouraged to control his own operating costs, budgeting himself on travel, telephone calls, and personnel. In this plan, he would not only include how he intended to develop his subordinates but also indicate—after a frank discussion of his own strengths and weaknesses with the materials manager—how he proposed to correct his own shortcomings.

With this approach, not only is responsibility for performance delegated to the lowest possible level, but the practice in planning is itself a management-development tool. Men become experienced in planning and administration while they are still in junior jobs. This permits management to test their managerial ability long before they advance to levels where their mistakes can seriously hurt the organization.

The materials manager's plan is a composite of the plans of his subordinates and would also be submitted annually. If accepted by top management, it would become a standard against which the department's performance would be measured. Performance measurements of individual parts of the plan might be made annually, quarterly, monthly, weekly, or even daily. In general, performance in achieving the qualitative goals would be measured less frequently than that in achieving the quantitative goals. For example, an annual or quarterly report would usually be adequate to measure progress in personnel development. On the other hand, deviations from operating budgets might be reported monthly, while price changes often are reported weekly or daily.

The quantitative phases of performance measurement get more attention for several reasons. Among them are:

1. Quantitative Data Is More Objective. It is based on operating statistics, whereas qualitative data reflects, in large part, the opinion of the observer. It would be hard for a materials manager to distort performance on cost reduction, where progress is measured in dollars and cents. But it would be very easy for him to exaggerate the progress he is making on such intangible goals as personnel development or improved supplier relations.

2. Quantitative Data Usually Changes Faster. Most of the materials management goals that can only be measured qualitatively are long-range in nature. Progress on them is usually so slow that it is pointless to attempt to measure it weekly or daily. On the other hand, progress on quantitative goals should be measured frequently, so that remedies can be applied immediately should performance fall short of expectations.

3. Quantitative Data Is More Directly Related to Company Profits. Top management has an immediate interest in such materials management goals as cost reduction, inventory turnover, etc., which can be measured quantitatively. Performance is directly related to day-to-day operating decisions. On the other hand, management is usually interested in qualitative goals only when it is planning for the future.

CONTROL OF OPERATING COSTS

Managements have been measuring how effectively purchasing agents and materials managers control operating costs for years. In fact, in the less progressive companies this is the only performance measurement that is applied to the materials department. The assumption is that the materials department is a service activity and should be interested primarily in providing its service at the lowest possible cost. Implicit in this assumption is the concept that the materials department is a clerical activity, and its performance should be measured in terms of how much it costs to process each purchase order, requisition, or production release. Accountants then carefully calculate the department's costs and divide them by the number of forms it processes. By this criterion, a purchasing department whose operating costs are equal to $10 for each purchase order it issues is considered more efficient than one that spends $12.

This is a false concept, of course. Control of operating costs is just one objective of the materials department, and not the most important one by any means. For example, the typical materials department can save $50 by buying materials at lower prices for every $1 that it can shave from its operating costs. And the best materials departments usually have rather high operating costs because they are willing to pay higher salaries to attract highly skilled personnel who are capable of doing an outstanding job of materials management.

Nevertheless, control of operating costs is still a fairly important objective. Were there no control, costs would soon get out of hand. Operating costs should be budgeted as part of the over-all materials plan. Performance can be measured in two ways: (1) Measurement of the productivity of the persons employed in the materials department with either absolute or relative standards. (2) Measurement of success in controlling direct materials department expenses by comparing actual costs with budgeted costs.

Control of Personnel

The materials department plan should include an estimate of personnel needed to achieve objectives. This estimate, if approved, becomes the department's personnel budget. Whenever possible, it should be based on objective criteria. For purchasing and material control jobs, the criterion may be the number of parts of a given type that a man can handle. For example, one company calculates that each buyer should be able to handle 250 complex parts and about 500 simple items; this company also needs one materials planner and two clerks for each 1,000 items that are controlled. Similar criteria can be applied to other materials activities. For example, personnel requirements in traffic, shipping, and receiving can be measured in terms of the number of shipments handled.

All the standards mentioned so far are relative. They are useful in determining personnel needs when work loads change. For example, if one buyer is needed for each 250 parts, we know that we must hire two buyers if 500 parts are added because of a new product. Absolute standards are more difficult to justify. How do we know that a buyer can't handle 400 parts, for example, instead of only 200? For some jobs, particularly the highly skilled ones, the answer is mostly a matter of judgment. The materials manager draws on his own experience and that of his supervisors, and he may also make comparisons with companies with similar materials management problems.

Absolute Measurements. More exact methods can be used to measure the less skilled jobs. Any job that involves doing something—as distinct from thinking about something—can be measured with conventional time-study techniques. The time-study man breaks the job into its basic components and calculates how much time it takes to perform each element at some standard of efficiency. Work standards can easily be set for such repetitive materials operations as typing purchase orders, filing various documents, processing various types of shipments and receivals, and so on. Many large corporations have made time studies of their highly repetitive materials jobs. A few even have introduced incentive pay on certain jobs. For example, one company boosted the productivity of its purchase-order typists by more than 20 per cent with incentive pay. Current output averages about 125 orders per typist per day.

It is difficult to make time studies of the less repetitive jobs. But they can be analyzed with ratio-delay studies. The first step in making such a study is to break the job into a series of simple elements that can readily be observed—walking away from the desk, talking to visitors, typing, talking on the telephone, doing nothing, and so on. Then an observer, unknown to the subject, notes the subject's activity at random intervals.

Usually several hundred observations are made over a period of several months.

A large appliance firm made such a study of secretaries and buyers in its materials department. Figures 20–1 and 20–2 show the results. Ratio-delay studies aren't foolproof, but they sometimes can give clues to improvements, both in the average performance of everyone performing the job being studied and in individual performance. For example, note in Figure 20–1 that the average secretary spent 10 per cent of her time on the telephone. Investigation might show either that the company

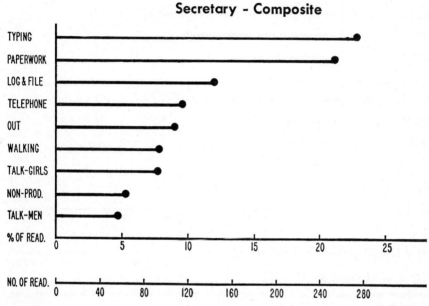

FIG. 20–1. This chart shows the results of ratio-delay studies made of ten buyers' secretaries. Managers get clues to performance when they compare studies of individual secretaries to this average.

was too lenient about personal calls or—as was actually the case at this appliance company—that secretaries were wasting too much time placing long-distance calls for executives, which could be handled more efficiently by the operator on the company's switchboard.

The studies also are useful for individual comparison of performance. Figure 20–1 shows, for example, that the average secretary spent 5 per cent of her time doing nothing, 10 per cent away from her desk, and 7 per cent talking to other girls in the office. One would have little doubt as to the efficiency of the secretary who spent 10, 15, and 10 per cent of her time on these activities respectively and correspondingly less on her more productive (and less pleasant) jobs: typing, paper work, and filing.

Usually there is an excellent correlation between ratio-delay studies of clerical workers and other evaluations of their efficiency. The least efficient secretary will have the highest average of nonproductive time. With the more highly skilled jobs, however, this may not be true. The best buyer may spend a greater percentage of his time doing nothing than the average buyer (see Figure 20–2), who spends only 4 per cent of his time

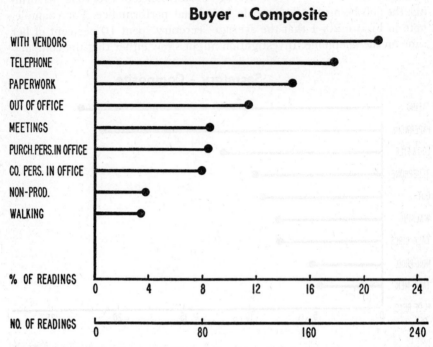

FIG. 20–2. This chart shows how the average buyer in a Midwestern appliance manufacturing company spends his time. It is based on ratio-delay studies of ten buyers in the purchasing department.

engaged in no apparent activity. The reason for this, of course, is that the best buyer may be able to perform routine tasks with dispatch and devote a greater part of his time to planning and generating ideas for cost reduction and product improvement.

Control of Direct Costs

The materials manager rarely has any problem controlling his biggest operating expense: wages and salaries. He gets his personnel budget approved and allows for salary adjustments. His performance will inevitably be satisfactory so long as he does not grant salary increases or increase his staff in excess of the budget.

Other expenses are harder to control. Travel and telephone expenses can easily get out of hand in a materials department, particularly if there are many unexpected quality and delivery problems with suppliers. Such expenses are heavy enough even when everything goes according to plan.

Contact must be maintained with thousands of suppliers. A materials department responsible for annual purchases of $30 million may have telephone and telegraph bills that exceed $2,000 per month. And it may spend as much as $20,000 per year on travel.

Telephone and travel expenses are controlled much as personnel expenses are. A budget for each is included in the over-all purchase plan. Standards are based on past experience. For example, both telephone calls and travel expenses would tend to vary with the dollar volume of purchases, the number of suppliers, and the number of employees in the department. Suppose that telephone expenses totaled $30,000 in a year when there were 100 persons in the materials department, 6,000 suppliers, and a $30 million purchase volume. Then a budget of $32,000 would not be unreasonable for a year when volume of purchases rises to $35 million, there are 110 persons in the department, and it is planned to introduce a number of new suppliers.

Most other expenses can be controlled in similar fashion. Expenses for office supplies, for example, should vary almost directly with either the number of persons employed in the materials department or the number of purchase orders and other forms being processed.

CONTROL OF PRICES

If a typical materials department cut its telephone bill or its office-supply expenses by 2 per cent, it might save a few hundred dollars per year. There would be no perceptible change in the company's profit margin. But if it could reduce the prices of all purchased materials by 2 per cent, profits would rise noticeably. As we saw in Chapter 1, in the average company with a 10 per cent profit margin every 2 per cent reduction in purchased materials cost brings a 10 per cent increase in profits. This is why price is perhaps the single most important objective in the typical materials department.

Performance in meeting the price objective can be measured in three ways: by comparing actual costs with the materials budget; by cost-reduction reports and bogies; and by price indexes.

The Materials Budget

Price performance is most directly related to over-all company objectives when actual costs are compared with a materials budget. Most well-managed companies try to budget sales and costs at least a year ahead. Such projections help management evaluate over-all performance in reaching profit and sales goals. Usually the cost department calculates standard unit material costs for each product. The materials budget is then calculated by multiplying these standard costs by proposed production volume for each product.

Performance is measured by means of variance accounts that show the difference between actual costs and budgeted costs.[1] Variances can arise both because the unit cost of the material was different from the plan or because usage (or scrap) varied. The former is the materials manager's responsibility; the latter is the manufacturing manager's (unless the scrap resulted from defective purchased material).

Top management often likes to use the materials budget to measure the materials department's performance because it is so directly related to the objectives of the business and neatly ties in the department with other company activities. However, the materials budget has serious shortcomings for performance measurement. These include:

(1) The materials budget includes only direct materials. Yet most companies spend substantial sums for indirect materials, which should not be overlooked in cost-reduction programs.

(2) Actual costs show up in variance accounts weeks or even months after they are incurred. This is because of the lag between the time material is ordered and the time it is finally used, after having been in inventory. Because different items have different lead times, it is extremely difficult to reconcile the usual cost department records with purchase records.

(3) Variance figures rarely, if ever, show why a price changed. Usually price increases and decreases are balanced against each other and are not segregated. In addition, cost department records often are not set up for item-by-item analysis, yet this procedure is essential for good materials management.

Cost-Reduction Reports

For the reasons above, most materials departments maintain their own controls over cost-reduction efforts. They cannot use cost department records.

The simplest, and one of the most effective, controls over purchase cost is a daily or weekly report of price changes on purchased materials (see the sample form in Figure 20–3). The report lists each item on which there is any price change, the reason for the price change, the amount of the price change, the percentage change, and the cost per month.

Each buying group normally makes its own report. Materials managers can use the reports both as a control and as a measure of performance. When the price for an item rises sharply, they can ask for an explanation. Similarly, when there is a sharp decrease, they may wish to know why the price was so much higher on the previous buy—or they may congratulate the buyer on a skillful job if he exercised considerable ingenuity in finding ways to reduce costs.

---

[1] The reader not familiar with this terminology should consult any accepted text in cost accounting or the *Cost Accountants' Handbook*, Theodore Lang (ed.) (New York: Ronald Press Company, 1947).

FORM O.O 128 (Rev 1/56)

WEEKLY REPORT OF PRICE CHANGES
PURCHASED PARTS AND MATERIALS
PRODUCTION ITEMS ONLY

X _____ DIVISION
DATE 10-19-57

PART NO OR MAT'L SPEC	PART NAME OR DESCRIPTION	SUPPLIER	% BUY	PURCHASE DATA						% OF CHANGE	REASON FOR CHANGE	PRESENT AVG. MO. REQ'MTS	EFFECT OF PRICE CHANGE Month
				OLD PRICE	LOT BUY	EFF DATE	NEW PRICE	LOT BUY	EFF DATE				
345675	Housing	A	100	.275	1000	1-56	.285	1000	10-56	+3.5	LAM	300	3.00
356305	Body	B	100	.960	300	1-56	1.017	300	10-56	+3.8	M	100	3.70
367557	Bracket	C	25	3.10	15000	3-56	3.01	15000	9-56	-2.9	M	15000	-1350.00
370752	Cap Screw	D	100	.43	2000	1-56	.45	2000	10-56	+5.7	LAM	735	14.70
370941	Bolt	E	100	.77	2000	1-56	.79	2000	10-56	+2.8	M	1045	20.90
383610	Brace	F	70	3.63	2000	3-56	3.46	5000	10-56	-4.9	N	1000	-170.00
381226	Valve	G	100	.57	BLKT	1-56	.59	BLKT	10-56	+3.6	M	41108	622.16
361754	Dowel	H	100	.205	BLKT	1-56	.216	BLKT	9-56	+5.2	LAM	1466	16.13
534516	Cover	I	100	.050	300	1-56	.052	300	6-56	+3.2	LAM	25	.05
740330	Valve	J	100	.2902	1000	8-56	.3250	1000	8-56	+12.0	LAM	525	18.27
737337	Fitting	K	100	.900	10000	5-56	.809	20000	10-56	-1.2	Q	6070	-66.77
739746	Gear	L	100	.0095	10000	7-56	.0092	10000	10-56	-3.2	N	4125	-1.24
35630	Plug	M	100	3.42	100/499	3-56	3.37	500	9-56	-1.4	M	300	-15.00

CODE FOR PRICE CHANGE
A - CHANGE IN MATERIAL COST
L - CHANGE IN LABOR COST
N - NEGOTIATED CHANGE
D - PRODUCT DESIGN CHANGE
S - SUBSTITUTE MATERIAL
Q - QUANTITY ONLY
O - OTHER, EXPLAIN

Courtesy Eaton Manufacturing Co.

FIG. 20–3. Weekly reports of changes in purchase prices help keep purchasing managers apprised of department performance on cost reduction and also expose any price increases that should be investigated.

Cost-reduction reports can also be used to measure performance of individual buying groups. Data can be accumulated by buying group and by reason for change and compared with budgeted price changes. The reports can be used to generate a healthy spirit of competition among the various buying groups. If each group has a cost-reduction target, then each will not only carefully study the report to see what progress it is making in meeting its own bogy but also be keenly interested in the progress of other groups.

Usually the cost-reduction target is originally determined as a percentage of purchase cost for each group. Percentages are helpful because they present fewer forecasting problems. For example, a 2 per cent quota would hold regardless of whether purchase volume were $10 million or $11 million whereas an absolute quota would be easier to meet if business were slightly better than expected.

Cost-reduction quotas of 2 to 3 per cent are fairly common. The targets then are translated into estimated absolute quotas, which are subject to change should actual dollar volume of purchases be different from forecasted volume. Different buying groups normally would get different quotas, both as a percentage of cost and in dollars. Ideally, the quota should reflect the cost-reduction opportunities of each group. For example, a group buying steel or other commodities where there is little price competition may have a quota of only 1 per cent. If its dollar volume were $10 million, the quota would be $100,000. Another buying group might have a 4 per cent quota. But its absolute quota would also be $100,000 if its dollar volume were only $2,500,000.

How is the quota determined? First, an over-all quota should be set for the entire materials department. It should be based on:

1. An Economic Forecast. If the outlook is for booming business, the quota will have to be quite low, since suppliers will be operating at near-capacity levels and will not be too responsive to cost-reduction efforts. On the other hand, if business is not too good, competition among suppliers will be keen.

2. Price Forecasts for Key Commodities. In many companies, a few commodities account for a large share of the volume of purchases. Predicted prices for these commodities should be taken into account when computing over-all cost-reduction quotas.[2]

3. Past Performance. This is one of the most widely used criteria. Managers naturally like to see some improvements each year. On the other hand, buyers sometimes complain that if they succeed in reducing costs for a number of years it becomes progressively harder to meet quotas because the opportunities for cost reduction keep diminishing.

4. Relation to Company Profit Objectives. Sometimes cost reduction is necessary if the company is to achieve desired profits. In some cases, top management may exert rather arbitrary pressure on its materials department to reduce costs in order to achieve these over-all profit objectives.

5. Opinions of Materials Personnel. The materials manager and each of his commodities specialists know from past experience and from "feel" of the market the cost-reduction quota that can reasonably be achieved.

After an over-all quota is agreed upon, individual quotas are set for each group, following the same basic criteria. Individual supervisors should have as much latitude as possible in setting their quotas. This boosts morale and stimulates effort to meet quotas, since they become bogies that the supervisor agreed were reasonable rather than targets imposed on him from above. Higher management sometimes finds, however, that it must stimulate supervisors to raise their sights in setting quotas. In some cases, supervisors try to make their jobs too easy; in a few cases, they're so eager to make a showing that they become overoptimistic.

Obviously, all price reductions are not the result of the buyer's efforts. Market prices drop through no effort on the buyer's part, products are redesigned to reduce cost, and so on. And price increases may reflect

---

[2] The principles of price forecasting were discussed in Chapters 6 and 7.

superior performance on the part of the buyer when they are held below the amount justified by increases in wages and raw material cost. Therefore, some evaluation of price changes is essential if they are to be good guides of purchasing performance. In a big company, this would be done by someone on the materials manager's staff, usually a purchase analyst

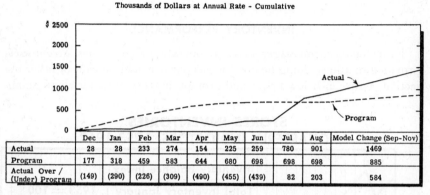

Thousands of Dollars at Annual Rate - Cumulative

	Dec	Jan	Feb	Mar	Apr	May	Jun	Jul	Aug	Model Change (Sep-Nov)
Actual	28	28	233	274	154	225	259	780	901	1469
Program	177	318	459	583	644	680	698	698	698	885
Actual Over / (Under) Program	(149)	(290)	(226)	(309)	(490)	(455)	(439)	82	203	584

FIG. 20–4. Charts that compare actual cost reductions with quotas can help stimulate interest in reducing prices, in addition to serving as measures of performance.

or value analyst. In a small company, the materials manager himself may have to do it.

Actual performance on price reductions attributable to buyer action can be charted against the savings objective for each buying group. Figure 20–4 illustrates how one company charts price-reduction progress for each of its buying groups.

Use of Indexes

Although weekly or daily price change reports are useful to keep materials management informed of price actions by subordinates, they are not ideal for performance measurement. There often are hundreds of price changes each month, even in small companies. Tabulating and evaluating each of them from a price change report is costly. In addition, errors are almost inevitable. Either buyers will incorrectly estimate usage in computing the monthly cost effect of the price change, or usage will change and their estimate will be inapplicable.

With a price index, on the other hand, estimates can be made with precision. In addition, they can be related directly to the cost of the company's products. There will be fewer errors and less clerical work, since a good index need contain only about 15 per cent of total items.[3]

Once the over-all index is established and a price-reporting system is operating, it requires relatively little effort to break up index items by

---

[3] How to make and use purchase-price indexes is described in detail in Chapter 7.

buying group so that each group has its own index. This permits comparison both for performance evaluation and to generate a spirit of competition. Purchase-price indexes can also be compared with the indexes of the U.S. Bureau of Labor Statistics and other organizations.[4] For instance, an index made up primarily of metal parts can be compared with the Bureau's wholesale price index of metals and metal products.

INVENTORY PERFORMANCE

Every materials manager strives to operate with minimum inventories, provided that in so doing he does not jeopardize achievement of other objectives (especially low prices and prompt delivery of materials to manu-

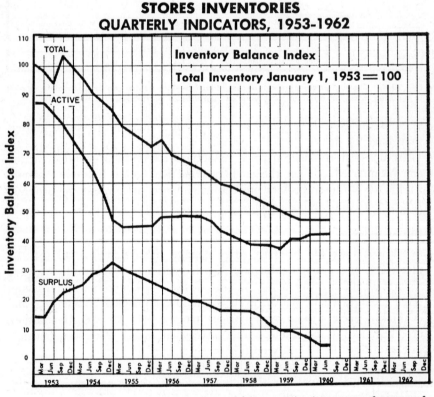

STORES INVENTORIES
QUARTERLY INDICATORS, 1953-1962

FIG. 20–5. Index numbers can sometimes be useful in comparing inventory performance of various buying groups or various plants within the same company. The index number would indicate the relative progress each unit has made in relation to some base period.

facturing when they are required). In some companies, inventory performance is measured simply by comparing present inventories with those of some base period.

---

[4] Many price indexes appear monthly in the *Survey of Current Business*, published by the U.S. Department of Commerce.

Figure 20–5 shows how a Southern textile firm measures performance in inventory management. Index numbers permit easy comparison of present inventory levels in each of its plants with inventory levels that prevailed during the base period. The lower the index number, the greater the progress that has been made in reducing stocks.

Though this measuring technique is simple, it can also be misleading, for it implicitly assumes that the need for inventories is constant from year to year in each plant. In most companies this would not be the case; the need for inventories would vary with the level of output. A more sophisticated approach is to set inventory standards for various levels of output and then compare actual inventories with these standards.

In general, the need for inventories does not rise in direct proportion to output. If $1 million in inventories is needed to maintain a production volume of $1 million per month, substantially less than $2 million in inventories will be needed for an output of $2 million per month. The inventory standard either can be for a specific investment or it can be measured as a rate of turnover (annual dollar volume of purchases divided by average purchased materials inventories). Whenever possible, inventory standards should be established for every subclass of inventory. Then the materials manager can compare actual performance with the standard and locate imbalances. It is possible, of course, to have too little of one class of inventory and too much of another class. Then over-all turnover figures would be in line with standards but individual turnover statistics would highlight imbalances.

Obsolescence should also be budgeted. The budget should be based primarily on past performance. But it should also reflect special conditions. For example, if obsolescence losses the previous year were unusually low because of special circumstances and higher losses will be inevitable during the current year, this should be allowed for in the budget. Otherwise materials personnel will be tempted to continue to carry inventories that should be declared obsolete. Special reports on inventory items for which there is little or no recent demand help the materials manager eliminate obsolescence.

SUPPLIER PERFORMANCE

Three major materials management objectives directly involve outside suppliers. They are prompt delivery, adequate quality, and favorable vendor relations. It is doubly important that performance in achieving these objectives be measured. It is essential not only to measurement of the materials department's performance but also to measurement of supplier performance by the materials department itself. Good buyers should regularly evaluate the performance of their existing suppliers. Not only should they visit supplier plants regularly, keep up to date on supplier finances and products, and so on, but they should try to keep objective records of supplier quality and delivery performance.

The Quality Objective

The materials department achieves its quality objective only when all supplier shipments meet standards and the cost of inspecting these shipments can be eliminated. Few materials departments can reach this ideal, but they can work toward it by selecting suppliers with good quality records and educating delinquent suppliers in quality procedures.

Every salesman will maintain that his company's quality is unsurpassed. How can the materials manager evaluate such claims objectively? He does so by analyzing records of his own company's receiving inspection reports. He may simply keep a record of rejects in the form of percentage of total shipments received from each supplier for each basic type of material. Naturally rejects will be higher for some items than for others. What is important is the trend of rejections for a given com-

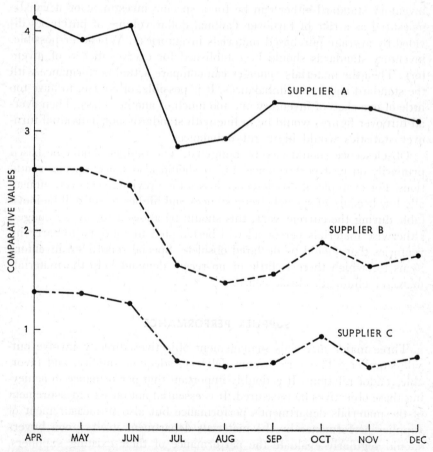

FIG. 20–6. Quality performance of competing suppliers can be measured by plotting rejects as a percentage of monthly shipments. This not only permits comparison of suppliers but also indicates whether or not a poor-quality supplier is showing any signs of improvement.

modity and the performance of competing suppliers on like commodities. If a supplier starts slipping on quality, the buyer first should warn him that he is falling behind his competitors. If there is no improvement, the buyer may be forced to give his next order to a different supplier.

Figure 20–6 shows the quality records of three competing suppliers. Each month the percentage of rejections by each supplier was plotted. The supplier with the highest rejection rate will first be warned—and he may even be shown the chart that compares his quality record with those of his two major competitors. If he fails to improve, the materials manager may try to locate a fourth supplier who can deliver higher-quality merchandise at the same or a lower price.

Tabulating the Results. Reports such as this are rarely made when the company does not have some means of tabulating quality statistics by machine—either with punched-card equipment or electronic data processing. With this equipment, data from inspection reports for every ship-

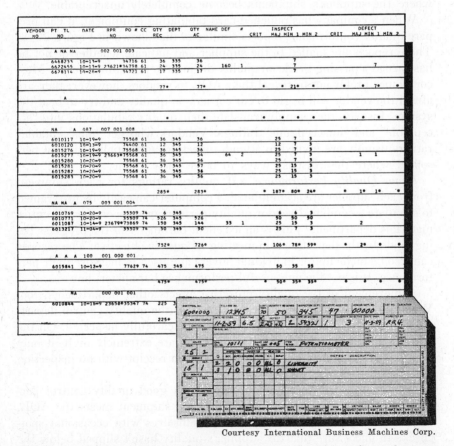

Courtesy International Business Machines Corp.

FIG. 20–7. Tabulating equipment facilitates measurement of vendor quality performance. Data from inspection reports is punched on cards and the equipment then calculates quality performance and prints the necessary reports.

ment is key-punched on cards (see Figure 20–7). The actual quality level, determined from the inspection reports, is then compared with the acceptable quality level (AQL).

Various formulas are used to make comparisons; typical is the following quality scoring formula used by an electronics company:

$$\text{Quality conformance} = 100 - \frac{30 \ (\text{per cent defective})}{\text{Acceptable quality level}}.$$

This formula is designed to give a "passing grade" of 70 when the supplier's quality meets the standard exactly. For example, if the AQL permits a 2 per cent rejection rate (i.e., two pieces out of a hundred do not meet the quality standard) and 2 per cent of a supplier's shipment is actually found defective, then quality conformance = 100 − 30(.02)/.02 = 70. Superior quality would earn the supplier a score higher than 70. Most companies regard any score below 70 as the point where the supplier's shipments become completely unacceptable.

When a company has punched-card tabulating equipment, it can prepare quality conformance reports similar to that shown in Figure 20–8. These reports are mailed to the supplier and indicate whether or not he has earned a passing grade on quality during the preceding month. Most companies prefer not to reveal their AQL to vendors, however; they are afraid the vendor will begin to cut corners on quality and try to beat the system. Instead, they simply translate their quality tabulations into "acceptable" and "unacceptable" ratings. Vendors who get "unacceptable" ratings usually are invited to attend a meeting with quality control personnel where they discuss ways to boost their quality.

Buyer Quality Performance. If quality ratings for each shipment from each supplier are accumulated, a computer can easily be programed to calculate a combined vendor quality performance report for the entire materials department. This is an excellent barometer of the progress being made by the department in meeting its quality objective. The records can also be made up for individual buyers and used to measure their performance. It is not the only useful performance barometer, however.

Achievement of the quality objective affects other departments, too. When quality is poor, the operating costs of the quality control department are high, since each shipment must be carefully inspected. On the other hand, when vendor quality standards are extremely high, it may even be possible to use purchased material on receipt with no inspection whatever.

Many companies "certify" suppliers with good quality control performance. These suppliers certify that each shipment meets the AQL, and the customer's inspectors content themselves with occasional spotchecks to make sure that the supplier's quality hasn't slipped below the certified standard.

When the materials department selects suppliers who meet quality

IBM **INTERNATIONAL BUSINESS MACHINES CORPORATION**

FORM 920-7967 2

<u>OWEGO, N. Y.</u>
PLANT LOCATION

PURCHASED PRODUCT QUALITY CONFORMANCE REPORT

TO:

ABC Company
J. Doe QC Manager
Hometown
New York

	PERIOD ENDING	VENDOR NO
	Nov 15 1959	00000

THE QUALITY CONFORMANCE INFORMATION BELOW REPRESENTS IBM's EVALUATION OF YOUR PRODUCTS UPON RECEIPT

QUALITY CONFORMANCE · SHIPMENTS

THIS PERIOD	LAST PERIOD	TWO PERIODS AGO	RECEIVED THIS PERIOD	ACCEPTABLE AS RECEIVED	UNACCEPTABLE AS RECEIVED
Acceptable	Acceptable	Unacceptable	18	17	1

SHIPMENTS LISTED BELOW WERE FOUND TO BE UNACCEPTABLE AS RECEIVED. YOU WERE ADVISED OF THE RESULTS BY THE REJECTED PURCHASE REPORT INDICATED. SHIPMENTS ACCEPTED AS RECEIVED ARE EXCLUDED FROM THIS LISTING.
*INDICATES SHIPMENT RETURNED

PART NUMBER	PURCHASE ORDER NUMBER	QUANTITY RECEIVED	SAMPLE QUANTITY INSPECTED	SAMPLE QUANTITY DEFECTIVE	REJECTED PURCHASE REPORT NO	*
6000000	12345	50	25	3	54321	*

Courtesy International Business Machines Corp.

FIG. 20–8. International Business Machines Corp. and other companies periodically mail reports to suppliers that indicate their quality performance. These reports can be generated easily if the company has data-processing equipment and is already calculating quality performance for internal use.

standards with little inspection, it is making a considerable contribution to profits. Some companies—most notably the General Electric Company —use the cost of operating the receiving inspection department as a barometer of materials management performance. The cost of shutdowns in manufacturing because of poor-quality purchased materials often can also be legitimately used as a barometer of materials management efficiency.

The Delivery Objective

Most shutdowns, however, result from the supplier's failure to deliver on schedule. Getting material is the most basic job in materials management. It is also one of the most difficult to measure objectively without data-processing equipment. Records of each shipment from each supplier must be tabulated. Figure 20–9 shows how one company plots delivery performance of its suppliers. Another company uses barometers—a time rating and a quantity rating—to rate its suppliers.

Time and Quantity Ratings. The time rating is calculated by comparing the date when a shipment is actually received to the date for which it

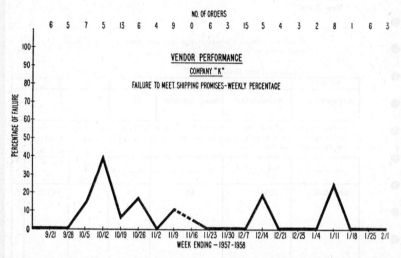

FIG. 20–9. Vendor delivery performance can be measured simply by dividing the number of times a vendor fails to keep a shipping promise by the number of shipments he makes. Listing the number of orders per week on the chart shows the significance of the failure. A high percentage of failures on a large number of orders is more serious than the same percentage of failures on a smaller number of orders.

was promised. Early shipments are penalized less than late shipments, because it usually is more desirable to carry excess inventory than to risk a stockout. The scoring is as follows:

  100—shipment received the week it was due or one week early.
  80—one week late or two weeks early.
  60—two weeks late or three weeks early.
  40—three weeks late or four weeks early.
  20—four weeks late.
  0—five or more weeks late.

Partial receipts also serve as a barometer of delivery performance. A supplier who must make a lot of unscheduled extra shipments in small quantities is not doing as good a job as a supplier who can accumulate the desired quantity and ship it according to schedule. Performance in avoiding partial shipments is measured by a quantity rating, which is calculated by dividing the number of scheduled receipts by the number of shipments actually made by the supplier.

The combined delivery performance rating is calculated by averaging the time delivery rating, weighted 70 per cent, with the quantity delivered rating, weighted 30 per cent.[5] For example, suppose a supplier is scheduled to make three shipments. His first shipment is two weeks early, his second scheduled shipment is received in two parts and the first part is two weeks late, and his fourth and final shipment arrives on schedule. The supplier's time delivery rating is equal to the average of his individual ratings—80, 60, and 100—or 80. Since he made four shipments when three were scheduled, his quantity delivered rating is 75. The combined rating equals 70 per cent of 80 and 30 per cent of 75, or 78.5.

This would not be good performance on most rating scales. The following scale is used by the New England company that devised this formula:

> 95–100 . . . . Excellent performance
> 90–94 . . . . Good
> 80–89 . . . . Fair
> Under 80 . . . . Unsatisfactory

Once a company is set up to tabulate delivery statistics, it can use them not only to measure supplier performance but also to measure how well the over-all materials department and the groups within it are doing in achieving the delivery objective. Performance of the department, of course, is equal to the combined performance of all suppliers on all shipments. Performance of individual groups within the department is calculated from statistics on the shipments for which they are responsible. With tabulating equipment, it is easy to key-punch receival cards not only with the vendor's code but also with the buyer's or expediter's code. Then it becomes a routine matter to run off not only delivery performance reports on suppliers but also on buyers, expediters, or some other organizational unit within the materials department.

Other Barometers. Delivery performance statistics may be fairly difficult to compile even when a company has data-processing equipment. Punched cards must be made up for each shipment, and equipment must be programed to run off the necessary reports. This is usually practical only if delivery performance reports are a part of an over-all data-processing system.

Other barometers of delivery performance may be easier to use. They involve studying the effect of delivery on operations rather than analyzing the delivery statistics. When delivery performance is poor, the internal operating costs of the materials department are high.[6] Travel and

---

[5] The reader should note that this weighting is quite arbitrary. Different companies would apply different weights, depending on what they believe to be the relative importance of the two factors.

[6] This also illustrates how various materials objectives are interrelated. If a materials manager successfully achieves the objective of getting suppliers to deliver promptly, he also achieves his objective of low department operating costs. But he may have to make some sacrifices to get prompt delivery.

telephone costs go up, and payroll costs rise because more expediters are needed. Each is a barometer of delivery performance.

Costs also rise in manufacturing, because scheduling of production is less efficient when materials are in short supply. Shutdowns also are more frequent. Many slowdowns in manufacturing are charged to variance accounts (in companies with standard-cost systems), which are designed to show why costs are higher than anticipated. If a company has a variance account for premium costs incurred on account of lack of material, this account in itself is a measure of the materials department's delivery performance. Of course, a barometer like this is not as useful as delivery statistics because its use is limited to measurement of department performance. It cannot easily be adapted to measure delivery performance of individual suppliers or buyers.

Vendor Rating

The best suppliers do more than meet quality standards and ship according to schedule. They offer shorter lead times than their competitors; their prices are lower; and they offer more new products, ideas, and miscellaneous services.

The Combined Rating. Various materials managers have attempted to weigh all these factors and develop numerical ratings for each of their suppliers. A supplier's price performance can be calculated by comparing his price with that of the lowest bidder on the order. A similar comparison can be made for lead time. In each case, the supplier's rating is calculated by averaging performance on a series of orders. The formulas are:

$$\text{Percentage of price performance} = \frac{\text{Lowest price or bid (any vendor)}}{\text{Actual price}}$$

$$\text{Percentage of lead-time performance} = \frac{\text{Shortest lead time (any vendor on comparable item)}}{\text{Actual lead time}}$$

Some companies consider only quality and delivery in developing composite delivery ratings. Others also take price and lead time into account. One company uses the following weighting to rate its suppliers:

> Quality. 40%
> Delivery. 20%
> Price. 35%
> Lead time. 5%

Such weighting is arbitrary and depends entirely on the materials manager's judgment of the relative importance of the various factors.

Favorable Relations. Such composite ratings may be useful as buying tools, and they also provide clues to how good a job the materials department is doing in terms of its objective of maintaining favorable supplier relations. But they don't tell the full story about performance on the latter objective. Part of it also shows up in cost-reduction reports. When supplier relations are good, vendors' ideas are stimulated.

Unfortunately, there is often a considerable lag before a successful vendor-relations program shows measurable results. This year's performance in developing supplier relations may show up in cost-reduction reports or quality statistics in succeeding years. So it is not possible to rely entirely on objective measures to determine whether or not the objective of favorable supplier relations is currently being achieved. The best the materials manager can do is to have a program and then report progress as best he can. For example, he may occasionally try to summarize the contributions that each supplier has made in suggesting new products or ideas, or in helping operating personnel with their problems. This would be a barometer of past performance and might provide clues to current performance.

DEVELOPMENT OF PERSONNEL

Survival is one of the most basic objectives of any organization. To perpetuate itself and the company of which it is a part, every department should strive to develop and train future managers. Historically, the materials department has done a rather poor job on this objective. Proof of this is the minute number of chief executives who are former materials managers. For example, the author of one study of the backgrounds of chief executives in big business did not even bother to list purchasing or materials management as a department through which one could advance to become a chief executive.[7] Presumably the category "operations and production" in this study embraced materials management as well as manufacturing. Only 40 per cent of the chief executives had this background (the balance came from finance, sales, legal departments, receivers in bankruptcy, personnel, and other departments), and undoubtedly practically all of them were from manufacturing or its equivalent in service companies.

One of the major reasons that materials departments have done such a poor job in developing chief executives is historical. As we saw in Chapter 1, it is only in the last fifty years that management has recognized the need for separate materials departments. And it is only quite recently that materials departments have developed enough stature and attracted enough high-caliber men to become logical training grounds for future top executives.

The materials department has done a better job in perpetuating itself by developing future purchasing agents and materials managers. Many, if not most, top materials managers have worked their way up through

---

[7] Mabel Newcomer, "The Big Business Executive," *Industrial Man*, W. Lloyd Warner and Norman H. Martin (eds.) (New York: Harper & Bros., 1959), p. 142.

the ranks of the materials department. The materials manager should always be grooming potential replacements for each of his key men. Personnel development is one of his most important objectives.

Unfortunately, it is not easy to measure year-to-year performance in achieving this objective. The results will be reflected in the performance of future managers, and it will be difficult, if not impossible, to trace them back to any particular period or program. The only practicable measure of year-to-year performance is to compare the materials manager's plans for achievement with those of previous years and to measure his actual progress in carrying out his plans.

The materials manager is interested not only in developing future managers but also in getting the best possible performance from every person in his department. His own performance should be measured by his success in reaching these goals. It is measured both by the programs he proposes for personnel development and by his ability to execute those programs.

High-Potential Employees

The materials manager's program should include regular appraisals of the performance and potential of every member of the materials organization. It should pay particular attention to development of the high-potential men who are the company's future managers. Figure 20–10 shows special appraisal forms used by the Ford Motor Company to evaluate high-potential employees in its management-development program.

To become "high potential," an employee must not only perform well in his present job; he must also show promise of being able to perform well in jobs with substantially more responsibility. He must have the personality, intellect, and education of a manager.

There should be high-potential men at almost every level of organization. This insures the orderly progression of competent executives that is essential to perpetuate the organization. In his annual report to top management, the materials manager should describe in some detail the progress being made by each of his high-potential employees. When there are insufficient high-potential men at any level in his organization, he should indicate how he proposes to fill the gap—through hiring new men, transfers, and so on.

Ideally, he should have replacements who are capable of filling any vacancies that might occur because of death, retirement, or resignation. Some managers use color-coded, phantom organization charts to help them plan. For each position, they list not only the incumbent but also his potential successors. Color codes indicate whether the potential successors are presently ready to handle increased responsibilities or whether they require additional training. For example, the top candidate for promotion might carry a green color code, which indicates he is ready to move on without any additional training or experience. Other candidates

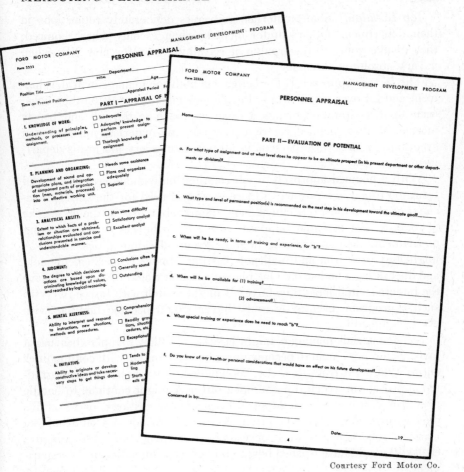

Courtesy Ford Motor Co.

FIG. 20–10. High-potential men capable of assuming greater responsibility are essential to a company's growth and survival. Ford Motor Co. uses this form to appraise the performance of the executives in its management-development program who are being groomed for future top-level jobs.

might carry yellow color codes, indicating that they are not quite ready. The materials manager should then make certain that these candidates get the training and experience needed to qualify them for future promotion.

Developing Managers

The materials manager should not assume that managers can be developed automatically, with no effort on his part. He should have a positive program designed to permit each employee to make a greater future contribution to company objectives. Included in this program would be such time-tested techniques as job rotation, special training programs, and special assignments.

Job Rotation.   Some materials managers deliberately rotate jobs in their department. Others prefer to make changes only when required; they dislike going to the trouble of retraining men for new jobs when it isn't absolutely necessary.

The former approach is the better one both for management development and for over-all efficiency. People inevitably get stale on their jobs; occasional job rotation brings a fresh approach to the job and boosts morale. With a planned rotation program, the materials manager can eventually train several persons in all phases of every job in his department.

With a planned approach to job rotation, individuals are transferred from job to job not only when there is a basic need for the shift, on account of promotions, retirements, and the like, but also for the mere sake of rotation. For example, suppose there are ten buyers in a purchasing department, each specializing in some group of commodities. Buyer A might buy gray iron and malleable castings; buyer B, permanent mold and die castings; and so on. One plan of rotation would be simply to have the buyers switch jobs; thus buyer B might switch with buyer A. With such a program, eventually every buyer would become familiar with every commodity.

Some materials managers might hesitate to follow this plan because it involves forcing a man to become immediately familiar with commodities entirely different from those he has handled. They prefer a more gradual approach, in which, for example, buyer A might continue to handle gray iron castings but would swap his malleable castings for buyer B's die castings. With this type of change, neither B nor A would have to learn a brand-new job all at once and, after enough of these changes, each still would have learned how to buy every commodity in the department.

Special Training Programs.   Each supervisor in the materials department should evaluate his subordinates. If there are gaps in their knowledge, he should try to fill them by means of training programs. High-potential employees should be encouraged to take special courses in night schools and take similar steps to broaden themselves. Many companies encourage such study by paying all or part of the tuition. Materials personnel should also be encouraged to participate in activities of such organizations as the National Association of Purchasing Agents, the American Production and Inventory Control Society, the National Institute for Governmental Purchasing, the National Association of Educational Buyers, and various traffic clubs.

Many companies have training programs designed to give a broad over-all understanding of company operations to young men fresh out of college. Figure 20–11 shows an outline of the training program of the Electronics Division of the Stromberg-Carlson Company. The materials

Typical Program Schedule

DEPARTMENT	ASSIGNMENT	WEEKS	DEPARTMENT	ASSIGNMENT	WEEKS
ENGINEERING	General Orientation (Projects, Design, Value, Systems Engineering, Project Control, Components and Materials, Services, Mechanical Design)	2	PRODUCTION ENGINEERING	General Orientation Industrial Engineering Tool Engineering Test Equipment Engineering Value Engineering Project Engineering or Assignment to one of the above areas	½ ½ ½ ½ ½ 4½
	Work Assignment (In one or more of above areas)	5			TOTAL 7
		TOTAL 7	PRODUCTION CONTROL	General Orientation Material Inventory Control Requisitioning and Scheduling Planning and Expediting	½ 1½ 2 3
INSPECTION AND QUALITY CONTROL	Purchased Materials Inspection Project Inspection Quality Control	1 1 1			TOTAL 7
	Work Assignment (One of the above areas)	4	MARKETING	General Orientation Military Marketing Industrial Marketing Contracts Administration Advertising	½ 3 1 2 ½
		TOTAL 7			TOTAL 7
PRODUCTION	General Orientation (Organization, Labor Relations, etc.)	1			GRAND TOTAL 49*
	Work Assignment (Capacity of Assistant Foreman)	6			
		TOTAL 7			
PURCHASING	General Orientation Value Analysis and Standardization Buying (Production) Buying (Engineering) Order Control	½ 1 1 1 ½			
	Work Assignment (One of the above areas)	3			
		TOTAL 7			

*The total of 49 weeks does not in all cases terminate the training of the individual. Depending upon the trainee's desires and qualifications and the needs of the company, the opportunity is afforded to spend two to four weeks in one or more of the following areas:

Plant Engineering
Value Engineering
Accounting
Research
General Services
Other-Operating Divisions

Courtesy Stromberg-Carlson Co.

FIG. 20–11. The materials department should participate actively in company-wide training both to recruit high-potential men and to indoctrinate future executives in other departments in the importance of materials management. As this chart shows, ²⁷ of the Stromberg-Carlson Company's training program is devoted to the materials management functions of purchasing and production control.

department should play an active role in such company-wide programs. In this way it can keep itself supplied with young high-potential men by regularly providing jobs for a few trainees who have completed the course. Also, trainees destined for other departments will be able to work better with the materials department if they know how it operates.

The materials department also can sometimes make a valuable contribution to the company's sales training program. Fledgling salesmen can learn how customers react to various sales approaches either by trying them out on purchasing personnel in their own company or by actually watching supplier salesmen in action. Several companies make their sales trainees serve a short stint in the purchasing department as a buyer's assistant. They not only can see other salesmen in action but also can objectively appraise the impact of each salesman on his customers.

Special Assignments. The materials manager often can use special assignments to test his subordinates. One assignment that can help develop future managers in two ways is that of organizing a training program. The subordinate who runs the training program is being developed, and the program itself helps develop others. High-potential men should be tested regularly with special assignments. These may include special reports, development of new procedures, participation in various company-wide activities (Community Chest drives, and so on), and various commodity studies.

GOOD RECORDS

The materials manager can sometimes achieve two objectives simultaneously when he assigns a high-potential man to audit the department's records. He is developing personnel and he also is making certain that the department's records and procedures are satisfactory.

Many materials managers prefer to have their records checked by someone outside the department, however. They have the company's internal auditors make detailed examinations; a few even use outside auditing firms. Auditors are experts in checking records and in detecting deviations from standard procedures. They can be used as an independent check on the materials department much in the same manner as they are used in the accounting department.

The internal auditor will first make a detailed review of the materials department's procedures in order to make certain that they provide adequate control. He will occasionally suggest changes that will either tighten control or cut costs. After he is satisfied with procedures, the auditor spot-checks a number of materials transactions to see if procedures have been complied with in practice. He then notes each case in which there is some deviation or in which records are incomplete. In a materials department, he would make a special effort to be absolutely certain that business was awarded to suppliers in the best interests of the company. For example, the auditor would expect to find clear records of each supplier's bid. If the contract were not awarded to the lowest bidder, he would expect to find evidence justifying the decision.

After he checked a satisfactory number of transactions, the auditor would make a report summarizing his findings. This report would provide an impartial measure of the department's performance in meeting its objective of having good records.

We have now covered measurement of performance of all of the basic objectives of a typical materials department. One question that may arise in the reader's mind must remain partly unanswered: How does one arrive at a combined rating that shows over-all performance in meeting all objectives? It would not be too difficult to calculate a combined rating.

All one need do is determine the relative importance of each objective, give it a percentage weight, and then calculate some cumulative performance rating for the over-all performance.

The writer believes, however, that such a combined rating would be almost meaningless. Not only is weighting of individual objectives arbitrary, but it would be necessary to combine objectives that can be measured quantitatively with those that can only be measured qualitatively. The writer believes that the only practical approach to performance measurement in materials management is to measure progress on each objective as accurately and impartially as possible. Then whoever is responsible for performance can be the judge of whether or not the department's efforts were directed toward the right objectives.

CASES

CASE 20–1. CONSOLIDATED BUSINESS MACHINES CORPORATION

Measuring Supplier Performance

George Matheson, president of the Consolidated Business Machines Corporation, is concerned about the company's choice of suppliers for sensor brushes, which are used in the company's data-processing equipment. Matheson occasionally plays golf with Harold Adams, president of the Adams Machine Company, one of the company's suppliers of brushes. Recently, Adams complained to Matheson that his firm has been having difficulty in getting its traditional share of Consolidated's brush business. On the last buy, Adams' firm failed to get any business even though Adams believed he was the low bidder. Matheson tells Adams that normally he doesn't get into the details of procurement but he promises to ask his purchasing manager, Sloan Howard, to investigate.

The following morning Matheson calls Howard and tells him of Adams' complaint. He says he doesn't want to influence the company's procurement policies but he does feel that Howard should investigate to make sure that Adams was treated fairly.

Howard discovers that Adams was indeed the low bidder on the last buy. Quotations for an order of 10,000 units were as follows:

Adams Machine Co.	$2.22
Burlington Electronics Co.	2.23
Zenith Tool & Machine Co.	2.25

Zenith and Burlington each got orders for 5,000 pieces. Zenith has done considerable development work on brushes, while Adams and Burlington have done very little. The quality and delivery records of the three suppliers on the last ten orders for the brush are as follows:

Supplier	Quantity Ordered	Quantity Defective	Delivery
Zenith	4,000	122	One week early
Burlington	4,000	92	One week late
Adams	3,000	120	On time
Adams	6,000	162	Two weeks late
Zenith	4,000	38	On time
Burlington	5,000	29	One week early
Adams	2,000	88	1,000 pieces on time; 1,000 pieces four weeks late.
Burlington	6,000	98	Two weeks late
Zenith	4,000	45	One week early
Adams	5,000	162	One week late

Consolidated's quality control department has set an acceptable quality level of 3 per cent on the brush.

Questions

1. Is Howard justified in eliminating Adams as a supplier of brushes?
2. In what respect is the complaint from Adams justified?
3. Prepare a report for Mr. Matheson explaining the decision to eliminate Adams as a supplier; use quantitative data as much as possible to support your position.

CASE 20–2.   CONTINENTAL AIRCRAFT CORPORATION

Choosing a New Materials Manager

Charles Harrington, vice-president in charge of materials of the Continental Aircraft Corporation, is looking for an assistant who can succeed him when he retires in two years. Harrington has three possible candidates for his job. They are: Robert Clement, 37 years old, materials manager of the company's California Division: Alex Dawson, 48 years old, materials manager of the Texas Missile Division; and Glenn Wilcox, 58, manager of materials research and administration on the corporate staff. Clement and Dawson report directly to the managers of their respective divisions and functionally to Harrington. Both men are highly regarded by their division managers. Wilcox reports directly to Harrington and has earned the respect of everyone on the corporate staff.

Clement is a relative newcomer to Continental. He has degrees in aeronautical engineering and business administration, and he joined the company just five years ago as an executive in the customer relations department. He was appointed assistant materials manager of the California Division two years later, and was made materials manager a year later. A young, aggressive executive, Clement has already racked up an enviable record at the California Division, which is the company's largest. Last year he exceeded his cost-reduction quota by nearly 20 per cent and managed to keep inventories from rising despite a 25 per cent increase in division sales volume. Clement is a good leader and morale in his department is high, although he sometimes is a little impatient with others when they fail to match his fast pace.

Dawson was Clement's predecessor as materials manager of the California Division. He joined the company as an engineering trainee shortly after he received his B.S. degree. His advancement in the organization was rapid, and he became materials manager of the California Division ten years ago. Harrington chose Dawson to take charge of materials activities at the rapidly expanding Texas Missile Division because of problems that were being encountered in producing satisfactory missiles. Before Dawson arrived, the division was plagued with both quality and delivery problems on purchased materials. Now, although costs are still much higher than Harrington believes they should be, suppliers are delivering on schedule material that meets the fantastically close tolerances required in missile manufacture.

Dawson has an excellent record for developing personnel. Clement was one of his proteges at the California Division, and other "alumni" who formerly worked for him now hold key posts both in other departments of Continental and in several outside companies. Compared with Clement, Dawson is much better at working with people, but he also has faults. Clement, in Harrington's opinion, has more imagination than Dawson, he drives both himself and his subordinates harder, and he may well have potential that will carry him beyond the position of top materials executive in some company.

Wilcox, the third candidate, is a real veteran of the company. He joined Continental 37 years ago as a draftsman, shortly after his graduation from college. His advancement has been steady if not spectacular. He has informally acted as Harrington's No. 2 man for more than ten years, and it is generally assumed that he will succeed Harrington. Wilcox has been employed strictly on staff work for the last ten years. He has spark-plugged a company-wide materials training program and has done an excellent job working out ticklish policy and procedures problems. Before that, he acted as assistant materials manager under Harrington. This was a line job, since at that time all of the company's products were made by what is now called the "California Division" and Harrington was its materials manager.

Questions

1. What qualities should Harrington look for in a successor?
2. Which, if any, of the three candidates should he choose?
3. When should he make his final decision?

Chapter 21

THE FUTURE OF MATERIALS MANAGEMENT

Automation is the single most important force that will shape the materials organization of the future. Automation in the office promises to change the materials organization by drastically reducing the number of clerical jobs and making new demands on the technical and managerial personnel in the materials department. Automation in the factory promises to make materials management more challenging and more difficult than ever before.

Millions of words have been written about the effect of automation on the labor force—whether it will cause widespread unemployment or create a bonanza of new, better-paying, highly skilled jobs. But the study of automation in materials management has been almost completely neglected, even though automation is certain to affect materials management as much as it affects the jobs of factory workers. In fact, it is entirely possible that many managements will wake up and discover that automation has created serious materials management problems while its effect on the labor force was greatly exaggerated.

The only thing that is really new about automation is the word itself, which was coined by Del S. Harder, vice-president in charge of manufacturing of the Ford Motor Company fifteen years ago. Harder used it to describe a process that has actually been going on for centuries— the gradual replacement of man by machine. The term "automation" caught on quickly and has now acquired a narrower meaning. For example, one expert, Professor Walter S. Buckingham, Jr., has defined automation as "any continuous and integrated production system which uses electronic or other equipment to regulate and co-ordinate the quality and quantity of production."[1]

It is now more or less generally agreed that the major difference between "automated" production and "automatic" production is feedback. In automatic production, the machine takes over the worker's manual duties but continues to be guided by an operator. An electric desk calculator is a good example of this. Once the operator tells the calculator what mathematical operations he wants performed by pushing the ap-

---

[1] "Automation and Technological Change," Hearings, Subcommittee on Economic Stabilization of the Joint Committee on the Economic Report, Congress of the United States (U.S. Government Printing Office, October, 1955), p. 32.

propriate buttons, the calculator obediently performs them. An electronic computer, on the other hand, is a good example of a tool for automated production. It can be programed to analyze basic data, make necessary calculations, and then regulate a process in accordance with the results of its calculations.

With automation, the machine "thinks for itself" and becomes at least partly self-regulating. It adjusts itself in relation to its own output. To do this, it must have some sort of feedback of operating data. For example, an automated machine tool may inspect its own output. If a certain dimension starts to exceed quality limits, this information is relayed back to the machine and the machine then adjusts itself so that the dimension is brought back within the desired limits again.

It is this kind of feedback that makes possible a workerless factory. It can also be applied to managing the factory. For example, several major chemical, petroleum, and steel companies already have facilities that have almost completely automated production machines capable of making their own operating decisions. Computers control the entire manufacturing process, insuring process control that is much more efficient than was ever possible before. Human operators sometimes stand by to take over if the control equipment should break down. But their days are numbered, even as stand-bys. Computer manufacturers are developing products so reliable that failures will become almost unheard of.

Such highly automated operations still are relatively rare. In the next decade they will be commonplace, according to most experts on automation. For example, John Diebold, a management consultant, testified before the Joint Economic Committee of Congress that automation had "arrived" and that its applications would become universal in many fields by 1970[2] (see Figure 21–1).

Labor leaders, economists, and many business executives are already alert to some of the problems automation will bring in the next decade. Inevitably the number of workers needed for production jobs will decline. The slack will have to be taken up by greatly increased output and broader employment opportunities in service industries (e.g., no one has yet figured out how to automate the barber out of business). Inevitably there will be dislocations. Automation may create a shortage of highly skilled labor while it is creating surpluses of semiskilled and unskilled labor. The equipment used in automation is complex and requires highly skilled technicians to design it, produce it, and maintain it.

The personnel problems that automation brings have been so thoroughly aired—there is even a Congressional subcommittee to study them—that management can hardly fail to solve them because of lack of advance warning. Not so with the materials management problems that

---

[2] *New Views on Automation*, papers submitted to the Subcommittee on Automation and Energy Resources, Joint Economic Committee, Congress of the United States (U.S. Government Printing Office, 1960), p. 79.

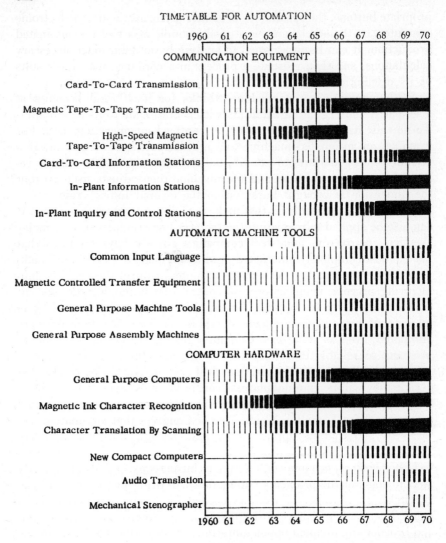

FIG. 21–1. Automation promises to become widely accepted in the next few years. It should be fully accepted for communications equipment by 1970 and at least moderately accepted for machine tools and computer hardware. (Source: John Diebold & Associates, as presented in a paper submitted to the Subcommittee on Automation and Energy Resources, Joint Economic Committee of the Congress of the United States, *New Views on Automation* [U.S. Government Printing Office, October, 1960], p. 107.)

automation brings. Automation in the factory will make materials management much more difficult than it has ever been. It will demand successful and imaginative application of the new techniques that will be made possible by automation in the materials department itself.

AUTOMATION IN THE FACTORY

The new automated factories appear remarkably free from problems. The machinery works quietly and efficiently; there is scarcely a worker in sight. Such plants look as if they should be low-cost producers, and they are. But they are not *no-cost* producers. Even though direct labor costs may have been virtually eliminated, all other costs still exist— purchased materials, administrative costs, maintenance and depreciation, interest and return on invested capital, and so on. In fact, some of these costs will be much higher in the automated plant. Its more complex equipment costs more to maintain. It also requires a greater initial investment, which means higher interest and depreciation charges.

As yet no one has built a workerless plant. But some of the highly automated plants in the electrical equipment, electronics, and auto industries provide clues as to what happens to costs when processes are automated. The following example is representative:

	Before Automation	After Automation
Material	$1.00	$1.02
Labor	.38	.04
Overhead	.57	.55
Manufacturing cost	$1.95	$1.61
Sales and administrative cost	.08	.08
Profit (to yield 20% return on investment)	.17	.38
Selling price	$2.20	$2.07

As expected, automation drastically reduces labor costs and also reduces total costs. Not so obvious, however, are these by-products.

1. Overhead Is Practically Unchanged. Although there is less indirect labor in the automated plant, what labor there is will be more highly skilled and higher-priced. The greater capital investment in automated equipment raises depreciation charges and probably also general maintenance and operating costs. Note the composition of the overhead changes. Fixed charges (depreciation, and so on) increase, while variable charges (mostly indirect labor) decrease. This makes costs more rigid than before.

2. Profit Requirements Are Greater. Automation requires a bigger investment in facilities. Naturally this means that profits on each unit produced must be higher to yield the same return on investment. In the example above, a 17-cent unit profit might be adequate, at standard volume, to provide a 20 per cent return on a $1 million investment in facilities. Suppose the investment in facilities increases to $2 million when production is automated. Then a 38-cent unit profit would be needed to provide a 20 per cent return on investment—assuming there is no change in volume of output.

In addition, many managers believe that automated facilities should earn a greater return on investment than nonautomated facilities (although competition may prevent this). The reason: the risks are greater with automation. In a completely unautomated plant, if a product doesn't sell management can simply lay off workers and minimize losses. With automation, it can't get off so easily. It is likely to be stuck with an enormous investment in equipment that isn't good for much of anything except making a product that no one will buy.

3. Purchase Costs May Rise.   When there are slight deviations in quality of parts and materials in a nonautomated plant, workers often are able to use the materials anyway by making minor adjustments. In a fully automated plant this might not be true. The automated equipment may not be able to compensate for off-standard materials; machines can never be as flexible as skilled human hands.[3] Inevitably, increasing automation will bring demands on suppliers to adhere more rigidly to specifications. This may raise costs of purchased materials slightly.

4. Costs Become More Rigid.   In a nonautomated plant, if a supplier fails to deliver materials of satisfactory quality the plant is shut down and the workers are sent home. This is costly enough. But in a fully automated plant, the costs of shutting down are many times greater. Since there are fewer workers, less can be saved by sending them home without pay. Substituted for the workers is a tremendous investment in equipment that goes right on depreciating, whether it's being used or not.

Let us see what happens to the costs in our example when there is a shutdown. In both the automated and the nonautomated plant, the material and direct labor costs can be largely eliminated; material isn't used and workers are laid off.[4]

Nevertheless, a supply failure even in the nonautomated plant can be costly. Note that the product in our example has a unit overhead cost of

---

[3] The writer observed an excellent example of this several years ago when touring the factory of a leading manufacturer of electronic data-processing equipment. Electronic control panel boards were being assembled and soldered on an automated line. The new process required just two workers to load and unload parts from the line. The old process had required more than a dozen workers, who assembled and soldered various components—capacitators, resistors, transistors, and so on—to the printed circuit panel boards. Now the job was done by machine. Only the machine wasn't working when the writer saw it. A shipment of capacitators had arrived, and some of them had wires that had been bent slightly in packing. Were the capacitators being soldered to the board by hand, this defect probably wouldn't even have been noticed. The workers would simply have bent the wires to make them fit when they soldered them to the panel board. With the automated setup, each capacitator with a bent wire shut down the line for ten or fifteen minutes. It jammed the magazine feed at one station in the line, and no sooner would it be unjammed by a worker when another bent capacitator would jam up another station. The problem was finally licked by packing and unpacking with special care to prevent the wires from being bent. Naturally this raised costs slightly.

[4] This is an oversimplification. Employers incur substantial labor costs even when they lay off workers. Union contracts call for supplementary unemployment compensation. In addition, state workmen's unemployment compensation benefits are paid from taxes levied on employers in proportion to their workers' needs for such benefits.

57 cents when made in a nonautomated plant. Perhaps 30 cents of this is fixed or nonvariable overhead, which is incurred regardless of whether or not the product is made. In addition, the company naturally loses its 17-cent unit profit when there is a shutdown. So its total loss on each unit not produced is 47 cents. If the plant has a standard volume of 1,000 units per hour, then the supply failure costs $470 per hour.

The costs of a shutdown almost double in the automated plant. The 55-cent unit overhead cost in the automated plant is a little lower than the overhead in the nonautomated plant. But much more of it—at least 45 cents—is fixed and nonvariable, incurred regardless of whether or not the plant operates. In the automated plant, the variable indirect labor cost that was incurred for inspectors, materials handlers, and so on, is replaced with nonvariable maintenance and depreciation expense needed because of the added investment in plant and equipment. As a result, the automated plant has 15 cents (45 cents minus 30 cents) more fixed and nonvariable overhead per unit than the nonautomated plant. In addition, the profit loss is greater when the automated plant shuts down. It is 38 cents instead of 17 cents, or 21 cents greater. Thus a shutdown in an automated plant results in a total additional loss of 36 cents (the 21-cent profit loss plus the 15 cents in extra fixed overhead) per unit. At standard volume of 1,000 units per hour, the supply failure in the automated plant is $360 per hour more costly than the same failure in the nonautomated plant. The total cost of the failure is $630 per hour.[5]

AUTOMATION IN THE OFFICE

Thus automation in the factory will put tremendous pressure on materials managers by increasing the costs of supply failure enormously. The use of computers and other automated equipment in the office will relieve some of this pressure. It permits the use of radically different materials management techniques.

It will also bring substantial changes in the organization structure for materials management. In Chapter 1 we saw that in most companies materials activities are not unified organizationally at present. The typical manufacturing company has separate purchasing, traffic, and production control departments. The only person responsible for all three activities in most cases is the company's president or general manager, and often he is much too busy with other problems to worry much about materials management. In the typical company materials get managed[6] mostly because the managers of the various materials activities have learned how to work together and because responsibility is divided

---

[5] Based on 45 cents for unit fixed and nonvariable overhead in the automated plant, plus 38 cents in unit profit, multiplied by 1,000 units per hour.

[6] But, in the writer's opinion, not nearly so well as they might be if materials activities were unified organizationally.

among them quite precisely by policies, procedures, tradition, and habit.

There are at least four reasons why this approach won't work in the future:

1. Computer Programs Will Stimulate Unification of Materials Activities. Computer programing is extremely costly. For example, one writer estimated that it could take as many as 20 man-years of programing to prepare materials records of engineered products for a computer because of the exceptions that must be taken into account.[7] Obviously, purchasing, production control, and traffic cannot develop programs independently of one another. Materials management must be considered an integrated activity in developing a single program. This, in turn, will help break down the functional lines between departments and help unify them organizationally. This has already happened in almost every company that has attempted to manage materials with computers so far. (The case of Fairchild Engine & Airplane Corporation discussed in Chapter 19 is a good example.)

2. Reports from Computers Encourage a Unified, Integrated Approach to Materials Management. Companies rarely invest in computers simply because they want to cut clerical overhead. They are every bit as interested in another objective: to speed the flow of information needed for making decisions. Computers permit daily inventory status reports in companies that formerly were forced to use monthly reports (issued up to a month late) as a basis for materials management decisions. Such rapid reporting is useful only if management is able to use it promptly in making decisions.

This is more likely to be the case in an integrated materials department organized by product or stage of manufacture.[8] In such an organization, one person can be delegated all the authority he needs to take action on most materials problems. This is not the case in the conventional materials organization with separate purchasing, production control, and traffic departments, particularly if these departments are not even unified under a common materials manager. In such an organization, basic materials decisions can be made only after there is some consultation among individuals in the interested departments. Inevitably, this is more time-consuming than if responsibility rested with one person who was responsible for all phases of materials management for a particular item. It is also more wasteful, since it causes several persons to check similar materials problems for identical products.

3. Manpower Needs Will Be Substantially Reduced. As we saw in Chapter 19, about 90 per cent of the materials jobs in a typical company are clerical. Ten years from now, less than 50 per cent will be clerical.

---

[7] Richard A. Clippinger, "Economics of the Digital Computer," *Harvard Business Review*, January–February, 1955, p. 78.

[8] These principles of organization and their application to materials management are discussed in detail in Chapter 4.

A materials department that requires 200 persons without automation will require no more than 100 persons with computers and other equipment taking over much of the routine work. This reduction will be felt more heavily in some functions than in others. It may, for example, virtually eliminate what is currently the biggest materials activity in terms of manpower, the production control department.

Computer programs already have been developed (e.g., at Fairchild Engine & Airplane Corporation, as described in Chapter 19) to take over all routine production control activities. Once the problem of data transmission is solved so that operators no longer are needed to record materials transactions on punched card or punched tape, clerical manpower needed to manage materials will be reduced further. As a result, the production control department will shrink so that its supervision ceases to be much of a problem.

The purchasing and traffic departments will also shrink, although not as much as production control. Suppliers of materials and transportation services must still be dealt with by people, but machines can take over much of the clerical drudgery in purchasing and traffic, including invoice checking, posting of records, and the like.

These reductions in manpower will make it more convenient to group these heretofore independent functions under a single manager.

4. Computers Will Reduce Flexibility. Computers are not as versatile as human clerks. Their programs must be carefully designed to allow for every exception. This makes programing costly and expensive to change. Materials management by computer will be practicable only if the authority for basic changes in policy centers on a single materials manager.[9] If materials management authority is dispersed, as it is in the conventional organization, there will inevitably be problems.

THE FUTURE ORGANIZATION

For all of these reasons, the materials management form of organization will be more popular in industry than it is today. While no more than 50 companies currently have integrated materials activities, with purchasing, material control, and traffic all reporting to a common manager, the writer is convinced that this number will grow enormously in the next decade. Hundreds and perhaps even thousands of companies will have integrated materials activities by 1970.

These materials departments should be quite different from present-day departments. Automation not only will drastically reduce the need

---

[9] This needn't mean that the materials manager should be directly responsible for operating the computer. That job can be done by a highly specialized service department. But a single materials manager should be the basic authority on what programs are devised for managing materials with the computer. The service department can then translate his instructions into an actual program for the computer.

for clerical help, but also will increase the need for highly skilled personnel. For example, few if any of today's materials departments are staffed with mathematicians. There is no need for them. Present-day materials management problems can be solved with arithmetic and high-school algebra. This won't be so in the future. Computers will permit the use of highly sophisticated inventory control formulas devised by trained mathematicians.

Similarly, the demand for economists in materials management will grow enormously. The inflexibility and high fixed costs that characterize the automated factory and office make it more important to forecast demand accurately. Computers will help economists in forecasting by digesting and analyzing complex statistics. Automation will also increase the demand for men with engineering backgrounds in materials departments. The tighter quality standards, closer scheduling, and more complex manufacturing processes that automation permits will require materials personnel with a real understanding of manufacturing and engineering.

No longer will it be possible—as it still often is today, particularly in smaller companies—to promote a man to the job of buyer or purchasing agent simply because he is a competent clerk in the stockroom and knows how to get along with people. Other qualifications will be required. A college degree will become almost mandatory, and advanced degrees will be commonplace, particularly in large companies. The opportunities then should be challenging enough to test the mettle of even the most talented.

SELECTED BIBLIOGRAPHY

Organization and Management

DALE, ERNEST. *Planning and Developing the Company Organization Structure.* Research Report No. 20. New York: American Management Association, 1952.

DRUCKER, PETER F. *The Practice of Management.* New York: Harper & Bros., 1954.

FAYOL, HENRI. *Industrial and General Administration.* London: Isaac Pitman & Sons, 1949.

HAAS, GEORGE; KRECH, E. M., and MARCH, BENJAMIN. *Purchasing Department Organization and Authority.* Research Study No. 45. New York: American Management Association, 1960.

LUSARDI, F. R. *Purchasing for Industry.* Studies in Business Policy No. 33. New York: National Industrial Conference Board, 1948.

NEWMAN, WILLIAM H., and SUMMER, CHARLES E. *The Process of Management.* Englewood Cliffs, N.J.: Prentice-Hall, Inc., 1961.

URWICK, LYNDALL F. *The Elements of Administration.* New York: Harper & Bros., 1943.

Forecasting and Planning

ABRAHAMSON, ADOLPH G., and MACK, RUSSELL H. (ed.). *Business Forecasting in Practice.* New York: John Wiley & Sons, 1956.

BACH, GEORGE LELAND. *Economics—An Introduction to Analysis and Policy.* 3d ed. Englewood Cliffs, N.J.: Prentice-Hall, Inc., 1960.

BAER, S. B., and SAXON, O. G. *Commodity Exchanges and Futures Trading.* New York: Harper & Bros., 1949.

DAUTEN, CARL A. *Business Cycles and Forecasting.* 2d ed. Cincinnati: South-Western Publishing Co., 1961.

DEAN, JOEL. *Managerial Economics.* New York: Prentice-Hall, Inc., 1951.

Evaluating and Using Business Indicators. AMA Management Report Number 25. New York: American Management Association, 1959.

GARDNER, ROBERT L. *How to Make Money in the Commodity Market.* New York: Prentice-Hall, Inc., 1961.

HAUSER, PHILIP M., and LEONARD, WILLIAM R. *Government Statistics for Business Use.* 2d ed. New York: John Wiley & Sons, 1956.

MOORE, GEOFFREY H. (ed.) *Business Cycle Indicators,* 2 Vols. Princeton, N.J.: Princeton University Press, 1961.

SAMUELSON, PAUL A. *Economics—An Introductory Analysis.* 5th ed. New York: McGraw-Hill Book Co., Inc., 1961.

SCHMECKEBIER, LAWRENCE F., and EASTIN, ROY B. *Government Publications and Their Use.* Rev. ed. Washington, D.C.: Brookings Institution, 1961.

SNYDER, RICHARD M. *Measuring Business Changes.* New York: John Wiley & Sons, 1955.

WASSERMAN, PAUL. *Sources of Commodity Prices.* New York: Special Libraries Association, 1960.

Purchasing Practices

ALJIAN, GEORGE W. (ed.) *Purchasing Handbook.* New York: McGraw-Hill Book Co., Inc., 1958.

CADY, E. L. *Industrial Purchasing.* New York: John Wiley & Sons, 1945.

DAY, JOHN S. *Subcontracting Policy in the Air Frame Industry.* Boston: Graduate School of Business Administration, Harvard University, 1956.

ENGLAND, WILBUR B. *Procurement: Principles and Cases.* 4th ed. Homewood, Ill.: Richard D. Irwin, Inc., 1962.

FARRELL, PAUL V. *50 Years of Purchasing.* New York: National Association of Purchasing Agents, 1954.

FARRELL, PAUL V., and AMMER, DEAN S. "The Truth About Military Buying," *Purchasing,* October, 1957, pp. 113–29.

FOULKE, ROY A. *Practical Financial Statement Analysis.* 3d ed. New York: McGraw-Hill Book Co., Inc., 1953.

HARLAN, NEIL E. *Management Control in Air Frame Subcontracting.* Boston: Graduate School of Business Administration, Harvard University, 1956.

HEINRITZ, STUART F. *Purchasing Principles and Application.* 3d ed. Englewood Cliffs, N.J.: Prentice-Hall, Inc., 1959.

HODGES, HENRY G. *Procurement—The Modern Science of Purchasing.* New York: Harper & Bros., 1961.

N.A.P.A. Handbook of Purchasing Policies and Procedures. New York: National Association of Purchasing Agents, 1939 (Vol. I), 1942 (Vol. II).

Procurement Handbook. Washington, D.C.: General Services Administration, Federal Supply Service, 1959.

WESTING, J. H., and FINE, I. V. *Industrial Purchasing.* 2d ed. New York: John Wiley & Sons, 1960.

WESTON, J. FRED (ed.). *Procurement and Profit Renegotiation.* San Francisco: Wadsworth Publishing Co., 1960.

Inventory Management

ABRAMOVITZ, MOSES. *Inventories and Business Cycles.* New York: National Bureau of Economic Research, 1950.

BROWN, ROBERT G. *Statistical Forecasting for Inventory Control.* New York: McGraw-Hill Book Co., Inc., 1959.

FETTER, ROBERT B., and DALLECK, WINSTON C. *Decision Models for Inventory Management.* Homewood, Ill.: Richard D. Irwin, Inc., 1961.

Inventory Management in Industry. Studies in Business Policy, No. 88. New York: National Industrial Conference Board, 1958.

MacNEICE, E. H. *Production Forecasting, Planning and Control.* 2d ed. New York: John Wiley & Sons, 1957.

MAGEE, JOHN F. *Production Planning and Inventory Control.* New York: McGraw-Hill Book Co., Inc., 1958.

MELNITSKY, BENJAMIN. *Management of Industrial Inventory.* New York: Conover-Mast Publications, 1951.

RITCHIE, WILLIAM E. *Production and Inventory Control.* New York: Ronald Press Co., 1951.

TODD, F. BEAMAN, and SCHARF, IRVING. "Profitable Inventory Levels," *Harvard Business Review*, September–October, 1953, pp. 101–8.

WHITIN, THOMSON M. *The Theory of Inventory Management.* Princeton, N.J.: Princeton University Press, 1953.

Traffic

COLTON, RICHARD C., and WARD, EDMUND C. *Practical Handbook of Industrial Traffic Management.* 3d ed. Washington, D.C.: Traffic Service Corp., 1959.

FOGG, CHARLES J.; WELLER, WALTER W.; and STRUNK, ARTHUR B. (ed.). *The Freight Traffic Redbook.* New York: Traffic Publishing Co., Inc., 1955.

KNORST, WILLIAM J. *Transportation and Traffic Management*, Vols. I–IV. Chicago: College of Advanced Traffic, 1947–49.

LOCKLIN, D. PHILIP. *Economics of Transportation.* 5th ed. Homewood, Ill.: Richard D. Irwin, Inc., 1960.

National Motor Freight Classification. Washington, D.C.: American Trucking Association (published periodically).

TAFF, CHARLES A. *Traffic Management: Principles and Practices.* Rev. ed. Homewood, Ill.: Richard D. Irwin, Inc., 1959.

Uniform Freight Classification. Chicago: Tariff Publishing Office (published periodically).

WILSON, G. LLOYD. *Freight Service and Rates.* Washington, D.C.: Traffic Service Corp., 1952.

———. *Freight Shipping Documents & Claims.* Washington, D.C.: Traffic Service Corp., 1952.

———. *Railroad Freight Rate Structure.* Washington, D.C.: Traffic Service Corp., 1951.

Make or Buy

CULLITON, J. W. *Make or Buy.* Boston: Graduate School of Business Administration, Harvard University, 1942.

"Does the Trend in Make or Buy Decisions Follow Market Conditions?" *Purchasing*, December, 1954, p. 71.

HIGGINS, CARTER C. "Make or Buy Reexamined," *Harvard Business Review*, March–April, 1955, pp. 109–19.

LEVINE, NORMAN P. "How to Know When to Make or Buy," *Purchasing*, January 5, 1959, pp. 72–74.

OXENFELDT, ALFRED G. *Make or Buy: Factors Affecting Executive Decisions.* New York: McGraw-Hill Book Co., Inc., 1956.

Cost Reduction and Price Analysis

AMMER, DEAN. "The Purchasing Department: Ford's Control Center," *Purchasing*, May 23, 1960, pp. 52–84.

BARNES, RALPH M. *Work Sampling.* Dubuque, Iowa: William C. Brown Co., 1956.

BRADY, GEORGE S. *Materials Handbook.* 8th ed., New York: McGraw-Hill Book Co., Inc., 1956.

BUZZELL, ROBERT D. *Value Added by Industrial Distribution and Their Productivity.* Columbus: Ohio State University, 1959.

CLARK, CHARLES. *Brainstorming.* New York: Doubleday & Co., Inc., 1958.

FERGUSON, ROBERT O., and SARGENT, LAUREN F. *Linear Programming.* New York: McGraw-Hill Book Co., Inc., 1958.

HEILAND, ROBERT E., and RICHARDSON, WALLACE J. *Work Sampling.* New York: McGraw-Hill Book Co., Inc., 1957.

Industrial Standardization—Company Programs and Practices. Studies in Business Policy No. 85. New York: National Industrial Conference Board, 1957.

KAPLAN, A. D. H.; DIRLAN, JOEL B.; and LANZILLOTTI, ROBERT F. *Pricing in Big Business.* Washington, D.C.: Brookings Institution, 1958.

LANG, THEODORE (ed.). *Cost Accountants Handbook.* New York: Ronald Press Co., 1947.

MILES, L. D. *Techniques of Value Analysis and Engineering.* New York: McGraw-Hill Book Co., Inc., 1961.

OSBORN, ALEX. *Your Creative Power.* New York: Charles Scribner's Sons, 1951.

STOCKTON, R. STANSBURY. *Introduction to Linear Programming.* Boston: Allyn and Bacon, Inc., 1960.

TERBORGH, GEORGE. *An Introduction to Business Investment Analysis.* Washington, D.C.: Machinery & Allied Products Institute, 1958.

WEISS, LEONARD W. *Economics and American Industry.* New York: John Wiley & Sons, 1961.

Automation and Data Processing

BRIGHT, JAMES R. *Automation and Management.* Boston: Graduate School of Business Administration, Harvard University, 1958.

BUCKINGHAM, WALTER. *Automation—Its Impact on Business and People.* New York: Harper & Bros., 1961.

New Views on Automation. Papers Submitted to the Subcommittee on Automation and Energy Resources, Joint Economic Committee, Congress of the United States. Washington, D.C.: U.S. Government Printing Office, 1960.

POSTLEY, JOHN A. *Computers and People.* New York: McGraw-Hill Book Co., Inc., 1960.

Miscellaneous

ALFORD, L. P. (ed.). *Cost and Production Handbook.* 3d. ed. New York: Ronald Press Co., 1955.

DICKERSON, M. B.; DILLAVOU, E. R.; and SCHUCK, H. M. *Business Law by the Case Method.* Englewood Cliffs, N.J.: Prentice-Hall, Inc., 1959.

GRAY, A. W. *Purchase Law Manual.* New York: Conover-Mast Publications, 1954.

TUCKER, SPENCER A. *Successful Managerial Control by Ratio Analysis.* New York: McGraw-Hill Book Co., Inc., 1961.

WYATT, JOHN W., and WYATT, MADIE B. *Business Law—Principles and Cases.* New York: McGraw-Hill Book Co., Inc., 1958.

INDEX

*This book has been set on the Linotype in 10
point Monticello, leaded 2 points, and 9 point
Monticello, leaded 1 point. Chapter numbers
and titles are in Spartan Heavy. The size of
the type page is 27 by 47 picas.*